THE COLLEGE PRESS NIV COMMENTARY

JEREMIAH-LAMENTATIONS

THE
COLLEGE
PRESS
NIV
COMMENTARY

JEREMIAH-LAMENTATIONS

TIM WILLIS, PH. D.

Old Testament Series Co-Editors:

Terry Briley, Ph.D.
Lipscomb University

Paul Kissling, Ph.D.
Great Lakes Christian College

 COLLEGE PRESS
PUBLISHING COMPANY
Joplin, Missouri

Library of Congress Cataloging-in-Publication Data

Willis, Timothy M.
    Jeremiah and Lamentations / Timothy Willis.
        p.   cm. — (The College Press NIV commentary. Old
    Testament series)
    Includes bibliographical references.
    ISBN 0-89900-892-5
    1. Bible. O.T. Jeremiah—Commentaries.   2. Bible. O.T.
    Lamentations—Commentaries.   I. Title. II. Series.
    BS1525.53.W55 2002
    224'.2077—dc21
                                                    2002067222

A WORD
FROM THE PUBLISHER

Years ago a movement was begun with the dream of uniting all Christians on the basis of a common purpose (world evangelism) under a common authority (the Word of God). The College Press NIV Commentary Series is a serious effort to join the scholarship of two branches of this unity movement so as to speak with one voice concerning the Word of God. Our desire is to provide a resource for your study of the Old Testament that will benefit you whether you are preparing a Bible School lesson, a sermon, a college course, or your own personal devotions. Today as we survey the wreckage of a broken world, we must turn again to the Lord and his Word, unite under his banner and communicate the life-giving message to those who are in desperate need. This is our purpose.

ABBREVIATIONS

AB . . . . . .*Anchor Bible*

BAR . . . . .*Biblical Archaeology Review*

CBC . . . . .*Cambridge Bible Commentary*

FOTL . . . .*Forms of Old Testament Literature*

HUCA . . . .*Hebrew Union College Annual*

ICC . . . . . .*International Critical Commentary*

Int. . . . . . .*Interpretation*

JBL . . . . . .*Journal of Biblical Literature*

JSOT . . . . .*Journal for the Study of the Old Testament*

LXX . . . . .*Septuagint*

MT . . . . . .*Masoretic Text*

NICOT . . .*New International Commentary of the Old Testament*

SBLDS . . .*Society of Biblical Literature Dissertation Series*

SBLMS . . .*Society of Biblical Literature Monograph Series*

VT . . . . . .*Vetus Testamentum*

WBC . . . . .*Word Bible Commentary*

ZAW . . . . .*Zeitschrift für die Alttestamentliche Wissenschaft*

Simplified Guide to Hebrew Writing

Heb. letter | **Translit.** | **Pronunciation guide**

Heb. letter	Translit.	Pronunciation guide
א	'	Has no sound of its own; like smooth breathing mark in Greek
ב	b	Pronounced like English B *or* V
ג	g	Pronounced like English G
ד	d	Pronounced like English D
ה	h	Pronounced like English H
ו	w	As a consonant, pronounced like English V or German W
וּ	û	Represents a vowel sound, pronounced like English long OO
וֹ	ô	Represents a vowel sound, pronounced like English long O
ז	z	Pronounced like English Z
ח	ḥ	Pronounced like German and Scottish CH and Greek χ (chi)
ט	ṭ	Pronounced like English T
י	y	Pronounced like English Y
כ/ך	k	Pronounced like English K
ל	l	Pronounced like English L
מ/ם	m	Pronounced like English M
נ/ן	n	Pronounced like English N
ס	s	Pronounced like English S
ע	'	Stop in breath deep in throat before pronouncing the vowel
פ/ף	p/ph	Pronounced like English P *or* F
צ/ץ	ṣ	Pronounced like English TS/TZ
ק	q	Pronounced very much like כ (k)
ר	r	Pronounced like English R
שׂ	ś	Pronounced like English S, much the same as ס
שׁ	š	Pronounced like English SH
ת	t/th	Pronounced like English T *or* TH

Note that different forms of some letters appear at the end of the word (written right to left), as in כָּפַף (*kāphaph*, "bend") and מֶלֶךְ (*melek*, "king").

Vowels in Hebrew (except where the ו is used to represent a vowel sound), are represented by "vowel points" added to the consonant. For example: הַ (*ha*, "the"). The letter *yod* (י, *y*) also becomes a *part of* certain vowel sounds, as in the conjunction כִּי (*kî*, "that"). Originally, Hebrew was written as "unpointed" text, with just the consonants. For convenience, the different vowel points are shown below on the letter Aleph (א).

אָ	ā	Pronounced not like long A in English, but like the broad A or AH sound
אַ	a	The Hebrew short A sound, but more closely resembles the broad A (pronounced for a shorter period of time) than the English short A
אֶ	e	Pronounced like English short E
אֵ	ē	Pronounced like English long A, or Greek η (eta)

א	i	Pronounced like English short I
א	î	The same vowel point is sometimes pronounced like אִ (see below)
א	o	This vowel point sometimes represents the short O sound
א	ō	Pronounced like English long O
א	u	The vowel point ֻ sometimes represents a shorter U sound and
א	ū	is sometimes pronounced like the וּ (û, see above)
אֵ	ê	Pronounced much the same as א
אֵ	ê	Pronounced much the same as א
אִ	î	Pronounced like long I in many languages, or English long E
א	ə	An unstressed vowel sound, like the first E in the word "severe"
א, א, א	ŏ, ă, ĕ	Shortened, unstressed forms of the vowels אָ, אַ, and אֶ, pronounced very similarly to א

JEREMIAH

INTRODUCTION

THE PLACE OF JEREMIAH IN THE OLD TESTAMENT

The Book of Jeremiah serves in many ways as the complement to the Book of Deuteronomy. They are similar at the linguistic level, as Jeremiah utilizes the vocabulary and ideas of Deuteronomy more than any other biblical prophet. But the connections between the two books run deeper than mere language. Deuteronomy sets the stage for Israel's entrance into the Promised Land. Jeremiah sets the stage for Israel's expulsion from the Promised Land. In Deuteronomy, Moses encourages God's people to be faithful to the LORD and obedient to his laws in order to live and prosper there. He warns them of the calamitous consequences that will occur if they do not (Deuteronomy 28), but he also promises them that the LORD will restore his people to their land, once they have restored proper faith in God in their hearts (Deuteronomy 29–30). Jeremiah explains, several centuries later, how the people have not been faithful to the LORD but have ignored his commands; therefore, they can expect the fulfillment of the warnings first uttered by Moses. But also like Moses in Deuteronomy, Jeremiah proclaims the LORD's future intentions to bring them back to their land and "restore their fortunes" (esp. Jeremiah 30–33).

Jeremiah is pivotal to one's understanding of the Old Testament, indeed of the whole Bible. He stands, first of all, at a crucial time in the history of God's people. For at least six centuries they have occupied the land promised to their ancestors. Even though their fellow Israelites to the north had been exiled by the Assyrians a century before Jeremiah's career, those in Judah who worship at the LORD's designated sanctuary in Jerusalem have survived. Furthermore, their economic fortunes have recently improved in tandem with a resurgence of worship and devotion to the LORD, the God who had brought them out of Egypt and established them in their land. But during Jeremiah's career, all of that changes. The people revert to their idolatrous ways, and the chosen city of Jerusalem is sacked by the Babylonians, who exile the vast majority of the nation's citizenry.

Second, Jeremiah is pivotal for an understanding of God's covenant relationship with his people. They stand under three covenants with God: the Abrahamic (the choice of a people to bring redemption to the world), the Mosaic (the establishment of that people as holy, living in a promised land), and the Davidic (the designation of a special royal family to lead the people). The Babylonian Exile would appear to mark the end of the latter two covenants; they no longer possess the promised land, and their king has no territory over which he can rule. Does this also mean the end of the first covenant? More importantly, does this mean that God's plan for the redemption of the world — inaugurated with the choosing of Abraham and his descendants — has been frustrated and now discarded? Jeremiah's prophecies address these issues, as well as some more immediate questions about what it means to be in a covenant relationship with God.

Third, Jeremiah's teachings are pivotal to a believer's understanding of the basic nature of the LORD. Exodus 34:6-7 gives an oft-quoted description of the LORD:

> The LORD, the LORD, the compassionate and gracious God, slow to anger, abounding in love and faithfulness, maintaining love to thousands, and forgiving wickedness, rebellion and sin. Yet he does not leave the guilty unpunished; he punishes the children and their children for the sin of the fathers to the third and fourth generation.

This description is borne out in the prophecies of Jeremiah. Although the majority of the book is about the punishing anger of the LORD upon his people for their prolonged unfaithfulness, it also points ahead to the future demonstration of his love and forgiveness. Jeremiah announces how the LORD is going to punish his people "to the third and fourth generation," but he also reveals that the LORD will restore his people, "maintaining love to thousands" (of generations). Ultimately, the latter overshadows the former. While the LORD does exhibit his anger at the unfaithfulness of his people, his more predominant characteristics are his mercy, love, forgiveness, grace, and patience. This is the overarching message of the Old Testament, and it is beautifully demonstrated in the teachings of Jeremiah.

THE WORLD OF JEREMIAH

Jeremiah became a prophet during the reign of King Josiah (639–609 B.C.), the most righteous king of the nation of Judah (2 Kgs 23:25). The twelve-tribe nation of Israel had split into two kingdoms – Israel/Ephraim to the north, Judah to the south – following the death of Solomon in 930 B.C.[1] The larger, northern kingdom had been conquered by the Assyrians of Mesopotamia in the middle of the 8th century B.C. Several thousand of its citizens migrated south into Jerusalem at that time. Their long-held feelings of distrust toward the House of David probably made them reluctant residents of the southern capital. This reluctance would have been dissipated by the miraculous deliverance of Jerusalem from the hands of the same Assyrians in 701 B.C., during the reign of the faithful king, Hezekiah (for more on those events, see Isaiah 36–37). This was interpreted as irrefutable proof that the LORD God of Israel had chosen David's house to govern his people.

Unfortunately, Hezekiah's faithfulness and the successes he won in regard to the Assyrians did not have the intended positive effects on the people. God had brought the Assyrians to discipline Judah, to punish them for social oppressions which God wanted them to stop. They eventually interpreted the events instead as a sign that God would never let an enemy destroy his Temple, that Jerusalem would stand forever against all attackers, regardless of the behavior of its inhabitants. This attitude is most evident in Hezekiah's son, Manasseh. His reign (696–642 B.C.) provokes the strongest condemnation from biblical writers (see on Jer 15:1-4; cp. 2 Kgs 21:1-18; 23:26-27). Hezekiah had relied on the LORD to prevent an Assyrian takeover of the land, but Manasseh effectively undermined the long-term effects of his father's faith. He ignored the laws of God through Moses, placed Judah under the domination of Assyria, and adopted Assyrian customs and religious beliefs. The tool God used for removing sinful activity from the nation became the primary catalyst for engaging in it. This Assyrian influence (and its accompanying political domination) lasted through the reigns of Manasseh and his son, Amon (642–640 B.C.), and into the reign of his grandson, Josiah (639–609 B.C.).

---

[1]Edwin R. Thiele, *The Mysterious Numbers of the Hebrew Kings*, 3rd ed. (Grand Rapids: Zondervan, 1983), pp. 67-78.

This political situation changed as Josiah grew up, because of the disintegration of power within the Assyrian Empire. By the time Josiah was an adult, he was effectively free to choose his own course; there was no longer any need to fear reprisals from Assyria. Josiah began with economic reforms. During the reigns of Manasseh and Amon, revenue was collected from Judah and sent to Assyria on a regular basis. Josiah retained those funds, using the money that had been going to Assyria to rebuild the cities and government buildings of Judah. One project involved refurbishing the Temple in Jerusalem. It was at this time (622 B.C.) that "the book of the covenant" was discovered (2 Kgs 22:1-10). Most scholars conclude that this was the Book of Deuteronomy (cp. Deut 30:10; 31:26).[2] Josiah, convicted by the words of the book, shifted the focus of his efforts from economic to religious reform (2 Kgs 22:11-23:24).

The righteousness of Josiah dominated the social landscape of Judah for the next decade, but it was already fading away by the time of his death in 609 B.C. (see Jer 3:6-10). His death constitutes a small aside in a much larger international drama that was being played out. The declining Assyrian Empire was being swallowed up by an emerging Babylon. Victories by the Babylonians at Haran (614 B.C.) and Nineveh (612 B.C.) pushed the Assyrians to the west and the city of Carchemish. Pharaoh Neco II of Egypt led his troops north through Judah to reinforce the failing Assyrian army. For reasons that are not revealed, Josiah marched out to intercept the Egyptians at the strategic pass near Megiddo. He was wounded in the ensuing battle and died shortly thereafter (2 Kgs 23:29-30; 2 Chr 35:20-24).

The effects of Josiah's death were far-reaching. Judah came under the control of Egypt, demonstrated most graphically when Pharaoh Neco dethroned Josiah's son Jehoahaz (Shallum) and replaced him with Jehoiakim, another son of Josiah (2 Kgs 23:31-35). Jehoiakim's reign (609-598 B.C.) was marked by political weakness and religious backsliding. Jehoiakim was placed on the throne by the Egyptians, but they relinquished their control over Judah when the Babylonians defeated them and the Assyrians at Carchemish in 605 B.C. It is at this juncture that Jeremiah first dictates his prophecies to Baruch, then sends them to Jehoiakim and his officials (Jeremiah 36). Some of Jeremiah's harshest criticisms come during these years

---

[2]M Cogan and H. Tadmor, *II Kings*, AB (New York: Doubleday, 1986), p. 220; T.R. Hobbs, *2 Kings*, WBC (Waco: Word, 1985), pp. 315-316.

(see Jer 7:1-15; 22:13-19), because Jehoiakim allowed the weeds of idolatry and other foreign worship practices — which Josiah had worked so hard to root out — to sprout again, choking out the faith and religious zeal of the people of Judah.

Jehoiakim was succeeded by his son, Jehoiachin (also called Coniah, or Jeconiah). His reign lasted only a few months. Even before he took the throne, a Babylonian force had set out for Jerusalem. When they arrived, they "arrested" Jehoiachin and some 10,000 government workers and leading citizens, carrying them back to Babylon. In Jehoiachin's place they installed his uncle, Zedekiah, as king (597–586 B.C.). He submitted to Babylonian domination for nine years, but eventually he attempted to form an alliance of resistance with several other small nations in the area. This provoked an all-out assault against Jerusalem by Nebuchadnezzar. After an eighteen-month siege, the city was sacked, Zedekiah's family was executed, and Zedekiah himself was blinded and led away to die in captivity (Jeremiah 39). All but a few of those who survived the destruction were led away with their king.

One of the few left behind by the Babylonians was Jeremiah. He placed himself under the care of Gedaliah, whom the Babylonians had appointed as governor of their new province of Judea. Gedaliah was assassinated several months later by a band of renegade Judeans who had managed to elude the Babylonian troops. Another band, fearing Babylonian reprisals, fled to Egypt, taking a protesting Jeremiah with them (Jeremiah 40–44). He apparently died there a few years later.

One can recognize two significant shifts in Jeremiah's prophecies as these events unfolded. The first half of his career is dominated by threats from the LORD about what will happen to Jerusalem and Judah if his people do not "amend their ways and their actions." These are not warnings, however, but only threats, because Jeremiah still speaks of the possibility that the people could avoid God's punishment if they would repent. This tone changes when Zedekiah comes to the throne. No longer does Jeremiah hold out any possibility that God might spare Jerusalem. Their future lies along one of four paths — captivity, death in battle, death from starvation, or death by disease ("the sword, famine, and disease"). This very dark message changes again during the final siege on Jerusalem. Jeremiah begins prophesying messages of hope after the exile, as if the exile is merely a dark tunnel through which they must pass. He points them to the light at the end of that tunnel, talking more explicitly and at some length about God's plans for the future restoration of his people under a new and better covenant.

JEREMIAH THE MAN

We know probably more about Jeremiah as a man than about any other Old Testament prophet. He comes from a family of priests that lived in the small town of Anathoth, a few miles north of Jerusalem. It is likely that these priests were descendants of Eli and Abiathar. That Aaronic line had served as chief caretakers of the Ark during the years of the judges and through the kingship of David (1 Sam 14:3; 22:20; 2 Sam 8:17; 15:24-29). Their arrogance regarding their position had provoked the anger of the LORD in the days of Eli and Samuel (see 2 Sam 2:27-36), prompting him to replace them with the Zadokite line. This transition was completed at the beginning of the reign of Solomon when Abiathar sided with Adonijah rather than Solomon (1 Kgs 1:7; 2:26-27). This places Jeremiah and his family at the end of a centuries-long rivalry with the priests who presided over worship in the Jerusalem temple, a rivalry which surfaces from time to time in Jeremiah's prophecies.

Jeremiah's ancestry made him something of an outsider to the religious and political establishments of Jerusalem. This situation naturally worsened when Jeremiah began speaking out against the corruption within those establishments, even making him enemies among his own relatives, who probably suffered ill feelings themselves from those whom Jeremiah criticized. Nevertheless, Jeremiah managed to have allies among those working in the palace, most notably Baruch the Scribe (Jeremiah 36, 45) and Ebed-Melech the Ethiopian (Jeremiah 38–39). Baruch is particularly significant because he plays the leading role in the actual writing of the Book of Jeremiah (see below). In fact, it is likely that God used the influence and reputation of Baruch in Judah at the time to see that Jeremiah's words were not forgotten.

Jeremiah's prophecies also reveal much about his internal turmoil as a prophet. He speaks of the abuse he suffered at the hands of palace and temple officials, the heartbreak of being criticized by his own relatives, and even mild rebukes from God himself for the way he complains at times. But most of all we see the heart of a man who grieves for the sin and then the suffering and humiliation of the people of Israel. He is a man who does not enjoy his work, because it involves the suffering and pain of people he loves dearly. He is "the Weeping Prophet," not because of the physical pain he himself is forced to endure (although there is some of that), but because he has to watch in frustrating agony as the ones he loves bring destruction down on their own lives, in spite of his many warnings.

JEREMIAH THE BOOK

The Book of Jeremiah provides us with more information about the process of how it came into being than any other book of prophecy. The events recorded in Jeremiah 36 are particularly informative, suggesting that the book developed in at least three broad stages. The story opens with a command from God to Jeremiah to dictate to Baruch the prophecies he had spoken over the preceding twenty-three years. This reveals that the prophecies of Jeremiah were not typically written down as they were spoken. So, the first stage in the development of the book was the oral delivery of the prophecies of Jeremiah, and the second stage was the committing of those prophecies to writing. But this is not the end of the process. The scroll containing prophecies from Jeremiah's first twenty-three years as a prophet was burned by King Jehoiakim, and Jeremiah had to dictate them to Baruch a second time. "And many similar words were added to them" (36:32).

This practice of adding "similar words" continued for many years after this event. This story reveals that Jeremiah first dictated some of his prophecies to Baruch in the middle of King Jehoiakim's reign (c. 605–604 B.C.). Jeremiah had been proclaiming inspired messages from the LORD for twenty-three years, but none were written down until this date. But this is only the mid-point in Jeremiah's career, who continues to prophesy until the early years of the Exile (c. 585–580 B.C.). It is obvious from the present form of the book, however, that Baruch did not simply leave that first (second) scroll intact and append later ones to it. The book in its present configuration consists of an interspersing of prophecies spoken before 605 B.C. and prophecies spoken after 605 B.C.[3] This indicates that some-

---

[3]For example, Jeremiah 21 is set at the beginning of the siege (588 B.C.); Jeremiah 22 contains a series of prophecies delivered to three of Judah's

one (probably Baruch) took the prophecies of Jeremiah and arranged them into their present order. It is likely that he also edited them by giving the historical setting for many of those prophecies. This process of *arranging* and *editing* is the third and final stage in the development of the book.

A couple of observations bring out the complexity of this final stage. First, the heading of the book (Jer 1:1-3) suggests that the book was completed when the city of Jerusalem fell to Babylon in 586 B.C. However, the narrative which begins in Jeremiah 37:1 and runs to the end of Jeremiah 44 relates events from Jeremiah's life for several years after that event. This suggests that the narrative in Jeremiah 37–44 might have been added to an already existing book which ended with Jeremiah 36 (or maybe Jeremiah 33; see comments). It is also possible that the opening verses do not mention the years after the fall of Jerusalem simply because there is no king within whose reigns those later prophecies can be placed (see on 1:1-3). A second obseravtion concerns the ending of the book. Jeremiah 52 parallels the ending of 2 Kings. Both conclude with a reference to an event that occurs around 560 B.C., some twenty years after the latest of Jeremiah's recorded prophecies. It is likely that the same editor (Baruch) appended chapter 52 to the book of Jeremiah several years after the rest of the book was completed (see comments on Jeremiah 52).[4]

Speculations based on these facts in no way undermine the assumed inspiration of these writings. They merely show the complexity of that inspiration. Inspiration is manifested at two or more

---

kings (over a span of a dozen years, 609–597 B.C.); the prophecy in Jeremiah 24 was delivered early in the reign of Zedekiah (596 B.C.?); while the prophecies and events of Jeremiah 25–26 originated in the early part of Jehoiakim's reign (609–605 B.C.).

[4]The production of this final stage is even more complex than this brief discussion suggests. The early Greek translation of Jeremiah (LXX) shows that some early Hebrew manuscripts preserved a different arrangement for some parts of the book than what one finds in the traditional Hebrew text, called the Masoretic Text (MT). The oracles against other nations (Jeremiah 46–51) are located after Jer 25:13 in the LXX, and they are in a different order. This has led to much speculation about the final stages of the formation of the Book of Jeremiah. I will not deal with those questions here, since we are working from the NIV translation. It, like all English translations, is based on the MT. For discussions regarding the differences between the MT and LXX, one can consult the critical commentaries (e.g., Jack R. Lundbom, *Jeremiah 1–20*, AB [New York: Doubleday, 1999], pp. 57-62).

chronological levels. First, Jeremiah is obviously inspired when he delivers his prophecies orally. Those words, and their meaning in their original historical context, can still be heard by us today. There is a separate "moment" of inspiration when some of those prophecies are first committed to writing at God's instruction. He has a purpose in mind for those prophecies at that moment in history which is not necessarily the same purpose as that for which the prophecies were originally spoken. Particular prophecies are chosen by God and presented through a new medium for a slightly different audience. The book itself constitutes yet another "moment" of inspiration. The author/compiler (probably Baruch) is inspired by God to present particular prophecies in a particular arrangement for the purpose of giving a written message from God to readers living long after these events had transpired. Some prophecies that were spoken originally at separate times and under separate circumstances are now placed side by side. Such placement has an intended (and inspired) effect on later readers.

This phenomenon is particularly noticeable in the first half of the book (Jeremiah 1–20). There are very few indications given as to the precise time or place in which the prophecies preserved there were originally spoken. It is likely that all or parts of prophecies from throughout Jeremiah's career were brought together in those chapters for thematic reasons. Thus, I will often remain ambivalent, when discussing those chapters, about whether a series of paragraphs were originally spoken at the same time by Jeremiah or were brought together and placed side by side later by Baruch. This should not affect appreciably the message received by the modern reader.

It is also important for the reader to be aware that the Book of Jeremiah is not a literarily homogeneous work. It consists basically of three types of literature: (1) prophetic oracles delivered in poetry, (2) prophetic oracles delivered in prose or sermonic form, and (3) biographical accounts about what Jeremiah (and some of his contemporaries) said and did. These three types are not always easy to distinguish. Generally speaking, the poetic oracles are found in Jeremiah 2–20 and 46–51, the prose oracles in Jeremiah 21–25, and the biographical sections in Jeremiah 1, 26–29, 34–44, and 52. This is only a generalization, though.[5] There are oracles — either poetic

---

[5] This list omits Jeremiah 30–33, a block of prophecies which illustrates well the subjectivity involved in these modern distinctions. All modern com-

or sermonic — within the biographical sections; there are sermonic oracles placed alongside poetic oracles (e.g., Jeremiah 7); there are poetic sections within sermonic oracles; etc. At times, it is even difficult for translators to decide whether a section is poetry or prose. A simple comparison of the NIV to any other modern translation will bear this out. So, while I will be following the NIV's lead in these matters, the reader needs to be aware that there is some level of subjectivity involved in the dividing of units and the determination of whether a verse is poetry or prose.

THE MESSAGE OF JEREMIAH

There are many facets to Jeremiah's message, so what follows is a sort of "bare minimum" of what he has to say. One major theme — often assumed more than expressed — is the sovereignty of God. He is sovereign over all nations. He has the authority to choose his prophet (Jer 1:5) and send him to prophesy "over nations and kingdoms" (1:10). He tests the thoughts of humans (12:3) and determines the fate of nations (18:5-11; 25:15-26; 27:1-11; 46:1–51:58). He is to be "heard" by all peoples. He also demonstrates his sovereignty over the people of Israel. They are not "the lost" — to borrow a later Christian designation — but the chosen people who have lost sight of what true devotion to the Lord means. They are a religious people, but a people with corrupt hearts. And they are Jeremiah's primary target.

The progression of Jeremiah's message to God's people can be seen in the shifts mentioned earlier. During the days of Josiah and Jehoiakim, Jeremiah delivers threats foretelling God's plans to send an "enemy from the north" that will come and devastate the land. God is threatening to send that enemy as punishment for two persistent types of sin: religious infidelity and oppression of the weak. The people exhibit the former through the worship of idols and the adoption of foreign practices in the worship of the LORD. The latter is manifested in the killing of the innocent, taking advantage of widows and the poor, and the uncompensated use of manual labor by the

---

mentaries set apart these chapters under such single, overarching labels as "Book of Hope" or "Book of Consolation," because of the positive tone and subject matter common to them. Chapters 30–31 consist almost entirely of poetic oracles; the remaining two chapters are entirely prose.

royal establishment.[6] In this first phase of Jeremiah's career, this destruction is spoken of as a threat, but it is destruction which still can be averted (but see comments on 15:1-14). This possibility hinges on the condition of their hearts when responding. If their hearts will change, if they will come to "hear" God's message and repent of their evil ways, then the plans for destruction will be suspended.

The possibility of deliverance is held out to the people until the days of Zedekiah. Then, the primary message becomes the inevitability of the destruction of Jerusalem and Judah. Zedekiah and his officials argue that God's punishment has already been meted out — upon those taken to Babylon with Jehoiachin. Jeremiah repeatedly refutes that interpretation of recent events; but he does not deny all reasons for hope. Instead, he says that hope for the people lies in those who are currently in exile. Israel's future lies in Babylon. Then, those there whose hearts change will return to their promised land, and the nation will enjoy a new beginning.

The positive side of this message overshadows all other themes in the final phase of Jeremiah's career. With the beginning of the final siege on Jerusalem, Jeremiah's message takes a decidedly optimistic turn. Hope lies with those in Babylon, and soon all who survive will be in Babylon. It is at this point that Jeremiah speaks of the "new covenant" between God and his people, with the emphasis again placed on the condition of their hearts. The eternal promises of God have not been retracted; they are merely being redefined by the One who is sovereign. The LORD is still "compassionate and gracious, slow to anger, abounding in love and faithfulness."

---

[6]These sins probably complemented each other in the lives of some in Judah. It is not the case that the Canaanite (the Baals) and Assyrian (the Queen of Heaven) religions promoted injustice and oppression. However, adherence to a different religion would have lent itself to such behavior. If someone with social power worshiped one god (Baal, for example) while a socially weaker individual worshiped the LORD, this would naturally have led the more powerful individual to believe that he would suffer no retaliation for his mistreatment of the weaker, since one would not expect his god (Baal) to defend a person who did not worship him.

There were also worshipers of Yahweh who oppressed their fellow worshipers. These are those who reduced devotion to God to times of worship, without living day-to-day lives of righteousness, justice, and mercy. These are the individuals who express surprise that the LORD might not protect them from the Babylonians as he had protected them from the Assyrians in the days of Hezekiah. These are those who rebuke and punish Jeremiah as a "traitor" when he insists that the LORD will destroy Jerusalem this time.

OUTLINE OF JEREMIAH

SELECTED BIBLIOGRAPHY

Bright, John. *Jeremiah*. Anchor Bible. New York: Doubleday, 1964.

Brueggemann, Walter. *A Commentary on Jeremiah: Exile and Homecoming*. Grand Rapids: Eerdmans, 1998.

Christensen, D.L. *Transformations of the War Oracle in Old Testament Prophecy*. Missoula, MT: Scholars, 1975.

Clements, R.E. *Jeremiah*. Interpretation. Atlanta: John Knox, 1988.

Dearman, J.A. "My Servants the Scribes: Composition and Context in Jeremiah 36." *JBL* 109 (1990): 403-421.

Deutsch, Robert. "Seal of Baalis Surfaces: Ammonite King Plotted Murder of Judahite Governor." *BAR* 25 (Mar–Apr 1999): 44-49, 66.

Holladay, William L. *The Architecture of Jeremiah 1–20*. Lewisburg, PA: Bucknell University, 1976.

_____. *Jeremiah 1: A Commentary on the Book of the Prophet Jeremiah: Chapters 1–25*. Minneapolis: Fortress, 1986; *Jeremiah 2: Chapters 26–52*. 1989.

Hyatt, J.P. *Jeremiah*. Interpreter's Bible 5. New York: Abingdon, 1956.

Lundbom, Jack R. *Jeremiah 1–20: A New Translation with Introduction and Commentary*. Anchor Bible. New York: Doubleday, 1999.

Martin, J.D. "The Forensic Background to Jeremiah III 1." *VT* 19 (1969): 82-92.

McKane, William. *A Critical and Exegetical Commentary on Jeremiah*. International Critical Commentary. Edinburgh: T. & T. Clark, 1986, 1996.

Nicholson, E.W. *The Book of the Prophet Jeremiah Chapters 1–25*. The Cambridge Bible Commentary. Cambridge: Cambridge University, 1973. *The Book of the Prophet Jeremiah Chapters 26–52*. 1975.

O'Connor, Kathleen M. *The Confessions of Jeremiah: Their Interpretation and Role in Chapters 1–25*. SBLDS 94. Atlanta: Scholars Press, 1988.

Overholt, T.W. *The Threat of Falsehood: A Study in the Theology of the Book of Jeremiah*. Naperville, IL: Allenson, 1970.

Parke-Taylor, Geoffrey H. *The Formation of the Book of Jeremiah: Doublets and Recurring Phrases*. SBLMS 51. Atlanta: Scholars Press, 2000.

Smith, Mark S. *The Laments of Jeremiah and Their Contexts: A Literary and Redactional Study of Jeremiah 11–20*. SBLMS 42. Atlanta: Scholars Press, 1990.

Thompson, J.A. *The Book of Jeremiah*. NICOT. Grand Rapids: Eerdmans, 1980.

Weinfeld, Moshe. *Deuteronomy and the Deuteronomic School*. Oxford: Oxford University, 1972.

JEREMIAH 1

I. INTRODUCTION (1:1-19)

Following the editorial superscription (1:1-3), the book opens with the prophetic call of Jeremiah (1:4-10), supplemented by two vision oracles for the people of Judah (1:11-12,13-16) and a message of encouragement for Jeremiah himself (1:17-19). There is an introductory formula ("The word of the LORD came to me") for the first three sections (1:4,11,13). The shift to the final section is marked in the Hebrew with an emphatic singular "you" (1:17). This yields the following ABB'A' structure for these introductory prophecies:

> encouragement to Jeremiah (1:4-10)
> vision oracle (1:11-12)
> vision oracle (1:13-16)
> encouragement to Jeremiah (1:17-19)

The purpose of the prophecies presented here is to set the tone for the entire book that is to follow. Four primary themes are evident. The strongest theme is for Jeremiah himself. This is the theme of encouragement in the face of opposition, stated most succinctly in the repetition of the LORD's statement, "I am with you and will rescue you" (1:8,19). Other statements directed toward Jeremiah reinforce this message: Jeremiah will say what the LORD commands (1:7,17); the LORD himself touches Jeremiah's mouth and places his words in Jeremiah's mouth (1:9-10); the LORD has made Jeremiah "a fortified city, an iron pillar and a bronze wall" against his opponents (1:18). Those opponents are identified as "the kings of Judah, its officials, its priests and the people of the land" (1:18). So, Jeremiah is being encouraged to stand up under the opposition which will arise from the leaders of his own people. The second theme is that Jeremiah's message will be a mixture of doom and hope. He is appointed ". . . to destroy . . . and to build . . ." (1:10). The LORD will destroy Jerusalem, but that will not be his final act; there

31

will follow a time of rebuilding. A third theme is the theme of the sovereignty of God. This is implied by the LORD's appointing Jeremiah "over nations and kingdoms" (1:10). This includes Judah, as well as many other nations. This theme of sovereignty is brought out particularly in the first vision oracle, when the LORD says, "I am watching to see that my word is fulfilled" (1:12). The second vision oracle brings out the final theme: God's punishment is a response primarily to the people's infidelity/idolatry (1:16). The exact nature of their sin is expanded and elaborated upon in the book, but this is seen as the root problem.

A. SUPERSCRIPTION (1:1-3)

1:1-3 The first three verses stand alone as a superscription to the entire book. This is typical of many prophetic books (cp. Isa 1:1; Hos 1:1; Joel 1:1; Amos 1:1; Micah 1:1; Zeph 1:1). This superscription differs from those others primarily in the fact that it is considerably longer. In spite of its greater length, this superscription is not comprehensive in its historical references. The three reigns mentioned (of Josiah, Jehoiakim, and Zedekiah) are the final three extended reigns of Judahite kings. However, two brief reigns which occurred between these longer ones are not mentioned,[1] and no reference is made to the reign of Nebuchadnezzar, the Babylonian king who conquered Jerusalem and ruled Jeremiah's homeland the last several years of his life. This suggests that the writer is being general in his choice of chronological markers for the prophetic career of Jeremiah.[2] This might explain why he fails to extend the time frame to include events which occurred after the fall of Jerusalem (Jeremiah 39–44).

The term **words** (v. 1) does not refer to individual words but to messages, prophetic oracles. A prophecy of Jeremiah from the LORD

---

[1]Jehoahaz ruled for three months before Pharaoh Neco of Egypt replaced him with his brother Eliakim/Jehoiakim (2 Kgs 23:31-35); and Jeconiah succeeded his father for three months before being exiled by Nebuchadnezzar and replaced with his uncle (2 Kgs 24:8-17). Jeremiah prophesies to/about both of these kings (Jer 22:8-12,24-30), yet they are not mentioned in this introduction.

[2]J.A. Thompson, *The Book of Jeremiah,* NICOT (Grand Rapids: Eerdmans, 1980), pp. 141-142.

commonly is introduced as "the word of the LORD" (1:4,11,13; 2:1,4; etc.). Jeremiah is identified as the **son of Hilkiah, one of the priests at Anathoth**. It is likely that these priests of Anathoth were descendants of Eli and Abiathar, priests who at one time presided over worship before the Ark but who were exiled to Anathoth early in the reign of Solomon.[3] This places Jeremiah in a rather unusual position as there is an almost automatic antagonism between Jeremiah and the Zadokite priests who preside over temple worship. This inbred antagonism explains the bitterness one senses in some of the conversations between Jeremiah and the temple priests (e.g., Jer 20:1-6; 29:24-32).

There is some discussion over the significance of **the thirteenth year of the reign of Josiah** (627 B.C.), the date that Jeremiah's career begins. Most commentators have taken this to be the year of Jeremiah's prophetic call, described in the succeeding verses. There are a few, however, who argue that this is the year of Jeremiah's birth.[4] There is nothing concrete upon which to base either position. The primary consideration is the number of prophecies spoken by Jeremiah during the reign of Josiah. This is a notoriously knotty problem, as there is only one explicit reference in the book to the speaking of a prophecy in the days of Josiah (3:6). Several prophecies in chapters 1-20 are variously dated throughout Jeremiah's career, but relatively few are placed by anyone within Josiah's reign. There is also a mention by Jeremiah in "the fourth year of Jehoiakim" (605 B.C.) that he had been receiving prophecies from the LORD for twenty-three years (Jer 25:3). This could be interpreted either as a reference back to his call or to his birth (since the LORD says, "before you were born I set you apart"; 1:5). The resolution of this issue is not crucial to our understanding of Jeremiah's words.

---

[3]William L. Holladay, *Jeremiah 1*, Hermeneia (Minneapolis: Fortress, 1986), pp. 16-17; Thompson, *Jeremiah*, p. 140; R.E. Clements, *Jeremiah*, Interpretation (Atlanta: John Knox, 1988), pp. 16-18; Lundbom, *Jeremiah 1-20*, p. 223; E.W. Nicholson, *Jeremiah Chapters 1-25*, CBC (Cambridge: Cambridge University, 1973), p. 20. Even if these priests were not from Eli's line, they would have had close contact with that line. Anathoth was not a large town.

[4]J.P. Hyatt, "Introduction and Exegesis," *Jeremiah*, Interpreter's Bible 5 (New York: Abingdon, 1956), pp. 779, 798; Holladay, *Jeremiah 1*, pp. 1, 14-15; cp. W. McKane, *Jeremiah*, ICC (Edinburgh: T. & T. Clark, 1986), pp. 3-5. For responses, see Thompson, *Jeremiah*, pp. 50-56; Lundbom, *Jeremiah 1-20*, p. 107.

B. THE CALL OF JEREMIAH (1:4-19)

1:4-10 The actual "call" of Jeremiah — from a form-critical point of view — entails only Jeremiah 1:4-10. It follows a pattern which one finds in several instances in the Old Testament, when a prophet or some other leader is chosen by the LORD. The pattern is this: (1) the LORD speaks or appears to the one being called; (2) the recipient voices some reason(s) why he/she is not fit for the task to which he/she is being called; (3) the LORD promises to make up whatever is lacking, so that they are fit; and (4) the person accepts the task or is given his first assignment. This sequence of events serves to demonstrate the person's humility. The person recognizes that, on his own, he is not able to do the job to which God is calling him. As he successfully fulfills that job, he and the reader are to recognize that he does so only because the LORD is working through him.[5]

The LORD's initial remarks to Jeremiah have long been of significance to biblical theologians. At first blush, it appears to be a straightforward claim of predestination, that the LORD decided before Jeremiah's birth that he would be a prophet, and there was nothing Jeremiah could do to thwart that decision. Two considerations should make one cautious about reaching firm conclusions too quickly, though. First, it is possible that this is an example of hyperbole, that God is overstating the fact to emphasize one aspect of it.[6] It could be similar to statements made by parents today, when they claim some-

---

[5]For some other examples, see the stories of Moses (Exodus 3–4), Gideon (Judg 6:11-18), Saul (1 Sam 9:15–10:8), and Isaiah (Isa 6:1-8). On this form, see N. Habel, "The Form and Significance of the Call Narratives," *ZAW* 77 (1965): 297-323; McKane, *Jeremiah*, pp. 11-14.

[6]In this case he is emphasizing that he, God, has chosen this path for Jeremiah; this is not a claim by Jeremiah for which he is wanting divine support. This is not to deny the veracity of the LORD's words, but simply to say one cannot deny him the right to use hyperbole to make a point, if he so desires. There are actually numerous examples of the LORD using hyperbole. For example, the LORD, speaking through Jeremiah, repeatedly says that the people worshiped idols "on *every* high hill and under *every* spreading tree" (2:20; 3:6; etc.). It is not necessary to argue that every single "spreading tree" in Judah had to be used as a place of idolatry to make this statement true. It is simply a way of saying that idolatry was widely practiced, that it was "everywhere." There is evidence from the ancient Near East that such hyperbolic claims were common for political and religious leaders. See Holladay, *Jeremiah 1*, pp. 27-28; Lundbom, *Jeremiah 1–20*, pp. 230-231.

thing like the following: "I knew my son was going to be a doctor from the day he was born." But even assuming that it is a straightforward statement of fact, one cannot deduce from this that God has predestined the life of every human being. Jeremiah might be the exception rather than the rule. Moreover, one cannot assume that Jeremiah was still without a say in the matter, that he could not reject the LORD's call. Otherwise, why would God need to encourage him?

In the Hebrew, each of the three lines in this verse ends with the verb — **I knew you . . . I set you apart . . . I appointed you.** This sort of parallelism is common in Hebrew poetry, indicating that the three verbs are to be understood as synonyms. The verb "to know" (יָדַע, yāda‘) is used here with the nuance of choosing someone for a special task (see the footnote in the NIV; cp. Amos 3:2), while also indicating a close, personal relationship between the chooser and the one chosen.[7] The verb for "set apart" (הִקְדִּישׁ, hiqdîš), is derived from a root meaning "holy." The form used here is often translated "make holy" or "sanctify." This passage indicates that "sanctification" is more than placing someone in an exalted state; there is also the expectation that the one sanctified will perform special tasks and responsibilities. The verb translated **appointed** literally means "gave"; it is different from the word for "appointed" in verse 10.

Jeremiah raises the objection that he is **only a child** (cp. 1 Kgs 3:7). The word for **child** (נַעַר, na‘ar) can refer to an unmarried male of any age, ranging from infancy (Exod 2:6; 1 Sam 1:22) to young adulthood (2 Sam 18:5,12), although it most often refers to an adolescent. The more common term for an infant is yeled (יֶלֶד; see 2 Sam 12:15-23). It is most likely that Jeremiah is a teenager when he makes this statement. Jeremiah's reason for making this point is not to disqualify himself solely because of his age, but because one's age influenced how seriously others would take them when they spoke. For example, Elihu hesitated to speak in the presence of Job and his friends because he was younger than they (Job 32:6-7). Similarly, Jeremiah recognizes that his age immediately makes the authority of his words suspect in the minds of his listeners.

God's response is an acknowledgment of this social connection between age and respect for one's words. The people will be inclined to ignore Jeremiah because of his young age, but Jeremiah is not going in his own name and is not speaking for himself. He

---

[7]Holladay, Jeremiah 1, p. 33.

goes where God sends him; he speaks what God commands. The exhortation, **do not be afraid**, is not backed up with a revelation about what will happen to him and that he will be happy with the outcome, but on the unqualified promise by the LORD, **I am with you,** no matter what happens (cp. Exod 3:12; Judg 6:12). The significance of this is immense. So often, people look for external, physical proof of God's presence in and approval of their lives when the only "proof" he might offer is that he is with them. Such proof cannot be verified; it is only known in the heart of the believer.

The LORD now touches Jeremiah's **mouth**, symbolically demonstrating that he is the LORD's "mouth" to his people. This places Jeremiah in an elite group among the prophets, as similar acts are reported only in the cases of Moses (Exod 4:10-17) and Isaiah (Isa 6:5-7). Further, what the LORD promises here fulfills the description of "the prophet like Moses" given in Deuteronomy 18:18.[8] This helps to explain why some associated Jesus with Jeremiah (Matt 16:14). The LORD appoints Jeremiah **over nations and kingdoms**. Indirectly, this assumes the sovereignty of God over all nations. But there are also at least two other significant conclusions to be drawn from this statement. On the one hand, in this statement the LORD claims authority over nations to punish them or bless them as he sees fit (Jer 18:1-11; 27–28; 46–51). This includes the "nation" of Judah (see Jer 25:17ff.). On the other hand, the LORD is also concerned to give encouragement to his people in exile, including those northern tribes who were exiled by the Assyrians a century earlier. This statement serves as encouragement by letting those in exile know that the LORD is still in charge of the kingdoms who hold them captive. If he says they will be released, they need not despair that he might lack the power and authority to do so.

The LORD claims (and demonstrates) his authority over earthly kingdoms by declaring what their fate will be. Jeremiah, speaking by God's authority, will proclaim God's plans **to uproot and tear down, to destroy and overthrow, to build and to plant** them. These six verbs

---

[8]The wording in verses 7 and 9 is very similar to that of Deut 18:18. The end of verse 7 literally reads, "And all which I command you, you will speak," and the end of verse 9, "Behold, I have given my words in your mouth." By comparison, Deut 18:18b reads, "And I will give my words in his mouth, and he will speak to them all which I command him." See Holladay, *Jeremiah 1*, p. 29; Thompson, *Jeremiah*, pp. 148-150; Nicholson, *Jeremiah 1–25*, p. 25; Lundbom, *Jeremiah 1–20*, pp 233-234.

form an interesting parallelism (see also 18:7,9; 24:6; 31:28,38-40; 42:10; 45:4). The first four denote destruction, while the latter two denote construction. The first and last are agricultural terms, while the four in between are used primarily regarding human structures. Viewed together, these six verbs constitute a sort of snapshot of Jeremiah's career. Jeremiah will prophesy the destruction of Judah (and other nations) during most of his career (**to uproot . . . and overthrow**), but toward the end he will shift to a more positive message of reconstruction for all of God's people (**to build and to plant**).[9]

1:11-12 This is the first of two vision oracles, of which there are a few other examples in Jeremiah (e.g., 24:3). These two are excellent examples of "sermon illustrations" that Jeremiah uses throughout his book. This one involves a Hebrew pun which the English reader cannot see. The terms for **almond** (שָׁקֵד, *šāqād*) and **watching** (שֹׁקֵד, *šōqēd*) are almost identical in Hebrew. By merely pointing to an almond branch, Jeremiah can make the point to his audience that the LORD is **watching** — is keeping watch like a guard over — his prophecies to ensure that they are carried out. There will be opposition to and refutations of Jeremiah's prophecies, but the LORD's words will not fail, because he himself will "see" to it.

1:13-16 This vision oracle introduces the "enemy from the north." The imprecision of the designation has led to several interpretations of what Jeremiah has in mind. The most likely referent for this "enemy" is Babylon as the Babylonian armies would normally march west from Mesopotamia into Syrian territory before proceeding south against Judah. There has been speculation, however, that this was originally a prophecy about Scythian incursions (Scythians lived north of Syria) into the region between the Assyrian and Babylonian dominions. The main impetus for looking for such an enemy is the fact that the Babylonians do not enter Judah until 605 B.C., more than two decades after Jeremiah's call. A more immediate fulfillment of this early prophecy would be welcome, especially to support the belief that Jeremiah began prophesying in 627 B.C. But the absence of clear biblical references to these Scythian incursions makes them a questionable fulfillment of Jeremiah's words.

---

[9]Walter Brueggemann, *A Commentary on Jeremiah: Exile and Homecoming* (Grand Rapids: Eerdmans, 1998), p. 26. There is a similar function in Isa 6:9-13 for Isaiah's career.

The balance of this prophecy in verses 15-16 seems to refer to the total overthrow of the city of Jerusalem which finally takes place in 586 B.C. Jeremiah prophesies that the LORD is going to **summon all the peoples of the northern kingdoms** and bring them against Judah (1:15). He makes the same prediction in 25:9, in that case specifying that Nebuchadnezzar of Babylon will be with them. He also says that **kings will come and set up their thrones in the entrance of the gates of Jerusalem** (1:15). A later description of the capture of Jerusalem includes the note that "all the officials of the king of Babylon came and took seats in the Middle Gate" (39:3). Jeremiah further prophesies that this "enemy" will come **against all the towns of Judah** (1:15). Scythian attacks would have been scattered incidents, while this sounds like a full-fledged invasion and subjugation. Related to this is the recognition that Jeremiah repeatedly links the coming of the Babylonian armies to the people's worship of other gods, which is mentioned in 1:16. This can be coupled with the fact that the people in Jerusalem seem to interpret the appearance of the Babylonians in Judah during the reigns of Jehoiakim and Jeconiah (605 and 598 B.C.) as the fulfillment of Jeremiah's warnings about coming destruction (cp. Jer 24:7-10; 27:16-28:4; Ezek 11:14-17). So, while it is possible that Jeremiah's "enemy from the north" might have referred to Scythians on certain occasions, the phrase in Jeremiah primarily refers to the Babylonians.[10]

1:17-19 The LORD now returns to the encouragement of Jeremiah as the focus of his attention. He has given Jeremiah a taste of what he will be prophesying to the people of Judah, and he recognizes that this will not be an assignment that Jeremiah will cheerfully accept. Like Isaiah, it would be natural for Jeremiah to ask, "How long, O LORD?" (Isa 6:11). So the LORD addresses this before Jeremiah even has a chance to react. He tells Jeremiah, **Get yourself ready!** Literally, this is, "Gird on your loins!" This is the language of war, of military preparation. Jeremiah is to expect a hostile audience. They will consider him a threat to their religious beliefs and wish to silence him, so he must be ready for a fight. The LORD then returns to one of the first things he had said in Jeremiah's initial call — **say to them whatever I command you** (v. 17; cp. 1:7). The prior statement by itself sounded like a statement of empowerment, as if

---

[10]Holladay, *Jeremiah 1*, pp. 42-43; Clements, *Jeremiah*, pp. 20-21; Nicholson, *Jeremiah 1-25*, p. 27; McKane, *Jeremiah*, pp. 19-21.

it would give Jeremiah the respect that he felt he lacked in talking to an older audience. Now we see that saying what the LORD commands will actually put him at risk. Even though these are the words of the LORD, they will not win for him acceptance; instead, they will have just the opposite effect. Rather than emboldening him, speaking the words of the LORD is a terrifying prospect.

This leads into the second half of verse 17. The reason why the word of the LORD is terrifying is because of the response it evokes from those to whom it is directed. It is the word of the LORD, but they will retaliate against the LORD's messenger for its contents. This rejection of the LORD's message is what threatens to **terrify** Jeremiah. The LORD "reassures" him initially with a threat of his own. If Jeremiah allows himself to be terrified by their threats of retaliation, then he will terrify Jeremiah even more. So, Jeremiah's only protection against those who would terrify him is to trust in the one who can terrify him even more.

In a sense, Jeremiah is just like his audience. He, like they, has to decide whether to trust in the LORD. They face the threat of the Babylonians, a threat which they can withstand only if they will trust wholeheartedly in the LORD as he reveals himself through the prophecies of Jeremiah. Jeremiah faces the threat of his own people, a threat which he can withstand only by trusting in the LORD.

The LORD does not wish to be respected because he is a greater threat, though. He does not wish to bully Jeremiah into obedience. Instead, he induces Jeremiah with promises of protection. He promises to make Jeremiah **a fortified city, an iron pillar and a bronze wall** (v. 18; cp. 15:20).[11] These are fortifications which will withstand the fiercest attacks. The LORD then spells out who the attackers will be — the leaders of his own people, in his own land. Now, in contrast to the threatening mood of verse 17, he promises protection against the threat, repeating what he had said earlier: **I am with you and will rescue you.** As before, he does not seek to minimize the threat. It is those with power in the nation who will be seeking to hurt and silence Jeremiah. And as before, he promises nothing concrete, only that, somehow, he will be "with" Jeremiah. He does not say how he will be with Jeremiah; he does not promise the avoidance of pain

---

[11]See Geoffrey H. Parke-Taylor, *The Formation of the Book of Jeremiah: Doublets and Recurring Phrases,* SBLMS 51 (Atlanta: Society of Biblical Literature, 2000), pp. 35-40.

and suffering. Rather, he gives a nebulous promise to "be with" Jeremiah, and he expects that to suffice. Acceptance of this call requires a measure of faith on Jeremiah's part. He will occasionally complain and worry about his physical well-being, and he even tries to avoid doing at times what the LORD demands of him. Yet he ultimately trusts in the LORD, prophesying what the LORD has revealed to him and relying on the LORD to be with him in the face of vehement opposition.

JEREMIAH 2

II. JUDAH BRINGS ABOUT HER OWN DESTRUCTION (2:1–6:30)

A. ISRAEL FORSAKES GOD (2:1–3:5)

It is impossible to be confident about the original oral extent and unity of the next several chapters of the book. Every commentator agrees that Jeremiah 7:1 begins a section that is separate and apart from what precedes it; but the unity/disunity of Jeremiah 2–6 is a matter of continuing debate. Most see a significant break early in Jeremiah 4 (either after 4:2 or 4:4), but then the unity of 2:1–4:4 is also debated.[1] The approach adopted here is to accept the major sections as designated by the NIV editors (2:1–3:5; 3:6–4:4; 4:5-31; 5:1-31; 6:1-30), and then discuss the contents of each major section as a series of smaller units. The determination of these smaller units is based on a combination of contents and linguistic clues. It is likely that some adjacent units were linked together by Jeremiah when he spoke them, before they were written down in this book form; others were originally spoken separately but were brought together by the book's inspired compiler.

2:1-3 This small unit has a double literary introduction. There is a narrative introduction (**The word of the LORD came to me**) in verse 1, then an oracular introduction ("This is what the LORD says")

---

[1]Holladay argues for the eventual unity (after much redaction) of all of 2:1–4:4 (*Jeremiah 1*, pp. 62-81; cp. Lundbom, *Jeremiah 1–20*, pp. 249-251). Clements divides Jeremiah 2 into a four-part "indictment": 2:4-13,14-19,20-28,29-37 (*Jeremiah*, pp. 27-28; cp. Thompson, *Jeremiah*, pp. 159-187; Brueggemann, *Jeremiah*, pp. 32-40). He puts 3:1-5 with the rest of Jeremiah 3; however, he also says that "the indictment proper extends as far as 3:5" (p. 23). Bright separates out 3:6-18 as a secondary unit. John Bright, *Jeremiah*, AB (New York: Doubleday, 1964), pp. 25-27.

in verse 2, which is omitted in the NIV. A similar double introduction in verses 4-5 points to a new beginning there, which justifies reading 2:1-3 as a separate unit.

As a whole, this unit serves to set up the metaphor of Jerusalem/Israel as the bride of the LORD. This metaphor is used throughout this section (2:1-3:5) and the next (3:6-4:4) as the primary metaphor for explaining the LORD's plans to bring destruction on Jerusalem. He is acting as a husband whose wife has been unfaithful to him. She has shamed her husband, and he responds to assert and restore his own honor. There are various possible implications to be drawn from the fact that he addresses **Jerusalem** here. It could simply be that "Jerusalem" represents the nation of Judah as a whole, just as "Washington" and "Moscow" can be used today in talking about relations between the U.S. and Russia. It could be that Jeremiah is directing his message at the political and religious leaders of the nation, since they are mentioned specifically in the closing verses of the preceding chapter (1:18). It could also be that the LORD singles out Jerusalem because the people had become convinced after Hezekiah was spared that the LORD would never allow Jerusalem to fall to her enemies (see Jeremiah 7). Or maybe all of the reasons mentioned are involved.

Jeremiah has inherited this metaphor from Hosea (see Hos 1:2-3:5). In the metaphor, the LORD and his bride are married at Mount Sinai with the establishment of the Mosaic covenant. The "honeymoon" comes in the sojourn in the wilderness, when the LORD says they **followed me through the desert, through a land not sown** (Jer 2:2). Both Hosea and Jeremiah describe this as a time when Israel loved the LORD deeply. No reference is made to complaining or rebellion; Israel relied on the LORD for her survival.

The continuation of the metaphor (v. 3) probably moves the reader into the period of the judges. There are several subtle nuances to these lines that one might possibly miss at first glance. To say that **Israel was holy to the LORD** has at least two nuances. He could mean to imply the special status of Israel, that it is separate and apart from all other nations. But holiness also implies special responsibilities (see on 1:5). They are holy in order to fulfill the promise made to Abraham that all of the world would be blessed through him and his descendants. Israel is then referred to as God's **firstfruits**. This seems to reflect the new agricultural life the people adopt after they enter their promised land. Just as they are harvesting their firstfruits, so they are the LORD's firstfruits. This line also implies the special status of Israel and her special responsibilities. They are not just fruit, but firstfruit. They are the farmer's most prized produce; they are expected to be of the highest quality. Further, there is the implication that they themselves are producing fruit in the way they live their lives. Their enemies were punished, not for Israel's sake, but so they could produce fruit for God's pleasure. According to Isaiah, the fruits God expected were righteousness and justice (Isa 5:1-7).

2:4-13 This unit, like the one before, begins with a double introduction. The initial call to **Hear the word of the LORD** (v. 4) is followed by the common prophetic formula, **This is what the LORD says** (v. 5). The unit falls into two parts (2:4-8,9-13) and may in fact have been two separate units originally. The first half gives a description of Israel's unexpected idolatry, which prompts (**Therefore**, v. 9) the LORD to **bring charges** against his unfaithful wife. In fact, the whole unit seems to borrow from the language of the courtroom. It begins as a plaintiff would begin when addressing those he is accusing: **Hear the word** . . . . In other words, "Listen to the accusations being made." At the transition in verse 9, the LORD twice uses the term רִיב (rîb), which is a term that carries the specifically legal sense of "file a lawsuit." This genre of "covenant lawsuit" is fairly common among the Hebrew prophets.

There are two sides to the central thought of this unit.[2] On the one hand, the LORD defends his own actions toward Israel, showing how he has acted as a good husband would act toward his wife. He is guilty of no **fault** that might explain her own shameful actions. The natural thing for the Israelites to do would be to call to mind how the LORD had delivered them from Egypt, cared for them in the wilderness, and provided a home for them (2:6-7). Then, they can be expected to respond with gratitude and praise, with justice and righteousness. They should be asking the question, "**Where is the LORD?**" (2:6,8). This is not a question of doubt, but a reminder. Each gener-

---

[2]There is a loose literary cohesion to verses 5-8 provided by two pairs of similar statements. The more obvious pairing comes in the form of the statement, "They did not ask, 'Where is the LORD . . .'" (vv. 6a and 8a). The other pairing comes in the references to idols (vv. 5b and 8b), although two different terms are used. In the former, he says, "They went after what is worthless"; in the latter, "They went after what does not profit." The NIV translation helps to bring out this subtle bracketing.

ation has been searching for a god who will protect them and provide for them, and the question would remind them of how the LORD had provided for them in the past. But no one asks the question.

This points to the other side to this unit, namely, how the people have repeatedly responded unnaturally. **They followed worthless idols and became worthless themselves** (cp. Ps 115:4-8; 135:15-18).[3] The LORD had carried them through a place of desolation and death into a place of fruitfulness and life. They received the gift of a fruitful and rich land by ruining it, spoiling it, defiling it with idols. They had turned to things that give no profit (**worthless idols,** v. 9) in their attempts to make a profit.

Adding insult to injury is the fact that those specifically entrusted with reminding the people of what the LORD has done for them lead the way in forgetting or ignoring the LORD.[4] The priests, who should have been leading the people in asking, "**Where is the LORD?**" do not ask the question. The legal experts (scribes) do not **know** the LORD, meaning they do not uphold (or maybe even consult) his teachings in giving their opinions on legal questions (see on 22:16). The **leaders** ("shepherds") have rebelled, when they should be the ones putting down rebellions. And the LORD's own prophets have deserted him and are prophesying on behalf of Baal. Instead of "going" where the LORD sends them (1:7), they are **following** ("going after") **worthless idols.**

The formal indictment the LORD brings is essentially one charge, but it is expressed in two ways. First, he challenges his audience to name any other **nation** that has been unfaithful to **its gods** the way Israel has been unfaithful to the LORD. None can be named. What makes this all the more tragic is Israel is the only nation whose God

---

[3] The term translated "worthless" in verse 5 is the same word (הֶבֶל, *hebel*) that is translated "meaningless" ("vanity") in Ecclesiastes, where it is often parallel with "a chasing after the wind" (Eccl 1:14,17; 2:11,17,26; 4:4; 5:16). The term connotes something that is not solid, that cannot be held. Thus, he is implying that their sins show them to be beings without substance.

[4] Four groups of leaders are singled out for this accusation: priests, "those who deal with the law," leaders, and prophets (2:8). This list sounds like a combination of the lists of religious leaders mentioned in Jer 18:18 and Ezek 7:26. The former mentions priests, sages, and prophets; the latter replaces sages with elders. The designation of "those who deal with the law" probably is a reference to scribes. Sages and scribes often worked hand in hand. The word translated "leaders" here is more literally "shepherds," and a correlation between shepherds and elders (Ezek 7:26) is well known.

is real; yet they are the only nation to "trade in" their God for another. Their God possesses **Glory**, yet they have put their faith in things that cannot profit, things that are **worthless**. So what Israel has done is not typical, even for nations who would have more reason to do it.

The LORD then reinforces this indictment with a metaphor, comparing himself to a **spring of living water** and the other gods to **broken cisterns**. This would have been a very vivid metaphor for the people living in that semiarid region of the world where water was a primary and perennial concern. Settlements naturally sprang up there around springs because they could provide water year round. Cisterns were dug and lined with limestone to supplement the natural water supply. They worked by catching the runoff from the seasonal rains and holding it during the long, dry months. But they could only hold enough to last for one dry season, and they were much more likely to become contaminated than springs. Moreover, the "cisterns" (gods) to whom the Israelites were turning for spiritual sustenance were broken; any nourishment they might have provided had seeped out, leaving the people with nothing. Yet the people continued to rely on them. Again, this is totally unnatural and irrational.

Each of the ways in which this charge is expressed carries with it a sense of incredulity. Who would have thought such a situation would develop? No one. This is completely unexpected, unnatural. And yet, we see people doing the same sort of thing today. We assume and look for "natural" and "logical" explanations for our successes and failures, rather than acknowledging the One who controls the fates of all. We yearn for answers to complex issues, resolutions to disagreements, the elimination of physical pain. But we look for answers from sources which cannot provide what we need. We turn to man-made chemicals and self-help schemes and short-sighted solutions, instead of looking to "the spring of living water" (cp. 17:13).

2:14-19 The beginning of a new unit is suggested here in the use of a triple question. Jeremiah uses this pattern several times, and it usually indicates the beginning of a unit (cp. 2:31; 8:4,22; 14:19; 49:1).[5] The first two questions expect "No" answers, but the third indicates that there are reasons to dispute those answers. These questions, in a roundabout way, assert that Israel is God's son and

---

[5]Lundbom, *Jeremiah 1–20*, p. 271.

would normally be able to claim better treatment and protection. They feel they have been treated like second-class citizens by God, and verses 15-16 reflect that kind of treatment.

The verbalizing of these questions allows the LORD to address other questions which the people of Jerusalem probably were asking. The degenerating military situation raised questions in the minds of the people about how the LORD was treating them. He gives the explanation for this turn of events in verses 17-19. The people feel that their "father" has forsaken them, but he states and then reiterates that it is they who are **forsaking the LORD your God** (2:17,19; cp. 2:13). What is unclear here is what they have done to forsake the LORD. It could be that they are looking to Egypt and Assyria for economic aid or military assistance against the Babylonians. It seems more likely that they have taken on the gods and worship practices of those nations. There is a play on the word "way" in these verses which has been lost in the NIV translation that suggests this interpretation, as does the wording at the beginning of verse 19. In verse 17, he questions why they have forsaken the LORD **when he led you in the way.** Then, verse 18 consists of a double question which more literally reads, "What to you is the *way* of Egypt/Assyria . . . ?" Israel has "forsaken" the way of the LORD (i.e., the way of life he has commanded) and walked in the ways of Egypt and Assyria. This use of "way" suggests something other than military assistance. Supporting this interpretation is the use of the term **backsliding** (מְשֻׁבוֹת, *m^ešubôth*) in verse 19. This term is used particularly in Jeremiah 3 to denote Israel as a "faithless" wife, a wife who has prostituted herself with other gods. So, they have "forsaken" their husband — their "spring of living water" (v. 13) — and they have drunk from another source. What looked like mighty rivers have turned out to be "broken cisterns."

Jeremiah's words in verse 19 imply that the people have learned a bitter lesson in the process, but one from which they are expected to learn. The terms translated **punish** and **rebuke** often carry a didactic nuance. Both are used elsewhere to denote the discipline that a parent gives to a child (יַסֵּר, *yissēr*; cp. Deut 8:5; 21:18; הוֹכִיחַ, *hôkîaḥ*; cp. Prov 3:12). We can deduce from this that the suffering which they are undergoing is not intended as the end or goal of God's plan for them, but as a means to an end.

The suffering which the people now face is a clear example of a bad decision coming back to haunt them. They have turned to other nations and their gods looking for help, but it is those nations who have let them down, in fact, who have turned against them and hurt them. They have forsaken the LORD, and so he has allowed them to suffer the consequences of that decision. They are experiencing the bitter taste of the fruits of their actions.

Certain statements in this unit would seem to suggest that it comes from a later time than the preceding unit. The LORD talks here about destruction that has already taken place, while the previous verses only describe the sins of the people that warrant punishment. Here, Israel has **become plunder** (2:14); **towns are burned and deserted** (2:15); Egyptians **have shaved the crown of your head** (2:16). This third statement suggests a time after 609 B.C., when an Egyptian force defeated Josiah at Megiddo and then replaced his natural successor with another son. It is even reasonable to assume that these words were spoken around 605 B.C. The people now view Egypt and Assyria as possible allies. Josiah went out against Egypt in 609 B.C., showing that he stood opposed to the Egyptian-Assyrian alliance; but by 605 B.C. the people in Jerusalem would have sensed that the Babylonians were a greater threat to them than the Egyptians. Moreover, any assistance which Assyria could have been expected to provide after 605 B.C. would have been negligible, so a date later than that becomes unlikely. Perhaps this unit has been placed here because the references to drinking the waters of Egypt and Assyria (2:18) echo the imagery regarding cisterns in verse 13.

These comments on the date of 2:14-19 raise other questions regarding the date of the previous verses. It could be that they come from the same time frame (609–605 B.C.), but they simply do not mention that the devastation of Judah has already commenced. But the absence of any reference to destruction is more likely to indicate a date prior to 609 B.C. To what events, then, is Jeremiah referring in 2:4-13? Two other possibilities present themselves. They could refer to the situation in Judah in the final days of Josiah's reign, when it appears that the positive changes accompanying Josiah's Reform (621 B.C.) were being exposed as superficial and cosmetic only (see on 3:10). It could also be that, in those verses, Jeremiah is speaking about the situation in Judah over the past several centuries and not just at the time he is speaking.

2:20-30[6] These verses consist of a hodgepodge of metaphors

---

[6]The references above (n. 1) indicate that it is more common to see a break after verse 28 rather than verse 30. My primary reason for doing so

depicting the rampant idolatry of the people. The people are servants of the LORD who have broken his **yoke** and removed their
bonds in order to serve another master; they have prostituted themselves **on every high hill . . .** (2:20); they are a **choice vine** that has
become a **wild vine** (2:21; cp. Isa 5:1-7); they are soiled with a **stain**
that cannot be removed (2:22); they are like a **swift she-camel** or a
wild donkey . . . in her heat that cannot be restrained (2:24); they
are disgraced like **a thief . . . when he is caught** (2:26). It is as if one
illustration is not enough to convey the totality of the corruption in
their lives. The unsubmissive servant conveys some dimensions of
the problem; but the prostituting wife suggests others, the wild vine
even more, and on and on it goes. Their sin is enduring and pervasive. **For you have as many gods as you have towns, O Judah** (2:28).
This is not something which has developed recently which the LORD
is seeking to eradicate swiftly, but something which he has witnessed
for many years and is willing to tolerate no longer.

It is helpful to isolate the statements of the people quoted by the
LORD in this unit. Brueggemann characterizes these as "false asser-
tions of identity."[7] They are that — and more. Each of them is a statement of rebellion and defiance toward the LORD. This is clear in the
first instance, as they pull off God's yoke and say, **"I will not serve
you"** (2:20); and it is clear in verse 25, when they seem to tire of hid-
ing their true sentiments from the LORD and pledge to go after foreign gods. The same element of defiance undergirds their other
statements. They deny that they have **run after the Baals** (v. 23),
effectively calling God (their accuser) a liar and challenging him to
prove his accusations. They defiantly turn from God and appeal to
the idols they have made as their divine parent and savior (v. 27).

The LORD then turns this defiance on its head in verses 28-30. He
challenges the people to call to their gods to save them from their
troubles (v. 28), troubles that come when the LORD punishes them
for their sins. They think that the LORD does not deserve their allegiance, that they will find more power in the false gods they have
made. So now God puts their reasoning to the test — by threatening
them himself. They will have to rely on the foreign gods they wor-

---

after verse 30 is the presence of the prose introduction in verse 31, a line
which Thompson simply omits as a marginal gloss (*Jeremiah*, p. 181) and
Holladay revocalizes to achieve a different reading (*Jeremiah 1*, p. 55).

[7]Brueggemann, *Jeremiah*, p. 38; cp. Lundbom, *Jeremiah 1–20*, pp. 275-276.

ship to protect them from their own God. This train of thought continues on in verses 29-30. The troubles that he is bringing on them evoke complaints; his people **bring charges against** him, as if he has broken his promises to them. The truth is, they have **rebelled** against him, and he is justified in bringing charges against them. And it is not as if they were caught off guard by his acts of punishment. He had sent prophets earlier who warned them to repent of their evil ways, but they had **devoured [those] prophets like a ravening lion**. He had struck them **in vain . . .** ; **they did not respond to correction**.

2:31-37 The beginning of this unit is also doubly marked stylistically. The brief rhetorical summons (**You of this generation, consider the word of the LORD**) is followed by another triad of rhetorical questions (cp. v. 14). The questions perpetuate the defiant element of the people's actions exhibited in verses 20-30. The questions anticipate negative answers, implying that the LORD has been like a garden (not a **desert**) to his people, that he has been their light (not **darkness**). They have been restless and dissatisfied with him for no reason, choosing to roam from him[8] rather than accepting what he provides for them. They fail to appreciate the blessings they have, and so they turn their attention to other possible sources of provision and protection.

The bitterness the LORD feels regarding Israel's infidelities reach a fever pitch in the middle of this unit. The people have **forgotten** him, meaning they have no regard for what he has done; they do not acknowledge him in their actions. He should have been treated as most precious, guarded and cherished like a woman's wedding trousseau; yet she has treated him like some cheap trinket, placed in the back of some drawer and forgotten. She has failed miserably as a wife, but she has excelled as a prostitute. **How skilled you are at pursuing love!** She is the expert; she has "written the book" on how to be promiscuous. She is the one who will be interviewed on the TV talk shows to give the most sought after advice regarding this topic, because **even the worst of women can learn from your ways**.

The LORD now fills out the existing picture of Judah's wrongs by amplifying one aspect of it and introducing a couple of others for

---

[8]The term translated "free to roam" (רוּד, *rûd*) does not intend a sense of breaking free of oppressive restrictions. Instead, it carries the sense that someone feels the urge to do something just to be doing it, perhaps out of a sense of boredom.

the first time. What he amplifies are the declarations of innocence, mentioned before only briefly in verse 23. They see the signs of God's anger, and they hear the accusations of wrong leveled by Jeremiah and other prophets; but they refuse to accept that the LORD has any justifiable reason to be angry with them (v. 35). The devastation they see around them must have some other explanation. The basis for such a claim of innocence is not spelled out until later when Jeremiah talks about the misguided confidence they place in worship (see Jeremiah 7). It is an important part of the picture, though, because it shows that the people had ample warnings and ample time to change their ways. It is not because they occasionally sinned that God decides to destroy their land and exile them, but because they persist in their sins after having been corrected and warned by him.

The elements introduced into this picture for the first time are charges of oppression and a reliance on the military support of foreign nations. God says they are stained with **the lifeblood of the innocent poor, though you did not catch them breaking in** (2:34). This is a fairly common sort of prophetic accusation, being a generic type of judicial corruption. The poor are charged falsely with some wrongdoing (in this case, theft) so that the wealthy can gain control of their property. The difficulty for the modern reader comes in understanding the connection between oppression and religious infidelity. The most likely connection is that commonality of religion naturally compels persons not to mistreat one another in other areas of life. The oppressive practices mentioned here suggest that the perpetrators did not feel a strong religious bond with those whom they oppressed, probably because there were other religious ties that superseded them. Another dimension added in these verses is the military/political dependence placed by Jerusalem in the powers of Egypt and Assyria (vv. 36-37). Whatever the external threat, they should be looking to the LORD — their Savior, the LORD of Hosts, he who brought them out of Egypt with a mighty hand and an outstretched arm — to protect them. Instead, they look to earthly powers, powers which historically have hurt them. It makes no sense.

JEREMIAH 3

A. ISRAEL FORSAKES GOD (2:1–3:5) (continued)

3:1-5 There is no consensus among scholars about whether to regard this unit as the end of the section in Jeremiah 2 or the beginning of the section running into Jeremiah 4. Perhaps it is simply the hinge in a long section encompassing all of 2:1–4:4.[1] The stylistic shift from poetry to prose in 3:6 might justify seeing a more significant break there, but to be consistent, one would have to explain why similar breaks are not demanded later in Jeremiah 3. Thematically, this unit perpetuates the husband-wife metaphor introduced in Jeremiah 2, but it also entertains for the first time the possibility for marital reconciliation, a theme which dominates the succeeding section. On the other hand, the section running from 3:6 to 4:4 seems to be viewing the northern kingdom of Israel and the southern kingdom of Judah separately. This would suggest a significant change in the message presented so far, because the people of God seem to be a single entity in Jeremiah 2. So, we will cautiously continue to follow the NIV's demarcation.

The hypothetical situation raised in Jeremiah 3:1 reflects the law recorded in Deuteronomy 24:1-4. This has received more than the usual amount of attention from scholars.[2] The law states that a man and woman who marry, divorce, marry others, divorce again, and then remarry each other are guilty of something "detestable in the eyes of the LORD." Brueggemann reaches the conclusion that, in what follows, the LORD effectively breaks his own law.[3] He married

---

[1]Holladay, for example, starts his discussion of 2:1–4:4 by saying, "One begins with the assumption that 2:1–4:4 forms a self-contained collection" (*Jeremiah 1*, p. 62); cp. Lundbom, *Jeremiah 1–20*, pp. 249-251.

[2]See J.D. Martin, "The Forensic Background to Jeremiah III 1," *VT* 19 (1969): 82-92; T.R. Hobbs, "Jeremiah 3:1-5 and Deuteronomy 24:1-4," *ZAW* 86 (1974): 23-29.

[3]Brueggemann, *Jeremiah*, pp. 42-43.

Israel at Mount Sinai; she has been unfaithful, prompting him to divorce her and send her into exile; later, he will bring her back and remarry her (3:6–4:4; cp. Hosea 2–3; Ezekiel 16). This is not a precise fit, however, because Israel is not said to have married another husband; she has **lived as a prostitute**.[4] But even that misses the point of the law in Deuteronomy and of this verse. The point of the law is that the marriage of the original couple is not "holy" the second time as it was the first. Even though the marriages and divorces along the way were all "legal," that still does not make them all "holy."[5] The whole process shows a lack of respect for the LORD's ways and wishes. Even though the marriages are "legal," marriage itself is being taken lightly, as if it is merely a matter of paper work. The point being made in Jeremiah 3:1 is this: If the remarriage of a man and woman defiles the land because one of them has been with one other partner, then the remarriage to someone who has had many other partners defiles the land exponentially more.[6] The issue at hand is not whether the LORD is subject to the laws which he has placed on humans, but the magnitude of Israel's sin.

Verse 2 emphasizes the multiplicity of Israel's infidelities, justifying the charge that she has **defiled the land**. Anywhere one looks, even on the **barren heights**, one can find a place where Israel has been unfaithful to her husband. The people have sold themselves **like a nomad**, like a street vendor, selling to anyone who happens to pass by. The LORD has not been passive about this behavior. Israel cannot say that they were unaware of his displeasure. He has stopped the **rains**, placing the nation in economic peril so that they would recognize their wrongs and repent (v. 3a; cp. Amos 4:7-8). But this has had no positive effect on Israel. Instead, she has tried to exploit the LORD's self-proclaimed natural mercy and love. She calls on him to forgive, to put an end to his wrath, but only so she can return to her evil ways (3:4-5). She talks about returning to him (v. 1), but she has no appreciation for how her actions affect the LORD. There is no true repentance here, only a desire to have the pain of punishment removed. God sees through this, and in the following section he calls the people to honesty.

---

[4]Thompson refers to this as a possible "loophole in the law" (*Jeremiah*, p. 191).

[5]The wife is already described as "defiled" before she returns to her first husband (Deut 24:4). This indicates that the defilement comes in the marriage to the second man.

[6]Holladay, *Jeremiah 1*, p. 113.

B. UNFAITHFUL ISRAEL (3:6–4:4)

This extremely important section on repentance distinguishes between the northern kingdom of Israel and southern kingdom of Judah in most of its units. At many points the language and images of 3:1-5 resurface, suggesting a strong connection to that previous unit. One cannot ascertain whether the units of this section were spoken as outgrowths of 3:1-5 or were placed after it because an editor noticed the similarities. The unit beginning in 3:6 is placed chronologically in the days of Josiah, which would place it prior to the date of 2:14-19, if not all of Jeremiah 2; and if 3:1-5 is a part of that section, then it too comes later than 3:6ff. In either case, the two sections complement each other very well thematically. The general flow of the units in this section is this:

3:6-10	the Lord describes the sins of Israel and Judah;
3:11-13	the Lord declares Israel more righteous and calls for her repentance;
3:14-18	the call for repentance expands to include Judah;
3:19-20	Israel's unfaithfulness in the past;
3:21-25	Israel's desire to repent;
4:1-2	the Lord calls for true repentance in Israel;
4:3-4	the Lord calls for true repentance in Judah.

3:6-10 The editorial introduction (3:6) places this unit **during the reign of King Josiah** (639–609 B.C.), and the reference to returning to the Lord suggests a time after Josiah's Reform (621 B.C.), even though the return was only in pretense (3:10). A date near the end of Josiah's reign is most likely. This date is most suggestive. Josiah is highly praised for his reform measures in the Book of Kings (2 Kgs 23:1-25; cp. 2 Chr 34:29–35:19) and in Jeremiah (Jer 22:15-16). The impression is left that conditions reverted to idolatry only after Josiah's death and were the result of his successors' weakness. This unit (3:6-10) reveals that the insincerity of the people's repentance was already surfacing in the days of Josiah, that their repentance never was wholehearted.[7]

This compact prophecy constitutes a sequel to the husband-wife metaphor used by Hosea regarding the LORD's relationship with the

---

[7]Thompson, *Jeremiah*, pp. 59-67, 196-197.

northern kingdom of Israel.[8] Through that earlier prophet, the LORD declared his intentions to exile the northern kingdom for its religious infidelity (Hos 2:2-13) and then win back the affections of his former bride (2:14-23). This is all summarized in Jeremiah 3:6-8a. Israel had **gone up on every high hill . . . and committed adultery there**. The LORD thought that she would **return . . . but she did not**; so, he gave her **a certificate of divorce and sent her away** into exile among the Assyrians. The LORD now reveals that he had a dual purpose in his harsh treatment of the northern tribes. His primary goal was to bring them to repentance; but he also had a secondary goal of bringing Judah to repentance.

This secondary goal moves to the fore in the second half of this unit (3:8b-10). The people in the south had been watching as events unfolded in the North, but somehow they missed the point. They saw what happened to their northern cousins (3:7b), but they assumed their own better fortunes were a result of their goodness or, more likely, because they worshiped in the right place (Jerusalem) and had the right royal family (the House of David). They failed to see that the northerners were exiled because of what they did, not where they did it. **Israel's immorality mattered so little to her** [Judah] (3:9), because Judah placed the blame for Israel's demise entirely on the externals of worship rather than on the internals of worship. This attitude of ignoring the sin and feeling specially blessed became more and more set as the seventh century progressed, until the people of Judah saw no comparison between their own actions and the actions of the North which had led to the Assyrian exile. Rather than being frightened by the possibility of divine retaliation, they were emboldened by the misconception they had an eternal endowment of divine protection. So, during the long reign of Manasseh, the people of Judah practiced idolatry even more than the people of the North had.

This attitude was not shared by Josiah. He instituted his reforms because he saw Judah's subservience to Assyrian domination as proof that the LORD was punishing his people for infidelity. He heard in the LORD's promises no guarantee of unconditional protection, and so he encouraged renewed faithfulness to the LORD. The people of Judah followed his lead because he was king and stopped their idolatrous practices, but they still did not see idolatry

---

[8]Ibid., pp. 194-195; Bright, *Jeremiah*, p. 26.

itself as the problem. There were telltale signs even before Josiah's death that the people still believed more in the power of their homemade gods than in the power of the LORD, and Jeremiah is confronting the people in this regard. **Judah did not return with all her heart, but only in pretense** (3:10).

A closer look at a few terms illuminates these ideas, terms which turn out to be central in many of Jeremiah's prophecies. One of these is a set of terms that come from a common root, שׁוּב (*šûb*), meaning "to turn back, return." Jeremiah uses this root in more ways than any other biblical writer.[9] He uses it in two senses here. First, he uses a passive form of it to refer to Israel as promiscuous. She is **Faithless Israel** (יִשְׂרָאֵל מְשֻׁבָה, *mᵉšubāh yiśrā'ēl*). In other words, Israel is she who is turned away from God. Only Jeremiah uses the term in this appositive way, and only in these verses (3:6,8,11,12).[10] Ironically, the LORD waits for this "turned" woman (and her sister) to turn again, to **return** (*šûb*) to him (3:7,10). Israel never does; Judah does, **but only in pretense**.

This introduces the second significant term in this passage — שֶׁקֶר (*šeqer*), translated "pretense, lie, false." Jeremiah uses this term more than thirty times, almost always in reference to the attitude or words of his opponents among the people. It denotes something that is not what it claims, a façade.[11] In this case, it is the repentance (*šûb*) of the people of Judah that is false. They lay claim to repentance on the basis of the external changes they have made in their worship. But they do not take it seriously; it is merely "for show." The proof for this is not given here, but it becomes apparent in the words and actions of the people during the reign of Jehoiakim.

Jeremiah characterizes this as repentance that is not **with all their heart** (3:10). This theme of "heart" is the third significant idea used in this passage and perhaps the most significant of the three in the book as a whole. Jeremiah almost certainly inherited this thematic element from the Book of Deuteronomy. It is a central theme

---

[9] For the most complete investigation of this term, see W.L. Holladay, *The Root Šubh in the Old Testament, with Particular Reference to Its Usages in Covenantal Contexts* (Leiden: Brill, 1958).

[10] This form of the root is used primarily in Jeremiah, elsewhere meaning "apostasy, faithlessness" (Jer 2:19; 3:22; 5:6; 8:5; 14:7; cp. Hos 14:5; Ezek 37:23; Prov 1:32).

[11] "'Falsehood' is what is without basis in the soul, what is hollow and rootless" (Holladay, *Jeremiah 1*, pp. 124-125).

there, and Jeremiah (and the compiler of the books of history — Joshua–2 Kings) uses it in strikingly similar ways. Best known is the command to "love the LORD your God with all your heart . . ." (Deut 6:5; cp. 2 Kgs 23:25). The people of Judah can claim to "love the LORD" on the basis of the sacrifices they offer to him in the temple. But they cannot claim to love him "with all their heart" because they are devoted to other gods as well, gods to whom they also offer sacrifices. Jeremiah will return to this idea shortly, and then at several crucial places throughout his ministry.

Jeremiah applies a special term to Judah here to compare her to **Faithless Israel**. He calls her "**her unfaithful sister Judah**" (בָּגוֹדָה אֲחוֹתָהּ יְהוּדָה, *bāgôdāh 'ŏḥōthāh yᵉhûdāh*; 3:7,8,10). The term translated **unfaithful** is *bāgôdāh*, derived from a root meaning "treacherous, deceitful" (cp. Judg 9:23).[12] The nuance here highlights the deceptiveness of Judah's actions; thus, in this case, the RSV translation might be more helpful ("her false sister Judah"). This information helps us see the comparison Jeremiah is making between the already-conquered northern kingdom and the threatened southern kingdom. The northern kingdom was conquered because it was openly unfaithful to the LORD, while Judah — who was supposed to learn from her "sister's" mistake — was unfaithful but tried to mask her unfaithfulness with a facade of faithful worship.

3:11-13 Once again, it is impossible to be certain about how to distinguish these units in order to understand the flow of thought. Many read verse 11 as the conclusion to verses 6-10 (based on the evidence presented in verses 6-10, the LORD has determined that **Faithless Israel is more righteous than unfaithful Judah**),[13] while others understand verse 11 as the premise and introduction to verses 12-13(18)[14] (because **Faithless Israel is more righteous than unfaithful Judah**, the LORD believes he stands a better chance with the North, so he appeals to them first to repent). Either is possible, but the latter is reflected in the NIV's paragraph division and is adopted here.

---

[12]There is another Hebrew root having the same letters that means "clothing, covering." It is unlikely that the two roots are related, but it is an interesting coincidence that English has developed a similar idiom for deception regarding clothing in the expression, "pull the wool over someone's eyes."

[13]Thompson, *Jeremiah*, p. 194; Holladay, *Jeremiah 1*, pp. 116-117; Clements, *Jeremiah*, pp. 34-35; Nicholson, *Jeremiah 1–25*, p. 43; McKane, *Jeremiah*, pp. 65-69; Lundbom, *Jeremiah 1–20*, pp 305-306.

[14]Brueggemann, *Jeremiah*, pp. 44-45.

The favorable comparison of Israel with Judah is not to be interpreted as a vindication of Israel (cp. Gen 38:26). She is not free of guilt. Such a comparison does not illustrate how the LORD goes about judging people; he does not lower his standards to some lowest common denominator. Israel is **more righteous**, but that does not mean that she is acceptable to the LORD as she is. The LORD is calling her, a **faithless** (מְשׁוּבָה, *məšubāh*) nation, to repent (**return**; שׁוּבה, *šûbāh*).

The reader must remember that the primary audience is the people of Judah. It is likely that they had developed an arrogant and "holier-than-thou" attitude toward the people of the North, because the LORD had exiled the North to Assyria. This section turns that attitude on its head, but then uses that reversal of perception to give hope to the people of Judah. These words are designed to humble Judah, so that the LORD can then exalt them. The people of Judah would have been angered that the LORD would consider them less righteous than the people of Israel, and the LORD's appeal to Israel would have added to that irritation. But then it also shows the LORD offering forgiveness to a people whom Jeremiah's listeners deemed to be beyond hope. If the LORD could extend forgiveness to those people, then they would believe that forgiveness was truly possible for themselves.

The LORD's call to repentance in 3:12-13 reaches back into 2:1–3:5 and reapplies some of the phrases used there. The initial call to **return** reminds the reader of 3:1. There, the LORD speaks of the possibility of returning as unthinkable because of the magnitude of their infidelity; yet now he calls to them, **Return, faithless Israel**. How can he do this in the light of their actions? Because he is **merciful**. He then responds to the question posed by Jeremiah's listeners in 3:5, "Will you always be angry?" (הֲיִנְטֹר לְעוֹלָם, *hăyinṭōr ləʿôlām*). His assurance in 3:12 (**I will not be angry forever**) uses the same Hebrew words (לֹא אֶטּוֹר לְעוֹלָם, *lōʾ ʾeṭṭōr ləʿôlām*). This forgiveness is not automatic, though. He tells the people to **acknowledge your guilt** ("know your iniquity"). In explaining what he means by their **guilt**, he alludes back to two statements made in the previous section: **You have rebelled against the LORD your God** (cp. 2:29), and **you have scattered your favors . . . under every spreading tree** (cp. 2:20). The concluding line (**and have not obeyed me**, "and have not listened to my voice") becomes a dominant theme later in the book (see especially Jeremiah 37–45).[15]

---

[15]Holladay, *Jeremiah 1*, pp. 118-120.

3:14-18 These verses expand the appeal for repentance to include Judah. In the preceding verses, he had said, "Return, faithless Israel"; now he says, **Return, faithless people**. This translation somewhat obscures the shift that is made. Jeremiah uses another form of the verb *šûb* in addressing his audience. In this instance, the form is שׁוֹבָבִים (*šôbābîm*). The doubling of the final *beth* of the root has the effect of suggesting repeated action, so that a rendering such as "ever-turning" might more vividly convey the intended sense. The word translated **people** here is most often translated "sons" in the Old Testament. So, the LORD is calling on his "ever-turning sons" to "(re)turn" to him; he wants them to stop turning away from him over and over again and turn in just one direction — toward him.

The recognition that he is now including Judah is made clear in verse 18 when he speaks of **the house of Judah** and **the house of Israel**. His comments there also suggest that this unit might come from a time much later in Jeremiah's career. He assumes here that Judah will be returning from exile in **a northern land**. Such an exile is not altogether certain until the days of Zedekiah, twenty years after the death of Josiah. This shows that the message of this section might be one that developed over several years, as the call for repentance to the North in the days of Josiah (3:11-13) is expanded to include Judah once the Babylonian Exile becomes inevitable (3:14-18).[16] This suggests how Jeremiah or Baruch could have reused an early prophecy. In its initial delivery, the prophecy in verses 11-13 could have been a direct appeal to northerners in Assyrian exile, or Jeremiah might have been utilizing the form of an appeal to others as an indirect way of humbling arrogant Judahites. Twenty or more years later, the same prophecy can be attached to another prophecy literarily, with the overall intent of showing that God's offer of mercy is still open to people who have truly been humbled by intervening events.

The other lines in this unit suggest some of the ways attitudes need to change in order for true repentance and restoration to occur. First, there is implied in the LORD's declaration, **"I am your husband"** (3:14b), that the people will have given up their promiscuous ways. He then promises that he will **choose** them and **bring** them back to his home in Zion. The former is more literally "take." It might carry a double meaning. The obvious one is that he will remove them from one place in order to bring ("take") them to

---

[16]Thompson, *Jeremiah*, pp. 199, 203; Bright, *Jeremiah*, p. 27.

another. But the word "take" is also common in the context of marriage, because a man "takes" his wife (cp. Gen 24:3-4; 25:1; 27:46; Deut 21:11; 22:13). The LORD has just declared himself to be Israel's husband, so his statement that he will "take" them might imply taking as a wife. In any case, there is a strong implication of divine initiative in this process.

The reference to **shepherds after my own heart** in 3:15 is probably an allusion to kings from the line of David or kings who exhibit a Davidlike character. David, like other monarchs of the ancient Near East,[17] is occasionally referred to as a "shepherd" for his people (2 Sam 5:2; 7:7; Ps 78:70-72), and Samuel had said of God's selection of David, "the LORD has sought out a man after his own heart" (1 Sam 13:14; cp. Acts 13:22). These two are brought together in Jeremiah 3:15, indicating that the LORD is planning either to perpetuate the Davidic Covenant (which started with "a man after God's own heart") or to establish another one on the same basis. Other statements regarding the Davidic Covenant in Jeremiah support the first interpretation (see Jer 33:14-26). The LORD goes on to describe these shepherds as men **who will lead you** ("shepherd you") **with knowledge and understanding**. The linking of **knowledge and understanding** is rare in Jeremiah. They are used together again only in 9:24, there to describe a proper reason for someone to boast: "that he understands and knows me . . . declares the LORD." That passage links such understanding to the performance of kind, just, and righteous deeds. If the same background holds for 3:15, the LORD is looking forward to the day when the royal establishment will be known for upholding justice and righteousness (cp. 22:1-4; 23:5; Isa 9:7; 16:5; 22:20-24; 32:1-8).

The main implications intended by the comments regarding **the ark of the covenant** and **Jerusalem** in 3:16-17 are not easily discerned. The two had been linked together for some time. Moses spoke often in Deuteronomy about "the place the LORD your God will choose as a dwelling for his Name" (e.g., Deut 12:11). That place was later revealed to be Jerusalem (see 2 Chr 5:5-6),[18] and "his

---

[17]For example, Lipit-Ishtar of Sumer and Hammurabi of Babylon wear this label. M.T. Roth, *Law Collections from Mesopotamia and Asia Minor* (Atlanta: Scholars Press, 1995), pp. 25, 77.

[18]The same passage links the choice of Jerusalem for this role directly to the choice of David and his house as king.

Name" apparently is associated with the ark (see 2 Sam 6:2). The
LORD says here that no one will think about the ark or miss it at all.
This is evidently a positive development, but that it would be so is a
surprise. The ark would seem to be a positive symbol of the LORD's
presence with his people. At least two explanations of how it
becomes a negative fixture should be considered. First, it is possible
that the people have come to equate the ark with an unconditional
assurance of the LORD's presence, replacing the symbol with the
reality to which it points. In other words, perhaps they have come to
believe that the LORD is "forced" to be wherever his ark resides (cp.
Jer 7:1-15; 1 Sam 4:3). It could be that they even worship the ark.
Just as they had come to worship the bronze serpent (2 Kgs 18:4),
perhaps they have elevated the ark itself to the level of an idol. A
second possibility is that the ark has come to be associated too
directly with the House of David. The northerners had a long tradition of animosity toward David's kingship, and their first king had
instituted policies for the specific purpose of dissuading his people
from worshiping in Jerusalem. If the ark represents David to them
(rather than the LORD), then it could have become a roadblock to
reunification rather than an aid. Finally, it is possible that both considerations lie behind Jeremiah's remarks.

These ideas are substantiated by the statement, **they will call
Jerusalem The Throne of the LORD**. The ark was thought of as the
footstool of God's throne, which suggested that the temple was his
palace (cp. Isa 6:1; Ezek 43:7).[19] But that imagery is not magnificent
enough, because people had come to equate the symbol of God's
throne with the other throne in Jerusalem — David's. In spite of
Solomon's words at the dedication of the temple (1 Kgs 8:25-29),
people had come to limit their concept of the LORD's kingdom. So
Jeremiah speaks of the entire city of Jerusalem as **the Throne of the
LORD**. The city replaces the ark in this role. The expansion of the
imagery from ark to city coincides with the expanded depiction of
the LORD's kingdom. He is not just the God of Israel, a mistaken
conclusion which might have arisen from a perceived connection
between the ark and the kingdom of David. By thinking of something larger as his throne, the notion that his kingdom is larger

---

[19]Holladay, *Jeremiah 1*, p. 121; G. von Rad, "The Tent and the Ark," *The
Problem of the Hexateuch and Other Essays* (New York: McGraw-Hill, 1966),
p. 108.

naturally follows (cp. Isa 66:1). It seems quite logical then for him to continue by saying, **all nations will gather in Jerusalem to honor the name of the LORD.**

Jeremiah normally uses the phrase, **follow the stubbornness of their evil hearts**, to describe the people of Judah. The word for "stubbornness" is related to "muscle," conveying the idea that someone is straining his muscles in resistance. The phrase denotes the people's unwillingness to "hear" or "obey" the LORD's words, and their persistent worship of idols (Jer 7:24; 9:14; 11:8; 13:10; 16:12; cp. Deut 29:19; Ps 81:12). This is the one place where that stubbornness — and the humble acquiescence which replaces it — refers to the worship practices of other nations.[20] The prediction that their stubbornness can and will break could be intended to inspire or shame an exiled people to do the same. Though exiled, those people are still God's chosen ones. In spite of the exile, the land of Israel is still **the land I gave your forefathers as an inheritance**. Yet now they are joined in their "inheritance" by humble believers from all the nations, people who have been blessed through God's chosen people.

The joining of **the house of Judah** and **the house of Israel** carries a couple of messages for the earliest hearers. First, it points toward the dissolving of barriers that have been raised between the people of Judah who remain in their land and the people of Israel who have already been exiled by the Assyrians. As we have mentioned before, the arrogance of the former is addressed several times by Jeremiah, yet it apparently is slow to go away. That is the broader implication of this note. The narrower implication is for the verses which follow. Israel is described as sinful yet repentant (3:19-25), and the LORD encourages her by calling for her true repentance (4:1-2).[21] Then, he turns his attention to Judah, calling for her repentance as well (4:3-4). If "the house of Judah" is truly to join with "the house of Israel," they must follow the example of repentance being set by their northern cousins.

---

[20]Holladay, *Jeremiah 1*, p. 121.
[21]Thompson, *Jeremiah*, p. 214, n. 30.

EXCURSUS

THE LORD'S COVENANTS WITH ISRAEL

These observations bring up the need to consider briefly the issue of covenant in the Old Testament. There are actually three covenants between God and the nation of Israel. The one with which people are most familiar is the Mosaic Covenant, established at Mount Sinai through the intermediation of Moses. It is subordinate to the prior Abrahamic Covenant. That covenant consisted solely of divine promises of numerous descendants and a special land in which they were to live, and that they would be a blessed people through whom all other peoples would be blessed. The only part played by them was that they would leave the fulfillment of those promises entirely up to God. The Mosaic Covenant was a conditional covenant, spelling out how those descendants were to live holy lives, so that they could remain and prosper in the land, because only from a state of holiness could they serve as the blessing to others that God envisioned. If they failed to meet the conditions of the Mosaic Covenant (the Torah), they could be expelled from the land promised to them. At issue in the career of Jeremiah is the Mosaic Covenant. The people have not been holy; therefore, God is calling for their expulsion from the land. This does not mean, however, that the Abrahamic Covenant is also in jeopardy. The promise of the land still holds. The message of Jeremiah is that the stubborn refusal of the people to obey the Torah necessitates their temporary expulsion; but they can return if their hearts change and become wholly obedient to the LORD.

The Davidic Covenant is a sort of mixture of the two other covenants. It consists of God's promise that David would "never fail to have a man on the throne of Israel" (1 Kgs 2:4; cp. 2 Sam 7:12-16; 1 Kgs 9:3-9; Ps 89:19-37). This is both unconditional and conditional. It is unconditional that the House of David is the royal line; it is conditional whether there will be a "throne of Israel" upon which one of David's descendants can sit. Obviously, whenever the nation did not control its promised land, there could be no "son of David" on the throne.

The ultimate fulfillment of the promises of these various covenants comes in Jesus and the Church (see Acts 3:24-25). Paul explains that the promise of "descendants" for Abraham refers to those who will "inherit" his faith (Gal 3:29). The writer of Hebrews shows that "the land" promised to Abraham and his descendants is not a geographical location, but a place of "rest" that one finds when one is "at home" with God (Heb 4:1-11). Similarly, we find that the ultimate "blessings" promised are spiritual rather than material or physical. By the same token, the ultimate meaning of the Davidic promise is manifested when Jesus is enthroned as an eternal king (Rom 1:1-4; Heb 1:3-9) whose throne rests in a heavenly temple in a "new" Jerusalem.

3:19-20 There is a clear shift here from promise of future restoration back to present accusation. It is also possible that there is a shift in audiences here. Now the **house of Israel** is addressed (v. 20). Based on the use of this label in verse 18, it seems justified to read this as a reference to the exiled people of the northern tribes. These two verses describe the LORD's past relationship with those tribes, which ended with their being exiled.

The most immediate link to the preceding verses is in the talk about the land that the LORD had given as an inheritance. There are many echoes of Hosea in this. The LORD gave them **a desirable land, the most beautiful inheritance of any nation**. He expected them to respond as grateful and obedient **sons** (v. 19), but they responded instead as an **unfaithful** wife (v. 20). The mixing of metaphors for Israel (sons and wife) is a bit surprising, but a plausible explanation arises from a simple comparison with Hosea. Hosea uses both metaphors in his indictment of the northern kingdom, and even seems to mix them when he uses both his wife and his children to represent Israel in the opening sections of his book (Hos 1:2–3:5; cp. 11:1-11). A similar mixing is evident in Jeremiah 3:1-5, where the metaphor of the wife (vv. 1-3) gives way to talk of God as Father (vv. 4-5).

The final lines of verse 19 make an interesting contrast to verses 4-5. There, the LORD says to the people of Judah, "**I thought you would call me 'Father' and not turn away from following me**." Those earlier verses reveal that they have been calling him "My Father," but that they then do turn away from him (again, cp. Hos 11:1-7). This indicates that their expected call to God comes from a place of insincerity. What he is looking for in verses 19-20, then, is people who will call to him in sincerity and truth, people whose lives will change as a result of their relationship to him.

3:21-25 Once again our attention is drawn to **the barren heights** (cp. 3:2). The association with prostitution and frivolity mentioned in verse 2 indicates that one might expect to hear sounds of carefree joy; but instead, one hears **the weeping and pleading of the people of Israel**.[22] They recognize that they **have forgotten the LORD their God**. They did not heed his commands to "remember" the things he did for them in getting them out of Egypt and settling them in their

---

[22]Holladay (*Jeremiah 1*, p. 123) proposes that the "weeping" here is done by God, who is weeping for Israel (cp. Jer 31:15).

land (cp. Deut 4:9; 7:18; 8:18-19). Particularly ominous (in hindsight) are the words of Deuteronomy 8:19-20: "If you ever forget the LORD your God and follow other gods . . . you will be destroyed for not obeying the LORD your God."

The LORD reveals his patience and forgiveness by repeating here the call for repentance (vv. 12,14). This instance brings together the ways in which Jeremiah uses the root **return** (*šûb*) earlier in the chapter. Quite literally, he says, "Return (שׁוּבוּ, *šûbû*), ever-turning (שׁוֹבָבִים, *šôbābîm*) sons, I will heal your being turned" (מְשׁוּבֹת, *mᵉšûbôth*). The nature of the response makes clear the nature of their sin, and the appropriateness of the warning in Deuteronomy 8:19-20. They are guilty of worshiping other gods.[23] They admit that **shameful gods have consumed . . . their flocks and herds, their sons and daughters** (3:24), that they have sacrificed those things to idols (cp. Hos 2:8; 2 Kgs 21:2-6). But now they realize that all that was a **deception** (שֶׁקֶר, *šeqer*; 3:23), that those idols possess no true power to help the Israelites. They confess, **we have not obeyed the LORD our God** (3:25). They now pledge to change all that because **you are the LORD our God** (3:22), and **the LORD our God is the salvation of Israel** (3:23).

---

[23]The references to "shameful gods" and "lie down in our shame" are probably allusions to Baal worship, as "Baal" and "shame" are sometimes interchanged. For example, Saul's successor is sometimes "Ish-bosheth" ("man of shame") and sometimes "Ish-baal" (2 Sam 2:9-10; 1 Chr 8:33; 9:39).

JEREMIAH 4

B. UNFAITHFUL ISRAEL (3:6–4:4) (continued)

4:1-2 The hurdle which the people of Israel must overcome is the temptation to replace the deception of their idols (3:23) with the deception of repentance (cp. 3:10). God says they must **return to me** (4:1; cp. 8:4). This is not a "return" to another form of deception, not even to the deception of prescribed worship or external obedience (cp. Jer 34:8-22). The return must be to the LORD himself. This requires something that goes deeper than one's actions, all the way to one's motivations and will. He calls on them to swear **in a truthful, just and righteous way . . . "As surely as the LORD lives"** (4:2). The recognition that God lives, that he truly exists and works in his world, leads one to live with truthfulness, with justice, and with righteousness. Those who live otherwise do not fully accept this basic truth. Instead, they relegate the LORD to the status of an idol, a being who exists in reality only in the minds of those who worship him. A return to the LORD demands the acceptance of a being outside oneself, a being with genuine power, power that supersedes one's own power and ability, power by which one can properly swear. The effects of such repentance extend beyond the people of Israel themselves to "the nations" mentioned in 3:17. When they see a truly repentant Israel, **the nations will be blessed by him** (the LORD). This reminds one of the promises of the Abrahamic Covenant (Gen 12:3; 22:18; 26:4). The practice of a true religion of the heart, as originally prescribed by Moses, would create a people through whom God could fulfill his promises to Abraham and his plan for rescuing humanity from its sinfulness and suffering.[1]

4:3-4 The LORD's words to the **men of Judah and the people of Jerusalem** are more menacing because they are not yet in exile. The

---

[1]Holladay, *Jeremiah 1*, pp. 128-129.

need for their repentance is more pressing, in view of the current circumstances. Failure to do so will cause God's wrath to **break out and burn like fire . . . burn with no one to quench it**. He mentions this because he realizes that he is talking here to a people who are experts at trying to deceive him with external acts of repentance. But he is a God who "searches the heart" (17:10), who knows that Judah "did not return to me with all her heart," that her acts of repentance under Josiah have been "only in pretense" (3:10). To overcome this deceptiveness, he tells his listeners, **circumcise your hearts** (4:4). This is nothing more than a call to their original religious faith. The Mosaic Covenant was from its inception spoken of as a covenant of the heart. Moses instructed the people to "love the LORD your God with all your heart" (Deut 6:4), to "fix these words of mine in your hearts and minds" (Deut 11:18), and to respond to being chosen by God by "circumcising your hearts" (Deut 10:15-16; cp. 30:6). Just like the Christian covenant, this was a covenant that concerned the heart; the problem, then, was that it was not being internalized and accepted as God had intended. It is ironic then that he calls them to **break up your unplowed ground** (4:3). That unplowed ground is their hearts, ground which should have been thoroughly cultivated and plowed as a result of previous warnings and disciplines of the LORD. Further, they are not to **sow among thorns**, probably referring to patterns of behavior which lead to idolatry. If they want to produce different results in their lives, they need to change their behavior.

This section reveals some very important ideas related to repentance. Jeremiah 3:11-13 shows that repentance is only possible because of the mercy and forgiveness of the Lord. Any act of repentance must come from the vantage point of humility. That humility comes when people are confronted with and then acknowledge the truth of their sinfulness, and the truth of God's sovereignty and power to save. The opposite of that humility is the "stubbornness" that Jeremiah mentions in 3:17. This is stubbornness against the Lord himself, not just resistance to authority in general. Conversely, repentance must be a return to the Lord, and not just a return to the institutions and patterns which he established.

The same principles must be applied to faith and the Church today. It is not enough for people to consider how many have been baptized or how many are in attendance at worship services or what ministries are supported. God "searches the heart." He calls for worship that truly is from the heart (Eph 5:19-20). Such worship cannot be judged solely on the basis of external appearance. What God calls for is a conversion of hearts, for persons to have their hearts truly cleansed and purified in baptism (Heb 10:19-25). Yet, we must recognize that this does have its effect in concrete, visible terms. It will have its effect in the way people live their daily lives, in ways of truth, justice, righteousness, mercy, and humility (cp. Hos 6:6; Amos 5:4-15; Micah 6:8). Anything less is "only in pretense."

C. DISASTER FROM THE NORTH (4:5-31)

The tone of this section is in marked contrast to the one preceding. There is hardly a mention of repentance, little hope for reprieve; only the pronouncement of impending doom, interspersed with expressions of grief. There is uncertainty about which Babylonian attack is the topic of discussion here. The certainty of attack might point to the final siege (588–586 B.C.; cp. 4:6 and 25:38). On the other hand, the attack envisioned here seems to be relatively swift, and there is a mixing of the slim possibility of hope for repentance with statements about the LORD's unwillingness to change his mind (4:13,27). These most strongly suggest the Babylonian attack of 597 B.C. (2 Kgs 24:10-16), after which any hope for Jerusalem seems to be dispelled by Jeremiah. A setting during earlier invasions (such as 605 B.C.; see 2 Kgs 24:1-2; Dan 1:1-2) is a less remote possibility.[2]

This section is divided into five units. The first (vv. 5-8), third (vv. 13-18), and fifth (vv. 27-31) are somewhat more objective in tone, describing in reporter-like fashion the devastation of the countryside and the nation's reactions. The second unit (vv. 9-12) and fourth unit (vv. 19-26) reveal the anguish which both Jeremiah and God feel toward those who are suffering. It is clear that a dialogue of sorts is going on between God and Jeremiah throughout this section, but it is difficult to be sure about who is speaking at certain points. This does not affect the basic interpretation, though. Both are involved in announcing the disaster that is coming, and both are grieved by the suffering the people endure.

---

[2]Thompson, *Jeremiah*, pp. 218-219; Bright, *Jeremiah*, p. 34.

4:5-8 This unit moves from the Lord's warning of coming destruction (vv. 5-6) to Jeremiah's description of the approaching army (v. 7) and call for a time of mourning in anticipation of its arrival (v. 8). The Lord's announcement is directed toward the two traditional segments of the southern kingdom, Judah and Jerusalem. The **sound**ing of **the trumpet** (שׁוֹפָר, *šôphār*) is a typical mode of alarm in times of war, signaling people to **gather** behind the walls of **fortified cities**. (The use of air raid sirens during World War II would be a close modern parallel.) The call **to go to Zion** is not just pointing people to Jerusalem, but to a second, specially-fortified district inside the walls of the city itself, where the palace and temple and other key structures were located.

Jeremiah portrays Nebuchadnezzar and his armies as a lion on the prowl, a destroyer of nations. This is a reference to the fact that Babylon's attacks on Jerusalem were part of a larger campaign of conquest that encompassed most of the eastern Mediterranean coastlands. He plans to lay waste your land ("set your land for desolation"; cp. 2:15). It is possible that Jeremiah has adopted the image of the lion from Hosea (Hos 5:14; 13:7-8). He uses similar imagery to describe Judah's final destruction in Jeremiah 25:38 — "like a lion he will leave his lair, and their land will become desolate . . . because of the Lord's fierce anger." There, the lion seems to be God rather than Nebuchadnezzar, although this is not certain. They are in some sense interchangeable in this regard, since the Babylonian king is working as God's agent (cp. 2:15; Isa 45:1). The people are addressed in verse 7 in the feminine singular (**your** land, **your** towns), that is, as a woman. This is most likely an example of the personification of Jerusalem (see vv. 14,18,31). Verse 8 shifts to plural addressees, calling on them to enter into formal mourning, to put on sackcloth, lament and wail. The shift from singular to plural might suggest a shift in speakers (meaning God's words continue through v. 7),[3] but such shifts are not uncommon. It is clear that verse 8 is spoken by Jeremiah, because the LORD is referred to in the third person.

The concluding lines of both parts of this unit (vv. 6b,8b) go together to justify the warnings about this impending calamity. The LORD explains that the attack is coming because he is **bringing disaster from the north, even terrible destruction** ("a great shatter-

---

[3]Holladay places 4:7 in the mouth of God as well (*Jeremiah 1*, p. 146).

ing") (v. 6b). This is not something determined by the Babylonians; it is the LORD's plan. Jeremiah then explains why the LORD is doing this: **for the fierce anger of the LORD has not turned away from us** (v. 8b; cp. 2 Kgs 23:36). There is only the most obscure of explanations given in this section for why the LORD is angry (see v. 22), so the section must be read in the light of those around it, where the sins of the nation are described in some detail. The last line here indicates that there was some reason for hoping the LORD might turn away his anger. The basis for that hope is revealed in the next unit (v. 10).[4]

4:9-12 This unit moves from a declaration by the LORD about Jerusalem's leaders (v. 9) to a complaint by Jeremiah that the LORD has deceived him (v. 10) to the LORD's assurance that the nation will be "blown away" by his judgments. These might not appear to flow together, unless one looks ahead to the following chapters (5:12-13; 6:12-15). Then one sees that this is the LORD's response to the predictions of false prophets and teachers in the nation. Those false leaders are **the king and the officials . . . the priests . . . and the prophets**. These are the very ones who are also guilty of promoting idolatry (cp. 1:18; 2:8,26). Later, he rebukes them for saying, "No harm will come to us" (5:12), and for saying, "Peace, peace . . . when there is no peace" (6:14; 8:11). The LORD is saying here (4:9) that the confidence exhibited by these leaders in their promises of peace will give way to discouragement and terror (**[they] will lose heart . . . will be horrified . . . will be appalled**). Their hopes are unfounded. Jeremiah's accusation that the LORD has **deceived this people and Jerusalem** is not based on what the LORD has revealed to him, but on what those false leaders are saying in the LORD's name. Jeremiah is, in effect, expressing the sentiments of other citizens of Jerusalem who would have been putting their faith in the assumed inspiration of those leaders.[5] The LORD's response clarifies his true message for **this people and Jerusalem**. The leaders apparently are comparing the approach of Babylon to a **wind** that winnows, that blows away

---

[4]There is some reason to connect this hope with Josiah's Reform. See ibid., p. 154.

[5]Thompson (*Jeremiah*, p. 222) compares Jeremiah's perspective here to his reaction to Hananiah's optimistic prophecy in Jeremiah 28. Jeremiah did not immediately question the veracity of those who proclaimed a different message; he always maintained a humble attitude regarding his calling.

worthless chaff (sinful elements among the population) and leaves behind good grain (themselves; cp. Jer 24:4-10; 29:15-19; Ezek 11:15). The LORD says the wind is blowing **from the barren heights** (probably an ironic allusion to the site of their religious adultery; cp. 3:2,21), **but not to winnow or cleanse**. His **judgments** call for something stronger, something that will blow all away.

4:13-18 The speaker in verses 13-15 is uncertain. The use of "us" and "we" suggests that he is one of the people, although this could be God quoting what the people say. The verb for **advances** (4:13) is the same as the one translated "has come out" in verse 7, which might indicate a common speaker for the two.[6] It is clear that verses 16-17 are the words of the LORD. The call to **proclaim it to Jerusalem** (4:16) is almost identical to "proclaim in Jerusalem" (4:5). The latter is introductory in 4:5, so a parallel function in 4:16 would be logical. These together suggest a transition in speaker from Jeremiah to the LORD at the beginning of 4:16.[7]

Jeremiah changes from the metaphor of the lion to connote Babylon to imagery evoked by the sight of the Babylonian **chariots**. They stir up dust **like the clouds**, speeding **like a whirlwind** . . . **swifter than eagles**. At the sight of it, the speaker and his listeners are struck with a common fear: **"We are ruined!"** This is the first of three times that this descriptor is used for Judah in this section (cp. 4:20,30). The word (שֻׁדָּד, *šuddad*) describes something that has been violently destroyed and no longer possesses any useful purpose (cp. Joel 1:10). The reaction to this realization is one of desperation. Jeremiah turns his attention for the moment from the approaching army and speaks to Jerusalem as a woman (cp. 4:7) with a soiled heart. He appeals to her to **wash the evil from your heart** (cp. 4:4) so that she can **be saved**. The same language is used by David in Psalm 51. He cries out to God, "Wash away all my iniquity" (Ps 51:2), and "Wash me, and I will be whiter than snow" (Ps 51:7). Instead of living with his sins, he prays "create in me a clean heart" (Ps 51:10) to "the God who saves me" (Ps 51:14). The same cleansing is the ray of hope for Jerusalem which never fades,[8] but it appears that her heart is still not ready to accept what God demands; she still **harbors**

---

[6]Holladay, *Jeremiah 1*, p. 157.

[7]Holladay places the transition between verses 14 and 15 (ibid., p. 158); so Lundbom, *Jeremiah 1–20*, p. 342.

[8]Thompson, *Jeremiah*, p. 225.

wicked thoughts. So, as if gesturing to her to look at the approaching disaster, he mentions the ever-nearing reports coming from the
regions just to the north — **Dan**, and then **Ephraim**.[9]

The LORD picks up the appeal in 4:16, as he had in 4:5. Jeremiah
has just spoken of **a voice . . . proclaiming disaster**; now the LORD
wants to **Tell this to the nations, proclaim it in Jerusalem**. The
nations are mentioned either because they are invaded before
Jerusalem is, or because he wants them (and the northerners scattered among them) to know what he has planned for Jerusalem. The
army that threatens **is coming from a distant land** (cp. 5:15), perhaps suggesting the breadth of the LORD's dominion. The explanation for the destruction comes in verse 17 — **she has rebelled
against me, declares the LORD**. The closest parallel to this is in
Hosea 13:16, suggesting another possible influence of that eighth-
century prophet on Jeremiah. One most often rebels (מָרָה, *mārāh*)
against the "commands" of the LORD (cp. Deut 1:26,43; 9:23; 1 Sam
12:14-15; Ps 78:56; 107:11; Lam 1:18). This points to a heart that
does not acknowledge the sovereignty of God nor trust him and his
love, that thinks it knows better than God what one needs in a given
situation (cp. 2:19). So, the LORD declares, **Your own conduct and
actions have brought this upon you**. This is not a result of the
LORD's weakness or unconcern; it is their own rebellion against his
loving sovereignty.

But the LORD is not unaffected by what is transpiring. He takes
no joy in seeing his people suffer. **How bitter it is** to him; **it pierces**
him **to the heart**. The "humanness" of the LORD moves to center
stage with these words. Or better, the fact that the emotions of grief
and anguish are part of the image of God becomes clear in passages
like this one. There is a slight wordplay involved in this in the
Hebrew. The "rebellion" (*mārāh*) of the people results in the LORD
being "bitter" (מַר, *mar*). The LORD is affected emotionally when his
people turn against him and then suffer the consequences. He does
not coldly and rationally stand by, knowing when the pain will pass.
Just as "Jesus wept," the LORD "weeps with those who weep." He
groans for his people. In so doing, he betrays the fact that he will
still be there to receive her, whenever she is ready to turn back to
him; his love for her persists through the pain, through the separa-
tion (cp. Hos 2:14-23).

---

[9]Ibid., p. 226.

4:19-22 Jeremiah and the LORD now take turns expressing the grief and heartache they both feel over the fate that confronts the people of Judah. Jeremiah opens with the expressions of deep emotion, using words such as **anguish,**[10] **writhe, agony** (4:19a). The LORD's **heart** was **pierced**, while Jeremiah's **pounds**, filled with **agony**. The next several lines begin and end with the sights and sounds of battle. At the first, he hears the **trumpet** (*šôphar*) and **the battle cry** (4:19b); at the end, he sees **the battle standard** and hears **the sound of the trumpet** (4:21). The question, **How long?** (cp. 4:14) with the latter accentuates the tone of despair in his voice. The lines in between reveal the swiftness of the nation's collapse. **Disaster follows disaster** ("shattering upon shattering"; cp. 4:6). There is no good news, no word of any success in any battle; every fortified city is broken.[11] All of this seems to have happened **in an instant . . . in a moment**. The Babylonian war machine is pushing forward at full steam.

The LORD's attention is focused elsewhere at the moment (4:22). He appears almost to be sitting, his face buried in his hands, wondering what went wrong. It is so obvious to him what should have been done, how easy it would have been for Judah to avoid this horrible fate. But **My people are fools**; . . . **they are senseless children**. Enveloping his comments is the word "know." He begins by saying, **they do not know me**; he ends by saying, **they know not how to do good**. Instead, **they are skilled in doing evil**. This is an example of an important concept in the Old Testament. Several writers talk about "knowing God," a phrase that has been picked up in modern Christianity but used in a rather nebulous way. For the Old Testament writers, to "know God" is to live a righteous and merciful life toward one's neighbors. It is a verb of action, not a verb of cognition. The clearest example of this comes from Jeremiah 22:15-16.[12]

> [Josiah] did what was right and just,
>> so all went well with him.
> He defended the cause of the poor and the needy,
>> and so all went well.

---

[10]Literally, "my bowels, my bowels!" See Holladay, *Jeremiah 1*, p. 160; Thompson, *Jeremiah*, p. 228; McKane, *Jeremiah*, p. 102.

[11]Holladay understands "my tents" and "my shelter" as a reference to the curtains in the temple (*Jeremiah 1*, p. 162). But this would lead to the conclusion that the LORD is the speaker in verse 20, which Holladay himself denies.

[12]Brueggemann, *Jeremiah*, pp. 58-59; McKane, *Jeremiah*, pp. 105-106.

> Is that not what it means to know me?
> declares the LORD.

The LORD's sorrow here is not so much for the suffering at hand, but for the oppression and injustice perpetrated by the people against their neighbors which has brought on this terrible disaster, disaster which could have been avoided.

4:23-26 Jeremiah speaks again in these verses, and again he focuses on the physical devastation going on. Each of these verses begins with the statement, **I looked**, showing their overall unity. On further reflection, one realizes that this repetition is part of Jeremiah's plan to describe the devastation in Judah as the undoing of God's creation (Genesis 1). Just as God "saw" (רָאָה, *rā'āh*) each day that his creation was "good," Jeremiah **looked** (*rā'āh*) at the destruction of that creation in the land of Judah.[13] The earth is once again **formless and empty** (cp. Gen 1:2). The **light** of the heavens **was gone** (cp. Gen 1:3,14-18). The land which he firmly established (Gen 1:9-10; cp. Ps 104:5) is now **quaking** and **swaying**. The **birds in the sky** and the **people** he had commanded to "be fruitful and multiply" (Gen 1:22,28) now are gone. The earth which he made into **a fruitful land** (cp. Jer 2:6-7) now has become **a desert** (cp. Gen 1:11-12). The LORD, who gave life to this land, has now taken life away, because his people have stirred up **his fierce anger** (cp. 4:8). The general flow of the creation account in Genesis 1 is from a lifeless world (Gen 1:1-2) to a world teeming with life (Gen 2:1-3). These verses assume that the reader understands that and uses that to describe the depopulation of the region.[14]

4:27-31 The final unit of this section opens with the LORD echoing the thoughts just expressed by Jeremiah. The created world reflects the devastation and sorrow experienced by the people of Judah. There is one thin ray of hope revealed in the statement, **I will not destroy it completely**; but that pales next to the description of

---

[13]One could even conclude that there is implied the sentiment, "I saw that it was evil," in contrast to Genesis 1. Lundbom, *Jeremiah 1–20*, p. 358. The Hebrew word for "evil" (רַע, *ra'*) can mean either "sin" or simply "hurt, disaster" (see Jer 18:8). See Brueggemann, *Jeremiah*, p. 61.

[14]Brueggemann, *Jeremiah*, pp. 59-60; Holladay, *Jeremiah 1*, pp. 163-164. This passage strongly suggests that the Genesis account of creation was known to Jeremiah and his audience, contrary to the opinion of many scholars who date the writing of Genesis 1 in the Exile.

the truly dark mood of these lines. The personification of **the earth** and **the heavens** (4:28) is nothing more than that. Other nations elevated these to the level of deities, but the biblical writers consistently personify them strictly in a figurative way as "witnesses" to what is going on between the LORD and his people (cp. Deut 31:28; Isa 1:2). Just as people today describe a time of sorrow as a "dark day" (whether it is cloudy or the sun is shining), the LORD says **the earth will mourn and the heavens above grow dark**. The more surprising aspect of this verse is the fact the LORD has **spoken and will not relent**. It is in his nature to **relent** (נִחַם, *niham*) in response to genuine repentance (18:7-10), but there are times when he decides that he **will not turn back** from the punishment he has planned (cp. 1 Sam 15:29,35; Jonah 3:10; Amos 7:1-9).[15] This is one of those times. Based on our understanding of the progression of Jeremiah's teachings on this subject, it is most likely that these words are expressed during the reign of Zedekiah.

There is no indication as to who is speaking in the closing lines (4:29-31).[16] Verse 29 consists of a fairly straightforward description of the terrified reactions of the population of Judah to the approach of Nebuchadnezzar's troops. **Towns are deserted** as people sneak **into the thickets** or **climb among the rocks**, anything to avoid capture by the prowling lion. Verses 30-31 juxtapose two images of women, images which represent the beginning and the end of Judah's relationship with foreign nations and their false gods. The first image is of a woman who is desperately trying to seduce a man, as a last-ditch effort to persuade him not to kill her. In fact, they have been lovers before; but now he despises her. Although she is **devastated** (*šuddad*; cp. 4:13,20), she still dresses in her finest clothes, puts on her jewelry and makeup, and tries to rekindle the passion that they once shared. But her efforts are **in vain**. This picture gives way to the picture of another woman. Instead of a woman in the throes of sexual ecstasy, we are confronted with **a woman in labor . . . bearing her first child** (cp. Isa 13:8; Nahum 2:10). This typically is the most difficult labor and most excruciating pain that a woman will ever endure. She is crying, groaning, **gasping for breath, stretching out her hands**. She is **fainting**, perhaps even expecting to die. The image is a vivid one. The pain is all-encompassing, and it is

---

[15]Holladay, *Jeremiah 1*, p. 168.
[16]Holladay assigns 4:29-30 to the LORD, 4:31 to Jeremiah (ibid., p. 150).

unavoidable. And she has no husband to comfort her (cp. Lamentations 1). In a sense, the labor she is having to endure is a result of her adultery. The lovemaking she had shared with foreigners has now borne fruit in the labor pains of conquest and exile.[17]

---

[17]Thompson, *Jeremiah*, pp. 232-233; Brueggemann, *Jeremiah*, p. 62.

JEREMIAH 5

D. NOT ONE IS UPRIGHT (5:1-31)

Once again, it is difficult to know how to divide this section into its original (oral) units. One cannot be certain that such divisions are even warranted. Verses 18-19, for example, seem to interrupt the natural flow of thought, shifting the reader's attention from impending disaster to restoration in the distant future. On the other hand, the refrain shared by 5:9 and 5:29 raises the possibility of the literary unity of most of the chapter. It could be that Jeremiah spoke two (or more) prophecies with the same refrain on different occasions, but then the editor of the book put the two side by side because of their common ending. It could be that the whole chapter preserves a lengthy prophecy which was delivered at one time. And it is possible that the inspired compiler of the book (Baruch) took a lengthy prophecy and placed some other words of Jeremiah within it to help readers see the message of the prophecy in the light of other prophecies of Jeremiah. The present demarcation of units is, therefore, somewhat subjective.[1]

The primary theme of the chapter is the lack of repentance. The people have been dealing with one another "falsely," the LORD has tried to "correct" them, but they "refuse" to change. This will naturally lead the LORD to call for calamity on the nation for its sinfulness. The chapter thus constitutes the next stage beyond the thought of 2:1-4:4, where repentance is called for in a more optimistic tone. The section on God's grief for his people's defiance in between (4:5-31) is

---

[1]Comparisons with previous commentaries reveal similar — but not identical — proposals. Holladay, *Jeremiah 1*, pp. 173-201 (5:1-9,10-17,18-19,20-29,30-31); Clements, *Jeremiah*, p. 41 (5:1-9,10-17,18-19,20-31); Thompson, *Jeremiah*, pp. 233-251 (5:1-9,10-19,20-31); Brueggemann, *Jeremiah*, pp. 62-69 (5:1-6,7-13,14-17,18-19,20-31); Lundbom, *Jeremiah 1–20*, pp. 371-413 (5:1-9,10-13,14-19,20-25,26-31).

now seen as all the more striking, as the LORD's faithfulness and love stand in stark contrast to the people's defiant apostasy (2:1–4:4; 5:1–6:30; cp. 44:15-19). While the LORD has been grieving over the disintegrating marriage with Israel, the people have become more entrenched in their religious adultery. The LORD's anger and frustration now have almost reached the boiling point.

5:1-6 The opening lines remind one of the story of Sodom and Gomorrah in Genesis 18.[2] In verse 21 of that chapter, God tells Abraham that he will go down to "see" for himself the wicked behavior of the cities, and then he will "know" that the reports about it are true. Here he tells people (the commands are plural) to **look around and consider** ("see and know") what is going on in Jerusalem. Of course, the reader knows — as one knows when reading Genesis 18 — that the one who is to **search** ("seek") **through her squares** will not **find** what he is looking for. The comparison with Sodom and Gomorrah makes Jerusalem look all the worse. In those doomed cities, God is unable to find only ten righteous persons; here, a search for just **one person who deals honestly and seeks the truth** is just as hopeless. There is a standard — a very low standard — that must be met if the LORD is to **forgive** his people and prevent the Babylonians from attacking, but it turns out to be too high.

What the LORD wants from his people is referred to in rather general terms, but terms which they would have understood automatically. He speaks of one who **deals honestly** ("does justice;" cp. Isa 1:17; Micah 6:8) **and seeks the truth** (or "faithfulness")[3] (5:1); he expects them to **know the way of the LORD, the requirements** ("justice") **of their God** (5:4-5).[4] These attributes point not just to the literal laws of God handed down through Moses, but even to the spirit behind those laws. Those laws call for "justice" and "truth" in specified cases, exercised by specified persons; but in so doing they indicate that the LORD looks for such qualities at all times in all his people.

He addresses this notion in verses 4-5. The (ludicrously) hypothetical idea is raised that it might be the uneducated (**the poor** and **foolish**) who have not upheld the LORD's commands, that the sins of

---

[2]Brueggemann, *Jeremiah*, p. 62; Holladay, *Jeremiah 1*, pp. 176-177; Thompson, *Jeremiah*, p. 236; Nicholson, *Jeremiah 1-25*, p. 59.

[3]Holladay, *Jeremiah 1*, p. 176.

[4]Holladay (ibid., p. 176), suggests that Jeremiah is drawing on Deut 32:4, where the qualities in Jer 5:1 are attributed to the LORD.

the people can be excused on the grounds the offenders were ignorant of what they were supposed to do. So, he turns to **the leaders**
("the great ones"), to the more educated individuals, who would certainly know the Law and be utilizing it in their daily lives;[5] but they
are no better. They have **broken off the yoke and torn off the bonds**
of God's laws, choosing instead to follow the ways of idols (see Jer
2:20; 27:2-11).

It is not as if this message is a surprise to the people. The LORD
has disciplined them previously for their unrighteousness. He **struck**
them and **crushed them** in order to awaken them to the LORD's feelings about their actions (v. 3), but they have not been attentive. They
have at times feigned repentance by swearing by the LORD (Josiah's
Reform; cp. v. 2), but it was purely superficial. The reality is they
refused correction, persisting in their wicked ways. The **therefore**
of this train of thought (5:6) should come as no surprise: they are to
expect an attack from their enemies, denoted in generic ways as wild
animals (cp. Hos 13:7-8).

5:7-9 This short unit takes us back to the main indictment in
chapters 2–4: religious adultery. Speaking like a judge pronouncing
sentence, the LORD begins and ends the unit with rhetorical questions. **"Why should I forgive you?" "Should I not avenge myself on**
such a nation . . . ?" (cp. 5:29; 9:9) The expected assent of the
"jury" for this sentence is intended to silence any objections, since
they are also the accused in this suit. Between these questions are
three charges which expose how Judah's idolatry is evidence of her
senseless ingratitude. First, they have **sworn by gods that are not**
gods. To swear by divine beings is to appeal to their power to back
up your own words. They have appealed to the power of beings
which have no power, thereby exposing the emptiness of their own
words. This accusation also exposes the falseness — the essential
powerlessness — of the oaths they swear by the LORD (5:2). Second,
they **committed adultery** with other gods, even though the LORD
supplied all their needs (5:7b). This accusation is just like that of
Hosea 2:2-13, where the LORD says that the people sacrificed to the
Baals, using the very products with which he had blessed them to

---

[5]In many passages describing the reading of the Law, groups of leaders
with judicial responsibilities are specifically identified as being present (see
Deut 31:28; Josh 8:33; 24:1; 2 Kgs 23:1-3). These passages also mention
their followers, so even they are really without excuse.

give thanks to someone else. Third, he compares the people to **well-fed, lusty stallions,**[6] who have all their needs met, yet still find it necessary to look elsewhere for pleasure. The hurt and anger which the LORD expresses are entirely understandable.

5:10-17 The first half of this unit (vv. 10-13) continues the comments about the LORD's feelings regarding the people's faithless ingratitude, while introducing two other elements which are common in Jeremiah's condemnations. One element introduced here is that any coming destruction will not be total (5:10); there will be a remnant, some **branches** of the vine left behind (cp. 2:21).[7] This element is not meant to soften the tone of the LORD's rebuke, but to give hope to later readers who will wonder about their own future. The second element Jeremiah introduces is the role played by other prophets. They see the warning signs of a Babylonian invasion, but they dismiss them and predict that all will be well (see Jer 28:6-9). In fact, their words (**He will do nothing . . .**) suggest that they see the sins of the people as sins, but they proclaim that the LORD will not punish the people for them.[8] They think the people have been given immunity. This notion is probably based on what happened to Jerusalem during the days of Hezekiah. That relatively recent event has put their perception of God out of focus; they do not see the whole picture, a picture based on what he has done throughout Israel's history. So, the very people who should be supporting Jeremiah are actually undermining what he has to say. The people who should be speaking for the LORD are actually denying his Spirit. They have a "spirit" (**wind**), but it is the wrong spirit.[9]

---

[6]The translation of the adjectives here is really uncertain, as this is the only instance of their use. The closest parallels suggest a meaning like "full-grown" or "healthy." For alternative interpretations, see Holladay, *Jeremiah 1*, pp. 180-181; McKane, *Jeremiah*, p. 119.

[7]It seems impossible to remove this element without also destroying the symmetry of the lines; so they cannot be considered secondary additions (Thompson, *Jeremiah*, p. 243; cp. Bright, *Jeremiah*, pp. 39-40). For this reason, one cannot be adamant about seeing verses 18-19 as a secondary insertion, even though many commentators do (see below).

[8]The reference to "sword or famine" (v. 12) uses the language of Jeremiah found primarily in prophecies from the reign of Zedekiah. This might indicate that this unit was spoken later than those preceding; but this criterion is too subjective for one to be sure.

[9]Thompson, *Jeremiah*, p. 244.

Therefore, at the beginning of verse 14, suggests that 5:14-17 is a continuation of the preceding verses, not an independent unit. Strengthening this impression is the statement, **Because** [they] **have spoken these words**. "These words" are the lies and baseless claims of the prophets mentioned in verses 12-13. The idea of injuring the people with these prophetic words (the words are **a fire**, the people **the wood**) is akin to Hosea's metaphor of the prophetic word as a "sword" and "lightning," which cuts and kills its hearers (Hos 6:5; cp. Heb 4:12). This points to the broader notion of the inseparability between words and actions in the biblical world. Words spoken by powerful individuals (God, the king, the prophet) carry such authority that they are not distinguished from the physical actions which carry out those words.

The judgment pronounced here on the people (5:15-17) refers specifically to the Babylonians, yet verbally it is highly reminiscent of Deuteronomy 28:49-52. There, Moses foretold that the LORD would "bring a nation . . . from far away, whose language you will not understand," who will "devour . . . livestock . . . and crops . . . ; they will leave you no grain, new wine or oil, nor any calves . . . or lambs;" and they will fight "until the high fortified walls in which you trust fall down." Jeremiah draws on this ancient prediction to get the people to see that the destruction he is announcing is totally consistent with the LORD's previous words.[10] The reasons for the destruction were clearly laid out in the book of the covenant, discovered in the days of Josiah, enforced by that righteous king, but ignored by the people. They are without excuse. They have come to put their trust in their own military might (**fortified cities**), rather than in their God (cp. Hos 10:13-14).

5:18-19 This brief unit appears to break with the surrounding units, both stylistically (prose, not poetry) and thematically (the promise of a remnant). The phrase **in those days** has been especially significant for some previous scholars as an indicator of "a later hand."[11] The assumptions lying behind such arguments are not as widely accepted today, however, and the presence of a similar exception clause in verse 10 shows that such a sentiment is not nec-

---

[10]Brueggemann (*Jeremiah*, p. 66) points to similarities in 1 Sam 8:11-17, which describe the policies of kings. These words might point to the collapse of the king's economic base.

[11]McKane, *Jeremiah*, p. 126.

essarily out of place in the present context.[12] Further, this unit does not speak of restoration, only preservation in exile. And finally, the need to explain the nation's predicament to other nations is not an uncommon rhetorical device in earlier passages (Deut 29:24-28; 1 Kgs 9:8-9; cp. Jer 16:10-13).[13]

The explanation for the exile (v. 19) is rather typical for the Old Testament. The people have **forsaken** the LORD (cp. Deut 29:25; 1 Kgs 9:9; Jer 16:11) and chosen to serve **gods** worshiped in other lands; therefore, they are forced to move to those other lands. In this, Jeremiah brings up again the accusation that the people are actually less zealous about their religion than their "pagan" neighbors. Other nations uphold the worship of their gods in their lands, even though those gods are man-made. But Israel does not uphold reverence for her God in her own land, even though he is the only true God (Jer 2:11).

5:20-29 This unit consists of a prophetic summons (vv. 20-21; cp. 4:5; 46:14; 50:2), a double accusation against the people (vv. 22-25,26-28), and a refrain calling for punishment (v. 29; cp. 5:9; 9:9). It could easily stand on its own.

The description of the people in verse 21 carried a deep (and harsh) meaning for **the house of Jacob**. They are a **foolish and senseless people**. The former term (סָכָל, *sākāl*) is applied by Laban to Jacob for leaving him without giving his farewells (Gen 31:28). It is also applied twice to King Saul (1 Sam 13:13; 26:21). Its use here might be taken as an affront to the Davidic House in particular. The second term literally means, "without heart." The heart was understood as the source of one's thoughts and motivations (see Deut 5:28-29; 7:17-18; 8:17-18; 9:4-5); one is guided by one's heart (see Ps 19:14). To be "without heart" is to have no sense of direction.[14] The subsequent charge that they **have eyes but do not see . . .** is taken over from Isaiah (Isa 6:9-10). These descriptors connote for that prophet idol-worshipers (cp. Ps 115:2-8; 135:15-18) who oppress the weak (see Isa 32:1-8). For Ezekiel, such behavior is a sign of willful rebellion (Ezek 12:2), and Jeremiah obviously concurs (see Jer 5:23). All these elements fit into Jeremiah's thoughts in this unit.

---

[12]Brueggemann (*Jeremiah*, p. 67) reads this as a sign of the LORD's own inner turmoil over what to do to the people he loves.

[13]Holladay, *Jeremiah 1*, p. 190.

[14]Brueggemann, *Jeremiah*, p. 68.

The LORD's first accusation is that the people do not honor and respect him as Creator. He has fixed **a boundary for the sea** (v. 22), and he continues to provide rain for a bountiful harvest (v. 24; cp. Job 38:8-11; Ps 104:9,13-15). The proper response should be to have hearts that **fear** and **tremble** before him (cp. Deut 5:29);[15] instead, they have **stubborn and rebellious hearts** (cp. Deut 21:18,20; Ps 78:8), which turn toward other gods (cp. Deut 7:4; 11:16,28; Josh 23:6-8). The consequence of this rebellious behavior is that the LORD has taken away the rains, and they have not enjoyed bountiful harvests (cp. Amos 4:6-11).

The second accusation (Jer 5:26-28) concerns social oppression, as the **rich and powerful** manipulate the economic and judicial systems to the detriment of the **fatherless** and the **poor**. They treat their weaker neighbors as birds, trapping them with some legal trick and then placing them in financial situations (**cages**) from which they cannot escape. As predicted in the Song of Moses, they **have grown fat and sleek**; now, they should expect him to judge and take his vengeance on his people, as he says in verse 29 (cp. Deut 32:15-18,40-43).[16]

5:30-31 The repetition of the refrain in verse 29 might indicate an intended conclusion of the section there. If that is so, the closing lines of this chapter might be better read as the introduction to the next. The concluding question — **But what will you do in the end?** — is answered in some sense by the directives of 6:1ff. On the other hand, these lines look back to comments earlier in Jeremiah 5, so they also serve well as a conclusion to what precedes. In that vein, the section closes with some finger pointing. The primary culprits are **the prophets**, who **prophesy lies** instead of the word of the LORD, and **the priests**, who **rule by their own authority** instead of by the LORD's authority. But the sickness that pervades Judah is not the fault of their religious leaders alone. The general population is also to blame because they do not speak out against these abuses of

---

[15]Holladay (*Jeremiah 1*, p. 196) notes a possible wordplay involving the Hebrew terms for "tremble" and "sand." Perhaps the reader is supposed to learn a lesson from the "sand" of the sea, which "trembles" at the command of the LORD. See also Thompson, *Jeremiah*, p. 248; McKane, *Jeremiah*, p. 129.

[16]There are several other allusions to Deuteronomy 32 in Jer 5:14-29. Again, the reason for drawing on such older texts is to convince the people that the LORD could destroy his people and still be true to his character.

power; in fact, they **love it this way** (cp. 26:7-9).[17] This reveals that the people were expected to know the commands and will of the LORD; they could not use the excuse that they were "poor" and "foolish" (v. 4) and thus unable to know what was expected of them. The whole nation was held accountable.

---

[17]Holladay, *Jeremiah 1*, p. 201.

JEREMIAH 6

E. JERUSALEM UNDER SIEGE (6:1-30)

The threat of invasion looms ever larger in this chapter. The transitions between most of the units are marked literarily by the repeated introductory formula, "This is what the LORD (Almighty) says" (6:9,16,22). There are two other formulaic lines in verses 6 and 21 which are very similar, but the differences indicate that those mark transitions within a single unit rather than the beginning of something new. The final unit (6:27-30) is distinguished by a definite shift in metaphors beginning in verse 27. It is likely that it functions as a conclusion to several sections, perhaps extending all the way back to the beginning of Jeremiah 2.

There is a slight but steady chronological shift within this section, suggesting a span of time extending from the reign of Jehoiakim to the reign of Zedekiah. The opening unit (6:1-8) speaks of preparations for battle, but a battle which can still be averted. The second and third units (6:9-15,16-21) speak of invasion as a more certain divine response to the unrepentant city. The fourth unit (6:22-26) goes the next step, describing the invaders as if they are already present in the land. The final unit reads as if the people have had their chance to repent, and the decision for exile is now irreversible. In spite of these slight differences, all of these units share the common theme of the LORD bringing a foreign army in wrath against Jerusalem as a response to the people's rejection of his words of warning.

6:1-8 These lines evoke a sense of urgency and anxiety with the verbal sounds of battle. The reader can almost see the alarmed eyes on the faces of the original recipients, hear their quickening heartbeats, feel their anguished breaths. Contributing to the sense of panic is the identity of the speaker. It is the LORD himself, their protector, who says, **Flee for safety!** But where to go? Those addressed are the **people of Benjamin**, the tribe to the north of Jerusalem. It might be significant that Benjamin was the one tribe which, centuries before, distinguished itself from the rest of the tribes and stayed with David's tribe.[1] All these years, the people of Benjamin have looked to Jerusalem for protection; it is the most heavily fortified city in the nation, and it is the dwelling-place of the LORD. But not now (cp. Jeremiah 7). **Flee FROM Jerusalem!** he says. The LORD then uses two wordplays as he continues sounding the alarm. The word for **Sound** (תִּקְעוּ, *tiqʻû*) is from the same root as **Tekoa**; and both words for **Raise the signal** come from the same root (שְׂאוּ מַשְׂאֵת, *śᵊʾû misʾēth*). The repetition of sounds in quick succession reflects the sense of urgency. The enemy comes **out of the north** (see 1:13), and it constitutes a **terrible destruction**.

The most terrifying aspect of this attack is that the LORD himself is leading it (v. 2). He is the one who will **destroy** the **beautiful and delicate . . . Daughter of Zion**. This designation might better be translated "Daughter Zion," as it intends to depict Jerusalem as a young woman. "Zion" probably refers to the innermost district of Jerusalem, where the temple and royal palace were located. Excavations at similar cities in the region suggest that there might have been a secondary defense wall around this part of the city, in addition to the main city walls.

The sense of **shepherds with their flocks** is not absolutely clear. This could be a reference to actual shepherds, bringing their flocks around the deserted ruins of Jerusalem for feeding.[2] But royal personages are often referred to as "shepherds" (see 2 Sam 5:2; 7:7; Micah 5:4-5), so this could be a reference to Babylonian leaders, stationing their troops all around the city.[3] The statement that they will pitch their tents would have pointed the Hebrew listeners back to verse 1, since the word for **pitch** (a tent) and the word for "sound (the trumpet)" are identical (*tiqʻû*).[4]

There are also two ways to understand verses 4-5. The subject changes from "I" to "we" in these lines. This might signal a change

---

[1]It might also be significant that Jeremiah's hometown of Anathoth was situated within the territory of Benjamin. Thompson, *Jeremiah*, p. 253.

[2]Brueggemann (*Jeremiah*, p. 70) sees shepherds as representative of the lowest rungs of society.

[3]Thompson, *Jeremiah*, p. 254; Holladay, *Jeremiah 1*, p. 206; Nicholson, *Jeremiah 1-25*, p. 67.

[4]Holladay, *Jeremiah 1*, p. 206.

in speakers, from the LORD to Babylonian soldiers. Then again, it might signal that the LORD is putting himself in the role of the one rallying the Babylonian troops, that they are joining together to attack the city. In either case, the main point of these lines is to suggest the urgent need for attack. The speaker does not want to wait another day before launching the attack. At first they say, **Let us attack at noon**. Then, when they realize they are too late for a noontime attack, they do not want to postpone it until the next day. They say, **Let us attack at night**.

The seeming inevitability of the attack in the preceding verses is tempered by the end of the unit. The LORD is certainly speaking still, initially continuing the siege language of the preceding verses with orders for the enemy to **build siege ramps**. But then he shifts to giving a rationale for such a siege (6:6b-7), accusing the inhabitants of **oppression, wickedness, violence**, and **destruction**. The verbs reflect the pervasiveness of the sins; the city **is filled with** them, it **pours** [them] **out** like **water**, they **resound in her**. The force of this string of verbal attacks is then softened in 6:8. Jerusalem is now told God's words of destruction are only threats, that they are to heed these threats "lest" he (**or I will**) finally abandon them and destroy them.

The final verse here seems rather dissonant from the prevailing tone of the section. It could be that these few verses (6:6-8) were originally spoken at an earlier time than those surrounding it, and that it was included here simply because of the reference to a siege in verse 6. Then again, it could be that these verses are original to the overall context, and that they are here to tell the reader to read this entire section as having a threatening tone of what *could* happen, but not as a direct warning of what *will* happen.

6:9-15 The LORD returns to a tone of inevitable destruction with verse 9. He orders those "gathering grapes" to **glean the remnant of Israel**. There will be no remnant in the land this time.[5] The rest of this unit then serves to justify such a harsh sentence. It is not a result of some irrational expectations the LORD has imposed on his people; rather, the fault lies with the people themselves. They do not listen to the LORD's words. **Their ears are closed**, or, more literally, "uncircumcised." There is additional "skin" covering their ears that should

---

[5]Thompson (*Jeremiah*, p. 257) takes this in a different way. He says that the harvester is looking for good fruit but is unable to find any. Thus, this verse parallels 5:1. But see Holladay, *Jeremiah 1*, p. 213.

have been removed. One cannot help but wonder whether this is a critique of religion that is entirely externalized, that the people have lost the true spiritual meaning of religious acts such as circumcision (cp. 9:23-24).

The allusion to circumcision might explain why verses 11-12 speak of only men suffering. In these verses, Jeremiah moves from boys (**children**) to **young men** to married men to elderly men in describing those who would be punished. The main component of the sentence pronounced here hits them where it will hurt them most: Their inability to defend and preserve **their houses, their fields,** and **their wives.** They will fail to fulfill their primary social roles — to head a home, and to protect their goods from theft and their families from harm.[6]

The LORD shifts his focus in 6:13 from all the men in the land to the religious leaders (**prophets and priests alike**). All the people are guilty of sin (**From the least to the greatest, all are greedy . . .**), but they have been heavily influenced in that direction by the **prophets and priests,** their religious mentors. Those leaders are greedy, and so they manipulate the cult system in such a way that they benefit financially at the expense of those who look to them to perform the prescribed ceremonies and to disperse economic aid (tithes) where needed. Moreover, these leaders minimize or explain away the signs that divine punishment is coming. They evaluate the sins of the people as minor offenses, and they dismiss warnings by others that the Babylonians are preparing for an attack (see 4:10). There is no room in their theology for a God who would throw them out of their Promised Land. The consequence of this "uninspired" behavior is that they in particular will suffer the fate the LORD has planned for Jerusalem.

6:16-21 This unit focuses the reader's attention on the bankruptcy of Israelite worship. In the process, it shows that the sacrificial system was only one aspect of the Old Testament concept of worship. The comments about sacrifices come toward the end of the unit, when he says, **Your burnt offerings are not acceptable, your sacrifices do not please me** (v. 20; cp. Hos 6:6; Amos 5:21-24). This is so, even though the people had literally gone out of their way to offer the best sacrifices they could. They had gone to Sheba and

---

[6]Brueggemann (*Jeremiah,* p. 72) notes that the three things to be lost (v. 12) are the same three that are not to be coveted, according to the Tenth Commandment. Holladay (*Jeremiah 1,* p. 216) points to a parallel in Deut 28:30.

India[7] to get the best incense and spices for sacrifices they could. But it is not the expensiveness of the materials used which make offerings pleasing to the LORD; it is the quality of the hearts of the worshipers. The corruptness of their hearts is recognized in the fact that they **have not listened to my words and have rejected my law** (v. 19). Exactly what they are ignoring and what they have rejected is not spelled out here. It almost certainly includes idolatry and social oppression, since those are mentioned most often in Jeremiah. It also includes their refusal to listen to the warnings of the LORD's prophets, the **watchmen** who have sounded **the trumpet** to warn of coming disaster (v. 17; see 7:25; Hos 9:7-8; Ezek 3:17).

Those watchmen, like Jeremiah now, had been calling the people back to **the ancient paths**, to **the good way**, where, the LORD says, **you will find rest for your souls** (v. 16; cp. Josh 1:13; Matt 11:28; Heb 4:1-11). This is a reminder that the Israelite prophets are not religious innovators, but restorers of an ancient faith. Furthermore, walking in those **ancient paths** is not simply a matter of following ancient and divine prescriptions regarding acts of worship. It has to do with a choice of following the LORD — in every aspect of your life — rather than following some other god or some alternate way of living (cp. 10:2; 18:15).[8] This imagery of **the good way** probably is to be traced back to Deuteronomy, where Moses repeatedly urges the people to "walk in all the way that the LORD your God commanded you" (Deut 5:33; 9:16; 11:28; 13:5; 31:29; cp. 30:15-20). This "way," **the ancient paths**, is the Law of Moses recorded in Deuteronomy and the rest of the Torah (see 7:5-7).[9] The LORD is calling them back to those laws. But this is more than the performance of certain external acts. He is calling them back to the attitude they held toward God's laws when they were given. That attitude is perhaps best exemplified in Deuteronomy 5:27, where the people tell Moses they will "listen and obey" whatever the LORD commands. The LORD's reply is to commend them for having such good "hearts," hearts that

---

[7]Holladay, *Jeremiah 1*, pp. 222-223.

[8]N.C. Habel, "Appeal to Ancient Tradition as a Literary Form," *ZAW* 88 (1976): 253-272.

[9]So Holladay, *Jeremiah 1*, p. 221. Brueggemann (*Jeremiah*, p. 73) mentions the use of "the way" in Israel's wisdom writings (cp. Lundbom, *Jeremiah 1-20*, p. 435). All of these together probably influenced how Jesus' listeners interpreted his self-designation as "the Way" (John 14:6) and the early designation of Christianity as "the Way" (Acts 9:2; 19:9,23).

listen to him. Now, in Jeremiah's day, the people say, **"We will not listen"** (Jer 6:17).

For their refusal to listen to the prophets or walk in "the good way," the LORD calls on other **nations** and the natural world (**earth**) to bear witness to the fact that the suffering he is bringing is just, and that those who will suffer were properly warned. This theme of warning concludes this unit in verse 21, but in a rather puzzling way. The LORD says he will set up **obstacles** (מִכְשֹׁלִים, *mikšōlîm*) over which the people will **stumble** (כָּשְׁלוּ, *kāšālû*). This might leave the impression God is devious and mean-spirited when he metes out punishment, but the purpose is to convey the sense that the people will feel humiliation. The same term is translated "they will be brought down" in verse 15; so these two units end on the same note (see also on 18:15).

6:22-26 This very somber and terrifying unit returns the reader to the battlefield setting of the opening unit of the chapter. Several themes common to Jeremiah appear in this relatively opaque passage. The enemy, of course, is the Babylonians. They come **from the land of the north** (meaning they enter the land of Judah from the north) . . . **from the ends of the earth**. The latter indicates that this relatively common expression is a hyperbole — at least it is from a modern perspective — referring simply to a nation lying at some distance from Judah. They strike fear in the hearts of their enemies, for they are not only a massive army, they are also **cruel and show no mercy**. They are so overwhelming, **like the roaring sea**, that hands which usually would strengthen in anticipation of a fight now **hang limp** (cp. 38:4). The image of **pain like that of a woman in labor** (v. 24) is most appropriate. This is pain which grips the entire body, and pain which cannot be avoided; **there is terror on every side** (v. 25). The imagery of the woman in labor is brought to its tragic conclusion in the final verse, as the joy that should follow the pain of childbirth is instead replaced with **bitter wailing** at the death of **an only son**. The only hope for the future of the family has been snuffed out.

6:27-30 The imagery of the final unit of this section paints a vivid picture of the situation in Judah, a picture which summarizes what has been said about Judah in the preceding parts. Jeremiah is a silversmith and Judah is a lump of raw **ore**, thought to contain precious metal encrusted with dirt and certain less precious metals (bronze and iron).[10] These less precious metals perhaps represent

---

[10]Holladay, *Jeremiah 1*, pp. 230-232; Thompson, *Jeremiah*, pp. 266-267.

the halfhearted worship (expensive sacrifices offered by immoral people; v. 20) mentioned previously. The silversmith has been smelting the ore, burning away the dross in order to extract the precious silver, a remnant. This process of smelting probably refers most immediately to Jeremiah's prophetic work, times when he has rebuked the people and called on them to return to the LORD. Unfortunately, after all this process has been completed and the dross has been burned away, there is nothing left. Just as he could not find "one person who deals honestly and seeks the truth" (5:1), now he can find no pure metal. The lump is of no use; the entire mass has been **rejected**.

It seems likely that this closing unit functions as the conclusion to more than just Jeremiah 6. We have already mentioned the thematic link back to the beginning of Jeremiah 5 (the absence of any good portion in Jerusalem). Several other links have been noted by other commentators.[11] One other is somewhat subjective. There is in these verses a definite mixture of anger and disappointment. The LORD is angry with the people and will punish them for the disappointment they bring; they will be thrown out. At the same time, he expected to find "precious metal" in them. He chose this ore because he thought it would contain something very valuable that he could use. He is profoundly disappointed that this has not been the case. This mixture of anger and disappointment pervades all of chapters 2–6. The announcements regarding the LORD's anger and threats/warnings of coming disaster predominate; but there is an unmistakable undertone of regret and disappointment that this is so. His heart is broken — not hardened — by what he sees in Jerusalem. He still wishes that something else could be done. And, as we will see later in the book, he has enough faith in Judah left to give them another chance in the not-too-distant future.

---

[11]W.L. Holladay, *The Architecture of Jeremiah 1–20* (Lewisburg, PA: Bucknell University, 1976), pp. 57-97; Thompson, *Jeremiah*, p. 266; but see Lundbom, *Jeremiah 1–20*, p. 447.

JEREMIAH 7

III. JEREMIAH'S CONCERN FOR HIS PEOPLE
(7:1–10:25)

A. FALSE RELIGION WORTHLESS (7:1–29)

There is a clear break when one moves into Jeremiah 7. The extended sections of poetic oracles end, and now a section of prose ensues. This section, which extends through 7:29, contains one of the best-known addresses by Jeremiah. It in many ways captures the core of Jeremiah's message.[1] The significance of the historical background of this message is great. It concerns the history of Judah as a whole, but also of Jeremiah's own family. Also, we know something of the posthistory to this event, because the audience's reactions to Jeremiah's words are described in Jeremiah 26. That account also places this section in its historical context: "early in the reign of Jehoiakim" (Jer 26:1; c. 609–605 B.C.). The destruction of Jerusalem is not absolutely certain at this time; there is still the possibility of repentance to avert that disaster.

There are four units to this section, distinguished from one another by who is being addressed. The first and main unit (7:1-15) records the sermon Jeremiah preaches to a crowd that happens to be in front of the temple. It is often called "Jeremiah's Temple Sermon." The LORD then shifts his attention to Jeremiah himself in the next unit (7:16-20), preparing him for a negative reaction from the crowd. In the unit that follows (7:21-26), his words are again directed to Jeremiah's audience, as he describes a long pattern of disobedience throughout the years. At this point, the LORD returns again to Jeremiah, warning him not to expect the present generation to be any different (7:27-29).[2]

---

[1]Brueggemann, *Jeremiah*, p. 78.

[2]Once again, the division into units is arbitrary. Several commentators

It is possible that the units beginning in verse 16 come from a later time than the sermon in verses 1-15, but have been placed here because of thematic similarities with what precedes.[3] Then again, it is possible that the entire section was one extended unit from the beginning. If the latter is true, the reader has to decide how the parts hold together, because earlier portions assume the possibility of repentance while later ones do not. Either the calls for repentance in the early parts are known to be futile, or (the more likely) there is an implied conditionality to the messages of devastation in the later parts. There is one very strong literary thread running through the whole section, though. This is the theme of "not listening." It is in the summary accusation in the first unit (v. 13); it is used sarcastically by the LORD in his first comments to Jeremiah (v. 16); it is used three times in the second accusation of the people (vv. 23,24,26); and it is used in the LORD's final comments to Jeremiah (v. 27) in a way that directly parallels its first usage. It is ironic, therefore, that Jeremiah's first words to the people in front of the temple are "Hear the word of the LORD" (v. 2). One would expect them, based on previous experience, to do anything but "hear."

7:1-15 This first unit is well structured. It begins with a narrative introduction (v. 1) to the record of a summons to hear a prophetic message (vv. 2-3). A twofold message is given in verses 3-4, which is then elaborated on in verses 5-7 and 8-15. In these elaborations, Jeremiah anticipates and undercuts the "official" responses to his words which temple functionaries might be expected to offer.

The formulaic narrative introduction appears here for the first time since 2:1. This is one of many reasons why some scholars speak of the unity of Jeremiah 2-6. The command to **stand at the gate of the LORD's house** and address the **people of Judah who come through these gates to worship the LORD** is likely to have carried great personal significance for Jeremiah. We mentioned in regard to the superscription of the book that Jeremiah's lineage probably included Eli's descendant, Abiathar. Solomon banished Abiathar

---

extend the unit beginning in 7:21 through verse 28. See Holladay, *Jeremiah 1*, p. 259; Brueggemann, *Jeremiah*, p. 82; Thompson, *Jeremiah*, pp. 286-289; Bright, *Jeremiah*, p. 58 Lundbom, *Jeremiah 1-20*, p. 479-480.

[3]Thompson (*Jeremiah*, p. 283) concludes that 7:16-8:3 were added secondarily, because there is no reference to them in Jeremiah 26; but this argument is not entirely consistent. Several items in 7:1-15 are not mentioned there either, yet Thompson does not see them as secondary.

and his descendants from serving in the temple (1 Kgs 2:26-27). The men of Jeremiah's immediate family are known as priests, but they still are not allowed to serve in the temple. One wonders how they were treated in the days of Josiah's Reform (see 2 Kgs 23:8-9,19-20). In any case, Jeremiah likely was viewed by the temple priests as something of an outsider, and almost certainly as a person out of favor with the LORD. The command to address the people in front of the temple — on their turf, so to speak — would have been interpreted as a direct challenge to the authority of the temple priests. The summons, **Hear the word of the LORD**, is a typical prophetic summons in the Old Testament (see Isa 1:10; Hos 4:1).

The basic message to the temple crowd consists of two points. The first is a call to repentance: **Reform your ways . . .** (v. 3). The second is not to be "deceived by" (i.e., read too much into) the presence of the temple (v. 4). The **deceptive words** are, **This is the temple of the LORD**.[4] This seems odd at first, because this building actually is the temple of the LORD. But the issue at hand is what truly makes a building the temple of the LORD?[5] Jeremiah's audience apparently assumes that calling his name over a place obligates him to protect it; Jeremiah shows that something more is needed. What is most important in this question is what significance the people attach to their claim that this is the temple of the LORD. They believe that the temple of the LORD is permanently inviolable by his enemies, that he will unconditionally protect it (and its city) against all attackers. Jeremiah's main task is to convince them that this is a false assumption.

The protasis of Jeremiah's first point (vv. 3,5-7) gives the conditions under which the LORD will continue to dwell in and inhabit Jerusalem. He says that the people must **reform** or **really change** ("make good;" see 4:22) their ways. The wording reminds one of the previously encountered call by the LORD to "walk in the good way"

---

[4]Holladay (*Jeremiah 1*, p. 242) adopts the plausible suggestion that the triple repetition of this statement means to imply that it is an example of "vain repetitions."

[5]A parallel challenge could easily be made to churches in the Restoration Movement. What truly makes a church a "church of Christ" or a "Christian church?" Or who are true "disciples of Christ?" R.E. Clements states the issue this way: "What is at stake [in Jer 7:1-15] is the . . . deeper theological point concerning the nature of the relationship that exists between God and all those religious institutions through which he may be approached by human beings" (*Jeremiah*, p. 46).

(6:16). The elaboration in verses 5-7 spells out what this means. The "good way," the "ancient paths" which they are to follow, is a life of righteousness, justice, and mercy, and a life which excludes other gods. The language he uses here draws heavily from the language of Deuteronomy. They are to "do justice between one another" (**deal with each other justly**; cp. 5:1; 22:15), particularly in matters concerning **the alien, the fatherless or the widow** (cp. the combination of these in Deut 10:18; 24:17; 27:19). These groups were those particularly at risk in the male-oriented society of ancient Israel,[6] and they are not being cared for in the Judah of Jeremiah's day. What is worse, they are being ignored by those who are worshiping the LORD. Part of the explanation for this might lie in the fact they worship other gods in addition to worshiping the LORD.[7] The lax attitude regarding their religious obligations to the LORD would also translate into a lax attitude regarding their social obligations to those at risk in their community.[8]

A technical question regarding the first point and its elaboration is the translation of the main clause of the apodosis. The reading in the NIV reflects the majority position: **then I will let you live in this place**. This reading has the support of most early Hebrew and Greek manuscripts. It expresses the primary implication of the identification of this as the temple of the LORD. Rather than simply say that he dwells in his own home, the LORD declares that, as a by-product of living in and protecting his own home, he will protect his people among whom he dwells. There is another reading possible, however, which is preserved in the early Latin translation (Vulgate) and certain Hebrew manuscripts. This reading retains the same consonants (which is all one finds in many early Hebrew manuscripts), but it applies different vowels.[9] The result is that the LORD says, "I will dwell with you in this place." One must then supply what is implied by this, namely, that the LORD will defend the people with whom he dwells. Thus, whether the

---

[6]Landed males enjoyed economic stability, because of the strong agricultural base in the region. The alien did not inherit land from a local family, nor did the fatherless; and the widow had no male obligated to protect her.

[7]Again, this is a sign they have left "the ancient paths." See Jer 18:15; Deut 5:7; 6:14; 7:4; 8:19; etc.

[8]Thompson, *Jeremiah*, pp. 278-279.

[9]The reading in the Masoretic Text (v. 7) is וְשִׁכַּנְתִּי אֶתְכֶם (*wešikkantî 'ethkem*); the Hebrew behind the Latin translation is וְשָׁכַנְתִּי אִתְּכֶם (*wešākantî 'ittᵉkem*).

protection of Israel assumed to accompany the LORD's dwelling in the temple is explicitly supplied (as in the MT) or merely implied (as in the Vulgate), the same idea is conveyed. The elaboration of the apodosis in verse 7 supports the majority reading, as it elaborates on where the people live, not where the LORD lives. This elaboration also heightens the sense of betrayal the LORD feels. The people are polluting the land by their actions, land which they possess only because the LORD gave it to them; they are worshiping other gods, gods other than the one who gave them the land.[10]

The second point is elaborated much more extensively. It is encapsulated to a large degree by talk about "trust." The short form of this point (v. 4) reads, **Do not trust in deceptive words and say, 'This is the temple of the LORD.'** The elaboration (vv. 8-15) begins with the accusation, **you are trusting in deceptive words**. Toward the end of this elaboration (v. 14), he refers to the temple as **the temple you trust in**. In between these two references to "trust," he explains how they are deceived by this talk about the temple (cp. 5:17). He accuses them of using the temple as robbers would use a hideout. They make a mockery of his house and his name (**this house, which bears my Name**; v. 10). They are guilty of breaking some of the central laws on which their relationship with God is based — five of the Ten Commandments — yet they still feel comfortable coming before the LORD as "good citizens" of his kingdom. They believe that they can get away with murder — literally — and still expect God to accept them because of their sacrifices. Their sacrifices have essentially become bribes.[11]

There is a pivot in verse 11, as the LORD shifts from accusation of wrong to pronouncement of judgment. The pivot clause (**I have been watching**) has a particularly ominous sound to it. The verb translated "watching" here is the very common word for "see." He is asserting that he, unlike other gods (and their worshipers), actually "sees" what is going on (cp. Isa 6:10; 37:17).[12] The result will be disastrous for this people.

---

[10]For further discussion, see Thompson, *Jeremiah*, pp. 276, 279; Holladay, *Jeremiah 1*, pp. 236-237. Holladay's own unique proposal is that the majority reading is correct in verse 3, while the minority reading should be adopted in verse 7.

[11]Clements, *Jeremiah*, p. 45.

[12]Holladay, *Jeremiah 1*, p. 247.

Jeremiah has a major hurdle to overcome, however, in trying to convince his audience that they have something to fear. They should have learned from what happened to the northern tribes that they could be defeated by foreign invaders (cp. 3:6-10). Instead, the conclusion they derived from that earlier event was that the LORD would always protect Jerusalem as he had then, that the presence of the LORD and the ark in the temple would repel any military force who came against it. Jeremiah reaches into his own past for an argument against this line of reasoning. Jerusalem was not the first resting place for the ark; it had previously resided **in Shiloh (where I first made a dwelling for my Name)**, under the care of Eli and his sons. The irreverent attitude of Jeremiah's own ancestors had led to the humiliating defeat of Israel's armies and the capture of the ark (1 Sam 2–4). The same irreverence now pervades the people of Jerusalem. They do not listen when the LORD speaks (through his prophets); they do not answer when he calls to them. **Therefore** (v. 14), these people are facing a repeat of what had happened to Jeremiah's people more than four centuries earlier.

Jeremiah pleads with them not to make the same mistake his people had made, but their pride prevents them from receiving his message. The religious leaders assume that their elevation and the demotion of Jeremiah's family reflect a permanent flaw in the latter and an unconditional preference for the former. Jeremiah's words directly challenge this assumption. He realizes that his ancestors' humiliation came as a result of not listening to the LORD and his prophets. Now the people of Jerusalem are not listening. Similarly, the people in Jerusalem have interpreted the fall of Samaria and the northern tribes as a sign of the LORD's undying preference for Jerusalem and rejection of the North, for no reason other than the presence of the Ark. **I spoke to you again and again, but you did not listen; I called you, but you did not answer** (cp. 7:27; 8:6). Jeremiah closes (v. 15) by challenging this rather arrogant attitude. What has happened to **all your brothers, the people of Ephraim** (the North), can happen to Jerusalem as well.[13]

7:16-20 This short unit is formulated as a private address to Jeremiah, but the majority of it concerns Judah. Verse 16 is directed to Jeremiah. There is a strong odor of sarcasm in the LORD's words, as he picks up on the preceding language of rejection. Just as the

---

[13]Brueggemann, *Jeremiah*, pp. 80-81.

people have not listened when he spoke to them, now he will not listen when Jeremiah speaks to him. Obviously, this is not a rebuff of Jeremiah, but an indirect rebuke of Judah. Because they do not listen to him, he will not listen to a righteous man praying on their behalf (cp. 15:1). The next three verses justify the LORD's attitude. The people's sin is everywhere (**in the towns of Judah and in the streets of Jerusalem**) and involves everyone (**children, fathers, women**). The LORD's somewhat baffling talk about **provoking me to anger** in verses 18-19 actually clarifies our understanding of it in another way. It is baffling because he talks about not being provoked to anger, but then he goes into an announcement about how he will pour out that anger on the nation (v. 20). What it clarifies is their understanding of the reason for the anger. A more literal reading of verse 19 would be: "Is it me they are provoking? says the LORD. Is it not them, for the sake of (or, with the result of)[14] shaming themselves?" The sense is that the one provoked has been shamed, and the anger is a response intended to protect or restore one's honor. The LORD is saying they have shamed him, but they have shamed themselves even more. So, because of the shame they have brought on themselves and their land, the whole land and all its natural inhabitants will suffer.[15]

7:21-26 The LORD directs his words once again toward the people. In these verses, he gets to the heart of long-held misconceptions about faith in the minds of the Israelites, but the sentiments he expresses apply to all worshipers of any time. He begins sarcastically again: **Go ahead, add your burnt offerings to your other sacrifices** (v. 21). He does not really want them to do this; he wants them to recognize that those things are not at the heart of worship, because their attitude about sin and the temple (7:9-11) reveals that that is what they believe. Instead, he makes a rather puzzling assertion: Following the Exodus, **I did not just give them commands about burnt offerings and sacrifices** (v. 22). The word **just** is not in the Hebrew text, but it is a good interpretation of what is meant. The truth is the LORD did give Israel commands about sacrifices, but he did not intend for the people to treat those commandments as the central or most

---

[14]Holladay, *Jeremiah 1*, p. 255.

[15]On the connection between humans and the rest of nature in destruction (and blessing), see Holladay, *Jeremiah 1*, p. 256. The principle goes back to the earliest chapters of Genesis.

crucial aspects of their worship. Observance of sacrificial laws was intended as one of many examples of a deeper principle: that the people were obedient to ("listened to") the LORD's commands (v. 23; cp. Isa 1:10-17; Hos 6:6; Amos 5:21-25; Micah 6:1-8).[16] But they were viewing it as a way to "keep the LORD happy," as a way to keep his attention diverted while they engaged in sinful activities. They thought the sacrifices would create a "smoke-screen" for their disobedience. He twice gives a direct charge of their refusal to listen in the accusation which follows (vv. 25-26). The persistence of their disobedience had been demonstrated in the fact the LORD had "called their bluff," sending prophets who informed them that the LORD was aware of where their hearts really lay. Thus the final charge is justified, when he says **they** [the more recent generations] **are stiffnecked** and even **more evil than their forefathers.**[17]

Before we judge these ancient Israelites too harshly, we should recognize some similarities in the history of Christianity, even in the Restoration Movement. Many doctrinal debates that have split churches have involved the outward forms of worship. It has often been considered most important to be "right" about what one can or cannot do within the time frame of worship assemblies, while consideration of whether individuals are motivated by a desire to do the will of God are ignored or second-guessed. What is worse, the "proprieties" of worship often overshadow the vulgarities of how the worshipers treat their fellow human beings (consider, for example, slavery). This passage should remind us to take a step back and consider the motivations of ourselves and everyone involved. We must always remember that an attitude of wanting to do the will of God — in every aspect of our lives — is to be honored above all else.

7:27-29 The LORD addresses Jeremiah directly again in this unit, and again he transitions quickly into a pronouncement against Judah. He tells Jeremiah that they will respond to Jeremiah the same way they have responded to him. They will **not listen to** him or **answer** him when he addresses them (v. 27), just as they did not "listen to" the LORD or "answer" him when he called to them (v. 13). Jeremiah is going to share with the LORD the heartache of loving a stubborn people. He then is told to issue an official proclamation

---

[16]Thompson, *Jeremiah*, pp. 287-291; Holladay, *Jeremiah 1*, pp. 261-262; Lundbom, *Jeremiah 1–20*, pp. 481-482.

[17]Holladay, *Jeremiah 1*, p. 263.

of the nation's status: **This is the nation that has not obeyed** [listened] . . . (v. 28). This is basically a repetition of what was just said in verse 27. Further, in a flourish that sends the reader back to 5:1, he announces that **Truth has perished**. There is no truth to be found, so call off the search.

There is then some ambiguity regarding verse 29. Someone is being told to present himself as a person who is in mourning. He is to cut off his hair and sing a lament over God's wrathful dealings with his people. The ambiguity concerns who is being addressed. The verbs are singular. Their subject could be Jeremiah, or it could be a generic subject, an indefinite "you." Either could fit in the context.

B. THE VALLEY OF SLAUGHTER (7:30–8:3)

This short section shares with the one preceding a bleak picture of the future of Jerusalem. It differs from it in many ways, though. First, the certainty of rejection (on the part of both Judah and then God) seems to contrast to the calls for repentance in the sermon. The reference to exposing the bones of the dead (8:1-3) points to the most extreme of military disasters. Second, many of the images and phrases employed to describe both the sin of the people and the LORD's punishment of them are different from those in most of Jeremiah 7.[18] The placement of this short section is probably best explained on thematic grounds. The prediction of the LORD's rejection and abandonment of his people (7:1-29) is most graphically illustrated in circumstances such as those described here (7:30–8:3).

7:30–8:3 There are two sins of the people mentioned here, in 7:30-31. The first is idolatry in the temple; the second, child sacrifice.[19] The omission of the other sins listed in 7:8-11 is striking here, although this is fairly common for Jeremiah in later chapters. This is the first time child sacrifice has been brought into the picture. The **Valley of Ben Hinnom** (later, "Gehenna") was located to the south

---

[18]One might consider the following list of phrases from 7:30-34, many of which are common in later sections of Jeremiah and in Books of Kings: "[they] have done evil in my eyes," "the high places," "the Valley of Ben Hinnom," "to burn . . . in the fire," "the birds of the air and the beasts of the earth," and "the voices of bride and bridegroom."

[19]This parallels most closely the description of the sins of Manasseh (2 Kgs 21:1-18).

of the city of Jerusalem (see on 19:1-2). It continued as a place of
unsanctioned sacrifice until the practice was stopped by Josiah
(2 Kgs 23:10; cp. Isa 30:33), but it apparently was revived after his
death. Because of its location downstream from the city, it had long
been utilized as a dumping ground for the city. It was said that fires
burned constantly there, as the people worked continuously to dispose of their refuse. These "perpetual fires" contributed to later biblical references to Hell/Gehenna as a place of eternal fire (see on
19:1-15). The region of **Topheth** is particularly associated with fire
and child sacrifice (see Isa 30:33; 2 Kgs 23:10).[20] The association with
burials is confined to Jeremiah (cp. 19:11). This designation has
been ascribed by archaeologists over the years to many such dumping grounds throughout the ancient Near East.

The practice of child sacrifice is thought to have infiltrated Israel
and Judah's religious practices from several of Israel's neighbors.
There is ample evidence of child sacrifice among the Phoenicians/
Punics, particularly in the Greek and Roman eras, and among the
Moabites in earlier years (see 2 Kgs 3:26-27). It is unclear how far
back this appalling practice began, as there is evidence of a connec-
tion between child sacrifice and "Molech the detestable god of the
Ammonites" (see 1 Kgs 11:5,7). It is first mentioned for certain in
Judah in the reign of Ahaz, father of Hezekiah (2 Kgs 16:3; cp.
17:17,31; 21:6; 23:10; 2 Chr 28:3).

The remainder of this section (7:32–8:3) contains the LORD's sentence on the people for their behavior. In typical biblical fashion,
the punishments decreed fit the crimes. The **Valley** where they sacrifice their children will become so clogged, there will be **no more
room**. This is a gruesome parallel to the sentiment of verse 21. The
other grim predictions in verses 33-34 are situations that would arise
if there were no children. There would be no one to protect the
gravesites of the dead, no bride and groom to be married. It is as if
the LORD has come up with a rather graphic way of saying that the
sacrifice of children makes no sense.

This trend continues in 8:1-3. The bones of the offending leaders (**the kings and officials of Judah, the priests and prophets and
. . . the people**) will be exposed, apparently because of a lack of

---

[20]"Topheth" is a transliteration of the Hebrew. Holladay translates it "firepit." For a fuller discussion, see Holladay, *Jeremiah 1*, pp. 264-270; Thompson,
Jeremiah, p. 450.

room. But now he goes further, hinting that their many prayers to the "hosts of heaven" (see 19:13; 2 Kgs 17:16; 21:3,5; 23:4,5) are going to be answered — when their bones are left in full view of those "hosts." Their bodies will become the **refuse** in the place of refuse, and **survivors** ("the remnant") **will prefer death**, when they should be rejoicing over the fact of their survival.[21]

---

[21]The horror of such an image is great. See Thompson, *Jeremiah*, p. 295; Holladay, *Jeremiah 1*, pp. 271-272.

JEREMIAH 8

C. SIN AND PUNISHMENT (8:4–9:26)

This lengthy section consists of units only loosely tied together
on thematic grounds. The time frame still appears to be the reign of
Jehoiakim (609–598 B.C.), although it is possible that some pieces
might have originated slightly earlier or later than this. It is difficult
to follow the train of thought at certain junctures, particularly
toward the end of Jeremiah 9. It appears there is, at times, a three-
way conversation going on, involving the LORD, Jeremiah, and the
people; but who is actually speaking is not always clear. Still, if one
steps back and looks at the units as pieces of a collage, a single picture does emerge. That picture is one of "sadness." The LORD is
"sad" because the people persistently refuse to repent. They in turn
are "sad" because of the suffering they are having to endure as a
result of their stubbornness. And the LORD is also "sad" because
their stubbornness reveals they still do not understand his true
nature and what it means to worship him.

8:4-13 This unit contains some of the most vivid and harsh accusations against the people in the book. The LORD essentially accuses
the people of being irrational, even "stupid." They do what is unnatural (v. 4), they show less intelligence than animals (v. 7), and yet
they consider themselves "wise" (vv. 8-9). The LORD's response is to
deprive them of all that they have, things which they have gotten
(families, property) — they think — by their "wisdom."

The LORD opens with a series of rhetorical questions (cp. 2:14,32).
The first two lead into a final pair of questions which tend to contradict the logic of the first two. This final pair gets to the heart of
the matter. The initial questions express something akin to one of
the basic laws of physics: "For every action there is a natural reaction." But it is the second of these questions that opens the way to
the final pair. The second literally says, "Will one turn (יָשׁוּב, *yāšûb*),

and not turn (*yāšûb*)?" The thought is that a person cannot "twist" in one direction and then hold their body in that twisted position forever; eventually, they must "turn" (back). This leads into the third question: **Why then have these people turned away?** (i.e., twisted without turning back). **Why does Jerusalem always turn away?** There is an intricate play on the root שׁוּב (*šûb*) in these lines (cp. 3:6-10; 4:1-2). The people should "turn" (*šûb*) and then "re-turn" (*šûb*). Instead, they are **turned away** (שׁוֹבְבָה, *šôbᵉbāh*; "ever-turning"); they **always turn away** (מְשֻׁבָה, *mᵉšubāh*; "are turned [continually]").[1]

The interrogator answers his own question in verse 5: **They cling to deceit; they refuse to return** (*šûb*). The term for **deceit** could also be translated "delusions" (cp. 23:26). It carries with it the sense of professing as true something that is known to be false in order to trick others, often with the intent of stirring up discord or even rebellion (cp. Josh 9:22; Judg 9:31; 2 Sam 9:27). The nature of this **deceit** is spelled out in verses 8 and 11.[2] It is because there are both deceivers and deceived (cp. 2 Tim 3:13) among the people that **they refuse to return** to the LORD (cp. 5:3). Neither is excused; both should know better.

Their stubborn refusal is a refusal to listen to **the requirements of the LORD** (v. 7), commands against idolatry and oppression of the weak. They are instead headstrong, **like a horse charging into battle** (v. 6). Their refusal to listen is in direct contrast to the LORD, who has **listened attentively**. Unlike the gods they worship, gods who "have ears but do not hear" (Ps 115:6), the LORD hears, but there is nothing to be heard. In this regard, the people show their stupidity, for they demonstrate that they know less than **the stork in the sky**.

Their stupidity does not prevent them from claiming to be wise, and they base that claim on what seems a very reliable foundation — **the law of the LORD** (v. 8). But the LORD says that possession of the Law is no guarantee of wisdom. This brings us to one of the most exasperating lines in the Book of Jeremiah. He asserts that **the lying pen of the scribes has handled** [the law] **falsely**. Who are these scribes? Why is their treatment of the Law so influential? In what way have they handled the Law that is "false?" Numerous suggestions

---

[1]Holladay reads this in a more specific way. For him, the prospect of "falling" and "rising" refers to Israel, while "turning" refers to the LORD. "And if Yahweh turns away from us, he will turn back to us, will he not?" Holladay, *Jeremiah 1*, p. 278.

[2]Cp. ibid., p. 279.

could be proposed regarding the nature of the offense here. Have the scribes turned the Law into a formula for economic success (see below, 9:3-6,23)? Have the scribes interpreted the Law to allow for rampant sin and even idolatry, as long as worship services in the temple continue (see 7:3-10; 9:3-6,12-14)? Have they given greater weight to external worship (sacrifices, rituals, etc.), while ignoring the more essential command to listen to the LORD (7:22-23)? Have they twisted God's conditional pledges of protection into unconditional promises? Whatever the correct answer, the people cling to this "deceit," this "false" reading of the Law.[3] Somehow, those who know the Law of the LORD the best have actually ended up rejecting it.[4] And in rejecting it, they have completely undermined any claim to wisdom (v. 9).

These self-proclaimed "wise men" have actually shown their foolishness (see 17:5-11). Since it takes wisdom to run a household, the LORD declares them unfit to continue as heads of their own households. Both their wives and their fields will be given to others (v. 10), others who truly are wise enough to oversee such things. This opens the way for him to repeat words of doom which he had spoken earlier (6:12-15).[5] At first glance, this seems surprising. But read according to the current arrangement of the book, it might point to something that would have been most significant to the original readers. The targets of the words in 6:12-15 are not specified. The illusion of "wisdom" which the "scribes" and others possessed might have led them to believe that Jeremiah had been talking about someone else. The repetition here might have been a notice to them that he had been talking about them in those other passages.

The LORD closes this unit with an additional warning of agricultural disaster (v. 13). These people have forgotten that their prosperity comes from the LORD. They have assumed instead that their own wisdom (derived from the Law) is the reason for their success (cp. Deut 8:17-18). The LORD has determined that he will remind them of the real source of their prosperity by taking it away from them.[6]

---

[3]These two terms are synonyms in Jer 23:26. See ibid., pp. 281-283, for a fuller discussion of this line.

[4]Thompson points to a distinction here between the "Law of the LORD" — which they know well — and the "Word of the LORD" — which they ignore. *Jeremiah*, p. 300.

[5]See Parke-Taylor, *Formation*, pp. 93-98.

[6]Brueggemann interprets this as a failure on the part of the people to produce the "fruits" God had expected of them (cp. Isa 5:1-7). *Jeremiah*, p. 90; cp. Clements, *Jeremiah*, p. 57

8:14-21 The next unit comes from a time when Judah is being invaded. The threatening words of the preceding unit are becoming reality. This is the LORD's response to the false message of the scribes, priests, and prophets. The unit seems at first to consist of a dialogue between the people and the LORD, but a closer look shows it is more complicated than that. The speakers are identified as "we" (vv. 14-16,20) and "I" (vv. 17-19,21). It is clear that "we" refers to the people; but the identification of "I" is less certain. In fact, it appears that both the LORD and Jeremiah speak in the first person here.

The people speak (vv. 14-16) from a position of despair. They are in the countryside when the enemy is first sighted, so they call to one another to flee for protection in cities surrounded by defensive walls (cp. 4:5). But even as they do so, they know it is a futile effort. **Let us flee to the fortified cities and perish there!** Their hopes for peace are being dashed. The emptiness of the assurances of "peace, peace" from their leaders is being exposed. The enemy invades from the north (**Dan** was the northernmost city in Israel), as Jeremiah had predicted. His words are being proved true; the words of his opponents are being proved false.

Verses 17-19 consist of statements by the LORD, enveloping Jeremiah's own words of anguish, who quotes the words of other sufferers. The LORD begins with a warning about **venomous snakes**. This most likely is not to be taken literally, but as a reference to the enemy now approaching.[7] It might also be an allusion to the story of the poisonous snakes sent by God to punish the people in the wilderness (Num 21:4-9). He had provided a way out of that punishment in the form of a bronze serpent. They, in turn, had elevated that serpent to the status of a god (2 Kgs 18:4). Perhaps this is a way for the LORD to say he is removing his protection from them, because of their unbridled idolatry.[8]

Jeremiah now speaks on behalf of certain exiles, **my people from a land far away.** This might be a reference to northerners exiled by the Assyrians, but it is more likely that these are former inhabitants of Jerusalem who had been exiled in one of the earlier Babylonian incursions (605 or 597 B.C.). Their statements, questioning the presence of the LORD in Jerusalem, expose a flaw in their theology. They

---

[7]Holladay, *Jeremiah 1*, p. 292.

[8]Thompson, *Jeremiah*, p. 303. Brueggemann explains this as the inevitability of suffering (cp. Amos 5:19). *Jeremiah*, p. 91.

had assumed that Jerusalem could not be destroyed (probably on the basis of what had happened in the days of Hezekiah) because it was his chosen city. Its impending destruction is interpreted by them as evidence that he does not keep his promises.[9] To this the LORD gives a swift retort: **they have provoked me to anger with their images, with their worthless foreign idols**. He has not been unfaithful to them; they have been unfaithful to him.

The people's reference to **harvest** and **summer** in verse 20 is somewhat enigmatic. It carries on the agricultural images of preceding verses, but its exact meaning is unclear. Unless there had been some prediction by false prophets that all would be well if they made it through that summer, there are three plausible interpretations. One would be to read it as a well-known saying, a saying used whenever people faced a situation of hopelessness.[10] Second, it could be that it is to be read figuratively. It could imply that the people think they have done what was needed to ensure God's blessings (a bountiful harvest, salvation from enemy attack), but now they see that they were wrong. Another plausible interpretation is to read this in the light of 9:22. The **harvest** here might not be a harvest of grain, but a harvest of men. There has been a "harvest," but not the one they expected. In any case, the despair in these words is contagious. The closing lines (v. 21) contain the words of either Jeremiah or the LORD, as they grieve over the suffering of the people.

---

[9]Thompson (*Jeremiah*, p. 305) says that the answer to the people's questions is positive; the LORD is king in Jerusalem. And it is as king that he shows his wrath by having his rebellious subjects punished.

[10]Thompson, *Jeremiah*, p. 306.

JEREMIAH 9

C. SIN AND PUNISHMENT (8:4–9:26) (continued)

8:22–9:11 The use of three successive rhetorical questions probably signals the beginning of a new unit in 8:22 (cp. 2:14; 8:4). The common theme of a speaker in anguish over the suffering of **my people** ties it to what precedes. The grieving (8:22–9:2) soon gives way to the assessing of fault (9:3-6), which prompts an additional pronouncement of judgment and grief (9:7-11).

As in 8:4, the first two questions draw the listeners' attention to a commonly accepted idea. **Gilead** was famous as a place of healing (cp. 46:11; Gen 37:25). The people apparently looked there for cures when all other remedies had failed. Like many hospitals today, it probably was where one went to get the best medical help available. Yet even that source is providing no comfort in this situation. The news that Judah's illness is undeniably terminal sends the speaker into the deepest of anguish.[1] His tears flow unabated, like a **spring** or a **fountain**; he weeps **day and night**. He is so sad and embarrassed; he wants nothing but to get away to some "cheap motel" in the desert, to separate himself from the one he loves because of the shame his adulterous wife has brought on him.

The condemnation becomes vitriolic in verses 3-6. This central portion is framed by talk of Judah not "knowing" the LORD (translated **acknowledge** in vv. 3 and 6), couched in language that is thickly nuanced. This is masked somewhat in the English translation. He says that the people, who have just been called **adulterers** and **unfaithful people** (cp. Hos 1:2), are "going out from evil to evil, and me they do not know." This is the language of marriage. A husband

---

[1]Who that speaker is in 9:1-2 is not clear. Verses 3-11 are certainly from the mouth of the LORD, but these first two verses could be from Jeremiah himself. Lundbom, *Jeremiah 1–20*, p. 535.

was said to "go in" to his wife to sleep with her (see Deut 22:13-14; 2 Sam 16:22), to "know" her (see Gen 4:1). But these people "go out" to other lovers, and away from their husband. They go **from one sin to another; they do not acknowledge** [know] **me, declares the LORD**. They even refuse their husband's amorous overtures; **they refuse to acknowledge** [know] **me** (v. 6).

This use of sexual euphemism thinly veils another nuance to the LORD's words. The expression, "know the LORD," connotes something very important to the teachings of Jeremiah. To "know the LORD" is more than being faithful to him in worship and keeping oneself unstained from the worship of idols. It also entails the doing of just and righteous deeds to one's fellow human beings (see below, 9:23-24, and 22:16). Thus the LORD's words here regarding "acknowledging" him indicate two pervasive sins among the people: their idolatry, and their oppression of the weak.

Oppression of the weak is part of what is implied by the repeated comments on "deceit" in these verses. It is through deceit ("the lying tongue") in legal affairs that the strong take advantage of the weak. Such deceit is also associated with scribal interpretations of the Law (8:8), suggesting corruptions of the cult might be in mind here as well. It apparently is difficult to separate these sins from one another.

The English reader is probably unaware of how personal and "unpatriotic" the words of verse 4 become. The translation (**For every brother is a deceiver, and every friend a slanderer**; cp. Lev 19:16) captures the sense of the line, but it misses the puns in it. The word for "deceiver" (יַעְקֹב, ya'ăqōb) consists of a doubling of the name "Jacob" (se Gen 27:35-36), and the word for "slanderer" (רָכִיל, rākîl) is very close to the name "Rachel" (רָחֵל, rāḥēl). So, a very literal translation would be, "For every brother really Jacobs, and every friend is (as) a Rachel." The LORD is sarcastically saying that the Israelites are "truly" living up to the names of their ancestors with their deceitful ways.[2]

Having laid out the accusation so eloquently, the LORD now turns to pass sentence on Jerusalem (9:7-11), drawing together sev-

---

[2]Jeremiah might imply something more here. The name "Jacob" was changed to "Israel" when he instructed his family to dispose of their idols (Gen 35:1-11). Perhaps Jeremiah is telling them to live up to their "new" name and not their original one. See Holladay, *Jeremiah 1*, p. 302.

eral images from preceding sections. He calls again for a time of refining (see 6:27-30). The reader knows that this **test** will yield no positive results; it will produce no useful metal. The LORD then returns to his most recent remarks about the people as deceitful liars (9:3-6). The deceitfulness of the people calls for the same response given twice before, that the LORD **avenge himself on such a nation as this** (5:9,29).

The fact that the Judge can so logically justify his sentence brings him no joy. He is condemning his chosen people, his wife, his children. And so he **weeps** and **wails** and **takes up a lament** for an uninhabited place. This is a desolate place, a desert wasteland, where no animal — domestic or wild — would even live. Tragically, this desolate place, this desert wasteland, is not some distant locale; it is Jerusalem itself (v. 11). This is why the LORD weeps. He, the creator of life, now is king over a place devoid of life, because he has had to banish its inhabitants.

9:12-16 This unit begins a pattern of reiterating particular issues touched on in preceding units. The first is the explanation for the impending disaster. Verse 12 serves as a challenge of sorts to the experts in the Law criticized in 8:8-9. They consider themselves to be **wise**, yet their "wisdom" does not enable them to fathom the reason for this devastation of Jerusalem. Such an event does not fit into their understanding of the Law; it does not fit into their theology. The LORD always blesses his chosen people; he never rejects them. Or so they think. This "wisdom" is really foolishness, so they can give no explanation for it.

The blame for this "foolishness" is placed in the most unexpected place. These "wise" experts have actually **forsaken my law . . . they have not obeyed** ["listened to"] **me or followed my law**. Instead of listening to the LORD and doing what he wants, they "do what is right in their own eyes" and **followed the stubbornness of their hearts** (cp. 7:24). Following that lead, they worship other gods. The result, commanded by the LORD, is the opposite of what they expect. They have eaten the sweet foods and drink offerings associated with Canaanite worship (see 44:19), but now they will **eat bitter food and drink poisoned water**. They have expected to live secure in the land God promised to Abraham, Isaac, and Jacob, but now he **will scatter them among the nations**. Their "wisdom" is truly folly.

There is a definite warning in these verses for some in the contemporary Christian community. The belief that God is a God of mercy but not also a God of wrath undergirds the thinking of several Christian groups. Many say that a God of love cannot condemn one of his creatures to suffer. They claim that theirs is a more "enlightened" understanding of God. Such a belief is not derived from the Bible, which presents a more balanced picture of the character of God. True, he is a God of mercy; but not of mercy only. He is also a God of wrath, a judge (see Exod 34:6-7). A sign of his supreme wisdom is his ability to hold these two poles of his character together in proper balance. Are Christians today really "wise" when they say this has changed?

9:17-22 This next unit expands on the theme of **lament** and **wailing** (see 9:1,10), as these two terms are used a total of five times in just four verses (9:17-20). It was traditional for women to wail over their fallen heroes after a battle. There were some who were "experts" at it.[3] The LORD summons all such women to this somber task, encouraging them to recruit their **daughters** as well (v. 20). Like the one weeping earlier, the **eyes** of these women **overflow with tears, and water streams from their eyelids** (v. 18). The destruction of **Zion** is complete, so their tears are unending. The commands in verse 20 to **hear** and **open your ears** highlights the disobedience of the people which has brought on this occasion for wailing. The people have not been listening to the LORD prior to this time; now they *must* listen. Because they refused to hear his laws, they now must hear his order to **wail** and **lament**. They have no choice.

The description of the invaders in verse 21 is quite graphic. They are not just enemy soldiers, but **Death** itself. It has entered their innermost quarters (**through our windows**) in the best-protected towns (**fortresses**). There is no escape. The women wail and lament because all the males have died — **children**, **young men**, and (adult) **men**. It should have been a time of great harvest, when grain and grapes were gathered (see 8:13,20). A harvest has been gathered, but it has provided nothing to nourish the people ("we are not saved"; 8:20). The women wail and lament, indicating they are now widows. There is no man to gather food for them. These widowed women are reduced to gleaning for their food; but even that is futile, because the fields have been completely defiled. **The dead bodies of men lie like refuse** ["dung"] **on the open field** (v. 22).

---

[3]Thompson, *Jeremiah*, p. 316; Holladay, *Jeremiah 1*, pp. 312-313; Nicholson, *Jeremiah 1-25*, p. 96.

9:23-26 The section closes with two "sayings" of the LORD, sayings which suggest how the people have misunderstood his will and
so lost their way. The first (vv. 23-24) points to a common misunderstanding of the Law. That misunderstanding places the Law
above the Lawgiver (the LORD). Just as the people have come to trust
in the temple (7:14), so they have come to trust in the Law. It is as
if they do not need the LORD any more. He has done his part by giving them the Law; now they are doing their part by carrying it out.
They think it is in the execution — the physical, external acts of fulfillment — that their success lies. They attribute their wisdom to their
understanding of the Law — as they interpret it — rather than
attributing it to the LORD; thus a man can **boast**[4] **of his wisdom**.
They attribute their strength to their adherence to the Law, rather
than attributing it to the LORD; thus a man can **boast of his strength**.
They attribute their wealth to their obedience to the Law — again, as
they interpret it — rather than giving the LORD the credit for making
them wealthy; thus a man can **boast of his riches** (cp. Deut 7:17-18;
8:17-18).[5] To the contrary, the LORD says one is truly wise, strong,
and wealthy when **he understands and knows me**. It is not the principles or precise commands of the Law themselves which give them
their authority and power. They bear authority because of who
speaks them, because they are the words of the LORD. To "know" the
LORD involves a deep, personal relationship with him. It leads a person to pattern their own character after his. This is why he goes on
to describe himself. The LORD **exercises kindness, justice and
righteousness on earth**, and the person who "knows" him will do
the same (cp. 22:15-16).[6]

The second saying (vv. 25-26) provides a concrete example of
what he means. The people of Judah naturally think of their circumcision as a sign of how they are different from those around
them. It symbolizes for them the law which they have, a law with its
own unique requirements. The LORD dismisses their distinctiveness
on the grounds it is superficial only. On the inside — in their hearts
— they are no different than those **uncircumcised** folk (and some

---

[4]The term translated "boast" in these lines is the word often translated
"praise" in the Psalms — *hallel*. These people "sing their own praises."

[5]Holladay, *Jeremiah 1*, pp. 317-318.

[6]See Thompson, *Jeremiah*, pp. 319-321 for a lengthy and moving discussion of these terms.

others who are circumcised) around them. They "fear the LORD" no
more than their idolatrous neighbors. Thus, the LORD is bringing
the Babylonians to **punish** all the "uncircumcised," a punishment
which will include the people of Judah.

Christian readers should realize that Jeremiah is speaking here
against a *misunderstanding* of the Law. Jeremiah attempts to correct
this misunderstanding in his prophecies. A similar misunderstanding arises later in Judaism and is confronted first by Jesus, and then
Paul. But it is a misunderstanding. The Law was not meant to be
read in a legalistic way, as if it contained a sort of magic formula for
success. Such a misunderstanding opens the door for "splitting
hairs" and finding ways to manipulate words ("the letter of the law")
that are actually in opposition to their original intent. Such an interpreter looks for ways to "get away" with something. The proper
interpretation begins in the heart of the recipient, as it is described
in Deuteronomy 5:28-29. Such a heart begins with the thought that
obeying the LORD is paramount; looking for "a way out" of what the
LORD demands does not enter into the process of interpretation.
The devotion this demands is aptly described as "circumcised in
heart" (cp. 4:3-4).

JEREMIAH 10

D. GODS AND IDOLS (10:1-16)

These sixteen verses paint contrasting pictures of the Lord and the idols being worshiped by the people (cp. Isa 44:9-20). Literarily, the section breaks into two parts (10:1-9,10-16). The first is introduced as an address to the "house of Israel," while the second is introduced as instructions to Jeremiah. Each of these parts breaks into four subparts, alternating between the belittlement of idols as things made by humans (vv. 2-5,8-9,11,14-15) and the exaltation of the LORD as Sovereign Creator (vv. 6-7,10,12-13,16). There is evidence that this section, too, is a compilation of prophecies made by Jeremiah at different times, but brought together here in the making of the book.[1]

10:1-10 The people of Israel are obviously influenced by the much larger nations around them. Those nations appear to have what Israel wants as a nation (power, prestige, respect), so it is natural for them to want to **learn the ways of the nations**. One of those **ways** is the way of idols. The LORD emphasizes, however, that idols are made of perishable things, implying that those who worship them are also perishable, in turn implying that those nations do not really deserve the respect they receive. Rather, **the customs of the peoples are worthless** (v. 3; translated "vanity" in Ecclesiastes); their

---

[1]Verses 12-16 are duplicated in 51:15-19, and the LXX version omits a few verses, while rearranging the order of others. Most curious is verse 11, because it is written in Aramaic rather than Hebrew. Some explain this phenomenon as evidence of a later insertion, but another explanation is just as plausible. Aramaic was the international language of the day (see Isa 36:11). Perhaps this (v. 11) is a saying that was to go out to all the nations; therefore, it is spoken in a language which the most nations would understand. For further discussion, see Lundbom, *Jeremiah 1-20*, pp. 593-595; Holladay, *Jeremiah 1*, pp. 324, 329-330. Holladay sees several links between these lines and the taunts of the Assyrians in 2 Kings 18-19.

gods are not to be feared (v. 5), but ridiculed. They are **cut, shaped, chiseled**, and eventually nailed down to keep them from falling over. They inspire no more fear than **a scarecrow in a melon patch**. They **cannot walk** or **speak** or **do any**thing **good** or bad on their own (cp. Ps 115:4-8; 135:15-18).

The first contrasting affirmations about the LORD (vv. 6-7) are bracketed by the statement, "There is no one like you" (מֵאֵין כָּמוֹךְ, *mē'ên kāmôkā*). The LORD is **great . . . mighty in power**, one to be revered. The people have regarded the **nations** in this way, but Jeremiah affirms that only the LORD is truly deserving of such respect. Moreover, he twice mentions those **nations** as being in subjection to the LORD. The LORD is *their* King, and even their wisest leaders are nothing in comparison to him. The people of Israel look to the nations, but the nations look to the LORD.

The reference to **the wise men of the nations** (v. 7) leads Jeremiah back to further ridicule of those nations (vv. 8-9). Those supposedly "wise men" are actually **senseless and foolish . . . taught by worthless** (see v. 3) **wooden idols**.[2] How can something made teach the thing that has made it? Yet this is what the so-called "wise men" do. Elaboration of the lengths to which these idolaters go to make their idols highlights even more how preposterous their beliefs are. The most expensive materials are used — **silver is brought from Tarshish and gold from Uphaz**,[3] cloths of **blue and purple** — and they are put together by **skilled workers** ("the wise"). What a waste of good talent and materials! All of these, some of the most precious items provided by the LORD in their culture, are made into objects of worship themselves. The Creator has been replaced by what the created has created, by that which will rot and decay.[4] In contrast, the LORD is the one who is **true, living**, and **eternal** (v. 10). These foolish and senseless nations tremble at **his wrath**. The people of

---

[2]Clements sees here a partial elaboration on the theme of true wisdom in 9:24. Clements, *Jeremiah*, p. 68.

[3]Holladay, *Jeremiah 1*, pp. 332-333; Lundbom, *Jeremiah 1–20*, p. 589; but see McKane, *Jeremiah*, p. 223.

[4]"In our day the comparable temptation may be the gods of militarism, of nationalism, of consumerism, of technology. . . . [The] temptation is to vest one's life hope in the things we ourselves generate, instead of receiving life as a gift from this One who stands beyond us and for us." Brueggemann, *Jeremiah*, p. 102. Stated more broadly, "Idol-worship tried to capture in material objects what is a spiritual experience." Thompson, *Jeremiah*, p. 328.

Israel (and contemporary Christians) should learn from the example and fate of these nations (see v. 2).

10:11-16 The contrasts between Creator and created, between worthless and worthy, continue in the second part of this section (quoted in 51:15-19). The false **gods** of the nations **will perish from the earth and from under the heavens**, which they **did not make** (v. 11).[5] But the God of Israel **made the earth by his power . . . his wisdom . . . his understanding** (v 12). He continues to demonstrate these characteristics in the awesome displays of the storm (v. 13). The fact that God made those things and they did not implies that they have no power or wisdom or understanding. This is stated explicitly in verses 14-15, where he describes the goldsmith and his idols as **senseless and without knowledge . . . a fraud . . . worthless, the objects of mockery**. He says **they have no breath in them**, implying they can give no life, no sustenance (v. 14). In fact, not only are they unable to give life, they are unable to sustain themselves; even **they will perish** (v. 15). The closing lines of this section then reiterate that **the LORD Almighty . . . *is* the Maker of all things**. Moreover, he has made **Israel, the tribe of his inheritance** (v. 16).

This concluding sentiment seems to have an edge to it. It should be a statement of boldness, an announcement accompanied by the cheers of an admiring and grateful people. The LORD, the God of Israel, is the one and only living God, the Maker of all things; and he has chosen one people — Israel — as his special inheritance. And yet, it is with a tear in the eye that this proclamation is made, because this special people does not worship the one and only living God who made them; they worship things which they have made.

E. COMING DESTRUCTION (10:17-22)

This short section is completely different in tone from the one preceding, resuming the message of punishment and grief from Jeremiah 9. A relatively brief oracle of doom (vv. 17-18) is answered by a personal lament (vv. 19-22). Many commentators extend this section through verse 25, but there appears to be a change of speakers between verses 22 and 23. Some believe that Jeremiah is speak-

---

[5]Holladay notes a pun here, between "perish" (אָבַד, *ābad*) and "make" (עָבַד, *ābad*). *Jeremiah 1*, p. 325.

ing on behalf of the nation in the prior section, but for himself in verses 23-25. The primary reservation is in regard to "my sons" in verse 20. Jeremiah never married, and therefore he never had children. For this reason, it seems more likely that the speaker beginning in verse 19 is someone else, probably Jerusalem personified. Supporting this suggestion is the fact that "you(r)" in verse 18 is feminine singular.[6]

10:17-18 The LORD's warning is addressed to **you who live under siege**. This strongly suggests a date late in the career of Jeremiah, most likely at the time of the final siege (588–586 B.C.). They are to prepare to leave their land,[7] and there is no hint that they will return. The LORD is going to **hurl out** the inhabitants of Judah, so that they are completely unprotected from their enemies.[8]

10:19-22 The lament of Jerusalem personified begins with medical language (v. 19), shifts to the imagery of shepherding (vv. 20-21), and concludes with a reaction to bad news (v. 22). The setting of siege still fits the sentiments expressed. The **injury/wound/sickness** afflicting the city at this time is fully accepted. It is **incurable**, and must be **endured**. There is no hope for repentance, no expectation of relief from the suffering. The patient looks for sympathy, but no remedy. In the same vein, the speaker talks of a **tent** that has been **destroyed**. This is the language of the shepherd who has lost everything.[9] His tent — his home — has collapsed, and he does not even have **sons** to survive after him, who might rebuild what he once had. Again, a strong sense of hopelessness pervades these words. The reason for this somber mood is the news that is coming **from the land of the north**. They can see for certain what will happen next. Jerusalem will cease to be a city, serving instead as **a haunt of jackals**, a den for creatures who live by scavenging off the bodies of the dead.

---

[6]Thompson, *Jeremiah*, p. 335; Clements, *Jeremiah*, p. 70.

[7]The exact meaning of the term for "belongings" is not known. It is likely a reference to a bundle of some sort, as depicted on several reliefs. Thompson, *Jeremiah*, p. 334.

[8]The verb for "hurl" is used in regard to a sling (Isa 22:17-18). The ending of verse 18 reads more literally, "so that they will find" (i.e., so that the Israelites' enemies can easily find and capture them).

[9]There are three terms drawn from the same root (רָעָה, *rāʿāh*, "to shepherd") used in these lines. First, there is no one to set up the shepherd's "shelter" (יְרִיעוֹת, *yᵉrîʿôth*). This is because the senseless "shepherds" (רֹעִים, *rōʿîm*) have not been seeking God's help. So, their "flock" (מַרְעִית, *marʿîth*) is being scattered across the hillsides.

F. JEREMIAH'S PRAYER (10:23-25)

10:23-25 The speaker does not explicitly identify himself in these verses, so one might argue that Jerusalem is still speaking here.[10] But the fact that he talks about himself as "a man" suggests someone different (see on v. 17), and Jeremiah is the most likely candidate. Most of this seems to be borrowed from other biblical passages. Verse 25 is very close to Psalm 79:6-7; verse 23 shares several terms in common with Proverbs 16:9, and verse 24 looks like an adaptation of Psalm 6:2.[11] All this suggests that Jeremiah draws on a rich history of lament to verbalize his own feelings at this most desperate hour of his career.

Jeremiah's words betray an internal struggle between acceptance of suffering and a desire for vindication and revenge. Jeremiah accepts the fact that he is going to suffer alongside his fellow Israelites, even though he is not guilty of the sins for which they are being punished. Such suffering is usually met with resentment (see 31:27-30), but Jeremiah exhibits the more faithful stance. Suffering is a part of life, whether "deserved" or not. The attitude of faith accepts such suffering, looking to God for comfort, not an explanation. This attitude continues in verse 24, as Jeremiah prays for mercy in the midst of his suffering. He sees the suffering as part of his education.[12] The LORD is "correcting" him, disciplining him (see Jas 1:2-8; 1 Pet 1:6-7). He prays only that his suffering will be meted out **with justice — not in your anger**. The ultimate purpose of such hardships is the building up of those who suffer, not their annihilation.

This attitude of acceptance and faith now turns to a call for vengeance (v. 25). Rather than **pouring out** his **wrath** on one of his own, the LORD is asked to "teach a lesson" to **the nations that do not acknowledge** ("know") **you, on the peoples who do not call on your name**. The people of Judah might not "know the LORD" (see 9:24), but neither do the peoples who are now attacking them. These peoples have **devoured Jacob**.[13] There are two possible motivations lying

---

[10]Holladay, *Jeremiah 1*, pp. 340-341; McKane, *Jeremiah*, pp. 233-234; Lundbom, *Jeremiah 1–20*, p. 609.

[11]Holladay, *Jeremiah 1*, p. 339.

[12]Thompson, *Jeremiah*, p. 337.

[13]The description of this destruction involves another set of wordplays in the final lines. The peoples "eat" (אָכְלוּ, *'āk°lû*) Jacob; they "eat him" (אֲכָלֻהוּ, *'āk°lûhû*) and "bring him to an end" (יְכַלֻּהוּ, *y°kalluhû*). The word for "his

behind such an appeal. One is the rather childish notion that the nations must be punished too, because they are just as deserving of this suffering as the Israelites. The other possibility arises from a concern about the LORD's reputation. These are nations that do not "know" the LORD, that do not worship him. They could easily arrive at the conclusion that this event justifies their lack of respect and faith in him, failing to see the true reason for Jerusalem's humiliation. But if the LORD later turns and corrects them, they will perhaps come to realize the true reason for this, thereby "learning" to respect and honor him themselves.[14]

---

homeland" (וֵהוּ‎, nāwēhû) is most often used to denote a shepherd's home, thus pointing the reader back to the shepherd imagery of verses 20-21.

[14]Clements, Jeremiah, pp. 70-71.

JEREMIAH 11

IV. VIOLATIONS, VIOLENCE, AND VISIONS (11:1–20:18)

A. THE COVENANT IS BROKEN (11:1-17)

This section lays out in basic terms the brokenness of the covenant relationship between the Lord and the people of Judah. The ideas expressed here are similar to those found in Jeremiah 7 and other prose texts, only in less detail. The fundamental "terms of this covenant" (v. 2)[1] are spelled out in 11:1-5, followed by a recounting of past covenant infidelities in 11:6-8, and an accusation of current infidelities in 11:9-13.[2] This fairly conventional structure is then supplemented by some comments by the LORD to Jeremiah (vv. 14-15) and by Jeremiah to the covenant people (vv. 16-17). Several commentators lump together Jeremiah 11-20 as a united block. One significant feature in these chapters, in contrast to Jeremiah 2-10, is the amount of material regarding Jeremiah's role and feelings in this unfolding tragedy. The closing verses of this first section elevate the visibility of this feature, and the next few sections propel it forward.

11:1-5 The LORD describes the covenant in terms of a curse. This approach probably is adopted because of the situation of infidelity and complacency which exists. The terms are very basic: **Obey me and do everything I command you.** There is no mention of what he might command. This implies that an obedient heart must exist

---

[1]Nicholson, *Jeremiah 1-25*, pp. 109-110. Many link this phrase to the "book of the covenant" found in the days of Josiah (2 Kgs 22:8-23:3; see Brueggemann, *Jeremiah*, p. 109, for main references; cp. Clements, *Jeremiah*, p. 76; Holladay, *Jeremiah 1*, p. 349).

[2]Some continue this unit to verse 14, because there is a shift from prose to poetry after that verse. Holladay, *Jeremiah 1*, pp. 349-353; Thompson, *Jeremiah*, p. 346.

a priori, and it must permeate the people's attitude toward their relationship with the LORD (cp. 7:22-23). The LORD could expect such an attitude because of what he had already done for the people (**I brought them out of Egypt, out of the iron-smelting furnace**; cp. Deut 4:20; 1 Kgs 8:51) and because of what he promised to do for them when they respond as they should. Those promises include a personal relationship (**you will be my people, and I will be your God**; cp. Deut 26:18-19; Hos 2:23; Jer 24:7; 30:22; 31:1,33; 32:38) and agricultural blessing (**a land flowing with milk and honey**; cp. Exod 3:8; 33:3; Num 14:8; Deut 6:3; 11:9; 26:9,15; 27:3; Jer 32:22). Jeremiah's affirmation (v. 5) demonstrates that he understands the terms and is willing to communicate them to the people.[3]

11:6-8 The recounting of past rebellion begins with an official "warning"[4] to **listen** and **follow** the covenant. This is the same warning that has been issued for generations. Its repetition here amounts to a final chance. He has **warned them again and again**, since the establishment of the covenant. So far, these people have not carried out their most basic obligation; **they did not listen or pay attention** (cp. 7:24,26; 17:23; 25:4; 34:14; 35:15; 44:5). Such a failure to listen indicates a deeper problem, that their hearts are not receptive (see Deut 5:28-29). Instead, their hearts are stubborn and evil (v. 8). The LORD has been responding to their stubborn resistance with lesser punishments: **the curses of the covenant**. One can now expect a more severe response.

11:9-13 The accusation gets more pointed, paralleling the more severe punishment that approaches. The attitude and actions of the people are called **a conspiracy** (v. 9; cp. 2 Sam 15:12; 2 Kgs 17:4), a coordinated rebellion against their king. It is a crime for which their ancestors were punished (v. 10), so they should expect no different reaction from the LORD. The way in which they have not **listened** is now specified as idolatry. God also specifies that the crime is identical to the one committed by **the house of Israel**, and the listener

---

[3]Holladay associates this language with the curses in Deut 27:15-26 (*Jeremiah 1*, pp. 349-350).

[4]In verse 7, the LORD says that he has "warned" the people repeatedly with these words. The word translated "warned" is sometimes translated "testified." The idea is that this is like a legally-binding obligation, one to which there are sworn witnesses ("heaven and earth"; see Deut 31:28; 32:1). The "warning" is a reminder of the covenantal obligations, a reminder which implicitly includes a reference to punishment for reneging on such obligations.

would recognize that Israel was exiled for that crime. Having laid out how deep-rooted is the crime, the LORD now shifts to describe the severity of the punishment (**Therefore** in v. 11 indicates the shift from accusation to sentencing). This will be a **disaster** ("evil") from which **they cannot escape** (v. 11). They have not "listened to" him, so he **will not listen to them** now if they cry out for his mercy. They might grow desperate over the LORD's unresponsiveness and cry out to the false gods they have been worshiping, but those will not be able to help either (v. 12). The sin is pervasive; everyone whom he addresses (the **towns of Judah** and **the streets of Jerusalem**; see 7:17; 11:6; 44:6,9,17,21) is guilty (v. 13). They can expect the punishment to be just as "pervasive."

11:14-17 The LORD now speaks directly to Jeremiah. He instructs Jeremiah again **not** to **pray for this people**,[5] reiterating that he **will not listen when they call** (cp. 7:16). This should be obvious, because the **distress** (רָעָה, rā'āh) which they will suffer will come in the form of a God-given **disaster** (rā'āh). This seemingly coldhearted attitude toward the suffering of his people is a thin facade for the anguish that the LORD actually feels. Jerusalem is his **beloved** (cp. Isa 5:1-7), yet she turns to sacrifice (**consecrated meat**) in search of help.[6] She **rejoices** in anticipation of a positive response, but that joy is just as futile as the sacrifices.

Jeremiah's response develops the metaphor of Israel as an **olive tree** (cp. Ps 52:8; Rom 11:17-24), perhaps deriving it from the vineyard song of Isaiah (Isa 5:1-7) and/or the horticultural imagery of Hosea (Hos 14:5-7). The LORD had planted this tree and been pleased with its progress at one time. But now, because **Israel** and **Judah have done evil** (rā'āh), he **has decreed disaster** (rā'āh) for them. They have been **burning incense to Baal**, so he will "burn" them, the branches of the unfruitful olive tree.

B. PLOT AGAINST JEREMIAH (11:18-23)

11:18-23 The situation of Jeremiah himself now begins to take center stage, in the first of Jeremiah's "confessions." These "confes-

---

[5]Clements (*Jeremiah*, pp. 78-79) speaks of Jeremiah in the role of prophetic mediator, as described by Moses in Deut 18:15-22.

[6]It is unclear whether these sacrifices are offered to idols or to the LORD. The latter would be an echo of the accusation in Jer 7:9-11.

sions" are personal laments, similar in form to many of the Psalms and the lament of Job in Job 3. These laments are often complemented by a response from the LORD. The fact that such a response is found in 12:1-6 has led most commentators to see 11:18–12:6 as a single section. On the other hand, there is a response by the LORD within these verses, and further lament and response in 12:1-6; thus, the NIV's delineation.[7]

The catalyst for this "confession" is most bitter. There are those of his own hometown (**the men of Anathoth**) who want to silence him. It is not difficult to imagine why this is. It could be a matter of "a prophet is not without honor except in his own country" (Matt 13:57; Mark 6:4; John 4:44). On the other hand, Jeremiah is opposed by virtually everyone with power in Judah. He has been prophesying against the whole nation. It is natural to assume that those who dislike his message would suspect his neighbors of sharing his sentiments. Those neighbors would want to distance themselves as far as possible from Jeremiah. They could easily plot against Jeremiah to redeem the "honor" of their town in the eyes of the rest of the nation.[8]

The exact nature of the plot against Jeremiah is not revealed, but the attitude of his opponents is clear. Jeremiah says that he **did not realize that they had plotted** to kill him. He had somehow been tricked into a sense of complacency, yet they had planned to turn against him and offer him up like a sacrificial **lamb** (cp. Isa 53:7-8). The quote in verse 19 suggests that they might have been planning legal action against him (the "shedding of innocent blood"). Not only do they want to kill Jeremiah, they want **his name to be remembered no more**. This is the language of complete disinheritance from the family (cp. Deut 25:6; Ruth 4:10).[9]

There is a marked contrast between the attitude of these opponents and the attitude of the LORD toward Jeremiah. The LORD is the

---

[7]See Holladay, *Jeremiah 1*, pp. 358-361, 365-368; K.M. O'Connor, *The Confessions of Jeremiah: Their Interpretation and Role in Chapters 1–25*, SBLDS 94 (Atlanta: Scholars Press, 1988), pp. 7-26; M.S. Smith, *The Laments of Jeremiah and Their Contexts: A Literary and Redactional Study of Jeremiah 11–20*, SBLMS 42 (Atlanta: Scholars Press, 1990), pp. 3-11. Bright (*Jeremiah*, pp. 89-90) moves 12:1-6 ahead of 11:18-23; cp. McKane, *Jeremiah*, pp. 253-254. The other "confessions" are located in 15:15-21; 17:14-18; 18:18-23; and 20:7-18.

[8]Thompson, *Jeremiah*, p. 351.

[9]Holladay, *Jeremiah 1*, p. 373.

only one acting as his faithful kinsman, as his redeemer in his time of need. The LORD reveals to Jeremiah the plot that is being conspired against him. Jeremiah appeals to him to avenge him against his enemies. Jeremiah does not have the power to avenge himself, but the LORD, **who judges righteously and tests the heart and mind**,[10] also avenges the wrongs plotted against Jeremiah; therefore, he has **committed [his] cause** to the LORD. The LORD responds favorably to this petition, in language which is most appropriate to the situation. Just as they have wanted to **destroy the tree and its fruit** (v. 19), the LORD promises to **punish them** and **their sons and daughters** (v. 22).[11] He will bring the **disaster** (*rāʿāh*) on them specifically, as he has already mentioned more generally for the nation (vv. 11,12,14). He even withholds from them the possibility of a **remnant**, which might have been part of their rationale for questioning his prophetic admonitions in the first place (see above). The warning that they will die **by the sword** and **by famine** is most typical of prophecies spoken by Jeremiah during the reign of Zedekiah, when all hope for Jerusalem has been lost.

---

[10]Literally, "the kidneys and the heart" (cp. 17:10; 20:12). See Parke-Taylor, *Formation*, pp. 13-18.

[11]Holladay speaks of this as ironic, because the LORD's plans for Jerusalem precede the plans of the men of Anathoth against Jeremiah. *Jeremiah 1*, p. 373.

JEREMIAH 12

C. JEREMIAH'S COMPLAINT (12:1-4)

Jeremiah verbalizes the sentiments probably held by every believer at some stage in his/her walk of faith (cp. Job 9, 21). There are some prior assumptions here, based on inappropriate generalizations of the LORD's words. These assumptions are that the righteous should prosper and live in peace and happiness while the wicked should suffer, constantly in need. Such assumptions lead to the thoughts expressed by Jeremiah here because reality argues against what he has assumed about God.[1] The specific occasion for this complaint is not certain. The situation described in 11:18-23 would fit (cp. 12:6), but we do not know whether that section has been placed in its present location to provide an occasion for this complaint, or because it actually was the occasion for it.

12:1-4 It is because Jeremiah has seen examples of the LORD's **justice** in the past that he feels confident and comfortable enough to broach this subject with him; yet he does question the LORD's justice in the present situation (v. 1).[2] He questions the fact that the wicked prosper while he himself is ever-faithful but oppressed, yet the LORD seems to do nothing to show his support for Jeremiah and his disapproval of Jeremiah's opponents. Will those others not conclude that they are in the right? That this situation is especially troubling to Jeremiah is seen in the way he devotes a dozen lines to describing the bad behavior of the wicked, while he gives only two brief lines to himself and two more lines calling for God's wrath upon the wicked (v. 3).

The characterization of the wicked is not as overt as one might assume at first glance. These **wicked prosper** and **live at ease**, but

---

[1]Holladay sees contrasts between Jeremiah's sentiments and the confidence of certain psalms (Psalms 1, 73; *Jeremiah 1*, pp. 376-377).

[2]Brueggemann, *Jeremiah*, p. 118.

that could be a sign of the LORD's blessings on them. Jeremiah says, in fact, that they prosper because the LORD has helped them (**You planted them**). They respond with words of gratitude, and it is only because of their treatment of Jeremiah that he knows that they are not fully devoted to him (v. 2).[3] The superficial and hypocritical nature of their relationship with the LORD might even be hidden to them. The one bit of proof Jeremiah gives (besides his own mistreatment at their hands) is their assumption that the LORD is not paying attention to the suffering of their land (v. 4). Jeremiah calls for their destruction (v. 3) in part to avenge his own suffering, and in part to bring an end to the suffering of nature in Judah which their wickedness apparently has precipitated.

D. GOD'S ANSWER (12:5-17)

The LORD's response consists of three parts. An initial rebuke of Jeremiah (vv. 5-6) quickly gives way to a series of metaphors regarding the imminent destruction of Judah (vv. 7-13). This is somewhat softened by the offer of future restoration (vv. 14-17), which might seem surprising. It would be logical to suggest that this final part was placed here by the book's compiler, perhaps implying to readers in Babylonian Exile that restoration is just as possible as destruction had been. It is also plausible to read the whole chapter as an original unit. Similar components of complaint, divine warning of destruction, and hope of restoration predominate in the Book of Habakkuk.

12:5-6 The LORD's rebuke suggests that Jeremiah's complaint is "premature." To put it in colloquial terms, "You ain't seen nothin' yet." He is going to be tested even more, so he needs to be tougher mentally. There has been general or official opposition to his prophecies, but now it is going to be worse because it is going to be his own relatives who persecute him. The LORD speaks of those relatives as traitors who cannot be trusted (cp. 9:3-4).[4] Such betrayal

---

[3]The phrase "far from their hearts" is, more literally, "far from their kidneys." The kidneys were thought of as the source of emotions. Jeremiah is saying they do not really feel ("believe") what they are saying.

[4]Many commentators conclude that 12:(5-)6 has been moved from the complaint in 11:18-23, that the words quoted in 11:19 are the proof that Jeremiah's brothers have betrayed him. See Holladay, *Jeremiah 1*, pp. 365,

would be difficult to swallow. To be opposed by his own family
would make him feel quite isolated.[5]

12:7-13 A dizzying array of images swirls by as the LORD speaks
condemnation on his **inheritance**. Judah is a defiant **lion in the forest, a speckled bird of prey**, a **vineyard**, and a **pleasant field** that
will be **trampled down** and **made a wasteland**. Two aspects of this
description of destruction stand out. One is its completeness. Judah
is to become **a desolate wasteland . . . parched and desolate . . . ;
the whole land will be laid waste** (v. 11). Invaders will devour it
from one end of the land to the other; no one will be safe (v. 12).
All their work will be in vain, as the curse on Adam (see Gen 3:17-
19) is completely realized in their case. The other predominant
aspect is that the true destroyer is the LORD. Even though there will
be **other birds of prey** and **wild beasts** who devour Judah, **many
shepherds** (v. 10) and **destroyers** (v. 12) who trample the land, they
are merely the instruments of God's wrath. His feelings toward
Judah are frighteningly transparent (**I hate her**, 12:8; cp. Hos 9:15).
He is giving Judah **into the hands of her enemies** (v. 7); **the sword
of the LORD will devour** the land (v. 11); their harvests will be fruit-
less **because of the LORD's fierce anger** (v. 13). The Babylonians are
to get none of the credit for their victory over Judah; it is wholly the
LORD's doing.

12:14-17 This word of hope is unusual, because it holds out hope
for Judah and her **wicked neighbors** (cp. Isa 2:1-4; 56:6-8; Micah 4:1-
3). These neighbors are mentioned occasionally, but almost always
in terms of how the LORD will wreak vengeance on them for hurting
Judah when she is down (cp. Psalm 137). The same fate awaits them
that awaits Judah (the LORD **will uproot them**; cp. 1:10), so the same
possibility for restoration is held out for them that is held out for
Judah (cp. 18:1-12). He will restore each of them **to his own inheritance** just as he will restore his own people (cp. Jer 48:47; 49:6,39).
He will **have compassion** on them just as he has compassion on
Judah (30:18; 42:12) in order for them to have hope. Judah has been

---

370-371, 380; Thompson, *Jeremiah*, pp. 355-356; McKane, *Jeremiah*, pp. 253-
254. Clements speculates that their opposition to Jeremiah arises when he
encourages people to surrender to the Babylonians (Clements, *Jeremiah*, p.
82; see Jeremiah 37–38). If this is correct, the LORD is reversing the accusations of "traitor" that they are lodging against Jeremiah.

[5]Brueggemann, *Jeremiah*, p. 120.

learning "the ways of the nations" (10:2); now the nations can learn the ways of Judah (v. 16). They must **swear by [his] name** (Deut 6:13; 10:20) and **listen** to the LORD (Jer 11:4,7; 13:15; etc.) just as the people of Judah must do when they return to the LORD. The more surprising aspect of this is that these **neighbors** will not simply be restored in their homelands; the LORD says, **they will be established among my people.**[6] They will live alongside the Israelites in their Promised Land. Then, through Israel, all the nations of the earth will be blessed (see Gen 12:3).

Implied in the LORD's words is a bold claim. The language of "inheritance" would have naturally suggested to the typical ancient Near Eastern listener that the gods of each nation gave each its "inheritance." The LORD's promise here shows that he is actually the one and only God, who gives each and every nation the "inheritance" that it has (cp. Deut 32:8-9).

---

[6]Literally, "they will be built in the midst of my people." This (along with "uproot") represents a dual verbal link to 1:10. Ibid., pp. 125-126.

JEREMIAH 13

E. A LINEN BELT (13:1-11)

13:1-11 This illustration is relatively straightforward, yet there are a few outstanding questions regarding its precise interpretation. The LORD instructs Jeremiah to hide a **linen belt**[1] in the ground, then retrieve it after an unspecified passage of time (**many days later**). The garment is soiled after being left outdoors for a while, even though it is put in a place (a **crevice**) normally thought of as protected (cp. 16:16).[2] Its damaged condition is used as an illustration of how Judah was protected and cherished by the LORD, yet it has been corrupted by its chosen disobedience and idolatry. The beauty of a new piece of clothing fades after it has been exposed for an extended time to the elements; in the same way, **the pride of Judah and the great pride of Jerusalem** are ruined by exposure to idolatry.

Two technical questions exist which influence the interpretation of this prophecy. The first is the location of the **crevice** where Jeremiah hides the garment. The NIV translation is **Perath**. Older translations read "the Euphrates" (see the footnote in the NIV). Either is possible. The primary objection to the reading "Euphrates" is that most references are to "the River Euphrates." The only (other) exception is in Jeremiah 51:63. Added to this is the distance Jeremiah would have to travel — twice — in order to perform this simple act. Because of the distance involved, some commentators

---

[1]The term for "belt" (אֵזוֹר, '*ēzôr*) is derived from the root meaning "to bind." This is not a "belt" in the modern sense. It probably refers to a sash, used for binding up ("girding") one's garments, or perhaps as a ceremonial garment (the wearing of linen is characteristic of priests). The fact that this garment is associated with "pride" suggests that it is worn on the outside, where it can be admired by others.

[2]Holladay, *Jeremiah 1*, p. 398.

have suggested that this was a mental illustration, a parable which was never actually acted out. This is made unnecessary, however, if one reads "Perath," or better, "Parah." The town of Parah is mentioned within a town list in Joshua 18:23, probably to be associated with Khirbet Farah,[3] just a few miles northeast of Anathoth and Jerusalem. Such a place would have been well-known to Jeremiah and his Jerusalem audience.

The condemnation of Judah and Jerusalem (13:9-11) expresses the sinful attitude in terms which are familiar to the reader of Jeremiah. The people **refuse to listen** to the **words** of the LORD (cp. 5:3; 8:5; 9:6; 15:18). They **follow the stubbornness of their hearts** (cp. 3:17; 7:24; 9:14; 11:8; 16:12; 18:12; 23:17) **and go after other gods** (cp. 1:16; 7:6,9,18; 11:10; 16:11,13; 19:4,13; 22:9; 25:6; 32:29; 35:15; 44:3,5,8,15). Had they been humble and faithful and listened to the LORD, they would have been a people of **renown and praise and honor**. This was the LORD's initial hope for this people (cp. Deut 26:17-19). **But they have not listened** (cp. 7:22-24; 11:4).

F. WINESKINS (13:12-14)

13:12-14 The placement of this oracle is strictly editorial. The imagery is completely different from what precedes or follows. It carries on the general message of the LORD's impending punishment, but his tone is more vehement than before. The only verbal link between this section and the preceding one is the root שָׁחַת (*šāḥath*; "ruin" in v. 9, "destroying" in v. 13).

The tone of the exchange between Jeremiah and his audience (v. 12) is not absolutely certain. The NIV translators have chosen to read the imperfect form of the verb as a subjunctive (**Every wineskin** *should be* **filled with wine**). It could also be read as a simple statement of present or future fact ("Every wineskin *is/will be* filled with wine"). The audience seems puzzled — even irritated — by this statement. Their response amounts to "Yeah; so what?" Why such a truism

---

[3]The reading in the Hebrew is פְּרָתָה (*peʾrāthāh*). The original final He of Parah would change to a Taw with the addition of an additional syllable. That syllable is a "directional He" ("toward Parah"). The transition from Hebrew "p" (Parah) to Arabic "f" (Farah) is common. Holladay, *Jeremiah 1*, p. 396; Thompson, *Jeremiah*, pp. 364-365; McKane, *Jeremiah*, p. 286.

would irritate them is not clear.[4] In any case, Jeremiah uses this comment to enter into an illustration of the LORD's plans for his people. They are the wineskins,[5] and the LORD is filling them with the by-product of wine: **drunkenness**. This drunkenness is an allusion to the LORD's wrath, as described in Jeremiah 25:15-29. The recipients of this divine wrath are Jeremiah's primary antagonists, who have been mentioned previously (see 1:18; 2:26; 8:1).

The vehemence of the LORD's language in verse 14 is a bit disconcerting. The NIV translation is perhaps misleading. The inclusion of "allow" (**I will allow no pity**) is a matter of interpretation. It implies that the LORD would normally feel compassion, but this time he is going to overrule himself. Such a mental struggle seems uncharacteristic of God. The reality is that "allow" is not in the text; it literally reads, "I will not spare [anyone]" (cp. 21:7). Still, this is very strong language. It is the same language used by David when he condemns to death the (fictitious) rich man who stole his neighbor's lamb (2 Sam 12:6). Moreover, it runs counter to other descriptions of the LORD's character (see Exod 34:6-7; 2 Chr 36:15). On the other hand, this attitude is presented by Ezekiel (Ezek 5:11; 7:4,9; 8:18; 9:5), and it reflects the attitude the people are told to have toward those who promote idolatry (Deut 13:8). Apparently, the point of no return has been reached; there is no more hope for repentance, and no more hope for salvation from the Babylonians.

G. THREAT OF CAPTIVITY (13:15-27)

This pessimistic section falls into three parts. The first is a mix of call for repentance and warning of destruction, concluding with Jeremiah's admission that he still weeps for this sinful people (13:15-17). There follows a brief statement to the king and queen, predicting their imminent humiliation (13:18-19). The perspective then

---

[4]See Holladay, *Jeremiah 1*, p. 403, for suggested interpretations.

[5]The translation "wineskin" is potentially misleading. These containers are to be smashed together and broken (v. 14). This hardly sounds like what one would do with "skins." The term used could also refer to jars or flasks, any container that might be used for holding liquid. Thompson, *Jeremiah*, p. 367; Holladay, *Jeremiah 1*, p. 402. Clements suggests that there is a thinly-veiled play on "wineskin" (נֶבֶל, *nebel*) and "fool" (נָבָל, *nābāl*). "Fools" (meaning the people of Jerusalem) are just as filled with wine as the wineskins themselves. Clements, *Jeremiah*, p. 86.

expands to include all of Jerusalem (v. 27), which is portrayed as a woman shamed after being caught in adultery (13:20-27). This imagery points back to the primary message of the opening sections (Jeremiah 2-6), only the occasional optimism found there is almost entirely absent here.

13:15-17 Jeremiah opens with some interesting use of the metaphors of hearing and seeing, popularized by Isaiah (Isa 6:9-10) and utilized by Jeremiah elsewhere (e.g., 4:19-26; 5:21). He begins with a call to **Hear and pay attention**. What is keeping them from this is they are **arrogant** ("high up"). They think that they do not need to hear anything more from the LORD. They have "heard" his optimistic messages from the past, messages of deliverance from invaders and of a remnant surviving the LORD's punishment (see Isa 36-37). They assume that the same messages apply to them now. Jeremiah tries to open their eyes to reality. He calls on them to **give glory to the LORD**. There is a double entendre here. This refers primarily to honoring the LORD. But "glory" and "light" are often associated images. The "glory of the LORD" which filled the tabernacle and temple was a bright light, enveloped by a column of cloud and smoke. The inference here is that, if the Israelites expect to see any light (**glory**) in their present situation, it will have to come from themselves; the LORD is not providing any light (cp. Amos 5:18-20; for the reverse image, see Isa 60:1-3). From him come **darkness** and **darkening hills** ("hills of twilight;" cp. Prov 7:9) and **thick darkness** ("the shadow of death;" cp. Ps 23:4) and **deep gloom**. The LORD, the Giver of Light and Life, is now withdrawing both.

Jeremiah does not gloat at this gloomy picture. The people might not listen — they might even seek to harm him for this "traitorous" message (see Jeremiah 12) — but Jeremiah's reaction is one of compassion and grief. He **weeps bitterly, overflowing with tears**, as he sees God's punishment on his audience. This is the attitude of the true prophet. These are his people, his brothers and sisters. He is not smug about his own relationship with the LORD, in contrast to the bleak future which awaits his hearers because they are estranged from him. Jeremiah is one of them; he wants to watch them reform, not watch them suffer in anguish.[6] Unfortunately, in contrast to his initial call to **hear and pay attention** (v. 15), they **do not listen** (v. 17).

---

[6]Holladay notes that one expects to find a divine word of condemnation here. Holladay, *Jeremiah 1*, p. 406.

13:18-19 The message **to the king** and **queen mother** (probably Jehoiachin and his mother, Nehushta; see 2 Kgs 24:8,15)[7] is brief and transparent. They are going to lose all sense of pride, represented by their **glorious crowns**.[8] The nation is to be humiliated. Everyone is going **into exile**, even persons in the remotest regions (**the Negev**). There will be no nation left to rule, nothing in which to take pride, no reason to wear a crown.

13:20-27 The shift to Jerusalem as addressee is signaled by the use of second person feminine singular verbs, beginning in verse 20.[9] The LORD addresses Jerusalem using a mixture of images, alternating back and forth between accusation of sin and pronouncement of judgment. The dominant image is that of the shamed adulteress (vv. 21-22,26-27). The initial allusion is somewhat veiled. He talks about Jerusalem hurting **like . . . a woman in labor** (v. 21). Such a description of agony is not unusual among the prophets, but this one seems a bit different. Jeremiah might be implying that Jerusalem truly is "in labor," but the cause of her pregnancy is her adulterous "alliances" with other nations and their gods. The use of this image in the rest of the passage is more typical. It was common to speak of the LORD as a man asserting his own honor in the face of his wife's infidelities. A husband did this by stripping her and exposing her (and her infidelity) to the community (cp. Hos 2:2-3; Ezek 16:35-42). The people of Jerusalem have been unfaithful in their worship of other gods (see 2:20-29; 3:1-10), so they will be forced out of their home. Previously, their **lot** had been to be the LORD's bride; their **portion**, this land. Now, their husband is sending them out of their home (v. 25). The LORD will "expose"[10] them (vv. 22,26-27), allowing the Babylonians to conquer them and plunder their land.

---

[7]Holladay, *Jeremiah 1*, p. 409; Clements, *Jeremiah*, p. 86; Thompson, *Jeremiah*, p. 370; Nicholson, *Jeremiah 1-25*, p. 125; Lundbom, *Jeremiah 1-20*, pp. 680-681.

[8]The word translated "glorious" here is the same word translated "of which you boast" in verse 20. It denotes something beautiful, something admired.

[9]There has been some uncertainty about the exact place of this transition. The verbs in the first half of verse 20 are vocalized as masculine plurals, even though the consonantal text preserves feminine singulars, as in the following verses. Some early translations insert "Jerusalem" in the first line to clarify.

[10]The root of the word translated "exile" (see v. 19) is גָּלָה (*gālāh*), meaning "to uncover, expose."

The adulterous wife is not the only image utilized here. Jerusalem is the shepherd or sheepfold whose prized **sheep** are about to be taken by **those who are coming from the north** (v. 20; cp. 1:14-15; 6:1). The people of Jerusalem are the **chaff** that is scattered by the **wind** (v. 24), because they are guilty of **many sins** (v. 22) . . . **accustomed to doing evil** (v. 23). Their sin is a part of who they are, just like a man's skin color or a leopard's characteristic markings (v. 23). They are horses, whose **lustful neighings** (v. 27; cp. 2:23-25; 5:7-8) betray their truly animalistic nature. Their treatment by the Babylonians reflects that true nature, for the Babylonians treat them as one treats animals.

The final line, then, brings this section to a fitting conclusion. At the beginning, there was talk of glory and pride. At the end, there is only dismay (**Woe to you, O Jerusalem**) and shame (**How long will you be unclean?**).

JEREMIAH 14

H. DROUGHT, FAMINE, SWORD (14:1–15:21)

The time for mercy has passed; the Lord has been long-suffering as long as he can. Now is the time "to uproot and tear down, to destroy and overthrow" (1:10). As destruction marches ever closer, the use of dialogue between the Lord and his people escalates. The tone of the people becomes more distressed, more desperate, and the tone of the Lord becomes more resolute, more determined to punish. The rhetoric is often reminiscent of the covenant language of earlier generations, but it is reversed. The Lord is now "rejecting" his "chosen" people. Instead of talk about prosperity and life, there are now predictions of ruin and death.

We are almost certainly in the reign of Zedekiah here.[1] This long section, although not necessarily a single unit originally, conveys the depth of the feelings held on all sides of the conversation in Judah at this heart-wrenching moment. With tears in his eyes, the LORD is handing over his Beloved, his chosen people, to cruel enemies. She is begging for just one more chance, but it will not be given. At the same time, the messenger's own safety is jeopardized. His perceived inability to intercede raises questions about the validity of his prophetic office.[2] The problem lies not with him, but with the people, whom the LORD now declares beyond help. Jeremiah is thus doubly pained. He is in anguish over the nation's impending doom, and he suffers harshly at the hands of his audience; so, the LORD speaks words of reassurance to him.

14:1-6 The chapter actually begins with a relative pronoun: "Which was the word of the LORD to Jeremiah" (cp. 1:2; 46:1; 47:1;

---

[1]Cp. Clements, *Jeremiah*, p. 96. Some argue that we are still in the reign of Jehoiakim (609–598 B.C.) here. Holladay, *Jeremiah 1*, pp. 427-429. The certainty of destruction is, in my mind, a characteristic of Zedekiah's reign.

[2]Clements, *Jeremiah*, pp. 90-96.

49:34). It perhaps serves to remind the reader of Jeremiah's prophetic commission, which is of issue in the middle of this section. This initial lament is expressed in terms of the sights and sounds of severe
drought. There is no rain in sight; even the **cisterns** (v. 3), designed
to capture the runoff rainwater and reserve it for normal dry spells,
have gone dry. **The ground is cracked** (v. 4). Wild animals are unable
to forage for enough food to stay alive (vv. 5-6). There is nowhere for
anyone to go for water. The people long for the sound of raindrops,
but all that one hears is a **wail**, a **cry** (v. 2), and the panting of **wild
donkeys** (v. 6). The people **languish** (v. 2); they are **dismayed and
despairing** (v. 3); **they cover their heads**, unwilling to watch the vegetation of their land shrivel up and blow away.

14:7-10 The people's words of repentance seem quite sincere —
and they probably are. But the LORD's response shows that they are
"too little, too late." They admit their sin, that it is **great** ("many"),
and it has been committed against the LORD himself. They turn now
to him, calling on him to save them **for the sake of** [his] **name** (v. 7),
to bring honor to his reputation and cause others to see the benefit
of relying on him. They **bear** [his] **name** (v. 9; cp. Deut 28:10), and
what happens to them will reflect on his power and character. They
acknowledge him as their **Hope**[3] and **Savior** (v. 8), but they do not
see him now fulfilling his obligations in that role. This puzzles and
discourages them. Is he not concerned about what the other nations
will think of him? He is their father, their protector and provider.
Yet he is acting as if he has no feelings for them, as if he never knew
them, as if their fate is of no concern to him. This is not the attitude
of a father; this is the attitude of a **stranger**, a **traveler** who is "just
passing through."

The statement, **You are among us** (v. 9), is particularly important. It is a double-edged sword. This could be a statement of confidence and hope. It is the language of tabernacle (Deut 23:14-16).
The one true God, the Almighty One, is in the midst of his people,
protecting them, providing for them. This is good news for a people
facing attack from a much larger enemy nation (Deut 7:17-24). But
it is also a warning. The LORD who is "among" them is a jealous God
(Deut 6:15). He will respond negatively against the presence of any

---

[3]There might be a double meaning here. In the Dead Sea scrolls, the term
for "hope" is parallel to a term for "pool." The LORD could be both a "hope"
and a "pool" of water during a drought. Holladay, *Jeremiah 1*, p. 433.

other gods "among" his people. He forbids the existence of various forms of "evil" among his people (Deut 17:2,7; 21:21), because he is dwelling among them. If he finds such evil, he will act to remove those who have introduced it to the land, even if those include his people. Therefore, their closing plea (**do not forsake us**) might not stem from wisdom. They should "be careful for what they pray for; they might get it."

The final verse of this unit gives the LORD's response to their appeal. He has heard the words of repentance before, yet that has never heralded the end of their infidelity. He has heard enough, so he does not accept their repentance now. Instead, he **will now remember their wickedness**. The sense of "remember" here is not merely to call to mind something from the past. It is to act toward someone as is warranted, to act in accordance with one's character in the light of the existing conditions (see Exod 2:24). The following line explicates what it means for the LORD to "remember" in this situation: he will **punish them for their sins** (cp. 31:34; Hos 8:13; 9:9).

14:11-16 The LORD's attention now moves from the people to Jeremiah himself. He expands on the admonition **not** to **pray for the well-being of this people**, an admonition which has been given twice earlier (7:16; 11:14; see on 15:1). He **will not listen**, as he has said before, and he **will not accept** their sacrifices (cp. Isa 1:10-15). The latter links this unit to the preceding one (v. 10). He expands on his earlier statements with the addition of the triad of destruction — **sword, famine, and plague**. This is the language of siege.[4] The strategic aim of a siege is to starve the besieged city into submission. Those who resist or try to elude the besieging army are killed (**sword**); those who remain in the city will hold out until all food is gone (**famine;** see Jeremiah 38), hoping their attackers lose heart before then; while they are confined inside the city, sanitation standards are severely compromised, making the spread of disease (**plague**) much more likely. This triad is one of the hallmarks of Jeremiah's message in the reign of Zedekiah (cp. 15:2; 21:7,9; 24:10; 27:8,13; 29:17-18; 32:24,36; 34:17; 38:2; 42:17,22; 44:12,13,18,27). All hope for deliverance is now gone. In their future lies only siege and captivity.

---

[4]This triad apparently was common in the Middle East. Thompson, *Jeremiah*, p. 382. For the most recent study, see Parke-Taylor, *Formation*, pp. 21-22, 201-202, 243-244.

Jeremiah responds (v. 13) to this message by asking the LORD about the words of other **prophets**. They too claim to speak for him, yet their message is one of hope and **peace**, not **sword or famine**. This is a clear example of the fact that biblical prophets were completely conscious as they carried out their prophetic ministry. Jeremiah raises a reasoned question. He has been hearing the words of other prophets, and he does not assume that their message is a false one.[5] Instead, when he receives a word from the LORD which contradicts the message he has already heard, he questions his received message. The LORD's response (vv. 14-16) is clear, yet Jeremiah still must choose to accept it, as his own listeners must choose to accept his message.

The LORD's response is that he has **not sent** those other prophets. Their message differs from the one Jeremiah has just received because those other prophecies originated in the prophets' own **minds** ("hearts"). The LORD did not send them with their message, so it consists of **lies . . . false visions, divinations**, etc. Their punishment fits their "crime." They will die **by sword and famine**, demonstrating most vividly that their words dismissing such a threat are empty. Sadly, these false prophecies will contribute to the humiliating deaths of others, as entire families will die and be left unburied (cp. Deut 21:23; 2 Sam 21:10; Ezek 6:5; 37:1; Amos 2:1).[6]

14:17-18 This brief unit extends the paired themes of **sword** and **famine**, revealing the LORD's own emotional reaction to the suffering which he himself has brought on his **virgin daughter** (i.e., one whom he loves dearly).[7] That reaction is to weep ceaselessly. This is a perfect example of "tough love." He is thinking of the nation as a single, unified entity. From this perspective, the calamity befalling Judah is seen to be a father's discipline of his daughter, intended to change eventually the behavior and attitude of the people. Such a perspective explains why the LORD has the emotional reaction that

---

[5]It is likely their message reflected the hopeful message of Isaiah, announced a century earlier (see ch. 37; cp. Brueggemann, *Jeremiah*, p. 137).

[6]Thompson, *Jeremiah*, p. 383.

[7]Holladay places the first line with the preceding verses, so that the following lines express Jeremiah's feelings. Holladay, *Jeremiah 1*, p. 436; cp. Thompson, *Jeremiah*, p. 385; Clements, *Jeremiah*, p. 92; Brueggemann, *Jeremiah*, pp. 138-139; Lundbom, *Jeremiah 1-20*, p. 712. However, the form of the line is typical of introductory statements.

he does. This is not a mere equation, where human sin yields divine punishment. The human suffering has been judged necessary by the LORD, but the sin that provoked it has not diminished the LORD's basic love for his people, even for the **prophet and priest** who have led the opposition to Jeremiah. In fact, it is because of his love for Judah that he has brought this suffering upon her. And it is because of his love for Judah that he weeps over her suffering.

14:19-22 This unit and the one following parallel verses 7-16. The people first give poetic expression to their remorse and humbly call for the LORD to deliver them from their enemies (14:19-22; cp. vv. 7-10). An introductory clause ("Then the LORD said to me," 15:1; cp. 14:11) marks the transition to the LORD's prose response, where he forcefully declares his intentions to punish the people (15:1-4; cp. 14:11-16).[8] There are even a few of the same terms and phrases used in the prior units which occur here as well (e.g., **we have sinned against you** [14:7,20]; **for the sake of your name** [14:7,21]; "sword and famine" [14:12,15-16; 15:2-3]).

The unit begins with a triad of rhetorical questions, a literary pattern seen before (2:14; 8:4,19,22). The first two expect negative answers (surely, the LORD does not **reject** and **despise** Judah); yet, the third reveals that the answers might be positive (their current afflictions seem to indicate he has rejected them). The thought of the LORD "rejecting" his chosen people (see Isa 41:9) contradicts notions about the faithfulness of God to his promises, in the minds of some. But this ("rejection") is exactly what is affirmed several times in Jeremiah (cp. 6:30; 7:29) and elsewhere (Ps 89:38). The LORD "rejects" those who "reject" him (see 6:19; 8:9; cp. 1 Sam 15:23,26; 2 Kgs 17:15,20). However, this "rejection" is usually understood as a temporary thing, a means to the goal of repentance and restoration (see 33:24-26). They are right to expect **a time of healing**, for the LORD is one who heals (see 17:14). They are wrong to expect it will come right away, though. This is a time to tear down, not a time to build; a time for wounding, not a time for healing.

The people again express what appears to be sincere remorse for their sins. They **acknowledge** ("know") their **wickedness** and **guilt** (v. 20). They appeal again to his **name** and his **covenant**, not their righteousness, as the basis for forgiveness (v. 21). They profess him as the true Creator, while the idols they had been worshiping are

---

[8]Brueggemann, *Jeremiah*, p. 140.

worthless (v. 22). Whether their remorse is sincere, we cannot judge; and this presents a theological problem for believers. There is a common assumption that "true" repentance would be followed immediately with divine blessing, that the LORD would have averted the Exile if the people were being genuine here. The succeeding unit indicates that this is not necessarily so. The LORD does not impugn the sincerity of their words, only that he will no longer hear them.

JEREMIAH 15

H. DROUGHT, FAMINE, SWORD (14:1–15:21) (continued)

15:1-4 The LORD's rejection of his people is stated in very strong terms. There were times in the past when he threatened to disown his people, but those times had been averted because of the presence and/or appeals of certain righteous individuals. Two classic examples are **Moses and Samuel**. Moses twice "stood in the breach" (Ps 106:23; cp. Exod 32:11-14; Num 14:13-23; Deut 9:19), serving as a sort of "defense attorney" for the people before the LORD. The people asked Samuel to pray on their behalf to avert the LORD's anger after they had demanded a king, rather than relying on him to save them (1 Sam 12:19). We noted earlier the literary parallel between Jeremiah 14:11-16 and this passage. The LORD's instructions there were to tell Jeremiah not to pray for the people. The reference to Moses and Samuel here suggests a parallel between those two previous prophets and Jeremiah.[1] They had prayed on the people's behalf; if Jeremiah is like them, he would be expected to pray on their behalf now. So the LORD's words regarding Moses and Samuel here are to imply that Jeremiah need not bother to pray for the people now. He would not change his mind for Moses and Samuel under the present circumstances, so he will not "hear" Jeremiah either.

The language of "going out" (**Let them go!** and **Where shall we go?**) carries a bittersweet tone (15:1-2; cp. Deut 1:28). This is the language of the Exodus, when the people "went out" of Egypt to travel to their Promised Land. He is telling them to "go (out)" again, only this time they are "going out" of their Promised Land. Their "destination" is one of four unhappy fates. But at least they have a choice.

Two sets of four fates are mentioned here (15:2-3). The first four are **death, the sword, starvation**, and **captivity**. The middle two are

---

[1]Thompson, *Jeremiah*, p. 387; Clements, *Jeremiah*, p. 94; Lundbom, *Jeremiah 1–20*, pp. 107-108, 720.

two of the three fates mentioned in 14:12. It is possible that **death** is given as a synonym of the third unhappy fate ("plague"). This makes **captivity** the only additional option listed here. It would be the most "favorable" option from Jeremiah's point of view. He repeatedly counsels people to surrender and enter into captivity to avoid the other fates (see Jeremiah 37–38). The other four fates are not mentioned as options. These are listed to represent the totality of the LORD's planned destruction. The use of **the sword** to represent military defeat is common in the Old Testament. References to **dogs**, **birds**, and **beasts** devouring the fallen in similar contexts are numerous (7:33; 16:4; 19:7; 34:20; cp. Deut 28:26; 1 Sam 17:44-46; 1 Kgs 14:11; 16:4; 21:24).

The final line of this unit is the most difficult to interpret in the context of Jeremiah as a whole. The statement is that the LORD will shame Judah **because of what Manasseh son of Hezekiah king of Judah did in Jerusalem.** The problem here is one of timing. Manasseh was the grandfather of Josiah; he died some fifteen years before Jeremiah's ministry began. This line seems to imply that the LORD had made an unalterable decision to destroy Jerusalem long before Jeremiah appeared on the scene. This raises a question, then, about why the LORD would have inspired Jeremiah to talk about the possibilities of repentance and the avoidance of destruction; yet those are part of the first half of Jeremiah's prophetic ministry. The same questions are raised when one tries to harmonize the teachings of Jeremiah with the Book of Kings (see 2 Kgs 21:10-16; 23:26-27; 24:3-4).

Three solutions can reasonably be proposed. The first is that the fate of Judah had been determined in the days of Manasseh. This would mean that Jeremiah's words about the possibility of repentance were hollow, that he said that, all the while knowing that repentance was never going to take place. Such a view raises serious questions, however, about the reliability of Jeremiah as a prophet. If one follows this line of reasoning, one can believe nothing the prophet says. A second view is commonly suggested by redaction critics, who believe the text was reworked over the years.[2] They argue in this instance that someone writing after the destruction of Judah diverges from Jeremiah's "interpretation," and that this exilic writer "interprets" the destruction as the LORD's judgment on Judah

---

[2]Clements, *Jeremiah*, pp. 94-96; Holladay, *Jeremiah 1*, p. 440; Lundbom, *Jeremiah 1–20*, p. 723.

for the heinous sins committed by Manasseh more than half a century earlier. They assume that the disagreement between this passage and others in Jeremiah which hold out the possibility of repentance indicates that there were at least two different writers, one being Jeremiah/Baruch and one being an exilic redactor. The problem with this view is that it denies the inspiration of one — if not both — of these writers. The third proposal is that it is the *deeds* of Manasseh which lead to Judah's destruction. The second half of verse 4 reads literally, "on account of Manasseh son of Hezekiah, King of Judah, because of what he did in Jerusalem." The second phrase is explanatory. It is the sinful deeds done by Manasseh — deeds which are replicated by Jehoiakim and Zedekiah, Josiah's sons — which lead to the destruction of Judah. **What Manasseh . . . did** is also what they did. Therefore, when Jeremiah talks about destruction **because of what Manasseh . . . did,** he is saying that the perpetuation of the sins of Manasseh in Jehoiakim and Zedekiah is leading to this calamity. The problem with this interpretation is that it is not supported by 2 Kings 24:3-4. The same language is used there as here, but with the additional note that "the LORD was not willing to forgive." This leaves the impression that the decision was made in Manasseh's day. On the other hand, there is also the implication that the LORD could have decided to be "willing to forgive," but he did not. Perhaps there was a chance that true repentance could have persuaded him to change his mind (see Jer 18:7-11), but now even that chance has passed (but see 2 Kgs 22:15-20).

15:5-6 The LORD addresses the people of Jerusalem directly in this brief unit, continuing the sentiment of inevitable punishment from the preceding verses. He employs a series of rhetorical questions to reveal that he will show no pity to Jerusalem. A pair of accusations against the people follow (they **have rejected** the LORD, they are **backsliding**), answered by a pair of statements in which the LORD pronounces his intention to punish them (he will **destroy** them, and **no longer show compassion**).

15:7-9 This unit reflects the bitterness the people will feel in the upcoming disaster. The LORD gives special attention to the grief of women.[3] The **widows** will be **more numerous than the sands of the**

---

[3]Such a message would do more than demoralize the women alone, because it would also haunt the minds of the men with thoughts of their inability to protect the women in their care.

sea; horrible sights will be brought to **mothers**; and **the mother of seven** will give up hope for her sons. The first and third statements reverse promises of prosperity spoken to previous generations (cp. Gen 22:17; 32:12; 1 Sam 2:5). A parallel reversal in nature is predicted. The **sun will set while it is still day**, rather than standing still to accommodate an Israelite victory (see Josh 10:12-14).

There is only one statement of accusation (v. 7), but it is of some significance. The people **have not changed their ways**. They have not "made good" their ways (7:3,5); they have not walked in "the good way" (6:16). Instead, they "perverted their way" (3:21) and walked in the "way of the nations" (10:2). Now, because they refuse to change, the LORD refuses to change his plans for their destruction.[4]

15:10-11 A quick exchange between Jeremiah and the LORD reminds the reader of the personal anguish Jeremiah endures as a result of delivering such harsh messages to the people of Judah (cp. 11:18-23). The preceding comments about grieving mothers leads into Jeremiah's remarks toward his own **mother**. Like Job, Jeremiah expresses the extreme thought that he would have preferred never to be born, considering his present predicament. It seems as if **the whole land** is against him. He expresses his frustrations in judicial terms. The terms translated **strives and contends** commonly refer to the bringing of lawsuits.[5] Some of the most common reasons for bringing suit against one's neighbor involve the lending of money (cp. Deut 24:10-11). Either the lender oppresses the borrower by making unfair demands regarding repayment, or the borrower defaults on the loan. When absolute evidence is not available, the plaintiff might issue a curse. Here he says they skip a step and issue curses without cause. The LORD responds with solid reassurance (v. 11). Those cursing Jeremiah now will petition him later for help. Ultimately, they will recognize his value.

15:12-14 The LORD now addresses his words to the people of Judah, but still on the general theme of the inevitability of destruction. The message is fairly straightforward, but a few notes of clarification might be helpful. The note that the unbreakable **iron** is **from the north** should remove any doubt that Jeremiah is talking about the Babylonians (see 1:14-15; 4:6; 6:1).[6] The reading **I will**

---

[4]Brueggemann, *Jeremiah*, p. 143.

[5]Thompson, *Jeremiah*, p. 392; Bright, *Jeremiah*, p. 106; Holladay, *Jeremiah 1*, p. 452.

[6]The reference to "iron" reminds some of Jeremiah's iron yoke (28:13-14).

enslave you to your enemies (v. 14) is not absolutely certain. The slightest of changes (a *daleth* to a *resh*) produces a different reading, reflected in several early manuscripts. This reading is "I will cause your enemies to pass by [you]." The sense of that reading is that those enemies would pass by, shaking their head at Judah's humiliation (cp. Jer 22:8; Isa 8:21; Ezek 5:14). The reference to **a land you do not know** (cp. 16:13; 22:28) is similar to "a people whose language you do not know" (5:15). Finally, the term for "kindle" (**my anger will *kindle* a fire**) is relatively uncommon in the Old Testament (cp. Jer 17:4; Deut 32:22; Isa 50:11; 64:2).

15:15-21 This section concludes with another of Jeremiah's "complaints."[7] Jeremiah addresses the LORD in verses 15-18, and the LORD responds in verses 19-21 (cp. 12:1-6). The tone of their respective remarks are mirror images of one another. Jeremiah's tone gradually shifts from appreciative to resentful, and then the LORD's tone shifts from accusatory to reassuring.

Jeremiah begins with words of petition (15:15). Unnamed individuals are persecuting him, and he appeals to the LORD because he believes the LORD is understanding and caring. He then defends his right to be heard, pointing to his past willingness to carry the LORD's message in a responsible and dignified manner (15:16-17a). This apparently was of the utmost personal significance to Jeremiah. Verse 16 literally begins, "Your words were found, and I ate them" (cp. Ezek 2:8–3:3). This sounds similar to statements about the discovery of the Law in Josiah's day (2 Kgs 22:13; 23:2).[8] It suggests that Jeremiah viewed his own internalization of the Law as fundamental to his personal faith and prophetic career. He had absorbed the Law into his own heart in ways which contrasted markedly to the response of the general population. This helps to explain why he now becomes more defensive. He had been ostracized for doing his job, enduring pain for carrying out the LORD's will. He complains bitterly, intimating that the LORD has not followed through on his promise to comfort Jeremiah in times of pain (15:17b-18). He has "eaten" the words of the LORD (15:16), and now he is looking for

---

This would give a more precise historical setting for this unit (the reign of Zedekiah; see Holladay, *Jeremiah 1*, p. 455).

[7]Some see verse 10 as the beginning of this confession. O'Connor, *Confessions*, pp. 27-44; Smith, *Laments*, pp. 11-15.

[8]Holladay, *Jeremiah 1*, p. 458.

some "water" (i.e., a sympathetic spirit) to wash down the food (15:18). He wears the LORD's name (15:16), so he looks to the LORD to defend him (cp. 14:9); the LORD's hand is on him, so he must speak (cp.1 Kgs 18:46; 2 Kgs 3:15; Isa 8:11; Ezek 1:3; 3:14,22; 8:1; 33:22; 37:1; 40:1).

The LORD's response shows that Jeremiah is making unwarranted accusations against the LORD. Just because his opponents have not yet been silenced, Jeremiah cannot assume that the LORD has abandoned him. He calls on Jeremiah to **repent** and **utter worthy . . . words** (15:19). He is the LORD's **spokesman** ("mouth;" cp. 1:9; Exod 4:1 6). The call to repentance reminds the reader of the LORD's appeals to the sinful nation in Jeremiah 3–4. In a sense, "Jeremiah has become the paradigm of salvation."[9] His own repentance and acquiescence to God will serve as an example to the people of how they are to react to his rebuke. The LORD then encourages Jeremiah to maintain his position against popular opposition, reassuring him that he will protect him. The language used here is the language of Jeremiah 1. The LORD will make Jeremiah **a fortified wall of bronze** (15:20; cp. 1:17-19); the LORD will **be with** him (cp. 1:8,19); he will **rescue** and **save** and **redeem** him (15:20-21; cp. 1:8,19).[10] By going back to the beginning, the LORD is reminding Jeremiah of how he has been with him over the many years of his ministry. He had told Jeremiah when he first called him that he would rescue him from his opponents. That opposition is getting more strident as the threat of Babylonian invasion looms ever larger. A bit of apprehension on Jeremiah's part is not surprising, but a firm rebuke and subsequent reassurance are necessary to bring Jeremiah back into balance.

---

[9]Clements, *Jeremiah*, p. 100; cp. Holladay, *Jeremiah 1*, pp. 463-464.
[10]Parke-Taylor, *Formation*, pp. 35-40.

JEREMIAH 16

I. DAY OF DISASTER (16:1–17:18)

There is a definite shift from prose to poetry at 16:19, which marks the division of this section into two parts. It is difficult, however, to ascertain the extent of originally independent units within each part. All of 16:1-9 holds together as a unit in which the LORD forbids Jeremiah to marry, as a message to the nation. Verses 10-13 contain a response to the people's anticipated reactions, justifying the punishment. This accusation is tempered by a promise of future restoration (vv. 14-15), a promise which itself is tempered by a return to accusation (vv. 16-18). It seems most likely that all of 16:1-13 originally comprised a single unit, but the continuations in verses 14-18 might have been created by the one putting the book together (vv. 14-15 also appear in 23:7-8). The second (poetic) half of this section moves back and forth between Jeremiah and the LORD. Jeremiah opens with a declaration of the LORD's unique divinity, in contrast to man-made idols (16:19-20). The LORD supplements this with his own words regarding idols (16:21–17:4). This is furthered by at least two "words" regarding the unique and ultimate sovereignty of the LORD (17:5-11), consisting of a nicely balanced juxtaposition of a curse and a blessing (vv. 5-8), an assertion by the LORD that he judges the heart (vv. 9-10), and a warning against the unjust accumulation of wealth (v. 11). Jeremiah responds to the LORD's words with his own warning to those who would ignore the LORD (vv. 12-13), and an appeal to the LORD to shield him from those who seek to do him harm (vv. 14-18).

16:1-13 The LORD gives Jeremiah disheartening instructions (vv. 1-4), calling on him to adopt a lifestyle that was looked upon as a curse in that culture. He is **not** to **marry** or father children, as a sign to his audience that there is no hope for any families who remain in Judah.[1] This prophetic message of doom stands in stark

---

[1]This is not a call to some higher plane of existence or self-denial for the

contrast to the LORD's use of birth announcements to give hope to
Isaiah's audience more than a century earlier (Isa 7:14-17; 8:1-4), and
in contrast to Jeremiah's own words to the exiles (29:6).[2] The certainty of defeat suggests a date of pronouncement during the reign
of Zedekiah, when Jeremiah repeatedly warned people of the inevitability of destruction at the hands of the Babylonians. This imminent destruction is described in a fourfold warning. Jeremiah's own
expressions of ignoble death (**deadly diseases** [see 14:18; Deut
29:22]; **sword and famine** [see 14:15]) alternate with more traditional ones, widely used in the ancient Mediterranean world.[3]

The mood of unrequited grief deepens in verses 5-7. The LORD
refers to traditional **funeral** rites[4] which will not be observed in the
days ahead. There will be no mourning of the dead, no show of
sympathy, no burial, no disfigurement to express one's grief (see
1 Kgs 18:23; Jer 5:7), no meals in honor of the deceased.[5] The LORD
is withdrawing his **love** and **pity** (cp. Hos 1:6) so completely from his
people that even their ability to grieve deserts them. As one might
expect, occasions for rejoicing also cease (vv. 8-9). The prime example of such an occasion is the wedding reception; so the LORD fore-
tells the cessation of those activities as well (cp. 7:34; 25:10; 33:11).
This brings the current warning of destruction full circle. The
instructions to Jeremiah that he is not to wed are but a single example of a general "warning" given by the LORD at this time.[6]

A pronouncement of judgment is typically followed with a justification by the judge. Verses 10-13 comprise that justification in this
case. The people ask, in mock innocence, **What wrong have we**

---

sake of a greater understanding. See Clements, *Jeremiah*, pp. 100-101;
Thompson, *Jeremiah*, pp. 403-404.

[2]Holladay refers to another possible contrast in the marriage of Hosea
and Gomer. *Jeremiah 1*, pp. 469-471.

[3]Concerns about the proper burial of one's family members lie at the
heart of the ancient Greek play, *Antigone* (cp. 1 Sam 31:11-13; 2 Sam 21:8-
14), while descriptions of bodies left to be eaten by "birds of the air and
beasts of the earth" are found in the writings of Homer, as well as the Bible
(Deut 28:26; 1 Sam 17:41-47; 2 Sam 21:10; Jer 7:33; 19:7).

[4]Jeremiah mentions here the *marzeah*-house ("the house where there is a
funeral meal"). There has been extensive research into this tradition in
Israel and Ugarit. For the primary studies, see the references in Holladay,
Jeremiah 1, p. 466.

[5]Thompson, *Jeremiah*, pp. 405-406.

[6]Brueggemann, *Jeremiah*, pp. 151-152.

done? The answer is the same answer that has been used to justify divine punishment in many preceding generations. They **forsook the LORD** and **followed other gods**. With these words the LORD had warned the first generations of Israelites to inhabit the land (Deut 29:25-28; Josh 24:16,19-20; cp. 1 Kgs 9:9). With these words he had justified the raising up of oppressors in the days of the judges (Judg 2:10-15). With these words he had justified the Assyrian exile of the northern tribes (2 Kgs 17:7,16). Now, with the same words, he is justifying the exile of his chosen people, Judah. The chosenness of God's people and the promises associated with that status require an additional justification be given. That addendum is the **stubbornness of** [the] **evil heart** (9:14; 11:8; 13:10; 18:12; 23:17; cp. Ps 81:12) of the current generation. This makes them worse than preceding generations (vv. 11-12). Their "stubbornness" is manifested in their refusal to obey ("hear"). This hints at the frequent divine accusation that the LORD had warned his people through his prophets, but the people had refused to "listen" to them (7:25; 25:4; 26:5; 29:19; 35:15; 44:4; cp. 2 Kgs 17:13-14).

16:14-15 The harsh words of judgment give way to a momentary promise of restoration. The tone of these lines seems out of place in the surrounding context of condemnation. It is likely, therefore, that these verses were uttered a few years later, after the people had entered into exile (cp. 23:7-8).[7] In that context, the people would read the preceding words as a reminder of the reason for their plight. In such a context, it would be easy for them to lose hope in the LORD. The current lines would encourage them to have hope; and placing this promise in this pessimistic context would only accentuate the possibility that the LORD could still show them mercy, even after being so angry with them.

The LORD draws a parallel between their subsequent return from Babylon and the Exodus from Egypt, saying the latter will pale in comparison with the former. For years, the LORD's spokesmen had promoted confidence in the LORD by referring to his great acts in the Exodus. He now promises them that they have something even greater to which they can look forward — their return to the Promised Land after exile.[8]

---

[7]Holladay, *Jeremiah 1*, p. 476; McKane, *Jeremiah*, pp. 373-374; but see Thompson, *Jeremiah*, p. 409; Lundbom, *Jeremiah 1-20*, p. 773.

[8]Brueggemann, *Jeremiah*, pp. 154-155.

16:16-18 This prose part closes with yet another metaphor about inevitable destruction. The LORD is sending **fishermen** and **hunters** after them, who will use "every trick in the book" to find and capture their prey. Once he captures them, he will **pay them double for their wickedness**, a harsh punishment which will be reversed when the people return from exile (see Isa 40:2). The justification for such a harsh judgment is, again, the worship of idols, "beings" which are **lifeless** and **detestable** "nothings."

16:19-20 The reference to idols in 16:18 opens the door to some of the most picturesque denunciations of idolatry in the book. Jeremiah begins with an appeal to the LORD and an ironically humiliating observation. The **time of distress** confronting Jeremiah has been precipitated by his attacks on the idolatry of the people of Judah. He calls on the LORD to defend him against the LORD's own people, who worship false **gods**.[9] Then he quotes the non-Israelites who made those gods to prove that they are false. They recognize that their gods are entirely "man-made."[10] The resulting picture shows "nonbelievers," who now acknowledge the emptiness of their own theology, trying to persuade the people of the one, true God to let go of the empty theology which the nonbelievers created and then abandoned.

---

[9]Actually, the words for "gods" and "idols" do not appear in this verse. More literally their words are, "Our fathers inherited a lie; vanity, and there is no profit in them." These terms are often used to refer to idols (cp. 2:5,8,11).

[10]It is likely that verse 20 contains "an ironic reversal of Gen 1:26." Holladay, *Jeremiah 1*, p. 482.

JEREMIAH 17

I. DAY OF DISASTER (16:1–17:18) (continued)

16:21-17:4 The LORD responds by pledging to "educate" his people (v. 21). Tying this unit together is the word "know" (יָדַע, *yāda'*), in 16:21 and 17:4. The LORD **will teach them** ("make them know") about his **power and might**, so that **they will know that my name is the LORD**. This is the language of the Exodus, when the LORD demonstrated his power to save his people from their Egyptian captors, making them "know that he is the LORD" (see Exod 7:5,17; 8:10,22; 10:2; 14:4,18; cp. Ezek 6:7,10,13,14; 7:4,9,27; etc.). He is "making them know" the same name now by exiling his people to Babylon, **a land you do not know** (7:4). The LORD is displaying now the same **power and might** he displayed in Egypt, and for the same purpose – to glorify his name (cp. Heb 13:8). But the results on his people are completely different.

The reason for this reversal of results on the people is their persistent and pervasive rebellion (17:1-4). Their sinfulness is **engraved with an iron tool . . . on the tablets of their hearts**. This suggests a contrast to clay tablets, which could be worked with a wooden stylus, and which could be "erased" and "corrected" before the clay hardened. These tablets are already hardened, and what is engraved in them cannot be altered (cp. Ezek 36:26). This also might suggest a contrast to the Ten Commandments, which were engraved on stone tablets, and which were to have been "on the hearts" of the Israelites since the day they entered the land (Deut 6:6; 11:18; cp. Jer 31:33). A further contrast lies in the accusation that their sin is inscribed **on the horns of their altars**, altars which should be dedicated to the worship of the LORD alone. Such inscriptions deprive their children of important knowledge about God. They do not "know the LORD," and they have not passed on that "knowledge" to their children. Their children know **the spreading trees** and **high**

hills where they go to worship idols, but they do not recognize the **mountain** (v. 3) of the LORD until it has been taken from them. They will lose their **inheritance** in their own land, which is the right of sons, and become slaves in a foreign land. They will come to **know the LORD** (16:21) when he exiles them to **a land** [they] **do not know** (17:4). The "name" of the LORD is a name of power, power that exhibits the LORD's mercy and love — as in the Exodus — but also his righteous **anger** (cp. 15:14;[1] Exod 34:5-7).

17:5-11 The LORD goes to the "heart" of the problem in these verses, expressing himself in terms which are most at home in a wisdom context. Verses 5-8 comprise a "didactic reflection,"[2] juxtaposing a curse and a blessing. The succeeding verses develop the topic of heart, which had been introduced in the contrast.

The topic of the contrast is trust. **Cursed is the one who trusts in man . . . but blessed is the man who trusts in the LORD** (vv. 5,7). The syntax of the two statements is identical; the only differences between them are in their first and last words. The state of being **cursed** is associated with **man**, and the state of being **blessed** is associated with **the LORD**. The term used for **the one** in verse 5 is translated **the man** in verse 7 (גֶּבֶר, *geber*). This term denotes a single male human being, while the term for **man** in verse 5 is the familiar Hebrew word, *'adam*, meaning "mankind" (the species). So the contrast here is between one who trusts in human power and ability to give life — in its fullest sense — and one who trusts in divine power and ability to give life. Trust originates in the heart. One's **heart** turns toward the one in whom one trusts, while it **turns away from** those deemed unable to provide help (v. 5; cp. Ps 118:8-9).

The outcomes of trust being contrasted here are illustrated with plants. **One who trusts in man** is compared with a desert **bush**. The environs in which such a bush lives are referred to as **wastelands, parched places, a salt land where no one lives**. Merely surviving in such a harsh environment is noteworthy; the **prosperity** indicated by fruit and seed is not forthcoming. The contrasting plant — **the man who trusts in the LORD** — is **a tree** rather than a bush. It grows in a well-watered place; **its roots** extend deep into the soil, finding much nourishment wherever they go. The same heat and drought that stunt the growth of the desert bush appear to have no effect on the

---

[1]See Parke-Taylor, *Formation*, pp. 23-31.
[2]Clements, *Jeremiah*, p. 105; but also Holladay, *Jeremiah 1*, p. 491.

tree. It is dark **green** with **leaves**, bearing **fruit** at regular intervals (cp. Ps 1:3).

The original hearers could not have missed the irony in this illustration. A "spreading tree" should have been a perfect reminder to the people of one who "trusts in the LORD," yet the people chose to worship other gods "under every spreading tree" (3:6). This was a common failing of the ancient Israelites — to interpret the clearest evidence of the LORD's power and love as a reason to worship some other (nonexistent) god. The same happens today, as God-given prosperity and spiritual gifts are credited to socio-economic theories or political programs or genetics or some other "objective" explanation.

This eloquent illustration also provides a reminder of another sort. Just as the bush and the tree face the same challenges (heat, drought) but produce far different results, so different people face the same challenges in their lives with far different results. The explanation for the different results is found in where their hearts turn to deal with those challenges. Those who turn to man-made solutions might survive, but their lives are unproductive, their spirits are quenched. But those who turn to the LORD flourish even in the most difficult of circumstances. They understand that life comes from the LORD, and they look to him to sustain and enrich their lives, whatever the circumstances (cp. Isa 40:27-31).

The key to this contrast is **the heart**, which is the topic of verses 9-11. The heart that "turns away from the LORD" (v. 5) is **deceitful**,[3] and no human can understand ("know") it. This is why people are wasting their time when they trust in humans; one human cannot fully fathom the heart of another. The LORD, on the other hand, cannot be deceived. he can **search the heart**. What he searches, he understands (cp. Acts 1:24; 15:8). One's **conduct** ("ways") is determined in the heart; so, the LORD judges the heart to determine the true motivation for one's words and actions. He understands the true motivation for the deeds that have led to one's current standing in life, and he affirms or condemns it accordingly. This is best illustrated in the lives of the rich (v. 11). Wisdom thinking (and we are in a wisdom context) held that the possession of wisdom led to prosperity, because wisdom comes from the LORD. One prospers by conforming his "ways" to the LORD's ways. But wisdom thinkers

---

[3]The term for "deceitful" is עָקֹב (*'āqab*), which is the root of the name Jacob (see 9:4).

were aware that many prosperous individuals did not respect the LORD's ways (see Job 21). How could this be? And how could this "injustice" be rectified? The answer is provided here. The LORD judges the heart, examining whether one has rightly gained their financial standing. If he has not, the LORD determines that fact and, in the end, exposes that person as the **fool** that he truly is.

17:12-13 These verses bring together much of what has just been said, calling on people to respond favorably to the words of the preceding units. (Whether this is a result of divinely inspired editing or was in the original proclamation cannot be ascertained.) The readers/listeners are to remember who is the true resident of the sanctuary in Jerusalem, which now bears the names of false gods on the horns of its altar (v. 1). His **throne** is **exalted**; he is the true **hope of Israel**. He is the one in whom their hearts should trust. He is **the spring of living water** (cp. 2:13) from which green trees draw their nourishment (v. 8). Those who **turn away from** (cp. v. 6) the LORD, who **forsake** (see 16:11) the LORD, have their home **in the dust**, "like a bush in the wastelands" (v. 5).

17:14-18 Another of Jeremiah's "complaints" is inserted at this juncture. This one is different from the previous ones in that there is no divine response recorded, which might be an indirect answer in itself.[4] Jeremiah's verbal attacks on the wealthy (v. 11) are sure to have been met with opposition from those with political power to wield. Their primary argument is that **the word of the LORD** — Jeremiah's prediction of doom — has not been **fulfilled**. That fulfillment is the only way that Jeremiah can prove he is a true prophet. As long as it is not fulfilled, these individuals can accuse him of slander against them. This seems to be the course they have taken, even to the point of punishing Jeremiah, who responds by calling on the LORD to **heal** and **save** him (cp. 1:8,19; 15:18-20; Ps 6:2,4). His response models for the Israelites the way they should have looked to the LORD for salvation. He says (literally) of the LORD, "You are my psalm." He is the one Jeremiah sings about in worship, while his opponents praise idols and wealth.

Jeremiah's accusers naturally believe they are right to accuse and punish him, so he must appeal to the LORD, his only "witness," to attest to his innocence. That innocence he declares in verse 16.

---

[4]Holladay, *Jeremiah 1*, p. 507; O'Connor, *Confessions*, pp. 45-52; Smith, *Laments*, pp. 15-18.

Then he appeals to the LORD again for help. He calls on him to protect him **in the day of disaster** (which he himself has predicted). As proof of his innocence, he asks the LORD to impose on his accusers the **terror, shame,** and **destruction** they intend to bring on him. This seemingly harsh and desperate request is actually a demonstration of faith. Jeremiah is leaving his fate in the LORD's hands, and he is leaving the fate of his accusers in the LORD's hands, instead of taking it into his own.

J. KEEPING THE SABBATH HOLY (17:19-27)

17:19-27 This prose oracle concerning the Sabbath is straightforward, unfolding in a logical succession. The LORD tells Jeremiah to speak at the city **gates of Jerusalem** (v. 19), reminding those who are going **in and out** of the ancient commandments regarding observance of the Sabbath (vv. 20-22). The LORD then accuses the people of ignoring those commandments (v. 23), and he presents them with two subsequent options: (1) they can correct their mistake and begin observing **the Sabbath** as commanded, resulting in prosperity for the king and the city (vv. 24-26), or (2) they can continue to ignore the Sabbath regulations and expect the destruction of the city.

The language of judgment in this oracle is similar to that of many passages in Jeremiah. The LORD's primary concern is that the people **did not listen or pay attention** (v. 23) to his commands regarding the Sabbath, and he calls on them to begin doing so now.[5] (The term for "listen" in v. 23 is the same word translated "obey" in vv. 24 and 27.) They have not been "listening" to the warnings spoken by Jeremiah and other prophets (cp. 7:24,26; 11:8; 25:4; 34:14; 35:15; 44:5). Rather, they have resisted like a **stiff-necked** farm animal, pulling away from doing the LORD's will (7:26; 19:15; cp. Deut 10:16; 2 Kgs 17:14). They have refused to **respond to discipline** (5:3; 7:28; 32:33; 35:13; cp. Deut 4:36). There is still the possibility for repentance, however, suggesting a date before the reign of Zedekiah. If they will **obey** ("listen to") the LORD, the royal court will prosper (**riding in chariots and on horses**), and people from all over the country will bring their **sacrifices** to Jerusalem.[6] If they do not, an

---

[5]Brueggemann, *Jeremiah*, pp. 165-166.

[6]The list of sacrifices (17:26) is unusual for Jeremiah and the "Deuterono-

unquenchable fire will **consume** the **gates** in which Jeremiah has been delivering his message.

The assumptions underlying this oracle are similar to those underlying Jeremiah's rebuke of the temporary manumission of slaves in Jeremiah 34. The LORD gave specific commandments through Moses after leaving Egypt, and he is holding the people accountable for carrying out those commandments. But one should not conclude from this that God is judging his people in a very mechanical, legalistic sort of way. There is a sinful attitude that runs deeper than a failure to perform certain actions. That is the attitude of "not listening" to what the LORD has to say, as discussed in regard to Jeremiah 7:21-26.[7] It is this basic refusal to submit to the sovereignty of the LORD, this refusal to respect his word simply because it is from him, which evokes his hot anger. The performance of the deed without the proper attitude would be rejected, because "the LORD searches the heart" (17:10). This seems to be the message of Jeremiah's Temple Sermon (7:1-15), where it is suggested that the offering of sacrifices should be interpreted as nothing more than a "bribe" to the LORD to protect them from harm for ignoring the Ten Commandments. This passage shows that the appropriate response is not the cessation of those rituals as "unnecessary" on legalistic grounds. The failure to fulfill the LORD's commandments (as in this case) is also a serious concern. But we must remember that it is so only because it points to a deeper problem: a basic rebelliousness against the LORD himself.[8]

---

mistic History" (Deuteronomy–2 Kings), which many associate literarily with Jeremiah. The pairing of "burnt offerings and sacrifices" is common in these and other writings of the Old Testament (e.g., Deut 12:11; Josh 22:26; Judg 20:26; 1 Sam 13:9; 2 Sam 6:17; 2 Kgs 10:24; Jer 7:22; cp. Exod 10:25; 18:12; 24:5; Lev 17:8; Num 15:3-8; Ezek 40:42). The linking of "grain offerings" with one of those is less regular (Josh 22:23,29; 1 Sam 3:14; 2 Kgs 16:13,15; Jer 14:12; 33:18; cp. Num 29:6,11,19), and even rarer in the case of "incense" (Jer 41:5; cp. Neh 13:5,9; Isa 43:23) or "thank offerings" (2 Chr 29:31; 33:16). For fuller discussion, see Holladay, *Jeremiah 1*, pp. 510-511.

[7]Some have suggested, in fact, that the gate of the people (17:19) is a gate leading into the temple, not a city gate. Holladay, *Jeremiah 1*, p. 509; McKane, *Jeremiah*, p. 416. This would further strengthen the connection between this passage and Jeremiah 7.

[8]"It is proposed that we have here a *pars pro toto* and that the sabbath law is representative of the whole covenant." Thompson, *Jeremiah*, p. 430; cp. Brueggemann, *Jeremiah*, pp. 166-167.

JEREMIAH 18

K. AT THE POTTER'S HOUSE (18:1-23)

The NIV editors place under a single heading two completely separate events, because both happen to involve pottery. (This might explain why the compiler of the book placed these accounts side by side.) Only the first event (18:1-23) actually takes place "at a potter's house." The second event (19:1-15) occurs in the Valley of Ben Hinnom, south of Jerusalem. Moreover, the confrontation between Jeremiah and Pashhur in Jeremiah 20 is a continuation of the Valley of Ben Hinnom episode; so, it would be more appropriate to place Jeremiah 19–20 under a single heading. I am separating chapters 18 and 19 for this discussion.

As we have seen in so many other cases, it is not certain that the contents of this section (18:1-23) were originally spoken at one time; they could have been brought together later by the inspired editor who gave the book its present form. The chapter falls into three parts. The first is a "vision oracle" (see 24:1-10), used as a general accusation of sinfulness against the people of Judah (18:1-12). A pronouncement of judgment by the LORD follows (18:13-17). It is logical for judgment to follow accusation, so it is quite reasonable to assume that these two parts did originate together. The verbalized rejection of the people is more likely to reflect a date during the reign of Zedekiah, rather than an earlier date. The third part of the chapter is another of Jeremiah's complaints (18:18-23). There are a few verbal connections — but no clear-cut thematic connections — between this complaint and the preceding verses. One could easily argue that it is here solely as the result of editing. The tone of Jeremiah's words is most similar to that in Jeremiah 37–38, so a date during the reign of Zedekiah again seems most likely.

18:1-12 This accusation of general sinfulness is one of several instances where the LORD uses an everyday event to reveal a profound message to Jeremiah, which he is to pass on to the people of Judah. The everyday event here is the making of a piece of pottery. Jeremiah observes as a potter works a lump of clay on his potter's **wheel**. Some imperfection in the clay causes the **pot** to be ruined before it is completed. The potter knows such a pot would be of no use to anyone, so he pounds the still wet pot back into an unshaped lump of clay and starts the process of **shaping** all over again (vv. 1-4).

The LORD then assumes the persona of the potter, speaking of Judah as the clay being worked in his hands (vv. 5-10). Other biblical writers use this metaphor in their teachings (Isa 29:16;[1] 41:25; 45:9; 64:8; Rom 9:21), and it is widely known by many Christians through Adelaide Pollard's hymn, "Have Thine Own Way." It could have been familiar to Jeremiah's audience through the prophecies of Isaiah, but there is a sense that it might not have been "well received" by that audience. The LORD begins addressing them with a rhetorical question: **O house of Israel, can I not do with you as this potter does?** The form of the question expects an affirmative answer; but the fact he asks it suggests that there was some doubt — probably based on their sinful actions — as to whether they actually accorded him this "right." The fact that he addresses them as **house of Israel** rather than "people of Judah" hints at the possibility he is appealing to their sense of obligation as an ancient covenant people, an obligation shared by the traditional clans of Judah and the many people who had fled from the North before Assyrian aggression more than a century earlier. This covenant relationship points to the cause of the people's misconception. They believe the covenant guarantees divine protection (cp. 7:1-15). Jeremiah contends the covenant also demands faithfulness to the ways of the LORD on their part (cp. Amos 3:2).

The core of this oracle is in verses 7-10. Like 17:5-8, these verses describe a stark contrast. The contrast here is between how the LORD responds to **evil** nations who **repent** (vv. 7-8) and how the LORD responds to good nations who "repent" and become evil (vv. 9-10). This is "basic doctrine" for Jeremiah. The LORD not only utilizes the vocabulary of Jeremiah's call (1:10), he dips back into the language of Jeremiah's Temple Sermon (7:3) in delivering this message. In so doing, he evokes a reminder to his audience of crucial mes-

---

[1]There are several verbal parallels between Jer 18:1-17 and Isa 29:16-17. Holladay, *Jeremiah 1*, pp. 521-522.

sages already given. The "basic doctrine" is that the LORD determines the ultimate fate of all kingdoms ("I appoint you over nations and kingdoms to uproot . . ." — 1:10); therefore, even the kingdom of Judah needs to "reform" ("make good") her ways — if she is doing evil — in order to receive the LORD's blessings (7:3).

The warning the LORD ultimately gives to the **people of Judah** (v. 11) is based on the basic affirmations made in verses 7-10. He picks up the words he had used in verses 7-8 to describe an evil nation, and he applies those to Judah. He **planned** (חָשַׁב, ḥāšab) to bring **disaster** (רָעָה, rāʿāh) against any nation that did **evil** (rāʿāh); now he is **preparing**[2] a disaster (rāʿāh) and **devising** (חֹשֵׁב, ḥōšēb) a **plan** (מַחְשָׁב, maḥšāb) **against** Judah (v. 11; cp. 36:3). To prevent this unwanted outcome, he appeals to them, **reform your ways and your actions** (see 7:3). The people's negative response (v. 12) is best interpreted in the light of 2:25, the only other instance in the book where the people say, **"It's no use!"** There, they go on to explain that they have decided not to heed Jeremiah's warnings, but will continue to worship idols instead. These, along with other sins detailed in the Temple Sermon, are the **plans** (מַחְשְׁבוֹת, maḥšᵉbōth) and the **stubbornness** (see 7:24 and 16:12 for other references) to which the LORD refers here.

This oracle is most significant, however, because of two theological tenets which form its backbone. The first is that the LORD deals with all nations according to the same "rules." All nations are blessed for being righteous; all are punished for being sinful; all are given the opportunity to repent. This fleshes out a little more of what the LORD meant when he told Jeremiah he would send him to "nations and kingdoms" (1:10). The basic message of Jeremiah to Judah is not case-specific; it could apply to any nation.

The second tenet is more controversial. It is the LORD's promise to **relent**[3] of the plans — for **disaster** (v. 8) or for **good** (v. 10) — he

---

[2]The term for "preparing" here is the term translated "potter" in verses 2-6 (a "potter" is one who shapes — or "prepares" — clay; cp. Gen 2:7). McKane, *Jeremiah*, pp. 421-422.

[3]The use of this verb נִחַם (niḥam) in reference to God raises questions throughout the Old Testament. The various modern translations of this term ("grieved," "was sorry," "relented," "repented," "changed his mind") do not clarify the situation. See Gen 6:6; Exod 32:14 (cp. Num 14:10-23); 1 Sam 15:11,29,35; 2 Sam 24:16; Jonah 3:10. For a brief but lucid discussion of the issues, see T.E. Fretheim, "Divine Foreknowledge, Divine Constancy,

has for a nation, if that nation changes its behavior. While this seems logical on its surface, it raises serious questions regarding divine omniscience and the veracity of prophets. In the hypothetical examples he raises, the LORD has already "announced" that he will do one thing, then he "relents" and does the opposite. This is a problem for prophets because such an announcement would most likely come through prophets. The reputation of those prophets is based primarily on whether they can accurately predict the future. If they "announce" something for the LORD, and the LORD subsequently relents of his announced plans, then the people will doubt the inspiration of those prophets. On the other hand, that is why the LORD sends prophets, and why they prophesy. They hope to persuade people to change their ways, in order to avoid what has been predicted.

This brings us back to the first theological dilemma, regarding divine omniscience. One assumption regarding divine omniscience is that it applies not only to knowledge of the past and the present, but also knowledge of the future. If God knows the future as perfectly as he does the past and the present, he would know prior to the original "announcement" how the recipients would respond. Problems of understanding God here ensue either way. If the recipients are going to reverse their behavior, and he knows that, then there is no true "relenting" on his part in response to their positive reception. He knows all along how they are going to end up, and so he does not really have to change his plans regarding them, only what he tells people regarding his actions. And if the people are going to persist in their behavior, and he knows that, then the warning or promise is a waste of time or a lesson for later audiences only, but not for the original recipients.

This can lead to much speculation for which there is no consensus resolution. Some explain this as God speaking in human terms for the sake of human understanding, but then one would also be saying that God is not really being truthful. Others say that God "chooses" not to know how people will respond, but one must still conclude from that that God has limited knowledge of the future. Others emphasize the notion that God must respect human free will in order to make faith genuine; but this suggests a certain type of

and the Rejection of Saul's Kingship," *CBQ* 47 (1985): 595-602; cp. Thompson, *Jeremiah*, p. 434; Brueggemann, *Jeremiah*, pp. 168-169; Clements, *Jeremiah*, pp. 113-114.

powerlessness, as God is "unable" to persuade the audience. Still others say principles of time do not apply to God, that he operates "outside" of time, that there is no distinction in his thinking between past, present, and future; but this just takes us back to the first proposal (that God is speaking in terms accommodated to human understanding). The primary theological concern in all this is to uphold the idea of divine sovereignty; but that seems to be compromised in some way by each of these solutions. God is restricted either by a human lack of understanding, by his own choosing (not to know the future), by human free will, or by time.

There is no clear solution to this complex issue which one can discern from this single instance. And it is not necessary to resolve it in order to fathom the intent of this particular oracle. Whatever the correct solution, the point being made here is that (1) people can change, and God will adapt his actions in response to those changes (cp. Ezek 18); and (2) the people of Judah have had plenty of warnings and plenty of opportunities to change their evil ways and avoid "disaster" from the LORD, but they have refused to do so. This leads to the following pronouncement of judgment.

18:13-17 The LORD's response to Judah's stubbornness is incredulity (vv. 13-15) and judgment (vv. 16-17). Half of the remarks of incredulity are in the form of rhetorical questions, typical of a "disputation."[4] **Who has ever heard anything like this? Does the snow of Lebanon ever vanish . . . ? Do its cool waters . . . ever cease to flow?** One would think that Judah's love for the LORD would be just as constant as snow on high mountains, yet they have **forgotten** him and worship **worthless idols** (cp. 2:10-13). This is another example where the words for "forget" and "remember" do not refer to cognitive memory but to acting toward someone as they deserve. The LORD deserves the worship of his people, yet they do not do so; they "forget" and worship idols instead.

These idols cause the people to **stumble in their ways and in their ancient paths**. The expression, "ancient paths," translates a different Hebrew term here (שְׁבִילִים, *šᵉbîlîm*) than in 6:16 (נְתִיבוֹת, *nᵉdîbôth*), but both are used as parallels to "ways" (דְּרָכִים, *dᵉrākîm*). The "main roads" and "highways" they are expected to take are "paths of righteousness" (Ps 23:3; cp. 18:20-24; 25:4-15), where they take care of the orphan and widow, where they worship the LORD

---

[4]Thompson, *Jeremiah*, p. 437.

with all their heart, where they honor the commands of the LORD in their daily lives (cp. Jer 7:5-9; Jas 1:26-27). Instead of walking in those "ways," they have "stumbled" (cp. 6:15,21; Hos 5:5) and gone off on secondary routes, full of danger. Here is an instance where taking "the road less traveled" is not a commendable choice.

The LORD begins to express his judgment in terms which would be typical for a conquered land (v. 16). It will be **laid waste** (12:11; 19:8; 33:10; 42:18; 44:12; 49:17; 50:13), subject to **scorn** (19:2,8; 25:9,18; 29:18; 51:37; cp. Lam 2:15; Micah 6:16; Zeph 2:15), and those who **pass by** will **shake their heads** in mourning (15:5; 16:5; 22:8-10; cp. 1 Kgs 9:8-9). He then introduces two other metaphors to describe his attitude toward Judah. First he speaks of himself as the wind, "scattering" his people like leaves, like sheep before a predator (9:16; 13:24; 23:2; 30:11; cp. Gen 11:4-9; Deut 4:27; 28:64; 30:3; Neh 1:8; Ezek 34:5-6; Zech 13:7). Then he speaks of turning his back toward them rather than his face (cp. Exod 33:21-23). This is the opposite of the famous Priestly Blessing — "the LORD make his face shine upon you and be gracious to you; the LORD turn his face toward you and give you peace" (Num 6:24-26). Instead of "smiling on" them, he will "give them the cold shoulder." He will punish rather than show grace; he will bring disaster rather than peace.

18:18-23 Here one finds threats against the life of Jeremiah (v. 18) and Jeremiah's response (vv. 19-23) in the form of a "confession" to the LORD.[5] The threats only loosely tie this unit to preceding lines in the chapter. The "plans" of the people to worship idols in verse 12 now give way to **plans** they are making **against** the life of **Jeremiah**. Similarly, the LORD said that the idols "have made them stumble" (יַכְשִׁלוּם, *yakšilûm*; v. 15); now, Jeremiah wishes for them to **be over-thrown** (מֻכְשָׁלִים, *mukšālîm*; v. 23) before the LORD. These create rather weak ties between this unit and the preceding ones.

Jeremiah's words form a direct response to the threats of the people in a couple of instances. The people tell each other to **pay no attention** to Jeremiah's prophecies (v. 18); then Jeremiah implores the LORD to **listen** ("pay attention") to his petition for help against those opponents (v. 19). They talk of honoring the **counsel** (עֵצָה, *ēṣāh*) **from the wise** (v. 19); he calls on the LORD to take notice of their **plots** (*ēṣāh*) against him (v. 23). These observations point to

---

[5]O'Connor, *Confessions*, pp. 53-59; Smith, *Laments*, pp. 18-22.

the greater message of this passage, that Jeremiah looks to the LORD to respond for him to the threatening words of his opponents.

The words of the people (18:18) indicate their assumption that **the priest, the wise,** and **the prophets** are the true "authorities" as to the LORD's will for his people, which puts them in opposition to the teachings of Jeremiah.[6] A similar triad occurs in Ezekiel 7:26, with "elders" there replacing **the wise** here. We can only guess at the exact nature of their opposition. The most likely explanations are that they are contradicting Jeremiah's warnings about the probable destruction of Jerusalem or his calls for repentance from sins which they have promoted/permitted (or both).

The solution is revealed by the contents of Jeremiah's condemnation. On the one hand, he calls for the LORD to punish them for rejecting his words. The people have **dug a pit to capture** him (vv. 20,22);[7] they have **hidden snares** for him; they have plotted to kill him. They have done this in spite of the fact he has spoken on **their behalf** before the LORD (cp. 15:1). It is only natural that he now call on the LORD to destroy them. However, he does so using the language of divine punishment which is so familiar in Jeremiah. In particular, the list in verse 21 of those who are to suffer (**children, wives, men** [= "husbands"], **young men**) matches that in 6:11-12, and the references to destruction by **famine** and **sword** in the same verse are becoming more and more familiar to the reader (see 14:12). What Jeremiah calls for is the fulfillment by the LORD of his previous warnings against the people. Although he will see no reason to gloat about it, the destruction of Jerusalem will mean personal vindication for Jeremiah as a prophet (37:18-20; cp. 1 Kgs 22:28).[8] As in the preceding complaint (17:14-18), there is no divine word here; that will come in the form of the Babylonian army.

---

[6]Brueggemann, *Jeremiah*, p. 171.

[7]The term for "pit" here is not the same as the one used in chapters 37–38.

[8]Holladay, *Jeremiah 1*, p. 528.

JEREMIAH 19

L. AT THE VALLEY OF BEN HINNOM (19:1-15)

The account of Jeremiah's oracle delivered in the Valley of Ben
Hinnom is recorded as a divine command to deliver the oracle
(vv. 1-13). The actual execution of the command is not recorded, but
that Jeremiah does carry out the command is not in question.
Jeremiah smashes a clay jar (v. 10) as an illustration of the message
he is delivering, and the oracle itself divides into two parts around
this illustration. The first part (vv. 3-9) precedes the breaking of the
jar, while the second part (vv. 11-13) follows it. Verses 14-15 record
his actions and an additional oracle following his return from the
Valley. The supplementary oracle reveals the people's rejection of
the main one. Jeremiah 20 reports events immediately following the
pronouncement of those oracles. The only verbal links to Jeremiah
18 are the references to a "potter" (v. 1; whether it is the same potter is not stated), the LORD's promise to "bring a disaster" (רָעָה,
rāʿāh; v. 3; cp. 18:8,11,17), and the mention of the people's "plans"
(עֵצָה, ʿēṣāh, v. 7; cp. 18:23). There are more extensive verbal links to
Jeremiah 7:16–8:3,[1] so there is no compelling reason to see an original unity between this chapter and the preceding one.

19:1-9 The LORD instructs Jeremiah to **buy a clay jar** (בַּקְבֻּק,
baqbuq)[2] and carry it to **the Valley of Ben Hinnom** (גֵּיא בֶן־הִנֹּם, gê' ben-
hinnōm). This valley lies to the south of Jerusalem, and it was used at
that time as the city's garbage dump (see on 7:31-32). It was said that
the fires of burning refuse there never ceased, so it was later associated with depictions of Hell or Hades. A variant form of this name
(Gehenna) is used in the New Testament in this way (Matt 5:22,29,30;

---

[1]Parke-Taylor, *Formation*, pp. 192-195.
[2]Probably used for dispensing water. Thompson, *Jeremiah*, pp. 447-448;
Bright, *Jeremiah*, p. 131.

10:28; 18:9; 23:15,33; Mark 9:43,45,47; Luke 12:5; Jas 3:6; 2 Pet 2:4). It is logical that the gate leading to this valley would be known as the **Potsherd Gate** (elsewhere called the Dung Gate?[3]), as broken pieces of pottery would be a normal part of a city's garbage. Jeremiah is to deliver his message to **the elders of the people and of the priests**. Why he calls on these leaders and not others is uncertain; the oracle itself addresses the **kings of Judah** as well (vv. 3,13). This partially explains, however, why the chief priest subsequently leads the way in demonstrating opposition to Jeremiah's oracles.

The first part of the oracle moves from a general announcement of disaster (v. 3) to a delineation of wrongs (vv. 4-5), then elaborates on the disaster that is approaching (vv. 6-9). The descriptions of both the sins and the punishment are vivid. The sins themselves are the same described previously in the book. The people are guilty of idolatry, which the LORD describes in four ways: they have **forsaken** the LORD (cp. 17:13) and made the Valley of Ben Hinnom **a place of foreign gods** (see 7:31-32); they have **burned sacrifices** there to those gods; they have shed **the blood of the innocent** (here a reference to child sacrifice — Jer 7:6,31-32; cp. Ps 106:38; 2 Kgs 21:16; 24:4 — or the killing of prophets — Jer 26:15); and they have **built the high places to Baal**. The ways in which the LORD elaborates on these offenses reveal how bad the situation has gotten. These are gods which were previously unknown in Judah, even though idolatry itself is not new. The people have not simply shed innocent blood, they have **filled** the city with it (cp. 2 Kgs 21:16; 24:4). He says the practice of child sacrifice, which seems prevalent, never even entered his mind (cp. 7:31; 32:35).

The same sense that this is an unprecedented time arises from the LORD's introductory comments on the city's destruction. He says the people's ears will **tingle** when they hear the announcement (v. 3). This expression is used in only two other places in the Old Testament: in the announcement of the fall of Eli's house (1 Sam 3:11), and in the initial announcement in Kings of the fall of Judah (2 Kgs 21:12). It points to something which will be received with incredulity and shock, because it goes against the current understanding of the nature of the LORD. He is rejecting his chosen priest, and then his chosen nation. The offense must be extremely grave to warrant such a turn of events. The gravity of the situation is further

---

[3]Thompson, *Jeremiah*, p. 448.

implied by the heaping up of grim forecasts in verses 6-9. Pieces of verses 5-7 and 11 are also in 7:31-33 (see there for further comment), but this passage adds to that earlier prediction. It is as if he is expanding on that oracle here, as if that other prophecy is not extensive enough in its description of the devastation to come.

The threat to **ruin the plans** of the nation (v. 7) creates an interesting wordplay in the text. The term for "ruin" comes from the same root (בָּקַק, *bāqaq*) as the term for "jar" (*baqbuq*).[4] The symbol of the frustration of the people's "plans" will also serve as a symbol of the "plans" the LORD has for them. Most of the remaining threats (vv. 7-9) are used elsewhere in Jeremiah,[5] but the use of ten of them together here heightens the sense of divine anger. The reference to cannibalism (v. 9) takes matters a step further. This is the first reference to this act of desperation in Jeremiah (cp. Lev 26:27-29; Deut 28:53-57; 2 Kgs 6:26-31), suggesting again the elevated severity of the present situation. Moreover, it stands as a morbid response to the child sacrifice of the preceding verses.

19:10-13 The full import of the location of this pronouncement comes out in Jeremiah's words following the shattering of **the jar** (v. 10). Just as one might **smash** (or "break," as in v. 10) a clay jar, so the LORD will **smash** Jerusalem. It cannot be "glued back together." What once was a useful and perhaps elegant item now is a worthless little pile of trash. He takes this imagery a step further in the references to **Topheth**, going even beyond what he had said in 7:30-33 (cp. 2 Kgs 23:10; Isa 30:33). Not only will Topheth be unable to contain all the corpses people will bring there, the entire city of Jerusalem will become a "Topheth," a firepit for rubbish (vv. 12-13). Josiah had "defiled" Topheth as part of his purge of foreign worship practices; now, all the houses in Jerusalem will be **defiled**, because they have made **the roofs** of those **houses** places of worship to foreign **gods** (cp. 32:29; 2 Kgs 23:12; Zeph 1:5).[6]

---

[4]Holladay, *Jeremiah 1*, p. 536; McKane, *Jeremiah*, pp. 445-446; Bright, *Jeremiah*, p. 131; Lundbom, *Jeremiah 1-20*, p. 840.

[5]For the expression "fall by the sword," see Jer 14:18; 20:4; 39:18; 44:12; for references to food for wild animals, see 7:33; 15:3; 16:4; 34:20. The expressions "devastate" and "be appalled" come from the same Hebrew root (cp. 2:15; 4:7,27; 5:30; 8:21; 18:16; 25:9,11,18,38; 29:18; 32:43; 34:22; 42:18; 44:12,22), as are the terms for "scorn" and "scoff" (cp. 25:9,18; 29:18). See Parke-Taylor, *Formation*, pp. 152-153.

[6]Holladay, *Jeremiah 1*, p. 541.

19:14-15 Jeremiah returns from the Valley to the area of the temple to reiterate his warnings and stress the inevitability of destruction. The long-standing threat of **disaster** is now very close to becoming a reality. This is because the people have refused to accept Jeremiah's words. They are **stiff-necked** (7:26; 17:23; cp. Deut 9:6,13; 10:16; Judg 2:19; 2 Kgs 17:14; 2 Chr 30:8; 36:13; Neh 9:16-17,29) and will **not listen** (cp. 3:13; 6:17; 7:13,24,26; 9:13; 11:8,10; 13:10-11; 17:23; 22:5,21; 25:3-4,7-8; 26:5; 29:19; 34:14; 35:14-17; 36:31; 37:2; 40:3; 42:21; 43:4,7; 44:5,23) to the divine warnings.

Looking back over the chapter, it appears that this oracle is building off the Temple Sermon in Jeremiah 7. That prophecy was delivered during the first half of the reign of Jehoiakim (c. 607 B.C.). In the present passage, Jeremiah "revisits" that earlier oracle when he "revisits" the temple.[7] The threats of that earlier passage have gone unheeded. Probably a decade or more later, Jeremiah reminds his audience of that earlier threat, but expressing himself now in more drastic terms. The people have refused to heed his warnings; the threat will soon become a reality.

---

[7]Thompson says the two oracles are contemporaneous, from early in the reign of Jehoiakim (*Jeremiah*, pp. 445-446). Holladay places 7:30-33 in the reign of Zedekiah (*Jeremiah 1*, p. 539).

JEREMIAH 20

M. JEREMIAH AND PASHHUR (20:1-6)

20:1-6 The story continues in Jeremiah 20. Reaction to Jeremiah's latest condemnation of Jerusalem is spearheaded by **Pashhur son of Immer** (see 38:1). Pashhur is a **priest, the chief officer in the temple**. Pashhur's opposition is both professional and personal. Professionally, Jeremiah is criticizing activities in the temple, which Pashhur oversees. Pashhur will naturally defend his own policies and practices in the face of Jeremiah's criticisms.[1] Personally, Pashhur and Jeremiah probably come from rival priestly families. Pashhur most likely comes from the line of Zadok, because he is a leading priest in the temple. Zadok's line replaced the Elide line as priests before the Ark during the reign of Solomon (1 Kgs 2:26-27; cp. 1 Sam 22:20-23; 2 Sam 8:17; 1 Kgs 1:7-8). Jeremiah traces his lineage back to the Elides ("the priests of Anathoth;" see on Jer 1:1-3). Pashhur could bolster his objection to Jeremiah with the assumption that the LORD had preferred Zadok's line over the Elides since the temple was built.

Pashhur places Jeremiah in **stocks**[2] at the northern end of the temple area, facing away from the Valley of Ben Hinnom. The text reports nothing of what Pashhur said to Jeremiah or to the people of Jerusalem to explain this official response. Jeremiah refers to him as one who **prophesied lies** (v. 6), but we do not know when this occurred. He releases Jeremiah after just one day of confinement.

---

[1]Brueggemann, *Jeremiah*, p. 179; Clements, *Jeremiah*, pp. 119-120.

[2]The form of these "stocks" is unknown. The term (מַהְפֶּכֶת, *mahpeketh*) occurs only here, 29:26, and in 2 Chr 16:10. It is derived from a root meaning "to turn (over)." It is unlikely that this is anything like the "stocks" of Puritan America. See Holladay, *Jeremiah 1*, pp. 542-543; McKane, *Jeremiah*, p. 460.

Jeremiah delivers an oracle against Pashhur when he is released, but the words against Pashhur (vv. 3-4a,6) envelope another general oracle against the whole nation (vv. 4b-5). The latter does not go into the detail typical of Jeremiah regarding the fall of Jerusalem. He mentions only death by the sword and captivity as possible fates for the inhabitants of the nation (cp. 15:1-4). He says more about the material wealth the Babylonians will take as plunder (v. 5; cp. 52:17-23) than he does about the people they will kill or capture. The greater thrust of the oracle targets Pashhur. He says the LORD has given Pashhur a new name to denote his legacy. Soon, people will think of Pashhur not as a high official, but as **Magor-missabib** ("terror on every side"; see 6:25).[3] He will be a **terror** to all those around him. No one will want to be known as Pashhur's associate, because all his family and friends will suffer at the hands of the Babylonians. They will either **fall by the sword** (v. 4) or **go into exile** (v. 6). The stated reason for this condemnation (besides the obvious displeasure with being placed in stocks) is that Pashhur has **prophesied lies** ("prophesied with falseness;" cp. 5:30-31; 14:14; 23:25-32; 27:9-16; 28:15; 29:8-9,21-23,31-32).[4] It is not surprising to find a priest uttering prophecies; Jeremiah, Isaiah, and Ezekiel all come from priestly families (see 1 Chr 25:1; cp. 1 Chr 6:33-43).

N. JEREMIAH'S COMPLAINT (20:7-18)

Jeremiah's final "complaints" (20:7-13,14-20) constitute a pair of passages reflecting the inner turmoil of a prophet.[5] He opens with a bitter expression of his plight as the unwelcome prophet (vv. 7-10), which leads into an imprecation for divine retaliation on his enemies (vv. 11-12), concluding with a short call to praise the LORD (v. 13). This combination is common, so the unity of these verses is probable (see 12:1-4; 17:14-18; 18:19-23). It is likely, but not

---

[3]For a fuller discussion, see W.L. Holladay, "The Covenant with the Patriarchs Overturned: Jeremiah's Intention in 'Terror on Every Side,'" *JBL* 91 (1972): 305-320; idem, *Jeremiah 1*, pp. 543-544.

[4]T.W. Overholt, *The Threat of Falsehood: A Study in the Theology of the Book of Jeremiah* (Naperville, IL: Allenson, 1970).

[5]O'Connor, *Confessions*, pp. 61-80; Smith, *Laments*, pp. 23-29. Several also isolate v. 13 as an independent doxology. See Holladay, *Jeremiah 1*, pp. 548-550; Clements, *Jeremiah*, p. 120; McKane, *Jeremiah*, pp. 480-481.

absolutely certain, that Jeremiah actually voices these sentiments shortly after his run-in with Pashhur. There is a strong link created by the reference to "Magor-missabib" (v. 10), a reference which would logically follow the events recorded in 20:1-6. But the connection could have been made by the book's compiler. Surprisingly, this complaint is followed immediately by a second, one which is reminiscent of Job's lament in Job 3 (vv. 14-18). Perhaps this doubling of complaints serves to mark the end of a long series of sections highlighting the prophet's own inner struggles (11:1–20:18).[6]

20:7-13 The exact nuance of verse 7 is difficult to ascertain. The verb translated **deceived** (or "persuaded") here can also convey the idea of "seduce" or "entice" (cp. Exod 22:15; Judg 14:15). Perhaps the best rendering in English would be "trick." Whatever the precise meaning,[7] the gist of his thought seems clear enough: he feels the LORD misled him in some way, that the LORD intended to hurt or embarrass Jeremiah by making him a prophet and forcing him to proclaim the message of doom that he has been proclaiming, even when his own good sense tells him he should not. The people have responded to his warnings with **ridicule, mocking, insult and reproach** (vv. 7-8; cp. 6:10). They do not respect him for telling the truth. They conclude he is wrong and an unnecessary, if not traitorous, discouragement, so they make fun of him to counter his prophecies.

Their plan seems to be working. Jeremiah feels beaten down, **overpowered**; others have **prevailed**. The LORD has "prevailed" over him (v. 7); he **cannot** ("prevail", v. 9); his human opponents plot to "prevail" over him, but they will not (vv. 10-11). Jeremiah tries to lighten his load by keeping quiet, simply refusing to utter the messages the LORD has given him, but that tires him out even more than responding to the ridicule of others. He speaks of a **fire** in his heart, imprisoned **in** [his] **bones**, a fire which cannot be quenched. This is not a literal "fire"; this is simply an overwhelming compulsion to say what the LORD has placed within him.[8]

---

[6]Clements, *Jeremiah*, pp. 73-75, 122-124.

[7]Holladay, *Jeremiah 1*, p. 552; Thompson, *Jeremiah*, p. 459 Bright, *Jeremiah*, pp. 132-133; Nicholson, *Jeremiah 1-25*, p. 169; Lundbom, *Jeremiah 1-20*, pp. 854-855.

[8]Thompson, *Jeremiah*, p. 460.

There are two striking elements in the remarks Jeremiah hears from those around him (v. 10). First, they are throwing back in his face the curse-name which he invoked on Pashhur. They are trying to transfer the object of that curse from the priest back to Jeremiah, saying *his* name is now "Magor-missabib" (v. 10; cp. v. 3); his family and friends can expect to suffer horrible fates.[9] A second element is more intriguing. Jeremiah overhears certain people plotting against him. They talk about his being **deceived**, that they would **prevail** over him. This is the language of Jeremiah's initial accusation against the LORD (v. 7). Taking these verses together, one sees that Jeremiah hears plots being fashioned against him, but he feels that it is all too late. The people want to plot against him, but he says the LORD has already done to him what those other people are planning. The LORD has already humiliated him ("prevailed" over him) more than they ever could. But the complaint does not go beyond the words themselves. Jeremiah has been griping about the cost of having the LORD with him, inside him; but he still turns to the same LORD to protect him against his opponents (vv. 11-12). He entreats the LORD to fight for him, to be with him in this struggle. He wants **vengeance** – and vindication – but he realizes that the LORD alone can give him those things (cp. 11:20). Only when the LORD has brought Jerusalem to ruin will Jeremiah have the personal respect he desires.

In this light, verse 13 does not appear totally out of place. Jeremiah has been asserting his confidence in the LORD to **rescue** him from his religious and political opponents. It is not surprising to find him praising the LORD in an anticipatory mode for rescuing him – this **needy** prophet – from those just-mentioned "mockers."[10]

20:14-18 The same general mood that makes sense of the praise of verse 13 makes this second bitter lament seem surprising. In spite of his deep, abiding faith in the LORD and the genuineness of his own confidence in the LORD, he still has his moments when he thinks life is too much to bear. The primary theme of this complaint is Jeremiah's wish that he had never been born. He expresses this theme in a variety of ways in these few verses, but primarily by reversing the normally joyful occasion of the birth of a baby. The mother carries the child until the time for it to be delivered, pro-

---

[9]There is also a parallel in Ps 31:13. See Parke-Taylor, *Formation*, pp. 48-51.
[10]Thompson, *Jeremiah*, pp. 457-458, 461-462; cp. Brueggemann, *Jeremiah*, p. 184.

viding a place for the child as it grows ever larger. Jeremiah voices the grotesque "wish" that such a state had become permanent in his case, that his **mother** had never been delivered of this child, that he had continued to grow inside her (vv. 14a,17). The "role" of the father at the birth of a son is to hear the good news of the birth (v. 15). Just as Jeremiah wishes his mother had never done her "job" and given birth to this baby, so he wishes that his **father** had never done his "job" of receiving **the news** about the birth of a son. But he gives the greatest attention to the one announcing his birth (vv. 15-17),[11] wishing he had never made the announcement, wishing on **that man** the destruction which the LORD had brought on Sodom and Gomorrah (**the towns the LORD overthrew**).[12] These remarks constitute the antithesis to a birth announcement; these are the things no one wants to hear. Yet Jeremiah implies by them that if those normally dreaded scenarios had occurred, they would be preferable to the **trouble** and **shame** which he actually has experienced in his life.

The possible inappropriateness of such sentiments on the lips of a prophet has been raised from time to time.[13] Jeremiah knew that this would be a thankless and physically demanding job when he was called to be a prophet (see Jeremiah 1). Nothing that happened to him could be considered "unexpected," because it was all essentially predicted by the LORD at the time of that prophetic call. This expression of frustration regarding the LORD and the task the LORD has placed on him suggests a less than admirable level of faith and acceptance for a "man of God." One might expect a strong remonstrance from the LORD, but none is forthcoming. This suggests a level of understanding and sympathy on the part of the LORD. He understands that Jeremiah is expressing a temporary feeling, a fleet-

---

[11]It could be a mere coincidence, but it is intriguing to consider the fact that Jeremiah is the LORD's "messenger," and he gives the greatest attention to the messenger in this scenario. People expect the messenger to bring good news, and he does. Yet Jeremiah curses him for that. This is similar to the fact that Jeremiah has been sent by the LORD, and he speaks the truth; yet the people curse him for being a good prophet who does his job. Cp. Brueggemann, *Jeremiah*, p. 186.

[12]Holladay, *Jeremiah 1*, pp. 564-565; Thompson, *Jeremiah*, p. 464; McKane, Jeremiah, p. 488; Nicholson, *Jeremiah 1-25*, p. 171; Lundbom, *Jeremiah 1-20*, p. 871.

[13]Holladay, *Jeremiah 1*, pp. 561, 566.

ing frustration. He understands that Jeremiah's tone will change significantly when the LORD fulfills his word and brings destruction on Jerusalem. Ultimately, the prophet's grief over the humiliation of his homeland will overshadow his personal trials.

JEREMIAH 21

V. DELUSION, DESTRUCTION, AND DEPORTATION (21:1–29:32)

A. GOD REJECTS ZEDEKIAH'S REQUEST (21:1-14)

Many scholars see this chapter as the beginning of a new block of material that extends through chapter 29. In this block, the tone is almost entirely negative, with destruction and death ever hovering over the reader's shoulder; the style is primarily prose, though not entirely so; and most of the passages are placed in a more specific historical context (see 21:1; 24:1; 25:1; 26:1; 27:1; 28:1; 29:1-2). The passages are not arranged chronologically, as the compiler moves back and forth among the reigns of Jehoiakim (609–598 B.C.), Jehoiachin/Jeconiah (598–597 B.C.), and Zedekiah (597–586 B.C.).

Jeremiah 21 is set during the final siege of Jerusalem, overlapping in some ways the material in Jeremiah 37–38. Exactly when during that eighteen-month siege these particular events take place is not clear, but more likely early than late. The chapter describes an inquiry by King Zedekiah (vv. 1-2), to which Jeremiah gives a three-part answer. First he addresses Zedekiah and his officials (vv. 3-7), then the people as a whole (vv. 8-10), then the members of the royal house (vv. 11-14). He advises them all that Jerusalem is doomed, and the only hope that any of them has for escape is through surrender to the Babylonians.

21:1-2 King Zedekiah sends two of his servants to **inquire of the LORD** through **Jeremiah. Pashhur son of Malkijah** (not the Pashhur of 20:1-6) stands in opposition to Jeremiah on another occasion (see 38:1-4), while **Zephaniah son of Maaseiah** comes to his aid on at least one occasion (29:24-32; see further discussion on 37:3). It is intriguing from a historical point of view to consider why Zedekiah sends **these officials**, and why he **sends** these officials. The information provided by the book reveals that one official is more sympathetic to Jeremiah than the other. Perhaps the king chose them so that together they could be trusted to return with an accurate accounting of what Jeremiah has to say. More intriguing is why Zedekiah would even seek an oracle through Jeremiah. We know there were many other prophets who would give an oracle more to the king's liking (see Jeremiah 23), yet he is opting to turn to the prophet who is more likely to say what the king does not want to hear. (The narrative in Jeremiah 37–38 reveals more about this aspect of these events, so a fuller discussion of it is provided there.)

The words of the royal inquiry reveal an optimism which, in hindsight, is unfounded. The inquiry probably comes early in the siege, because the king is hoping the Babylonians will abandon the siege. They actually do leave for a while (see on 37:3-5), but it turns out to be a very temporary reprieve. The failure to mention that here suggests a preceding date.[1] The mere fact that the king expresses such optimism shows a measure of faith in the LORD which is admirable. The expression **perform wonders** (v. 2) is applied particularly to the Exodus in the Old Testament (see Exod 15:11; Ps 77:11,14; 78:12; 106:7,22; cp. Josh 3:5; Judg 13:19; Ps 40:5; 105:2), suggesting the king is looking for a similarly miraculous deliverance in his own hour of distress. Even in the face of the overwhelming Babylonian armies, he still holds out faith in the power of the LORD to rescue his people. Such faith in another "exodus-like moment" had probably been reinforced by the city's experience in the days of Hezekiah (Isaiah 36–37; 2 Kings 18–19; see on Jer 37:3-5). Sadly, the actions of the people (which Jeremiah has been criticizing for decades) show that this is also a faith which does not carry with it a sense of obligation to walk in the ways of the LORD in "everyday" situations. It is a one-sided faith, a faith in a God of power, but not a faith in a God of holiness. Christians today exhibit a similar attitude when they look to God for healing or for victory in some sporting event or for a financial windfall, but who think little of the moral and ethical responsibilities of being children of God.

21:3-7 Jeremiah's message to the king (vv. 3-7) must have been very demoralizing. He mentions the imminent deaths of the city's inhabitants with his typical triad of **plague, sword and famine** (v. 7a). But building up to that point, he also describes what appar-

---

[1]Holladay, *Jeremiah 1*, p. 570.

ently is insurrection from among Zedekiah's own troops, as his own **weapons of war** will be **turn**ed **against** him (v. 4). What is worse, the LORD himself is **fight**ing **against** Jerusalem. It is not Nebuchadnezzar whom the people of Jerusalem should fear, but the LORD. He uses traditional sayings about the LORD as warrior to make this point. The LORD says, **I myself will fight** (v. 5); but he will not fight against Israel's enemies as on other occasions (cp. Exod 14:14; Josh 10:14). He will fight against his own people. The **outstretched hand and mighty arm** with which he vanquished Egypt and Israel's other enemies in past generations (Exod 6:6; Deut 4:34; 5:15; 7:17-19; 9:29; 11:2; 26:8; 1 Kgs 8:42; 2 Kgs 17:36; Ps 136:12) will now be turned against Jerusalem. In this situation, he will hand them over to someone who will not show them the **mercy** and **pity** and **compassion** which the LORD has so graciously shown them at other times (cp. Exod 34:5-7; Num 14:17-22; Ps 78:38). The king has no reason for optimism, no reason to hope for a miracle. He must prepare to meet his God (Amos 4:12).

21:8-10 The message Jeremiah addresses to the people does contain an element of hope, although one that probably did not sound very appealing to his hearers. He holds out for them **the way of life and the way of death**. The Law spoke of "the way of life" as something that would bring them happiness in their own land (cp. Deut 30:15-20), while "death" was to be found outside the land. Jeremiah expands on the latter by mentioning yet again the triad of **sword, famine or plague** (v. 9), forms of destruction which they will now find in their land, not outside it. For "the way of life," he offers but a single avenue: **surrender to the Babylonians**. Life is now to be found outside the Promised Land, not in it. The LORD's purpose is being accomplished through the Babylonians, not against the Babylonians (as the people of Jerusalem want). He gives the reasons why this is their only option for life, in verse 10. He has **determined** to bring **harm** to the **city** ("I have set my face against this city for evil"), and he promises that the Babylonians will **destroy** the city **with fire**.

21:11-14 The final part of this message, **to the royal house of Judah**, still calls for justice and righteousness (cp. 7:5-7; 22:3,15-16). This was a central responsibility of kings (cp. Deut 16:18-20; Psalm 72; Isa 9:6-7; 11:1-4; 32:1-8). It is surprising to find a call for it here, though, because destruction is inevitable and justice will do nothing to deflect it. Verse 12 suggests that punishment might still be averted, but that seems unlikely, given the inevitability of destruction which has permeated Jeremiah's prophecies for the past several years and which dominates the next couple of verses.[2] Perhaps verse 12 is to be read relatively, in the vein of Jeremiah's "hopeful" words to Zedekiah in 38:17-18. There he holds out the possibility that Jerusalem will not be burned, that some portion of the punishment might be averted. The city will still be captured, but not utterly destroyed (see on 38:17-18). The double mention of **fire** as the means of destruction in these verses might support such an interpretation.[3] Moreover, the second half of verse 12 is identical to part of Jeremiah 4:4.[4] That verse warns of the LORD's **wrath** coming, if the people fail to circumcise their hearts. Perhaps he is saying here that they have not done so (as evidenced by continuing oppression), and so they should fully expect punishment.

Whatever the case, the certainty of divine punishment resumes in verse 13. The people are speaking confidently of their defenses, defenses which have held against all previous attackers. **Who can come against us?** they ask. Such confidence rests on the belief that the LORD is with them, as he has been with them before. The **rocky plateau** ("rock of uprightness") on which they live conveys a double meaning. On the surface level, it refers to the topography of Jerusalem, set on a hill surrounded on three sides by valleys (cp. 31:40; Ps 26:12). On a deeper level, it can refer to the LORD. The LORD is often referred to as a "rock" (cp. Deut 32:4,15,18,31; 1 Sam 2:2; 2 Sam 22:3,32,47; 23:3; Ps 19:14; 28:1; 31:2; 61:2; 62:2,6,7; 78:35; 89:26; 92:15; 94:22; 95:1; Isa 26:4; 30:29; 44:8; Hab 1:12), and he acts with "uprightness" (cp. Isa 11:4; 45:19). He has been their "rocky plateau," upon which they have enjoyed safety and security. However, this time is different, because this time he is **against** them. He will make sure they are punished "according to the fruit of [their] **deeds**" (cf. 7:3,5; 17:10; 18:11).

---

[2]Most commentators link 21:11-14 with 22:1-9, rather than 21:1-10, partly on the basis of this inconsistency. See Holladay, *Jeremiah 1*, pp. 575-577; Thompson, *Jeremiah*, p. 470; Brueggemann, *Jeremiah*, pp. 188-189; McKane, *Jeremiah*, p. 506; Bright, *Jeremiah*, p. 144.

[3]Holladay resolves the anachronism here by splitting this oracle into two — verses 11-12 he dates to the reign of Jehoiakim, verses 13-14 to a later date (*Jeremiah 1*, pp. 575, 577). Otherwise, one would have to say the LORD suffers a momentary lapse, or that he says this to stress the lack of repentance on the part of the kings.

[4]Parke-Tayler, *Formation*, pp. 62-64.

JEREMIAH 22

B. JUDGMENT AGAINST EVIL KINGS (22:1-30)

The door to Jeremiah 22 is pushed open in 21:11, when Jeremiah addresses "the royal house of Judah." This chapter consists of a series of oracles directed to each individual king from Jeremiah's career, except Zedekiah. It is possible that 23:1-8 is meant to serve in that capacity.[1] The royal object of every other unit is relatively certain. Verses 10-12 are addressed to Shallum (22:11), Josiah's son, who was deposed by the Egyptians and replaced with Jehoiakim (Shallum = Jehoahaz; cp. 2 Kgs 23:31-35).[2] Verses 13-23 level a longer prophetic attack against Jehoiakim (= Eliakim; 2 Kgs 23:34), while the rest of the chapter (vv. 24-30) denounces the evil practices of King Jehoiachin, who reigned only three months. This leaves only 22:1-9 in temporal limbo. It would make sense to say that these verses were addressed to Josiah, the father of Shallum and Jehoiakim, and the king in the early years of Jeremiah's career. Verses 6-9 seem at first glance too harsh to fit the reign of Josiah, so perhaps they are to be connected with the comments on Shallum (vv. 10-12). Then again, they could date from the first five years of Jeremiah's prophetic career, before the discovery of the book of the covenant. Also, Jeremiah does have a relatively negative assessment of the state of the nation at the end of Josiah's reign (see on 3:6-10), so perhaps these words were spoken then. The opening of verse 6 most likely marks a transition within a literary unit, rather than the introduction of a new unit (cp. v. 11); so verses 1-9 will be treated here as a single piece. The first five verses — like verses 6-9 — could fit the reign of any of the kings before Zedekiah, including Josiah.

22:1-9 This oracle is divided into three parts syntactically, each beginning with **This is what the LORD says** (vv. 1,3,6). The first part

---

[1]Brueggemann, *Jeremiah*, pp. 194, 207-208.
[2]Holladay, *Jeremiah 1*, p. 590; McKane, *Jeremiah*, pp. 522-526.

consists of instructions to Jeremiah to speak in **the palace,** followed by his summons to those in the palace to **Hear the word of the LORD.** In this case, the audience is the Davidic **king,** his **officials** ("servants"), and his **people.** Other passages in Jeremiah indicate that it is the failure of these specific groups of people to obey such a summons that lies at the heart of the nation's problems. The nation's political leaders refuse to hear the LORD (cp. 36:31; 37:2).

The primary appeal (v. 3) is for the royal establishment to uphold the cause of the oppressed. In general terms, this is "to do justice and righteousness." This is a common theme in the Old Testament, occurring at least once in every section.[3] "To do justice and righteousness" is for individuals to correct the wrongs done by one man against another ("justice") and to do what is **right** themselves ("righteousness"). These wrongs were most commonly done by the wealthy and powerful at the expense of their weaker neighbors. Kings and their judicial appointees were particularly held responsible for seeing that the cause of the oppressed weak was defended (Ps 72:1-4,12-14; Isa 9:7; Jer 33:15). The remainder of verse 3 expands on this general principle in terms which would have been well-known to Jeremiah's listeners. The **alien,** the **fatherless,** and the **widow** are the most commonly mentioned victims, as they have no land-owning male to protect them in this patriarchal, agrarian society. Concern for these groups is particularly prominent in the laws of Deuteronomy, where the personal example of the LORD and the experiences of the people provide motivation for "doing justice and righteousness" (Deut 10:17-19; 14:28-29; 24:17-22; 26:12-15; 27:19). Again, it is particularly important for royal personages to carry out these responsibilities (cp. Deut 17:18-20).[4] The judgment upon those who **shed innocent blood** provides an additional element to this traditional picture. It is used especially to condemn the innovations of Manasseh (2 Kgs 21:16; 24:4), probably the practice of child sacrifice (see on Jer 19:4-5).

---

[3]The pairing of "justice and righteousness" occurs in the Pentateuch (Gen 18:19), the Historical Books (2 Sam 8:15; 1 Kgs 10:9; 1 Chr 18:14; 2 Chr 9:8), the Psalms (Ps 33:5; 72:2; 89:14; 97:2; 99:4; 106:3; 119:121), the Wisdom writings (Job 29:14; 35:2; 37:23; Prov 1:3; 2:9; 8:20; 21:3; Eccl 3:16; 5:8), and the Prophets (Isa 1:21,27; 5:7; 9:7; 16:5; 28:17; 32:16; 33:5; 56:1; 59:9,14; Jer 4:2; 9:24; 33:15; Ezek 18:5,19,21,27; 33:14,16,19; 45:9; Hos 2:19; Amos 5:7,24; 6:12; Micah 7:9).

[4]Brueggemann, *Jeremiah,* p. 195.

Verses 4 and 5 lay this responsibility squarely at the feet of the **kings** and **their officials and their people** (cp. v. 2), in ways which are reminiscent of the choice given by Samuel to the people when they first adopted kingship (1 Sam 12:14-15), and reminiscent of the choice offered by the LORD to Solomon regarding his covenant with David (1 Kgs 9:4-9). There are two clearly delineated options. Either obey the LORD's **commands** and succeed, or ignore them and face destruction. The difference here is that the terms of success or destruction are applied strictly to the royal establishment. If they do right, they will continue to serve as kings (v. 4); if they do wrong, **this palace will become a ruin** (v. 5).

The balance of this oracle (vv. 6-9) expands on the warning of verse 5. The language regarding the Davidic Covenant (see 2 Sam 7:8-16) probably explains the necessity to focus more attention on this alternative and its outcome. Read in isolation, some of the talk regarding the LORD's covenant with the house of David could lead one to believe that they held an unconditional claim to the throne, and an unconditional promise of the LORD's protection of Jerusalem. The unfolding of events during the reign of Hezekiah certainly could have supported such beliefs (see on 7:9-15).[5] Therefore, the LORD makes very clear the possibility of destruction. He talks about destruction of one part of the palace to predict the destruction of the whole. The regions of **Gilead** and **Lebanon** were sources of wood, wood that had been used in the building of the palace and the temple in Jerusalem. They probably were some of the most highly prized aspects of the royal buildings (see v. 15; cp. 1 Kgs 7:2-5), yet he says the timbers from those areas will be used for common firewood (see Ps 74:4-8). If he does not regard as salvageable the wood of the palace, he also does not regard its human inhabitants as salvageable. Then, he reminds them of the inherently conditional nature of the Davidic Covenant, by reiterating the words spoken to Solomon when the temple was first built (see Deut 29:24-28; 1 Kgs 9:8-9).[6] They have known for centuries that it was necessary for them to remain faithful to the LORD, but they have **forsaken** him and **have worshiped and served other gods** (cp. Jer 1:16; 2:13,17,19; 5:7,18-19; 9:13-14; 16:10-11; 19:4-5). This is the other side

---

[5]Clements, *Jeremiah*, p. 130.

[6]For an Assyrian parallel to the question-answer form, see Holladay, *Jeremiah 1*, p. 585.

of the coin of disobedience. They disobey by promoting oppression and the worship of foreign gods. This places them in violation of the Mosaic Covenant, and so they should expect to see the curses of that covenant (Deuteronomy 28–30), even on Jerusalem.

22:10-12 This lament for **Shallum** (= Jehoahaz) is relatively straightforward. The account of his three-month reign takes up only a few lines in Kings and Chronicles because Pharaoh Neco captures him and carries him away to Egypt before he is able to do anything of note (2 Kgs 23:31-34; 2 Chr 36:2-4). In this oracle, Josiah is **the dead king** (killed by Neco's troops near Megiddo; 2 Kgs 23:29-30; 2 Chr 35:20-24), and Shallum is **him who is exiled**. Jeremiah says Shallum deserves to be mourned the most, because he will die in exile, not in his homeland. Not to be buried in the land of one's birth added indignity to the death of the deceased.[7] As such, Shallum serves as a warning to the people. Although they might feel "fortunate" still to be alive after various Egyptian or Babylonian attacks, they will come to prefer death (and burial) in their homeland to life (and burial, later) in exile.[8]

22:13-23 Jehoiakim is another king for whom the people **will not mourn** (v. 18), even though he will die in his homeland like his father, Josiah. The oracle concerning him is the lengthiest of this collection, perhaps showing the degree of disobedience on his part. It is broken into two halves by the transitional clause, **Therefore this is what the LORD says about Jehoiakim . . .** (v. 18). The first half (vv. 13-17) issues an accusation of sin against the king in the form of a woe-oracle. The second half (vv. 18-23) pronounces a judgment against him.

The indictment charges Jehoiakim with oppression of the poor and weak. He would appear to be a successful king to the casual observer, so one is surprised to hear Jeremiah pronounce a woe-oracle about him. It comes because of the means by which Jehoiakim has achieved his wealth. He has gotten his wealth and prestige at the expense of his subjects (cp. Isa 5:8-10). He has built **his palace** with the most expensive **cedar**, as a show of wealth and power; but he has also built it **by unrighteousness** and **injustice** (v. 13; contrast to

---

[7] In this regard, one might consider the cases of Jacob (Gen 49:29–50:14) and Joseph (Gen 50:24-25; Exod 13:19; Josh 24:32).

[8] Jeremiah changes his message later, however, when he talks of hope for those in exile and doom for those remaining in Judah (see Jeremiah 24).

vv. 3,15), sending his workers away without pay (cp. 1 Kgs 5:27-28). His father was "a tough act to follow," so Jehoiakim set out to show himself a true king. He "spruced up" the palace, adding new **rooms** and painting them royal **red** (v. 14). He was a "man of vision," but his was a vision built on **dishonest gain**, **shedding innocent blood**, **oppression and extortion** (v. 17). In these ways, he took on only the material trappings of kingship, while ignoring truly kingly character. The basis of that kingly character, exemplified by his father, was to **know** the LORD.

Jeremiah 22:15-16 give the clearest explication of how Jeremiah understands the meaning of "know the LORD" (cp. 2:8; 4:22; 9:3,6; 10:25; 24:7; 31:34). He says that Josiah showed that he "knew" the LORD by "doing justice and righteousness," by standing up for **the poor and needy**.[9] Jehoiakim's actions are the opposite of Josiah's. He might claim that he "knows the LORD," but his actions betray the truth of the matter. The same, sadly, could be said of so many believers since Jeremiah's day. It is this type of misunderstanding on the part of the Pharisees and scribes which leads Jesus to pronounce "woes" upon them (Matt 23:13-39). Concerns about confusing religious zeal with materialism lie behind Paul's words to the rich in 1 Timothy 6:17-18 and James's remarks to the "religious" in James 1:26-27. Like Zedekiah, such people see the LORD as a God of power (to give them wealth), and not a God of holiness (see on 21:1-2).

The judgment pronounced on Jehoiakim falls into two parts. The first (vv. 18-19) laments the absence of a lament for the king at the time of his death. None will turn to his **brother** or **sister** to voice their grief (**Alas**). None will lament the fall of one so recently high up. His burial will be the burial of the lowest creature, thrown out with the trash (cp. 36:30).[10] The second part of the pronouncement

---

[9] See also Exod 5:2; Judg 2:10; 1 Sam 2:12; 3:7; 1 Chr 28:9; Job 24:1; 36:26; Ps 36:10; 87:4; Isa 19:21; 43:10; Dan 11:32; Hos 2:20; 5:4; 6:3; 8:2; 13:4. These passages fill out the biblical understanding of "knowing the LORD;" they do not contradict what Jeremiah says. Several of them use "knowing the LORD" in reference to an acknowledgement of his sovereignty. This is a necessary prerequisite to "doing justice and righteousness," which Jeremiah is talking about here. Those who "know the LORD" acknowledge and submit to his authority, seeking to conform their lives to his ways, which include justice and righteousness. Cp. Brueggemann, *Jeremiah*, pp. 200-201; Thompson, *Jeremiah*, p. 479; Holladay, *Jeremiah 1*, pp. 598-599.

[10] This ignoble end for Jehoiakim is not borne out in the historical record (2 Kgs 24:6). Thompson, *Jeremiah*, p. 480.

of judgment (vv. 20-23) begins and ends with a reference to
Lebanon. The addressee now is Jerusalem ("you[r]" is feminine
here).[11] This part begins with instructions to **cry out** in anguish
toward Lebanon, **Bashan**, and **Abarim**, three corners of Judah's
range of influence (Lebanon to the north, Bashan to the northeast,
Abarim to the southeast). These are Judah's **allies**, who have been
crushed by their common enemy. The people of Jerusalem have a
false sense of security, security most likely based in God (again, see
7:11-15); but they have not **listened** to (= **obeyed**) the one in whom
they profess to trust. So instead of resting secure in his care, they are
being "driven away," **ashamed and disgraced**. **Lebanon** is mentioned a second time at this point, representing the conspicuous
wealth of the capital.[12] It is the **cedar** timbers from Lebanon which
adorn the palace. Jerusalem should remind one of a wealthy queen,
resting peacefully in luxuriant surroundings. Instead, she sits doubled over with **pain** in the face of her inevitable devastation.

22:24-30 Jeremiah's remarks concerning **Jehoiachin** actually
appear to be a combination of two originally separate oracles. The
first is an oracle about Jehoiachin as the LORD's rejected signet ring
(vv. 24-27; cp. Hag 2:23), the second about him as a Davidic king
without an heir (vv. 28-30). The break between the two is clearly
marked by the triple rhetorical question formula used several times
in the book to introduce an oracle (cp. 2:14,31; 8:4-5,19,22).

The first oracle is presented in the form of an oath. The typical
oath formula is, "As the LORD lives" (e.g., 4:2; 5:2; 23:7). Here, it is in
the first person, because the LORD is swearing by himself (cp. Heb
6:13-17). He refers to Jehoiachin[13] as his **signet ring**. This ring would
bear the official seal of its bearer, carrying his authority. He would use
it to stamp a clay seal on a letter or some other object being sent, iden-
tifying the item as his property. Such a ring was closely guarded.[14] But

---

[11]For this reason, many commentators regard these verses as an editorial
addition to the oracles addressing the kings. So Brueggemann, *Jeremiah*,
p. 202; Clements, *Jeremiah*, p. 135; McKane, *Jeremiah*, pp. 539-540.

[12]Brueggemann, *Jeremiah*, pp. 202-203.

[13]This king is designated by three names in the biblical text. Here, he actually is "Coniah" (cp. 37:1; Esth 2:6); elsewhere, either "Jehoiachin" (Jer
52:31; 2 Kgs 24:6,8,12,15; 25:27; 2 Chr 36:8,9; Ezra 1:2) or "Jeconiah" (Jer
24:1; 27:20; 28:4; 29:2; 1 Chr 3:16,17). All come from the same Hebrew
root, meaning "May the LORD endure/establish."

[14]Holladay, *Jeremiah 1*, p. 605.

the LORD swears he will **hand over** this ring to the **Babylonians**, a people whom the people of Jerusalem **fear** (the root here is the same as that in "Magor-missabib," 20:3-4). Just as he has already talked about the ultimately sad fates of Shallum (vv. 10-12) and Jehoiakim (vv. 18-19), he now describes the ultimate fate of Jehoiachin (vv. 26-27). The LORD will **hurl** him, along with his **mother**, into another land. Like Shallum, he **will die** away from his birthplace and suffer the indignity of burial in a foreign land; "he will never return" (vv. 10,11,27).

The second oracle continues some of the themes of the first, this time considering the fate of Jehoiachin in regard to the dynastic promise made to David. This disgraceful fate is an "in-spite-of" fate. In spite of his royal status, his burial will be disgraceful. In spite of the divine promise to David, divine protection will be withdrawn from Jehoiachin. The rhetorical questions ask if Jehoiachin is worth no more than a **pot** (עֶצֶב, '*eṣeb*), not the term used in 19:1,10). The expected answer is No. After all, he is a king, in the line of David. Yet, like a pot, he is to be **hurled out**, thrown away. Moreover, now it is **his children** — the future of the Davidic line — who are to be thrown out with him. This leads to a poignant plea: **O land, land, land, hear the word of the LORD!** The triple address is highly unusual (cp. 7:4), indicating the deep distress felt by the speaker. The initial summons ("hear") is quite common as the introduction to a prophetic oracle (2:4; 5:21; 6:18; 7:2; 10:1; 11:2; 19:3; 21:11; 22:2; 29:20; 31:10; 34:4; 44:24; cp. Isa 1:10; 28:14; Ezek 20:47; 25:3; Hos 5:1; Joel 1:2; Amos 3:1; 4:1; 5:1; Micah 1:2; 3:1; 6:1). It also points to the basic problem of Jeremiah's audience — they have not "heard/listened to/obeyed the word of the LORD." The triple appeal intends to get the attention of an audience that has grown accustomed to ignoring what they are supposed to "hear" from the LORD. The main portion of the oracle (v. 30) reveals the broader implications of this judgment, and why the speaker is so distressed. The exile of Jehoiachin affects the Davidic Covenant. The promised eternal dynasty appears to be coming to an end. They will make no record of children (though he has several; 1 Chr 3:17) who might succeed Jehoiachin **on the throne**. The wording of this pronouncement even contains an altered version of the traditional promise to David. In that promise the LORD had literally stated, "A man to you (David), sitting on the throne of Israel, shall not be cut off" (see 1 Kgs 8:25; cp. Jer 33:17; 1 Kgs 2:4; 9:5). Now he says, "A man, sitting on the throne of David, shall not prosper." Only the verb has changed. The import of this oracle could not have escaped the Davidic kings. Jeremiah was announcing the termination of the divine promise on which their claim to the throne rested. It is no wonder he is regarded by them as a traitor.[15]

---

[15]Brueggemann, *Jeremiah*, pp. 196, 204-205. Subsequent prophecies will show that this is actually hyperbole. The absence of a Davidic king from the throne will be only a temporary situation, as the LORD reaffirms his oath to maintain the dynasty (see 23:5-6; 33:14-26).

JEREMIAH 23

C. THE RIGHTEOUS BRANCH (23:1-8)

This short section consists of three originally separate oracles (vv. 1-4,5-6,7-8). The first and third are in prose, the second is in poetry. The first is another woe-oracle (cp. 22:13), the second and third share the introductory formula, "The days are coming." It is likely that all three come from the reign of Zedekiah (597–586 B.C.), which would explain why they are brought together here.[1] These complete the series of oracles against the kings and their officials.

23:1-4 The initial woe-oracle focuses attention on **the shepherds who tend my people** (cp. Ezekiel 34; Zech 11:4-17). The first half issues an indictment and judgment against them (vv. 1-2) while the second half shifts to a divine promise to reverse the negative impact of these shepherds. The metaphor of the king as shepherd is fairly common in ancient Near Eastern literature.[2] Biblical writers apply the shepherd imagery to David and his descendants (see 2 Sam 5:2; 7:7; 1 Chr 11:2; 17:6; Ps 78:71; Ezek 37:24; cp. Isa 44:28; Micah 5:4; 7:14), and depictions of the LORD as shepherd are part of the broader understanding of the LORD as Divine King (Gen 49:24; Ps 23:1; 28:9; 74:1; 78:52; 79:13; 80:1; 95:7; 100:3; Isa 40:11). Together, these reveal an important aspect of the Israelite understanding of kingship. Like their neighbors, the Israelites conceived of their kings as shepherds, "tending" the people in their care. They also conceived of the LORD as their shepherd, the Chief Shepherd. He was ultimately responsible, and he possessed authority even over those earthly shepherds. This had the effect of limiting the authority of Israel's kings more than in other nations, in the minds of the

---

[1]Holladay, *Jeremiah 1*, pp. 614, 617, 621; Thompson, *Jeremiah*, pp. 486-487; McKane, *Jeremiah*, pp. 560, 566.

[2]There are examples going back at least to the days of Hammurabi, who would have been a contemporary of the biblical patriarchs.

Israelites. The **shepherds** mentioned here would include the king and members of the royal family, first of all, because many administrative posts would have gone to the king's relatives. It would also include other royal appointees, who were entrusted by the king with "caring for" and "tending" the people of Judah (cp. 22:22). The accusation made here is that the shepherds have not been doing their job properly. They have not been "tending" the sheep; they have been **destroying and scattering** the sheep, and **have . . . driven them away and not bestowed care on them** (vv. 1-2).

The LORD then makes some intriguing wordplays regarding this accusation. First, he says he will **bestow punishment** ("bestow care") **on you** (the shepherds). They have not "taken care" of the sheep, so he will "take care" of them (in a punitive sense).[3] He will respond to the "evil of their deeds," deeds which they should have "made good" (cp. 7:3,5). He then shifts the perspective to talk about how he will correct the negative practices of these shepherds. He says he will **gather** the scattered sheep. Surprisingly, these are sheep which he — not they — **have driven** away (v. 3). He is using the term "driven" in two senses here. He has accused the shepherds of "driving" the people to worship other gods, "scattering" them to the high places that dot the countryside (cp. Ezek 34:6). In response, the LORD has "driven" the nation into exile in other lands.[4] But now he will "gather" what he has "scattered," returning them to **their pasture** (the Promised Land of Israel). There they will flourish ("be fruitful and multiply"), because the LORD will bless them as he blessed humanity in the beginning (Gen 1:28) and after the Flood (Gen 8:17; 9:1,7), and as he blessed the patriarchs (Gen 17:6; 35:11; 48:4). Completing this picture, he will appoint new shepherds, **who will tend them** as righteous officials should.

23:5-6 The theme of setting things right continues in the second oracle. There is no specificity about when these things will happen (in Hebrew, there is no article with "days"), only the assurance that they will. This promise concerns the Davidic monarch alone, but his

---

[3]There are several other wordplays in English which approximate the contrasting nuances here. See Thompson, Jeremiah, p. 487; Holladay, *Jeremiah 1*, p. 614. Also, the Hebrew word for "be missing" (v. 4) comes from the same root.

[4]The exile to which the LORD is referring here could be the partial exile of the nation with Jehoiachin in 597 B.C., or in anticipation of the full exile that takes place at the end of Zedekiah's reign (586 B.C.).

role invariably concerns the entire nation. In the mode of a royal birth announcement (cp. Isa 7:14; 11:1-9), the LORD promises the coming of a "New David." Yet what he expects of this king is nothing new (cp. Lev 26:5). His primary characteristic will be righteousness. He will be a **righteous Branch** (cp. 33:15; Zech 3:8; 6:12), he will "do justice and righteousness" (cp. 22:3; 1 Kgs 10:9), and his name will be **The LORD [Is] Our Righteousness**. The emphasis on righteousness strongly hints that this future monarch will represent the antithesis to King Zedekiah. Zedekiah's name means "righteousness of the LORD" or "the LORD is righteousness," yet his rulership does not reflect that name. This oracle declares that some future monarch will live up to this name, that he will truly exemplify the righteousness of the LORD in his kingship. This will yield positive consequences for both **Judah** and **Israel** (v. 6), pointing as well to the future restoration of the united kingdom (cp. Ezek 37:15-28).[5]

One could interpret this as a messianic prophecy, predicting the kingship of Jesus Christ. It is not necessary, however, to insist on that narrow interpretation alone. Certainly Jesus rules his kingdom in righteousness, and in that sense he "fulfills" the words of this oracle. On the other hand, God probably is not thinking solely of Jesus here. These words are general enough to have multiple applications; they simply culminate in the kingship of Jesus. Jesus fits the mold of the ideal king envisioned by ancient Israelites, but he was not expected to be the only Israelite king to exemplify these characteristics.[6]

23:7-8 The third oracle forecasts a New Exodus (cp. 16:4-5). This shows the completion of a cycle begun in Jeremiah 21:1-2, where Zedekiah inquired about the possibility of the LORD performing "wonders" again, as he had in the days of Moses. He now reveals that he has something even greater than the Exodus from **Egypt** in mind. He speaks of a change in the traditional oath pattern among the Israelites. It was typical, when swearing an oath by a deity, to refer to an event or characteristic that best demonstrated the deity's nature and power, as an indication of his ability and willingness to confirm the oath (see 1 Sam 14:39; 2 Sam 4:9; 1 Kgs 1:29; 2:24; 17:1; 18:15; 2 Kgs 3:14; 5:16). For the LORD, one such event had been the Exodus. Now he plans to do something even greater — return his

---

[5]Holladay, *Jeremiah 1*, p. 619.
[6]Ibid., pp. 619-620; Thompson, *Jeremiah*, p. 491; Brueggemann, *Jeremiah*, p. 207.

people from exile to their Promised Land. This will result in the alteration to the traditional Israelite oath, as it is stated here.

D. LYING PROPHETS (23:9-32)

The inspired compiler of the book follows the preceding oracles regarding kings with a series of oracles "concerning the prophets" (23:9a). The division of this block (23:9-40) into two sections by the NIV editors is strictly arbitrary. These two sections contain a total of four oracles regarding prophets who prophesy falsely. The first two are composed in poetry, the latter two in prose. The first (23:9-15) accuses "prophet and priest" (v. 11), then royal prophets (vv. 13-14) of promoting "adultery" and "wickedness" among the people; the second (23:16-24) refutes the message of "peace" proclaimed by certain false prophets; the third (23:25-32) rebukes prophets who falsely claim to have received divine revelation through dreams; the fourth (23:33-40) rebukes those who falsely claim to have received an "oracle of the LORD."

23:9-15 One could easily argue to divide this oracle into two or even three smaller units. Jeremiah expresses his grief over the damage done by false prophets in the opening lines (v. 9),[7] then the LORD gives two accusations (vv. 10-11,13-14), each followed by a pronouncement of judgment (vv. 12,15). Each pronouncement is introduced by **Therefore**. One could read Jeremiah's words of grief as an introduction to the oracle which immediately follows; but they could also be an independent piece, functioning in their present position as an introduction to the entire block of oracles concerning false prophets. Similarly, one could read each accusation-judgment sequence (vv. 10-12 and 13-15) as a separate oracle.[8] On the other hand, the themes of "adultery" (vv. 10,14) and "ungodliness" (vv. 11,15) link verses 13-15 back to verses 10-12. This points to a complementarity between the two accusation-judgment sequences, consequently suggesting the unity of verses (9)10-15. Also, the whole passage echoes the thoughts

---

[7] The quotation marks in the NIV reflect an interpretation which has Jeremiah speaking through verse 10. The reading in Hebrew suggests, however, that the transition from the words of Jeremiah to the words of the LORD occurs between verses 9 and 10. Holladay, *Jeremiah 1*, p. 625; Thompson, *Jeremiah*, pp. 493-494; McKane, *Jeremiah*, p. 569.

[8] Holladay, *Jeremiah 1*, pp. 624-625.

of Deuteronomy 29:19-28, and the LORD might be alluding to that passage in these remarks.

Jeremiah is staggered by the prophecies he proclaims (v. 9). There is no sense of self-righteousness or satisfaction over the fate of his opponents. He is not happy to see his fellow-prophets suffer, even though they have made him suffer and he has called on the LORD to seek vengeance on them. The grief he feels knocks him to his knees. When the LORD asserts his holiness, a human cannot but **tremble**.

The LORD enters an accusation of adultery (v. 10), but the identity of the accused and the nature of the adultery are momentarily delayed. The first piece of evidence is **the curse** that the sin yields on the land in the form of a drought. This echoes the remarks regarding "curses" in Deuteronomy 29:20. In that context, the LORD warns that the land will become "a burning waste of salt and sulfur— nothing planted, nothing sprouting, no vegetation growing–. . . like the destruction of Sodom and Gomorrah" (Deut 29:23; cp. v. 14, below) if the people are guilty of turning to other gods. The designation of idolatry as adultery is well-established in Jeremiah (see 3:8-9; 5:7; 9:2; 13:27; cp. Hos 2:2; 7:4), so it is most likely that idolatry is what he has in mind when he accuses the people of adultery here. The land has been "emptied" (of vegetation) because it is **full (of adulterers)**.

The additional element here is the highlighting of the influence of **prophet and priest**[9] in promoting idolatry in the land (v. 10c-11; cp. 5:30-31). They are **godless** (חָנְפוּ, *ḥānᵉphû*); their **course** is **evil** (רָעָה, *rāʿāh*), and they use their **power** over worship in the **temple** to do **wickedness** ("evil," *rāʿāh*) even there (cp. 7:8-15). These charges are directly countered in the judgment stated in verse 12. The LORD will make the "course" of these religious leaders flow into a **path** (cp. 12:1) that is **slippery**. He will respond to the "evil" (*rāʿāh*) of which he has twice accused them by bringing his own **disaster** (*rāʿāh*) upon them. This will be an extended calamity: **the year they are punished** ("taken care of;" see 23:2).

The second half of the oracle (vv. 13-15) clarifies these remarks. There is a string of parallelisms here between the accusation against

---

[9]The word "prophets" in verse 10 is not in the Hebrew text, only an indefinite "they." By recognizing that verse 10 is part of the LORD's remarks (and not Jeremiah's), we see that "they" are identified in the next verse, as "prophet and priest" (but see v. 15).

Samaria (v. 13) and the accusation against Jerusalem (v. 14ab). As seen in other passages (like 3:6-13; 7:8-15), there was a misguided confidence held by the people of Jerusalem, who thought the chosen status of Jerusalem gave it unconditional protection. The prophecies of Jeremiah show that the people have made more of these distinctions than was justified. He talks of what he **saw/has seen** . . . **among the prophets** of both capitals. One is **repulsive**, the other **horrible**; the two are equally sinful. One involves **prophesying by Baal**, the other is called **adultery**; these are two designations for the same offense (cp. Hos 4:12-14). One group **led astray** the northern tribes, the other has encouraged none in the south to **turn from his wickedness**; either way, their followers are on the wrong path (cp. 18:11). In the concluding line of verse 14, he summarizes this accusation by comparing the two capitals to **Sodom** and **Gomorrah** (cp. Deut 29:23; Isa 1:9-10). The fate of such cities is obvious. The pronouncement of judgment which follows focuses attention on the immediate problem: **the prophets of Jerusalem**. Those in Samaria were "taken care of" long ago. The fate that befell them can now be expected by those in Jerusalem. The LORD then reuses an earlier statement of judgment for idolatry, saying the people will **eat bitter food and drink poisoned water** (9:15); but he places the blame for the people's **ungodliness** (חֲנֻפָּה, *ḥănuppāh*) directly on the shoulders of the prophets.

23:16-24 In this passage Jeremiah advises the people to ignore the oracles proclaimed by the false prophets. Theirs is a message of peace (cp. 4:10; 6:14; 8:11) and freedom from injury (cp. 4:6; 5:12; 11:11) in direct contradiction to the message Jeremiah has been proclaiming. But Jeremiah's message is not simply a "They said/I said" argument. In the middle of this passage (v. 21), the LORD himself enters into the debate, corroborating Jeremiah's message.[10]

Jeremiah characterizes the message of the opposing prophets as **false hopes** ("vanities," as in Ecclesiastes). Those hopes are probably

---

[10]Some go so far as to separate verses 16-20 and 21-24, because of the shift in speaker (from Jeremiah to the LORD; so Holladay, *Jeremiah 1*, pp. 633-634). There are strong verbal links between the two parts, however, and verses 21-24 seem to presuppose information which one finds only in verses 16-20 (e.g., "these prophets"). It is also possible that verses 23-24 serve to introduce verses 25-32, rather than concluding these verses (so Thompson, *Jeremiah*, p. 500; Clements, *Jeremiah*, p. 142; Brueggemann, *Jeremiah*, p. 213; Nicholson, *Jeremiah 1-25*, pp. 198-200).

derived from the unfounded belief that the LORD would always protect his people, no matter what their behavior (cp. 21:2). But their
words are empty, with no more substance than the air they use to
voice them. Like the true prophets of the Bible, they **speak visions**
(see Isa 1:1; Obad 1:1; Nahum 1:1), but their visions originate in
their own "hearts" (cp. 12:2), **not from the mouth of the LORD**
(v. 16). By way of contrast, the LORD is about to express **the purposes of his heart** in the form of a **storm** or **whirlwind** of anger
(vv. 19-20). Jeremiah extends this antithetical use of "heart" in his
depiction of the prophets' receptive hearers as those who **follow the
stubbornness of their hearts** (v. 17; cp. 3:17; 7:24; 9:14; 11:8; 13:10;
16:12; 18:12). One set of evil hearts is listening to another, rather
than seeking to know the heart of the LORD.

But how is one to know if a prophet's message is true or false?
The answer given here is simple, yet one that cannot be verified. A
true prophet (like Jeremiah) is one who has actually **stood in the
council of the LORD** (vv. 18,22). This parallels the typical royal
courts of the ancient Near East. A king's "council" consisted of the
king and his advisors, something like a president's cabinet in
America today. The king would sit on his throne at the head of a
table, with his advisors seated on either side of the table before him.
They would meet together to discuss various matters in need of
attention, and for each matter the king would pronounce the final
decision. During their discussion, messengers ("servants") would
stand away from the table, listening to the discussion and occasionally providing pertinent information. When the king pronounced a
final decision, he would commission one or more of the attending
messengers to take the decision and deliver it to those who needed
to hear it. In similar fashion, God was thought to discuss matters
with his angels, while prophets listened in. Once a decision was
reached, God would commission a prophet to take the message to
whatever people needed to hear it. (An excellent example of this
appears in the story of Micaiah, 1 Kgs 22:19-23; cp. Isa 6:1-8.)
Jeremiah accuses these false prophets of making up their own message, rather than getting it from the LORD. None of them has actually stood in the LORD's council, so they are ignorant of his anger
and of his plans to punish his people.

The LORD corroborates Jeremiah's accusation in verses 21-22.
Those other prophets did not stand in his council to hear what he
said, and so he **did not send** them (cp. 1:7) with the **message** they

have been proclaiming. If they had been privy to the LORD's council as Jeremiah had been, they would have opposed the behavior of the people, calling on them to repent; instead, they have been reassuring the people that the LORD will protect them. They have not "turned" the people from their sins (v. 22), which explains why the LORD will not "turn" from his anger (v. 20). The LORD closes his remarks with a thinly-veiled warning to these false prophets, that they especially cannot hide (cp. Psalm 139) from the storm of wrath he is bringing against his people. In this he contrasts himself to those prophets. They claim to have seen visions, but what they actually "saw" were products of their own imaginations. He, on the other hand, has actually "seen" what they have been doing, and will act accordingly.

23:25-32 The message of these verses is very similar to the ones preceding. The false **prophets** are again rebuked for **prophesy**ing from their own "hearts" (**minds**; v. 26), rather than proclaiming a message from the LORD. The latter would expose the sinfulness of the people, rather than comforting them (vv. 29,32; cp. 23:22). Their portrayal of the LORD is out of balance. He is purely a God of mercy and forgiveness. This is contrary to the LORD's **name**, which denotes a coupling of mercy with punishment for sin (see Exod 34:5-7).[11] They are causing people to **forget** that name by talking about the LORD's merciful protection only. They provide "proof" of the truthfulness of their lies by repeating each other's words.[12] The assumption is that two or three "witnesses" who agree must be true. A prophet is supposed to be the "mouth" of God (Exod 4:14-16; 7:1), but they **wag their own tongues** (v. 31). They claim to be speaking in the name of the LORD (v. 31), yet he actually did not **send** them (v. 32).

The primary difference between these verses and those immediately preceding is the medium by which the prophets receive divine messages. The preceding verses assume the medium of a "vision," while this assumes a **dream** (cp. Deut 13:1-5). The formative difference between the two probably is negligible. The truly distinguishing characteristic is the source of each. Just as one speaking visions (v. 16) was speaking from his own heart rather than God's, the dreamer is reporting *his* **dream** rather than a **word** spoken from the LORD. The contrast (v. 28) between **straw** and **grain** refers to the

---

[11]Thompson, *Jeremiah*, p. 501.
[12]Holladay, *Jeremiah 1*, p. 645.

difference between false prophecy and true prophecy, not between different modes of prophecy; either is legitimate (or illegitimate), depending on its source. The **fire** and **hammer** (v. 29) are metaphors for ways in which the LORD destroys a worthless oracle. The designation of these false prophecies as **lies** — in contrast to the "truth" (v. 28, **faithfully**) of the LORD's word — reminds one of Jeremiah 8:5,8; the lack of **benefit** to the hearers is reminiscent of Jeremiah's previous remarks about Baal-worship (2:8).

E. FALSE ORACLES AND FALSE PROPHETS (23:33-40)

23:33-40 This prophecy is tightly constructed around a series of conjunctive particles. Verse 33 begins with the indefinite particle, וְכִי ($w^ek\hat{i}$, "when, if"). This is complemented with וְאִם ($w^e\hat{i}m$, "although, and if") at the beginning of verse 38. This sequence is common in Israelite case law. The first particle introduces a main law while the second introduces a subordinate case (e.g., Deut 19:1,8). This construction suggests two complementary parts to these verses (23:33-37 + 38-40). The first part can be further subdivided into two subparts, as the near-repetition of verse 35 in verse 37 indicates cohesion to those verses. Each verse begins with the particle, "thus" (כֹּה, $k\bar{o}h$), and the two contain a pair of questions which only slightly vary from one another. The result reveals the following structure to the passage:

(a) Verses 33-34 — a dual pronouncement of judgment (**I will forsake . . . and I will punish . . .**) on those who claim to be uttering divine oracles;

(b) Verses 35-37 — the transformation of a mutual inquiry among the other prophets (**"What has the LORD answered?"**) into an indictment against them; and,

(c) Verses 38-40 — a direct accusation against those wrongfully claiming to utter divine oracles, leading into another dual pronouncement of judgment (**I will forget you and cast you out. . . . I will bring upon you everlasting disgrace . . .**).

There is a significant translation problem in these verses, which the NIV editors reveal in part by mentioning alternative translations in the footnotes. The focus of the LORD's remarks concerns claims and questions regarding **the oracle of the LORD**. There is some uncertainty about the translation of this phrase, though. The Hebrew root of "oracle" (מַשָּׂא, *maśśā'*) is נָשָׂא (*nāśā'*), meaning "to lift, carry." The noun form most often means "burden, tribute" (see Jer 17:21-22), but it can also refer to a message "lifted up" for people to hear, thus an "oracle" (see Isa 13:1; 15:1; 17:1; 19:1). The latter meaning is the one adopted in the NIV, but other translations adopt "burden" (for example, the RSV), emphasizing the idea that a proclamation from the LORD is a "burden" which only a "strong" prophet can carry. The fact that the LORD specifically refers to prophets and priests in this context makes the "oracle" nuance more obvious here, but the underlying nuance of "burden" must not be ignored.[13]

Other wordplays, syntactical abnormalities, and uncertain readings add to the complexity of this passage. The key syntactical problem comes in the second half of verse 33. The LORD is giving Jeremiah instructions about how to respond to a query from the people. The NIV gives a second question as the response (**"What oracle?"**) but this cannot be right. The Hebrew text, as it currently stands, has the direct-object marker (אֵת, *'eth*) preceding this question. This would imply that the question itself is the direct object of **say (to them)**, but such a construction is unprecedented. The more logical solution is to recognize that this awkward clause arose when a copyist incorrectly divided the words in this clause.[14] The correct word divisions are reflected in the LXX and Vulgate translations. They reveal that the earlier Hebrew reading was אַתֶּם הַמַּשָּׂא (*'attem hammaśśā'*; "you are the oracle"), rather than אֶת־מַה־מַשָּׂא (*'eth-mah-maśśā'*; "What oracle?"). The clearest explanation for such a statement comes in verse 39, where another Hebrew wordplay emerges. All through this passage, the LORD talks about "the oracle of the LORD." The root of "oracle" is the verb, *nāśā'* ("to lift up"). In verse 39, the LORD declares that he will **forget** the people. The root of this word is נָשָׁה (*nāśāh*), which is almost indistinguishable from the verb for "lift up," which lies at the root of "oracle." The people are asking, "What is the oracle of the LORD?" The answer is, "You are the oracle" (מַשָּׂא, *maśśā'*), because the LORD is going to "forget (*nāśāh*)

---

[13]This intimates the "heavy" responsibility one assumes when one serves as a spokesman for the LORD. For a fuller discussion of this, see W. McKane, "מַשָּׂא in Jeremiah 23,33-40," in *Prophecy: Essays Presented to Georg Fohrer on His Sixty-Fifth Birthday*, ed. John A. Emerton, BZAW 150 (Berlin: Walter de Gruyter, 1988), pp. 35-54.

[14]The origin of the confusion is easy to discern, as the same sequence of consonants occurs in the preceding clause.

you and cast you out." The link between verses 33 and 39 is confirmed by the repetition of the phrase, אֶתְכֶם נָטַשְׁתִּי (*nāṭaštî 'ethkem*; translated **I will forsake you**, in v. 33, and **I will cast you out**, in v. 39).[15] Thus, this passage turns a question of the people into its own pronouncement of judgment. The remainder of the passage merely expands on this pronouncement.

If one follows the references to "oracle (of the LORD)" through the entire passage, a relatively clear picture emerges. The initial question of the people (v. 33) is directed toward Jeremiah: **"What is the oracle of the LORD?"** They ask him because they believe the LORD really speaks through him, or because they plan to use his own words against them. Those asking the question turn out to be the answer to that question; they themselves are **the oracle**. That "oracle" is that he will **forsake** (נָטַשׁ, *nāṭaš*) them. The focus then shifts to the other prophets (v. 34), who falsely claim to speak the LORD's oracles. The LORD promises to **punish** ("take care of") the one who so misuses his name. In this, he reaches back to 23:1-4 and makes use of the language of judgment employed there. Thus, there is a verbal connection between the final passage regarding the kings and the final passage regarding false prophets. The LORD then shifts the scene slightly (vv. 35-37), exposing their noninspired prophetic function by quoting their own words. These false prophets ask each other what the LORD has said (**"What is the LORD's answer?"**), thereby exposing the fact that they themselves have not had the LORD's words revealed to them. What should be **the oracle of the LORD** actually turns out to be a man's own words. He forbids them to **mention** ("cause to remember") **the oracle of the LORD**, because they actually **distort the words of the living God**. This evokes Jeremiah's question, **"What is the LORD's answer to you?"** (v. 37) The additional "to you" suggests that Jeremiah is confident that the LORD has made known to him an "oracle of the LORD," but he does not see the same reason for confidence in these other prophets.

The presumptuous misuse of the name of the LORD leads to the direct accusation and indictment of verses 38-40. The false prophets preface their remarks with the claim, **"This is the oracle of the**

---

[15]The primary sense of this verb is "forsake, abandon." Some interpret this with a derived nuance of "toss aside," and therefore read "burden" instead of "oracle." Still, the "burden" being spoken of is understood to be a message ("oracle") from the LORD. See Thompson, *Jeremiah*, pp. 503-505.

LORD," even though the one thing the LORD did reveal to them was that they must not make such a claim. The LORD then uses a word-play on the root of "oracle" (*nāśā'* and *nāśāh*) to usher in a final pronouncement of judgment (vv. 39-40). He repeats his threat to **cast out** (*nāṭaš*; see v. 33) his people; he then reverses their message. Instead of an everlasting kingdom and people, now they will have **everlasting disgrace—everlasting shame**. The "oracle" they proclaim will not be remembered (see on v. 36); instead, their "shame" will be.

JEREMIAH 24

F. TWO BASKETS OF FIGS (24:1-10)

This brief "vision oracle"[1] provides classic examples of Jeremianic terminology, while providing some valuable insights into the mood in Jerusalem during the reign of Zedekiah. It follows a simple outline, similar to the oracle regarding the potter and clay (18:1-10; cp. 1:11-14). There is a brief description of what Jeremiah "saw" (vv. 1-3), then a transition to oracle (v. 4) introduces an exposition of the positive (vv. 5-7) and negative (v. 8-10) implications of what Jeremiah sees.

The editor reveals that this event takes place in the reign of Zedekiah, probably earlier rather than later (c. 597-594 B.C.).[2] Early in the year 597 B.C., King Jehoiachin (here, "Jeconiah") and some 10,000 royal administrators and workers were exiled to Babylon, after only three short months on the throne. The Babylonians placed his uncle, Zedekiah, on the throne in place of Jehoiachin (2 Kgs 24:8-17). Jeremiah has been prophesying for some time that the LORD would send an "enemy from the north" to punish Jerusalem for her sins, and now it has happened. One might expect this to cause those left behind to change their ways, as Jeremiah had been calling on them to do; but this was not to be the case. Zedekiah and his advisors view the exile of Jehoiachin as the fulfillment — the complete fulfillment — of the LORD's warnings through Jeremiah. They conclude that the LORD has now punished the guilty parties, leaving behind those favored by him, in possession of a city which enjoys divine protection (see Ezek 11:14-15). This oracle serves to contradict that unfounded attitude of confidence. It is an early

---

[1]The designation "vision" is used rather broadly here. This is not a vision in the sense of something seen that is not physically present; rather, it is "seeing" a deeper significance in some common item or everyday event (but see Holladay, *Jeremiah 1*, pp. 656-657; Clements, *Jeremiah*, p. 145).

[2]For discussions of authenticity, see Holladay, *Jeremiah 1*, pp. 656-657.

example of Jeremiah advising the people left behind to surrender to the Babylonians (cp. 21:9; 38:2,17).

24:1-10 What Jeremiah sees are **two baskets of figs**, sitting **in front of the temple** (vv. 2-3). The figs in one basket look delicious, the others are completely rotten. There is no explanation for why they are there, and there is no significance to the fact they are in front of the temple. The focus is on the baskets of figs. One basket represents Jerusalem, the other represents Babylon; the figs are the people of Judah who live in those cities. Zedekiah and those with him in Jerusalem would naturally assume that they are the "good" figs, while Jehoiachin and those with him in Babylon are the "bad" figs. Jeremiah sees it differently.[3]

The LORD talks first about the **good figs**. These are the people already in Babylon. He does not refer to them as "good" in a moral sense.[4] He has not separated out those in Judah who are righteous and rewarded them by removing them from danger. He speaks of them as "good" because they will receive "good" from him. They represent the future for the LORD's people, not because they are righteous, but because the LORD plans to work through them to create a new and more faithful people. He has not forsaken them, even though they have forsaken him (16:11); he has **sent** them **away** to Babylon, showing his control over their fate there. Now he promises he will protect them there, in order to inspire them to love him. Surprisingly, his promises are to those not currently living in "the land of promise."[5] Nevertheless, as before, their righteousness will come as a response to his prior blessing. His actions on their behalf will teach them to believe in him and obey him, just as the miraculous deliverance from Egypt produced those results in their ancestors (see Exod 14:31; 19:3-6; Josh 24:2-15; Ps 105:42-45).

The language of restoration (v. 6) reverberates with themes and language found elsewhere in Jeremiah. At his call the LORD told Jeremiah he would "uproot and tear down, destroy and overthrow, build and plant" (1:10; cp. 18:7,9). The vast majority of his messages to the people have heralded coming destruction. It would be logical for someone to conclude that a king and his subjects who have been exiled to Babylon are recipients of destruction, such as Jeremiah has

---

[3]Brueggemann, *Jeremiah*, p. 217.
[4]Contra Brueggemann, *Jeremiah*, p. 218.
[5]Clements, *Jeremiah*, pp. 146-147.

been predicting. But the LORD now turns their thinking on its head, as he declares Jehoiachin and his subjects to be the recipients of his favor, as he talks of (re)construction through them. Them he will **build**; them he will **plant**. They — not Zedekiah and his officials — will stand strong against opposing forces; they will grow and flourish in their land. And the people can trust in these words of reconstruction, because they have seen how Jeremiah's previous words of destruction have been proved true.

The language of restoration also has roots that extend back to Moses (v. 7). There is a threefold statement here about genuine faith. The first and third emphasize the importance of "heart," while the second makes its home in the Israelite understanding of marriage. The expression, **give them a heart to know me, that I am the LORD**, is unique (cp. 31:34; 32:39), but it is merely an expansion of a common expression that originates in the story of the Exodus. There, the LORD describes the significance of several of the plagues by saying, "By this they/you will know that I am the LORD" (Exod 7:5,17; 8:22; 9:29; 14:4,18). Through the plagues the people came to know the power and glory of the LORD, that he was worthy of their ultimate respect and gratitude. Knowledge is something held in one's heart, in the thinking of the ancient Near East; so, to have a heart that "knows the LORD" is to recognize his sovereignty in the acts he performs and then submit to his will. This "knowledge" was held by Josiah (22:15-16), but somehow it had been lost by the general population and other kings (see 2:8; 4:22; 9:3,6). Through the acts he would perform to restore them to their land, the LORD will once again gain the respect and obedience he deserved from his people (cp. Ezek. 15:7; 16:62; 20:42,44; 28:26; 34:27; 37:13,28; 38:23; 39:28; Hos 6:3; 8:2; 13:4). This restoration will culminate in a new declaration of the original "wedding vows" made between the LORD and his people in the days of Moses (Deut 26:16-19; Hos 1:9-10; 2:23; Jer 7:23; 11:4; 30:22; 31:1,33; 32:38). The people will be faithful to him alone; **they will return to me with all their heart** (cp. Deut 30:10; 1 Kgs 8:48; 2 Kgs 23:25). In this, the reader must see the reversal of Jeremiah's prophecy in 3:6-10. He points to the "divorce" he had given to the northern kingdom for their failure to return to him, and he hints at a similar judgment for the southern kingdom for its "half-hearted" repentance (3:10). He looks forward here to a day when repentance will be "wholehearted" (cp. 29:13), when the people will finally be faithful to the LORD as he has always wanted.

The pronouncement of exile and destruction against Zedekiah and those with him (24:8-10) forms a nice balance to the preceding pronouncement of restoration and reconstruction. The **figs** in the basket of Jerusalem are **poor** (*rā'āh*, "bad"; cp. "disaster" in 18:8). Again, this is not to be taken in a moral sense. They are the recipients of **bad**, but they are not morally worse than those who have already been exiled. All of these "figs" have been "bad" in the eyes of the LORD; some are simply more "fortunate" than others in how the LORD will use them to achieve his ultimate will with his people. The difficult aspect of this for them to accept is that the only "safe" place is in Babylon, the land of their enemies. They expect **Jerusalem** to be safe (based on past experience), and if not there, perhaps **Egypt**. But neither of those will escape the wrath of the LORD in this instance (see 42:13-18).

To emphasize the certainty of destruction, Jeremiah piles on the descriptors of dismay and humiliation (vv. 9-10).[6] First he lists three pairs of "curses" to describe the fate of the people (**abhorrent/ offense, reproach/byword, ridicule/cursing**; cp. 29:18; 42:18; 44:8,12; cp. Deut 28:25,37; 1 Kgs 9:7), curses which will come on them **wherever I banish them**. The sobering effects of these terms are furthered by another recitation of the typical Jeremianic triad of destruction (**sword, famine and plague**; cp. 14:12), fates which will come on them **until they are destroyed from the land.**

---

[6]Holladay, *Jeremiah 1*, pp. 659-660.

JEREMIAH 25

G. SEVENTY YEARS OF CAPTIVITY (25:1-14)

This passage has been pivotal in studies of the production of this prophetic book. The prophecy in it is dated to the reign of Jehoiakim, and it is similar to the Temple Sermon (7:1-15) in its central message and themes. However, the promise of an eventual return from exile and the prediction of Babylon's own humiliation (vv. 12-14) seem premature in comparison with other prophecies of Jeremiah. The third-person reference to Jeremiah in verse 13 adds to the impression that the book's editor, Baruch, has penned some of these lines, prompting many scholars to conclude that an originally negative oracle by Jeremiah has been supplemented with later positive elements.[1] The first eleven verses fit well the fourth year of Jehoiakim's reign (605 B.C.), but the mention of the humiliation of Babylon as something already described by Jeremiah and written down (vv. 12-14) fits better the reign of Zedekiah (see 27:7; 29:10; 51:59-60). Perhaps the references to "seventy years" in verses 11 and 12 prompted Baruch to place these two oracles side by side. We will examine the passage here as a bringing together of prophecies originally spoken on two separate occasions.

25:1-11 The first eleven verses fall into three main parts. The narrative introduction (vv. 1-2) gives the setting for the words to follow. Jeremiah brings the typical charges of apostasy and rebellion against the people of Jerusalem (vv. 3-7), and he follows those charges with a pronouncement of divine judgment at the hands of the Babylonians (vv. 8-11).

---

[1]Further complicating matters is the evidence of the LXX. The reference to Jeremiah's oracles "against all the nations" (v. 13) is followed by those oracles (Jeremiah 46–51) in the LXX. There is no consensus among Jeremiah scholars as to which arrangement is the more original. See Holladay, *Jeremiah 2*, pp. 5, 23-24.

The **fourth year of Jehoiakim** was a pivotal one in Jeremiah's career. The same date is the setting for the dictating of Jeremiah's first scroll to Baruch (36:1-4). There is a strong sense that it marks the culmination of a major phase in the career of Jeremiah, and in the history of Jerusalem.[2] Jeremiah has been warning them for many years that the LORD would bring destruction on them for their idolatry and other sins; in this year, the people get their first real taste of what Jeremiah has been forecasting for them. After this, there should be no reason to doubt the veracity of his words.

Jeremiah's message is very simple: The LORD sent him to warn the people, and the people **have not listened**. They have not listened to Jeremiah (v. 3), they **have not listened** to other **prophets** the LORD sent (v. 5); therefore, they have not listened to the LORD (v. 7; cp. 7:24-26; 11:8; 13:11; 29:19; 35:15; 37:2; 44:4; 2 Kgs 17:13-14). The message attributed to other true prophets (vv. 5-6) is very similar to Jeremiah's message in his Temple Sermon (also see Deut 8:2; 13:10). They have called on the people to **turn** (cp. 3:14,22; 4:1) from their **evil ways**, if they wish to **stay in the land** promised to them. The people have been assuming that the promise of land is unconditional, and so they have felt free to break God's laws, even those "at the top of the list" — the laws against the **worship** of **other gods**. Jeremiah and these other prophets remind the people that the realization of those divine promises is conditioned on their positive response, as stated in the laws of Moses. Their prophetic warnings are nothing more than a call to restore their original relationship with the LORD, a relationship in which they enjoy his promised blessings. The failure of the people to heed these warnings results, in essence, in self-inflicted hurt (v. 7).

The LORD had previously threatened to punish his people with "disaster from the north" (1:14; 4:6; 6:1), but he had not explicitly identified who that northern enemy would be — until now. Now that the Babylonians are actually approaching Jerusalem, the LORD clarifies what he has been intimating for twenty-three years. The people could have averted this, if they had taken to heart his previous threats. But now, **because you have not listened to my words**, he says, the northern enemy is coming. A foreign king (**Nebuchadnez-**

---

[2] Some have equated an early version of Jeremiah 1–25 with that first scroll. The LXX inserts the oracles against other nations after verse 14, strengthening the sense that this is the end of a major portion of the book.

zar) will function as the LORD's **servant** to carry out his decrees. Such a bold claim "must have been galling to the Judeans,"[3] who prided themselves in being the chosen people of the LORD. They have come to expect the LORD to bring them honor and glory, but the results of his present actions will be humiliation and a loss of life's everyday pleasures. Rather than being a people that is admired and emulated, they will become **an object of horror and scorn**. No one will want to be like them. The cozy sights and sounds of "home" — a newlywed couple full of hopes for the future; the making of food and a light in the window, inviting in guests — will vanish from the land. Instead, it will become as uninviting as the desert (cp. 12:11-12). This time of desolation will be long, lasting **seventy years**. This number could be taken literally, as a round figure (the first returnees from exile came to Jerusalem sixty-seven years after this prophecy), or it could be taken more figuratively, as a reference to something most adults would never live to see (in contrast to the predictions of other prophets; see 28:3).[4]

25:12-14 This dark reference to seventy years of desolation is now turned into a message of hope. The **seventy years** will eventually be completed, and then the LORD will turn his attention to punishing Babylon (cp. 27:7). He will **punish** ("take care of"; see 23:2,34) **Babylon** as he has punished Judah. The **Babylonians** believe they are in control of their fate; but these lines assert that, because Nebuchadnezzar is the LORD's servant, the LORD determines the extent of his success (cp. Isa 10:5-23). The Babylonians will suffer the same fate as they have inflicted on other **nations** (v. 14). The LORD refers to a fuller delineation of Babylon's offenses and the punishment that will follow. These prophecies are recorded in Jeremiah 50–51. Again, the fact that they are mentioned here as not only spoken, but **written in this book**, indicates the relatively late date of these lines.

H. THE CUP OF GOD'S WRATH (25:15-38)

The remainder of this chapter reveals that Judah's humiliation is part of a larger plan, a plan to punish many nations for their sinful

---

[3]Brueggemann, *Jeremiah*, p. 221.
[4]Thompson, *Jeremiah*, pp. 513-514; McKane, *Jeremiah*, pp. 627-628.

practices. This basic message is developed using two primary metaphors. One is described in prose, the next in poetry. The first is the metaphor of drunkenness. The sinful nations will become drunk with the suffering they will endure, and so they will stumble and fall to the ground (vv. 15-29). This metaphor becomes a common one for referring to the level of suffering endured by the people at the hands of the Babylonians (see Lam 4:21; Ps 75:8; Isa 51:17; Ezek 23:32-34; Hab 2:16; Rev 14:10).[5] The second metaphor depicts the LORD as a lion stalking his prey, spreading disaster wherever he goes (vv. 30-38). This metaphor he probably inherited from earlier prophets (see Hos 5:14; 11:10; 13:7; Amos 3:8).

25:15-29 The development of the metaphor of the **cup** is relatively straightforward. The LORD is announcing his intention to intoxicate many lands with war (vv. 15-16). One initially takes such a drink because of the joy it is expected to bring; but then it turns into something that humiliates. In similar fashion, these **nations** enter into military conflict with Babylon in hopes of gaining glory and honor for themselves, but they are humiliated in the end.

Following this general pronouncement, Jeremiah gives a list of the many nations the Babylonians are destined to conquer (vv. 17-26). This list begins with **Judah**, describing the destruction of God's people in typical terms. This must have been especially difficult for the people to accept, not just because the LORD is punishing them, but because they are placed at the head of a list of "the nations" (= "the Gentiles"). One other surprising element in this is the final phrase of verse 18: **as they are today**. The temporal perspective here is that Jerusalem has already been laid waste. This suggests a date during the exile, but that would seem to be contrary to the impending nature of the destruction described in later verses (see v. 29). Perhaps this one clause intends to update the prophecy, after the destruction of Jerusalem. The list that follows (vv. 17-26) points to the vastness of the Babylonian Empire. It includes **Egypt** (which was beaten but not actually conquered by Babylon), the peoples surrounding Judah (Phoenicians, **Philistines**, Moabites, Edomites, etc.), the Arab tribes to the south, the Elamites and Medes to the north and east, and other kingdoms to **the north**. The final victim is

---

[5]Some suggest an origin in the bitter water ordeal of Num 5:11-31. Thompson, *Jeremiah*, p. 516; W. McKane, "Poison, Trial by Ordeal and the Cup of Wrath," *VT* 30 (1980): 474-492.

Babylon itself, mentioned in the form of the cryptogram, **Sheshach** (like "the land of Magog" in Ezek 38:2; cp. Jer 50:39,41,57).[6]

After this long aside, the main train of thought resumes in verse 27 (the repetition in v. 27 of a clause from v. 16 — **because of the sword I will send among them** — indicates this resumption). The possibility is raised here that some nations will try to avoid this destruction, perhaps by surrendering to the Babylonians without a fight. While this had been a possibility at an earlier stage (see 26:2-3), the LORD now rules it out completely. All nations must **drink** of **the cup** he has prepared. If the LORD's chosen people (**the city that bears my Name**; v. 29) cannot escape his wrath, then no other nation can expect to escape (see 1:5,10; chaps. 46–51). The LORD's anger burns against all sin, not just against his people when they sin. The sin and resultant suffering of his people simply is more distressing. They have enjoyed a closer relationship with God, so they should act differently than others. When they do not, it is all the more noticeable.

25:30-38 The development of the second metaphor (Yahweh as a roaring lion) actually is one of several raised in three oracles ("words"). The first (vv. 30-31) and third (vv. 34-38) share the common notion of the LORD as a roaring lion; the second (vv. 32-33) speaks of **a mighty storm** spreading over many nations. It is possible that these three actually constituted a single oracle originally, with the "mighty storm" a hyperbole of the lion's roar. There are other images suggested in these oracles as well, so it is probably unnecessary to distinguish between oracles based on these differences. They all share in common the basic idea that the LORD is "noisily" expressing his anger.

The first part speaks of the LORD as one who will **roar, thunder** ("give his voice"), and **shout,**[7] whose noise rings through **the earth** as a **tumult** (cp. Amos 1:2; 3:8; Joel 3:16). The piling up of these images furthers the message of these lines. The point Jeremiah is conveying is that the LORD will come in a very intimidating way, striking fear in the hearts of those whom he is approaching. Each of

---

[6]The location of "Zimri" (v. 25) is unknown. Thompson identifies "Sheshach" as an Athbash for Babylon (שֵׁשַׁךְ = בָּבֶל). This is an encoding method where one uses the alphabet in reverse (A = Z, B = Y; in Hebrew א = ת, ב = שׁ). Thompson, *Jeremiah*, p. 518.

[7]The comparison to "those who tread the grapes" is a bit puzzling. Obviously, this was known to be a noisy enterprise, but the reason for this has been lost.

these on its own is intimidating, but mentioning them one after another heightens the sense of the LORD's overpowering force to a fever pitch. All of this is part of his decision to execute judgment on these sinful nations. As the divine judge, he is **bringing charges against** them, and then he will carry out the sentence imposed upon them (**put the wicked to the sword**).

This sense of carrying out a sentence on criminals underlies the metaphor of the storm in the following verses. The **tumult** that **will resound to the ends of the earth** (v. 31) arises in conjunction with the bringing of formal charges. Those punished fall victim to the **mighty storm** that comes **from the ends of the earth** (v. 32). Moreover, those punished are left to rot out in the open, rather than being **buried** with honor. Such treatment in death was understood to be the fate of criminals.

The balance of this section returns to the lion metaphor and develops it further.[8] The **lion** was of particular concern to **shepherds**, as it picked off stray sheep from the flock. Jeremiah heightens the common level of anxiety regarding this well-known danger by speaking of the danger to the shepherds themselves. He tells the shepherds to **Weep and wail**, but not because they are going to lose some of their flock to a marauding lion. In this instance, the lion is hunting for the shepherds. It is common to speak of sheep being slaughtered, but now it is the shepherds. Such a warning must have carried particular significance to the royal establishment. Their ancestor, David, had been chosen to "shepherd" the LORD's people (2 Sam 5:2; 7:7). Now, the LORD is the lion, hunting down those whom he appointed. This is not a killing of hunger, but of **fierce anger**.

---

[8]The lone exception is the mention of shattered pottery, in verse 34 (cp. 19:10-11).

JEREMIAH 26

I. JEREMIAH THREATENED WITH DEATH (26:1-24)

Jeremiah 26 begins a small collection of biographical narratives. In these, accounts of the words Jeremiah proclaims are combined with incidents of opposition to his proclamation (Jeremiah 26–29; cp. chapters 37–45). These events span more than twenty years of his career and so are merely representative of how people (do not) receive the prophet's message. In this first narrative, we return to the time when Jeremiah delivers a message to those entering the temple (26:1-6; cp. 7:1-15). Religious and community leaders respond by calling for his death, and they bring him before certain royal officials for a trial (26:7-11). Jeremiah defends himself by asserting that he speaks in the name of the LORD (26:12-15). The officials and elders are swayed by this defense, citing Micah as a precedent (26:16-19) and calling for Jeremiah's release (26:24). The editor (Baruch) inserts a note here about another prophet whose own story suggests that Jeremiah's fate was not necessarily a foregone conclusion (26:20-23).

26:1-6 Most critics agree that this chapter provides a sequel to the Temple Sermon in Jeremiah 7:1-15.[1] Here we are told the message is delivered to those coming to the temple **early in the reign of Jehoiakim**. This could be anytime between 609 and 605 B.C.[2] The LORD instructs Jeremiah to proclaim a message in front of the temple (26:2; cp. 7:2-3), in the hope each of those coming to worship

---

[1]Holladay, *Jeremiah 2*, pp. 101-103; Thompson, *Jeremiah*, p. 523; Brueggemann, *Jeremiah*, p. 233; Clements, *Jeremiah*, p. 154.

[2]Some commentators date this to Jehoiakim's accession year (so Holladay, *Jeremiah 2*, p. 103; Thompson, *Jeremiah*, pp. 523-524). However, the note in 28:1 identifies the "fourth year" of Zedekiah's reign as the same year as "early in the reign of Zedekiah" (27:1). Holladay attributes this to a textual error, but perhaps "early" refers to "the first half" or something similar to that.

there will **turn from his evil way** (26:3; cp. 7:3,5-7), and then the
LORD will "turn" from **the disaster** he has planned (cp. 18:7-10). The
details concerning the changes they need to make are not given here
as they are in the Temple Sermon. The main message here is about
the need to **listen** (26:4-5; cp. 7:13) to the LORD's **law** and **the words
of my servants the prophets** in order to prevent the fate of **Shiloh**
(26:6; cp. 7:14) from being repeated in Jerusalem.[3]

26:7-11 The reaction of Jeremiah's audience is immediate. They
call for Jeremiah's execution on the basis of his comparison between
Jerusalem and Shiloh. One can easily see why the temple **priests**
would be incensed with Jeremiah, because they naturally see themselves as preferred by the LORD and Jeremiah's family as rejected by
the LORD (see comments on 7:14 and the significance of Shiloh). The
priests are joined here by **the prophets and all the people** (v. 7).
These prophets almost certainly included those whose message contradicts Jeremiah's own (cp. 37:19). These are the same groups who
had entered into a covenant pledge with King Josiah, when he initiated the great reform a generation earlier (2 Kgs 23:1-3), and these
are the same groups to whom Jeremiah addresses his remarks on
false prophecy in Jeremiah 23:33-34. They apparently have their own
interpretation of how the LORD is working out his will in the lives of
the people of Jerusalem. The **people** would naturally listen to those
other prophets and priests, because they would see the fact that those
individuals are in power as proof of the LORD's favor on them.[4]

---

[3]The major differences between the Temple Sermon and the message
recorded here are (a) the possibility of averting disaster is in a main section
of the Sermon, while it is in the introductory instructions to Jeremiah here;
and (b) the destruction of Jerusalem on the basis of nonreceptivity is stated
unconditionally in 7:12-15, while it is conditional here. (On the other hand,
the tenor of the Sermon as a whole is conditional.) There are various ways
to explain the fact that there are differences between these two accounts.
One is to say the two messages are different parts of the same prophecy. A
second is to assume that one rendition is a verbatim recording of what
Jeremiah said, while the other is merely a summary. In that vein, it is even
possible that both texts are summaries of what Jeremiah said. Finally, it is
possible that Jeremiah delivered the same central message in front of the
temple on several occasions, and that these two passages preserve two similar but chronologically disparate prophecies.

[4]Holladay, *Jeremiah 2*, p. 106; Thompson, *Jeremiah*, p. 525; Brueggemann,
Jeremiah, p. 234.

It is intriguing to consider the vehemence of their reaction, however, when one considers the overall religious behavior of the
nation. Jeremiah's accusations against them most likely include a
well-founded charge of idolatry (7:9). Why would people who practice idolatry be so defensive about the worship of the LORD? Perhaps
our incredulity arises from a mistaken perception of idolatry, based
on biblical commands about it. Those commands typically pit worship of the LORD in direct opposition to the worship of any other
deities as an either/or proposition. There is plenty of evidence to
suggest, however, that ancient Israelites often mixed worship of the
LORD with the worship of foreign deities. In the minds of many of
them it was perfectly acceptable to worship the LORD in one place
and some idol in another. A major hurdle for the biblical prophets
and writers was to convince their audiences that this really was an
either/or situation. It is possible that, in Jeremiah's day, the people
had come to associate the LORD exclusively with the Jerusalem temple and the House of David while allowing for the need for other
deities in other places and in other aspects of their lives not directly tied to the monarchy. One can certainly see how there might be
parallels to such a way of thinking among Christian groups today
where faddish programs, hobby-horse doctrines, compromises to
cultural preferences, and other innovations tend to mix the message
of the gospel with man-made ideas and understanding.

Unnamed royal **officials** come to the temple to hear the case.
This shows the close ties between the religious and royal establishments. Jeremiah has prophesied against the temple and against the
city of Jerusalem (v. 6), but it is the latter which is of greatest concern to these officials (v. 11). This message is considered an act of
treason or sedition. A prophet who proclaims imminent divine punishment on a city without warrant might discourage some local citizens and military personnel whose support would be crucial during
a military crisis.[5] For a smaller city like Jerusalem, this could turn the
tide of a battle. Besides, there are many other prophets (who work
in the palace) whose message contradicts Jeremiah's (see above).
These officials are accompanied by **all the people** (v. 11). It is unlikely these are the same people who just made the accusations with
priests and prophets against Jeremiah. These might be "some of the
elders of the land" (v. 17), who voice part of the verdict in the case;

---

[5]Holladay, *Jeremiah 2*, pp. 105-107.

but the information provided does not clarify the situation (see v. 16). The general population could have been easily swayed by the false prophets and priests, while the elders were more level-headed in this situation.[6]

26:12-15 It is somewhat surprising that Jeremiah's defense works here. He begins by reiterating the call for repentance he has prophesied before the temple (vv. 12-13; cp. 7:3-11; 26:2-3). All that he adds to this is the threat they will be guilty of shedding **innocent blood**, if they have him executed (cp. 7:6; 19:4; 22:3,17). Why this concern would sway their decision here is not clear, as the example of Uriah (vv. 20-23) demonstrates.

26:16-19 Those hearing the case deliver their verdict in two parts. First, the officials and people call for Jeremiah's release because **"he has spoken to us in the name of the LORD our God."** Why this is now reason enough for Jeremiah's release is a mystery. In their initial accusation, the people had charged Jeremiah with prophesying the destruction of Jerusalem "in the LORD's name" (v. 9). The rationale is developed more fully in the precedent cited by the **elders**. They point to the example of **Micah**. He prophesied the destruction of Jerusalem (Micah 3:12), but he was not executed for delivering such a message. Instead, his message brought about repentance on the part of King **Hezekiah**, which led to forgiveness from **the LORD** and the sparing of the city from **disaster**. The implication is that the people have charged Jeremiah prematurely. He has, after all, prophesied this message in a conditional mode. The destruction prophesied is contingent on how the people react to Jeremiah's message, not on the fact he has delivered it. Thus, the elders can conclude their remarks by saying, **"We are about to bring a terrible disaster on ourselves"** (cp. 44:7). If no disaster comes, they can credit themselves with that. If it does come, Jeremiah is shown to be a true prophet of the LORD and therefore free from prosecution as a false prophet.[7]

26:20-23 The editor obviously inserts a sort of footnote here for the benefit of later readers, yet it is one which complements rather than disrupts the narrative as a whole. The note is about another prophet, **Uriah son of Shemaiah**,[8] who is a true prophet like Jeremiah.

---

[6]For a fuller discussion of "people" in this passage, see ibid., pp. 104-105.

[7]See Clements, *Jeremiah*, pp. 156-160; Brueggemann, *Jeremiah*, pp. 234,236.

[8]We know of two men named Shemaiah from this time, either of whom

He too **prophesied in the name of the LORD** (v. 20) about the disaster coming on Jerusalem; but for some reason, **King Jehoiakim** took particular offense at Uriah and his message. He had him extradited from **Egypt** by an official embassy and brought back to Judah for execution.[9] The reader is left wondering why Jeremiah is spared when Uriah is not. Perhaps Baruch wanted to bring out the true gravity of Jeremiah's situation for the reader.

26:24 There is then one other historical note disclosed: Jeremiah enjoys the support of **Ahikam son of Shaphan**. This Ahikam had been commissioned by Josiah to authenticate the "book of the Law" discovered in the temple, which had sparked Josiah's great religious reform (2 Kgs 22:12,14). This Ahikam had heard a warning similar to Jeremiah's from the prophetess Huldah (2 Kgs 22:15-20). We do not know what role he plays in Jehoiakim's court, but the fact that this note seems to be juxtaposed to the preceding one regarding Uriah suggests that he still holds enough power to help Jeremiah avoid the fate that befell other prophets in similar situations.[10]

One other aspect of this narrative which we cannot minimize is what it teaches about biblical prophecy. Micah is a prophet whose example is cited in support of Jeremiah. Interestingly, the prophecy cited is one which was not fulfilled; and it is that nonfulfillment which gives Jeremiah's message credence in the present situation. Micah had declared that Jerusalem would be destroyed, but the repentance of Hezekiah averted that disaster. Clements tries to circumvent this by asserting that Micah's prophecy referred to the destruction in 586 B.C.[11] Such an interpretation would completely undermine the use of Micah's prophecy as an argument in Jeremiah's defense. What Micah's prophecy shows is that, unless specifically stated otherwise, a prophecy's fulfillment was known to be contingent on the people's response to it (see 18:7-10). This is fascinating because the primary test of a prophet's veracity was his abil-

---

might or might not be this Shemaiah. One was an official in Josiah's palace (2 Chr 35:9); the other was a false prophet (Jer 29:24-32).

[9]At this time, Judah was under Egyptian hegemony (2 Kgs 23:31-35). On this point, see Thompson, *Jeremiah*, p. 527.

[10]His brother, Gemariah, urged Jehoiakim to heed the written warnings of Jeremiah (36:10,25). Another brother, Gedaliah, was appointed governor by the Babylonians after Jerusalem fell (39:14). Holladay, *Jeremiah 2*, pp. 109-110; Thompson, *Jeremiah*, p. 528.

[11]Clements, *Jeremiah*, pp. 156-157.

ity to announce the LORD's intentions accurately. If a prophet announced destruction, and yet such destruction did not come, one might logically question that prophet's inspiration. Such an expectation must be tempered by a consideration of the LORD's self-proclaimed character — that he is "merciful and gracious, slow to anger. . . . yet he does not leave the guilty unpunished . . ." (Exod 34:6-7). Jeremiah's own words make this same understanding explicit, because they present the LORD's message in a conditional mode. It is this conditionality which the elders affirm — and which the people ignore in their accusation — in their call for Jeremiah's acquittal.

JEREMIAH 27

J. JUDAH TO SERVE NEBUCHADNEZZAR (27:1-22)

The next two chapters record two parts of a single story from Jeremiah's life. These events occur early in the reign of Zedekiah (597–586 B.C.), later specified as the fourth year (28:1) of the reign of Judah's last king (594/593 B.C.).[1] King Nebuchadnezzar of Babylon has recently sent another force to Jerusalem for a brief mission. That force takes the new king, Jehoiachin (= Jeconiah/ Coniah), as their prisoner, along with ten thousand leading citizens of the nation (among them, Ezekiel). They then place Zedekiah,

---

[1]Several Hebrew manuscripts actually read "Jehoiakim" rather than "Zedekiah" as the king in 27:1. All subsequent references are to Zedekiah, though (27:3,12; 28:1). It is likely that a copyist accidentally substituted Jehoiakim for Zedekiah here because of the following designation, "son of Josiah" (see 26:1).

There is some uncertainty about the date of these events. It was common in Mesopotamian records to designate a king's accession year as "early" in his reign. Greek manuscripts for 28:1 omit any reference to "the fourth year," leading some commentators to conclude this series of events takes place a few years earlier. So Brueggemann, *Jeremiah*, p. 240. More are swayed, however, by the omission of the introductory clause, "early in the reign . . ." in the Greek of 27:1. They see the reference to "the fourth year of Zedekiah" as more likely to be original. So Holladay, *Jeremiah 2*, pp. 114-115; Thompson, *Jeremiah*, pp. 531-532; Clements, *Jeremiah*, p. 160.)

On the other hand, the implicitly rebellious nature of the meeting reported here between Zedekiah and the foreign envoys seems out of place in the first year of this king's reign. Nebuchadnezzar placed Zedekiah on the throne. He would not immediately turn against the ruler who had made him king. Babylonian records show that Nebuchadnezzar had to deal with several enemy armies between 596 and 593 B.C. Also, there is a reference to Zedekiah going to Babylon in the same fourth year of his reign (Jer 51:59). It is plausible to conclude that these envoys — and then Jeremiah — are advising Zedekiah as he prepares to leave.

Jehoiachin's uncle, on the throne. Now, certain envoys come to Jerusalem from the neighboring countries for some sort of conference. The fact that Jeremiah advises them to submit to Babylon suggests that a central topic being considered is a possible attempt to break free from Babylonian domination. The LORD instructs Jeremiah to put on an ox's yoke to illustrate Babylonian control. Thus attired, Jeremiah delivers three messages, one for the foreign envoys (27:4-11), a supplementary message for King Zedekiah (27:12-15), and a warning to the priests and people of Jerusalem about false prophets (27:16-22). His primary message is that they need to accept Babylonian control. This elicits a response from the Gibeonite prophet, Hananiah. He tries to "modify" Jeremiah's message with a prophecy of his own, announcing a quick end to Babylonian hegemony and breaking the yoke Jeremiah has been wearing (28:1-4,10-11). This announcement Jeremiah cautiously accepts (28:5-9). The LORD soon repudiates Hananiah's message, however, pronouncing judgment on him for misleading the people. He dies just two short months later (28:12-17).

27:1-3 This narrative opens with another example of Jeremiah using "visual aids" to communicate his message (cp. 13:1-11; 19:1-13). The metaphor of a **yoke** in reference to political or religious control is well-represented in the Old Testament (Lev 26:13; Deut 28:48; 1 Kgs 12:4-14; Isa 9:4; 10:27; 14:25; Ezek 34:27; Nahum 1:13; cp. Matt 11:29-30).[2] Jeremiah makes strong use of it by actually putting a yoke on himself. He delivers his message to representatives of five neighboring nations. From the south and east are **Edom** (descendants of Esau) and **Moab** and **Ammon** (descendants of Lot). From the northwest are the Phoenician city-states of **Tyre** and **Sidon**. It is unclear whether Jeremiah appears before all the foreign envoys at once, or individually.

27:4-11 The message to these envoys consists of a general decree (vv. 4-7) and a warning to those who ignore it (vv. 8-11). It begins with a bold claim of military and cosmic power by the LORD. The reference to his **outstretched arm** (v. 5) is the image of a king leading his troops into battle. For the Israelites, it especially evokes memories of the Exodus from Egypt (Exod 6:6; Deut 4:34; 5:15; 7:19; 9:29; 11:2; 26:8). Jeremiah links it to the role of LORD as Creator (cp.

---

[2]S. Dean McBride, "The Yoke of the Kingdom," *Int.* 27 (1973): 273-306. For a helpful description of a yoke, see Holladay, *Jeremiah 2*, p. 120.

32:17).[3] Because he has created "the world, and all who live in it" (Ps 24:1), he controls the fate of the nations in it (cp. Isa 45:1-7). **Babylon** is the central player at present. **Nebuchadnezzar**, the Babylonian **king**, is the LORD's **servant**. What he does he does as the LORD's agent, carrying out the LORD's will, not Nebuchadnezzar's will. It is this fact that should make these officials recognize the inevitability of what Jeremiah announces.[4] The LORD, the Creator-God of the Universe, is moving against these nations. There is no escape. **Even the wild animals** ("animals of the field") will be placed under Nebuchadnezzar's yoke, domesticated by him. These "wild animals" might be symbols for the various kings and/or nations represented by these envoys (e.g., the lion was a symbol for the House of David). The fact they are "wild" might refer to their refusal to submit to this domesticating yoke. It is more common to conclude, however, that this indicates the completeness of Babylonian control, control that encompasses the most "peripheral" of creatures.[5] There is an element of hope, though. Babylonian domination will last only three generations. Then, the Creator of the Universe will raise up others to topple Babylon (v. 7).

Two previous passages in Jeremiah come to mind in the transition at the beginning of verse 8. One is the statement by the LORD to Jeremiah at his call, when he appointed him to be a prophet "over nations and kingdoms" (1:10). The other is the message regarding prophecy and repentance in Jeremiah 18:7-10. The LORD asserts there that he might issue a prophecy about any "nation or kingdom," announcing either doom or salvation. Both imply the LORD's sovereignty (based on his function as creator; see v. 5) over all "nations and kingdoms." The present passage is another assertion of that sovereignty.

It is from this stance that the LORD announces his intentions regarding these various nations. They all must submit to Babylon, just as an ox submits to the yoke. The only "alternative" he offers to these other nations is the same fate he has been offering to Judah —

---

[3]Holladay, *Jeremiah 2*, p. 119; Brueggemann, *Jeremiah*, p. 242.

[4]There might also be an almost subliminal message here involving the word "serve" (עָבַד, *'ābad*). Nebuchadnezzar is the LORD's "servant," and these nations are to "serve" him. The Babylonian king prospers as a servant, perhaps implying that they will prosper too, if they follow his example of servanthood.

[5]Holladay, *Jeremiah 2*, p. 121; Thompson, *Jeremiah*, p. 533.

the sword, famine and plague. This triad is a chief characteristic of Jeremiah's message during Zedekiah's reign. Its utilization here demonstrates that the LORD is "no respecter of persons." He punishes all who refuse to submit to his will. The primary reason for such resistance is a contrary message by other religious advisors. In Judah, these are the "false prophets" (see below and 23:9-40). These neighboring nations have a variety of similar advisors — **diviners, interpreters of dreams, mediums**, and **sorcerers** (v. 9; cp. Deut 13:1-5; 18:9-13). All of these, like the false prophets of Judah, are advising their kings to resist Babylon, perhaps assuring them of divine deliverance as well. The LORD refers to such messages as **lies**, and he advises those nations' leaders not to **listen** to those messengers (vv. 9-10; cp. 6:13-15; 23:25-26). The "reward" for "listening" to the LORD instead is a lighter "yoke." The Babylonians will still be victorious, but they will allow those whom they conquer to **remain** in their native lands (v. 11).

27:12-15 Jeremiah gives the same message in essentially the same terms to **Zedekiah**. Unlike Judah in the days of Hezekiah, the imminent fate of Judah is no different than the fate of the other nations. Judah is to **bow . . . under the yoke**, so that they will not suffer **the sword, famine and plague**. They too are not to **listen** to false prophets among them, because those prophets are **prophesying lies**. He makes no mention of a possibly lightened "yoke," though that might be assumed (see vv. 7,22).

27:16-22 The subsequent warning about the **lies** of Judah's false prophets is unusual in a couple of ways. It is one of the rare occasions in Jeremiah when the prophets and the priests do not represent a unified front. Here, the **prophets** are speaking words of reassurance to the **priests**, rather than the two speaking in unison to the rest of the people. This is probably because the message is in regard to something of particular concern to the priests. The Babylonian force that came to Jerusalem in 597 B.C. had looted the temple, taking away some of the valuable items kept there. Some of the more significant articles had been left behind (**the pillars, the Sea, the movable stands**; see 1 Kgs 7:13-51).[6] The false prophets are giving a

---

[6]It is impossible to infer from this what was actually taken. One might assume that central articles not mentioned here are those that were taken. This would include the menorah, the table, the incense altar, and the Ark of the Covenant. Such an argument from silence is hardly proof, though. The conclusion that they took the ark is particularly suspect. The ark was

message of hope, promising the imminent recovery of the **articles** already taken (v. 16). The LORD has not sent them (cp. 23:16-18,30-32), however, so their words carry no weight. Jeremiah's message is that things will get worse before they get better. Nothing will be recovered in the near future; rather, more will be lost (vv. 18-22). The people want to show their willingness to "trust" in the LORD, but they trust only as long as the result will be their own deliverance from foreign rule. Jeremiah asserts that "trust" involves leaving everything — even the outcome — up to the LORD's discretion.

The final pronouncement regarding the temple articles is rather verbose. The introduction takes up three verses (vv. 19-21). The subordinate clause describing the articles taken is so long, a resumptive clause is needed in verse 21 to return the listener to the original train of thought. The effect is to heighten the anticipation in the listener about what is being announced. What they expect is a word of doom, and that is what they receive. But it is also here that the LORD finally utters a word of hope for the temple. One can almost see the priests collapsing to the ground under the weight of Jeremiah's words as he builds up to the pronouncement, yet he closes on a note of hope. The LORD announces that the Babylonians will take all the articles of the temple to Babylon, where they will remain for an unspecified length of time; then they will be returned. The LORD himself will **come for them** and **bring them back** to Jerusalem (cp. v. 7).

This is a very strong promise, one which should be no small comfort to those who are listening. The people have been basing their hopes (and probably accepting the message of the false prophets) on the basis of the nation's past experiences with the LORD. They know him as a God of mercy and forgiveness. Jeremiah's message has been virtually devoid of that, while the oracles of the other prophets could have been reminding the people of the LORD's miraculous deeds on Israel's behalf in the past. This final note of hope shows that the LORD is still true to his name (see Exod 34:6-7). The difference in Jeremiah's message is a matter of timing.[7] The false prophets

---

the primary indicator that the LORD was still "present" among his people. Several texts tie it directly to the presence of the "glory of the LORD" (1 Kgs 8:1-11). Ezekiel talks about the "glory" leaving Jerusalem when the city is captured in 586 B.C. (Ezek 10:1-19; 11:22-23). It is more likely that the Babylonians took the ark away then.

[7]Brueggemann, *Jeremiah*, pp. 250-251, n. 25.

believe they can predict on their own when the LORD will do what he will do; Jeremiah reminds them — and us — that only the LORD knows when he will act.

JEREMIAH 28

K. THE FALSE PROPHET HANANIAH (28:1-17)

[The chronological setting for this chapter was discussed with chapter 27.]

28:1-11 Hananiah's counteroracle constitutes an "official" response to Jeremiah's message. We do not know exactly how much time has elapsed since the scene in chapter 27 closed, except that it cannot have been more than five months. It most likely was within the same week, because Jeremiah is still wearing the yoke (vv. 10-11) he had used to illustrate his message. **Hananiah** delivers his oracle **in the house of the LORD**, and Jeremiah has just been talking about the articles confiscated from the temple. Hananiah delivers the message **in the presence of the priests and all the people** (cp. v. 5), and Jeremiah has been warning those very groups not to listen to the words of the prophets (27:16). Hananiah, like Jeremiah, speaks in the name of **the LORD Almighty, the God of Israel**. We know how the story ends, so we know that he speaks falsely here; but not even Jeremiah knows this yet (see vv. 5-9).

Hananiah's oracle begins and ends with the promise that the LORD will soon **break the yoke** (vv. 2,4) which Nebuchadnezzar is placing on the shoulders of Judah and the other nations. Jeremiah mentions elsewhere an exile of seventy years (25:11-12; 29:10), and it is likely that Hananiah is responding directly to that prediction when he says it will end **within two years** (v. 3).[1] He then predicts the return of the **articles** of the temple, along with the **king** and those exiled with him. This reflects a different "spin" than what one finds in chapter 24 and the oracle of the baskets of figs. There, the people in Jerusalem assume that King Jehoiachin and his fellow exiles

---

[1]Jeremiah's letter to the exiles (29:1-23) constitutes a broader response to Hananiah's prediction, which might explain why Baruch places it next in the book.

are those who are being punished by the LORD for their infidelity, while Zedekiah and those left are a "remnant" with which the LORD will rebuild his nation. Hananiah's oracle pins the hopes for Judah's future on the restoration of Jehoiachin as king. We are not told the reason for this shift.[2]

The articles of the temple and Jehoiachin's entourage have been removed to Babylon. They represent the heart and soul of Judah's society, and so those left behind are "scrambling" to make sense of what is transpiring. These items and people also represent (from Jeremiah's perspective) the areas in which true devotion to the LORD has been most insidiously compromised. The royal ideology has been around for centuries, reminding the people that the LORD "chose" Jerusalem as his city and the House of David as the shepherd of his people (2 Chr 6:4-6; Ps 78:66-72). The deliverance of Jerusalem in the days of Hezekiah confirmed this.[3] The people have taken this too far, however, seeing the LORD's promise as an unconditional guarantee that the LORD would always protect this city and this dynasty from foreign attack. The message of the prophets, like Jeremiah, is that true faith in the LORD is a requisite response. The failure to respond in faith results in a forfeiting of one's right to enjoy the blessings promised by the LORD.

Jeremiah's response to Hananiah's message is one of cautious optimism. Hananiah says what Jeremiah would like to hear: that the LORD will soon return the temple **articles** and the **exiles** from their captivity. His acceptance is tempered, however, by his own experience with prophets and prophecy (vv. 7-9). He calls on Hananiah to **listen** (for a change) to what he has to say from that experience. He points out that prophecies about impending military disaster are usually accurate, implying that it often does not take divine help to recognize when a powerful nation is about to take over a weak nation (see Deut 13:1-5, in this regard). The more difficult prophecy is the sort that Isaiah made when he assured Hezekiah that the Assyrians would not capture Jerusalem even though they had captured every other city they had attacked (Isa 37:9-35). Jeremiah knows that the LORD can bring "peace" again, if he so desires, so he does not dismiss Hananiah's prophecy outright. But he himself has received no such word from the LORD, so he is guarded in his affirmation of Hananiah's hopeful word.

---

[2]Holladay, *Jeremiah 2*, p. 128.
[3]Brueggemann, *Jeremiah*, p. 251.

Hananiah then reasserts his message symbolically by smashing **the yoke** Jeremiah has been wearing. He reiterates the two main points of his oracle as he does so. He shatters the yoke to symbolize how the LORD intends to **break the yoke of Nebuchadnezzar** from all the nations now under his control. This will happen **within two years**, not the seventy years Jeremiah has been announcing.

Jeremiah's attitude here is quite commendable. Hananiah's message contradicts the tone and content of the several messages he has been receiving and prophesying, yet he does not quarrel with Hananiah until he has first heard from the LORD. If he were to respond without waiting for the LORD's own response, he would be just as guilty as Hananiah of prophesying presumptuously. He knows that he has truly been receiving the word of the LORD, and that word has even included warnings about false prophets, who proclaim "peace" when there is no peace (6:13-15; 23:16-18). He could easily have cited precedents to refute Hananiah's message, but he does not because he knows the ways of the LORD. He knows the LORD is a God of mercy, so Hananiah's message would not be out of character for the LORD. He also has learned how to wait for the LORD to respond to his own critics, so he does not have to fear an opposing word from a rival prophet. The LORD will reveal the truth in due time.[4] This is much like the attitude Paul counsels Timothy and Titus to adopt in their discussions with opposing teachers (2 Tim 2:14-26; Titus 3:9). Such an attitude can grow only in a heart filled with faith in God and humility about one's place in God's world.

28:12-17 The LORD's response to Hananiah's word is directed first to the message (vv. 13-14), then to the messenger (vv. 15-16). He begins by reaffirming and strengthening his earlier message to Jeremiah regarding the image of the yoke of Babylon. The "weaker" image of a **wooden yoke** is now replaced with the "stronger" image of an **iron yoke**. This shows that Babylonian domination will persist, even in the face of repeated opposition and attempts to break it. This word of judgment is sure; the LORD is emphatic. He closes with another reference to the subjugating of **wild animals** (see 27:6). None will be able to evade the Babylonian onslaught.

The LORD then focuses directly on Hananiah. The primary message to this prophet hinges on the word "send" (שָׁלַח, šālaḥ).[5]

---

[4]Clements, *Jeremiah*, pp. 166-168.
[5]Holladay, *Jeremiah 2*, p. 126.

Jeremiah declares to him, **The LORD has not sent you** (v. 15; cp. 29:31). Now, for his presumptuous message, the LORD will **remove** him ("I am sending you from on the face of the ground;" v. 16). The LORD had not "sent" him before, but he is "sending" him now. He is a prophet who has been "lying" to the people; they **trust in lies**. The LORD even accuses him of preaching **rebellion**. This must have sounded odd to Hananiah and his supporters. Hananiah is telling the people that the LORD will deliver them (miraculously, if necessary) from the control of the Babylonians. If the people believe Hananiah and trust in the LORD to deliver them, they will naturally assume that their attitude demonstrates their loyalty to the LORD. Yet he says an attitude that expects divine deliverance in this situation constitutes rebellion, not faith. This is so, because he (and they) is not listening to what the LORD has to say. He is generating his own words of comfort, giving expression to his own "wishful thinking" (cp. Deut 18:20-22). The true prophet "listens" (cp. 28:7,15; **Listen, Hananiah!**) to whatever the LORD has to say.[6] Because Hananiah does not listen, and because he is doing harm "in the name of the LORD" rather than good, the LORD pronounces a swift death sentence on him. The final verse (28:17) reports the fulfillment of that sentence a mere two months later. It also hints at the inevitable fulfillment of the preceding oracle regarding the "iron yoke" of Babylon. Jerusalem will fall to Nebuchadnezzar; there is no hope for a reprieve.

---

[6]Brueggemann, *Jeremiah*, pp. 251-253.

JEREMIAH 29

L. A LETTER TO THE EXILES (29:1-23)

This chapter reveals another method for delivering prophetic messages: by mail. King Zedekiah was sending couriers to Nebuchadnezzar in Babylon, and the prophet has them take a letter to the exiles living there (29:1-3). The letter consists of five parts, each beginning with, "This is what the LORD (Almighty, the God of Israel,) says" (vv. 4,8,10,15,20). Jeremiah begins with a call for the people to "make themselves at home" in Babylon (29:4-7), a message which runs contrary to the message being spoken by other prophets (29:8-9). His own message is that the future offers prosperity for those in Babylon (29:10-14), but death and destruction for those remaining in Jerusalem, in spite of what others might be saying (29:15-19). This leads to a concluding pronouncement of condemnation against two leading false prophets (29:20-23). The letter reveals that there are others like Hananiah among the exiles in Babylon. The following episode (29:24-32) demonstrates how there were some attempts to coordinate this opposition to the message of Jeremiah.

29:1-3 We do not know the exact date for the sending of this letter, but the reference to the exile of Jehoiachin and others (v. 2) suggests a time soon after that event (c. 597–596 B.C.). The letter is addressed to the nonroyal leaders among the exiles: **the surviving elders** ("the rest of the elders")[1] . . . **the priests, the prophets, and all the other people.** These groups have represented Jeremiah's opposition in previous episodes (26:7), so one would not be too optimistic about a positive reaction to the letter. The two individuals who carry the letter (**Elasah son of Shaphan and Gemariah son of Hilkiah**) come from families that played important roles in Josiah's reform

---

[1]Holladay proposes the interpretation "preeminent" for "rest of" (cp. Gen 49:3). Holladay, *Jeremiah 2*, p. 140.

efforts (see 2 Kgs 22:4-13; 23:4). These families appear to have been more sympathetic than others in the palace to Jeremiah's message (cp. 36:10-16).

29:4-7 Jeremiah advises the exiles to do the things that communicate the permanence of a society. They are to **build houses**, rather than live in tents; they are to **plant gardens**, rather than "eat what grows by itself" (Isa 37:30); they are to arrange marriages for their children, which points to long-term financial commitments. Most surprising, they are to **seek the peace and prosperity of the city** of their captivity (cp. Psalm 137). Even though this has a selfish component to it (**if it prospers, you too will prosper**), it runs contrary to their natural inclination.

This passage reflects something that becomes an important component of Jewish and Christian life in the centuries that follow. In most cases, these believers have found themselves to be the minority in their society. They have little influence over the moral and ethical tone of the culture in which they find themselves. They see themselves in a struggle with much in the society. It is important to see what this passage teaches, and what it does not teach. This passage reminds believers that their general economic welfare is tied to the society in which they live. For this reason alone the LORD tells them to pray for the city in which they live. They are not expected to promote or even condone the standards of their society. They are to pray for it for their own sake.

29:8-9 Attention shifts here to the immediate concern of this letter. There are other prophets living among the Babylonian exiles who are promoting the position held by prophets like Hananiah in Jerusalem. Jeremiah does not give the exact message they proclaim, but it is fairly easy to deduce it from what he writes here. He repeatedly accuses them of **prophesying lies** (vv. 9,21,23). Such "lies" in Jeremiah are most often words of hope and appeasement, when the LORD's true message is one of devastation and punishment (see 5:12,31; 6:13; 8:8,10; 14:14-15; 20:6; 23:14,25,26,32; 27:10,14-16; 28:15). This fits the context of Jeremiah's letter as well. These other prophets "prophesy lies," while Jeremiah speaks of "the sword, famine and plague" which the LORD is sending (vv. 17-18). Almost certainly, they are assuring the exiles that they will soon return to their homeland. Jeremiah has the unpleasant task of dashing their hopes.

29:10-14 Jeremiah now softens the blow of this harsh rejoinder of others' "false" reassurances with his own "true" message of reassurance. He quickly passes over the fact that the return is **seventy years** away (v. 10) to get to many words of comfort and encouragement. He opens and closes the balance of this section with the assurance that the LORD intends to **bring . . . back** those who have been exiled (vv. 11,14). He speaks of the LORD's **gracious promise** — a promise of prosperity, a promise of **hope and a future**. Although they are to settle down for a while in Babylon, their "future" is not to be found in Babylon, but back in Jerusalem; Babylon is a temporary way-station. The LORD's promise to their ancestors about a land still stands, but its realization is postponed for the present generation.

The LORD makes it clear, however, that this is a reciprocal relationship. He promises them prosperity and a future, but he also expects reverence and devotion from them. He indicates this in a series of five verbs. He expects the people to **call . . . and come and pray . . . seek . . . and find** him (vv. 12-13). This is the language of temple worship (see 1 Kgs 8:27-51), so there is an implicit promise here of the restoration of the temple. There is also an expectation of something which has been missing from their worship. He says to them, **you** [will] **seek me with all your heart**. This is what was missing from their worship in the days of Josiah (cp. 3:10), but what has always been required of them (Deut 6:4-5; 10:12; 11:13; 13:3; 26:16; 1 Sam 12:20; 1 Kgs 2:4; 8:23; 2 Kgs 23:3). Such expectations would never change.

29:15-19 It is necessary to "read between the lines" of verses 15-16, but what is left unsaid is fairly obvious. Jeremiah juxtaposes the words of the exiles against the words of the LORD. The exiles merely mention the presence of certain **prophets** among them (v. 15), and the LORD declares the imminent humiliation of Jerusalem and the Davidic monarch (Zedekiah; vv. 16-18).[2] Perhaps it is significant that the people claim **the LORD has raised up** the prophets whom they mention; perhaps this implies their belief that the LORD is doing something positive for them. Regardless, it seems clear that the message of the prophets has to do with the glorification of Zedekiah and the people still in Jerusalem (cp. Ezek 11:14-16) because the LORD's response to their words are his own words of

---

[2]Actually, verses 16-20 are missing from the LXX. The sequence then is from the assertion "the LORD has raised up prophets for us in Babylon" (v. 15) to a naming of those prophets (v. 21). This rendering leaves no real clue as to what is "false" about the prophets' message. See Holladay, *Jeremiah 2*, pp. 135-136.

judgment against them. The basic tenor of this message parallels the message regarding the articles of the temple in 27:19-22. The false prophets there are announcing that the articles already confiscated will soon be returned to reside with the articles still in the temple. The LORD responds that the articles still in Jerusalem will soon be joining those in Babylon. Here, he gives the same message regarding people. Jehoiachin and the other exiles will not rejoin their kinsmen back in Jerusalem. Instead, Zedekiah and those still in Jerusalem will soon be joining the exiles in Babylon.

The wording of verses 17-18 shares a great deal with the wording of 24:8-10. Jeremiah refers to those remaining in Jerusalem as **poor figs that are so bad they cannot be eaten** (v. 17; cp. 24:8). Twice he pronounces the triple fate of **the sword, famine and plague** (vv. 17-18; cp. 24:10). He also supplements this common formula with five other terms for humiliation, three of which occur in 24:9-10 (**abhorrent, cursing, reproach**). It is likely the exiles have already heard of Jeremiah's illustration of the baskets of figs.

Verse 19 informs the letter's recipients of the reason for this announced judgment. Once again, the problem is a failure to "listen" to the word of the LORD, which he sent repeatedly **by** [his] **servants the prophets**. They not only did wrong, they failed to heed the LORD's warnings when he pointed out their wrongs. Interestingly, the LORD reminds the exiles that this is why they are already in Babylon. It seems that they too tend to compare themselves to their fellow Israelites. Zedekiah and the people still in Judah were seeing themselves as better than those already exiled, which prompted the proclamation of the oracle of the fig baskets (24:1-10). The reference to that oracle here might make the exiles think they rate higher in the LORD's eyes than those "poor figs" still in Jerusalem. Jeremiah informs them that both groups are guilty of the same sin. The exiles are the "good figs" only in the sense that they are those to whom the LORD promises to "do good." To participate in the "good" of Israel's future, all must pass through Babylon.

29:20-23 Jeremiah concludes his letter with a direct reference to two prophets in Babylon who are contradicting his words. The two are **Ahab son of Kolaiah and Zedekiah son of Maaseiah**. Neither is mentioned elsewhere in the Old Testament. The latter could be the brother of Zephaniah, who is mentioned in verse 25; but this is in no way certain. If they are brothers, they sit on different sides of the political table.

Jeremiah first announces the LORD's sentence against them (vv. 21-22), then he identifies their offenses (v. 23). The sentence on these prophets has parallels elsewhere in Jeremiah. There are several instances like this one, where the LORD promises to **hand them over** to the Babylonians (see on 38:3). It is a bit unusual here, because this is the language of capture, and they already are captives. He also says he will **put them to death**, which is a fairly generic sentence (11:22; 20:5-6; 21:6,9; 28:16). The form of death (by "roasting," קָלָה, *qālāh*), has precedents in Babylonian law.[3] Finally, he spells out how they will be used as part of a **curse** (קְלָלָה, *qᵉlālāh*) yet another allusion to the oracle of the two baskets of figs (cp. 24:9). The actual accusations against them are a bit unusual. One is no surprise: **in my name [they] have spoken lies**. This is the standard accusation against prophets who try to contradict Jeremiah's message (5:31; 20:6; 23:25; 27:15). There is also the unexpected charge of **adultery**, yet one which accompanies charges of lying elsewhere in Jeremiah (7:9; 9:3).[4] By way of conclusion, the LORD declares himself **a witness** (v. 23). He is a witness both to their sin and to the letter.

M. MESSAGE TO SHEMAIAH (29:24-32)

The text supplements Jeremiah's letter to the exiles with two oracles regarding priestly reactions to it. The first reveals the nature of the priestly response (vv. 24-28), the second gives the LORD's response to it (vv. 30-32). In between, we discover that Jeremiah has at least one ally among the priests, "Zephaniah son of Maaseiah" (cp. 21:1; 37:3). This priest is a man of some importance, as he is the primary addressee of the letter. He is a supervisor over the temple (v. 26), in the same capacity as Pashhur several years earlier (20:1). Like Ahikam (26:24), he thwarts the efforts of those who try to silence Jeremiah.

29:24-28 The priestly response to Jeremiah seeks to negate Jeremiah's message by classifying him as a **madman** (אִישׁ מְשֻׁגָּע, *'îš mᵉšuggā'*; cp. 2 Kgs 9:11; Hos 9:7). **Shemaiah**, a priest already in exile, calls on **Zephaniah**, a **priest** still **in Jerusalem**, to fulfill his duties to

---

[3]Thompson, *Jeremiah*, p. 549.
[4]Some propose this is hyperbole. Holladay, *Jeremiah 2*, p. 144; Brueggemann, *Jeremiah*, p. 262.

silence **any madman who acts like a prophet**. The punishment he
mentions is essentially that employed by Pashhur, in an earlier
attempt by a priest to silence Jeremiah (20:1-6). He then cites the
message of Jeremiah's recent letter (v. 5) as "proof" that he is a madman.

29:29-32 After Zephaniah has warned him of these maneuver-
ings by Shemaiah, Jeremiah receives a judgment oracle against the
priest from the LORD (vv. 31-32; cp. 22:30). He accuses the priest in
the same terms used to accuse Hananiah (**I did not send him, and**
[he] **has led you to believe a lie**; cp. 28:15). The pronouncement of
judgment points to the primary deficiency in the faith of these early
exiles. Like the false prophets to whom they are listening, they want
a speedy cessation to their suffering. They believe correctly that the
LORD is merciful and will deliver them from their exile, but they do
not want to have to wait for that deliverance. "Only in retrospect,
after an interval of some decades, did the words of Jeremiah begin
to take on a more optimistic and reassuring note."[5] True faith in the
LORD means trusting in him to do not only what he deems best, but
when he deems best. Jeremiah tries to encourage them to "wait on
the LORD," but they — as usual — are not listening. Their refusal to
listen has brought the exile on them; it will also prevent them from
enjoying the end of the exile.

---

[5]Clements, *Jeremiah*, p. 172.

JEREMIAH 30

VI. HOPE FOR THE FUTURE (30:1-33:26)

A. RESTORATION OF ISRAEL (30:1-31:40)

The general allusions in chapters 25 and 29 to a return from exile after seventy years are like a thin ray of light, just visible through the space under a closed door. With Jeremiah 30-33, it is as if that door is briefly opened and the full brilliance of hope shining behind it is allowed to radiate out on the dismal scene of gloom that suffocates Zedekiah's reign. The words of hope within these chapters helped to sustain succeeding generations through the exile and beyond, and the fulfillment of certain passages in the life of Christ and the work of the Church have inspired and sustained Christian believers down through the centuries.

These four chapters are most commonly known as "The Book of Consolation," "The Book of Hope," or "The Book of Comfort." Their overwhelmingly hopeful tone stands in contrast to the themes of sin and judgment which predominate in most of the rest of the book. The divine command in 30:2-3 indicates that the "words" which follow hold together as prophecies of hope for restoration after exile. This theme continues through the end of chapter 33, after which there is a return to more negative themes.[1] The material within this block falls into two primary sections along general lines of literary form. The first half (chaps. 30-31) is comprised mostly of poetic oracles, the second half (chaps. 32-33) consists almost entirely of prose narrative. In this general way, these four chapters parallel the literary form of much of the rest of the book (poetry predominates in chaps. 2-20, prose in 21-29 and 34-45). The date of

---

[1]See comments on 34:1-7 for seeing that passage as a transition from these "words of hope" back to the more common themes of sin and punishment.

composition for the oracles in chapters 30–31 is uncertain. There
are several references to the return of exiles from the northern
tribes (see 30:4, and subsequent references to Jacob/Israel, Samaria,
and Ephraim), which have their closest parallels in oracles from the
end of the reign of Josiah (612–609 B.C.; see 3:6-18). It is possible
that Jeremiah has taken some of his early prophecies about the
restoration of the northern tribes and brought them together with
more recent oracles regarding Judah, for the purpose of providing
greater hope for the people in Jerusalem during the time of the final
siege (588–586 B.C.).[2] The narratives of chapters 32–33 clearly date
the prose sections to the final eighteen months of Zedekiah's reign,
when Jerusalem was under siege from Nebuchadnezzar's armies for
the last time (32:1-2; 33:1). It is easy to understand why such a message of hope and comfort would be most appropriate during a time
of such great distress.

There are approximately a dozen "sayings" within chapters
30–31. The beginning of each is marked in most instances by the
formula, "This is what the LORD says" (30:2,5,12,18; 31:2,7,15,16,23,
35,37). There are three other prophecies introduced by the formula, "The days are coming, declares the LORD" (31:27,31,38).[3] The
presence of these literary demarcations suggests that these "sayings"
were delivered at different times, but we cannot know how disparate
those times were. This does not mean, however, that the book's editor (Baruch) has arbitrarily united originally independent prophecies, the sum of which is different in message from the original
intent of each. Rather, there is a commonality of themes among the
various units, reflecting an interdependence which existed among
them from the outset. The combining of these various units into a
cohesive collection merely makes obvious the common message of

---

[2]So Holladay, *Jeremiah 2*, p. 156; Thompson, *Jeremiah*, pp. 551-555; Parke-
Taylor, *Formation*, p. 126. This too would parallel what seems to be going on
in much of Jeremiah 2-20, where "early" and "late" prophecies are woven
together.

[3]Jeremiah 31:26 speaks of Jeremiah "waking up" (from a prophetic vision
or dream). The next unit begins, for the first time here, with the clause,
"The days are coming." The note in 31:26 probably referred originally only
to the oracle immediately preceding (31:23-25); but its placement in the
sequence of "sayings" now gives it a larger structural function as well. It
seems to serve as a marker of a transition from one group of sayings to
another. See McKane, *Jeremiah*, pp. 808, 811. The significance of such a shift
is unclear.

all the prophecies recorded here. The fact that these prophecies might have been spoken at any time in Jeremiah's career — even at times when his main message consisted of indictments for sin and threats of imminent divine punishment — indicates how the mercy of the LORD is always part of his ultimate plan, even when his anger burns most hotly.

30:1-3 The first "saying" introduces this entire section in a couple of ways. First, the LORD instructs Jeremiah to record **all the words I have spoken to you**. This is similar to the instructions given to Jeremiah in 36:2, when the LORD tells the prophet to dictate to Baruch a scroll containing the prophecies he had spoken prior to that time (605 B.C.). Verse 3 suggests, however, that this scroll will contain only those prophecies having to do with the return from exile. The instructions in chapter 36 go on to refer to "every disaster" the LORD intends to bring on "Israel, Judah and all the other nations." It seems that he intends this scroll to encourage in the same way he intends the other to serve as a warning. Second, these verses prepare the reader for the prophecies that follow by using the two introductory formulas used in those prophecies (**This is what the LORD . . . says**, v. 2; **The days are coming, declares the LORD**, v. 3).

30:4-11 This initial prophecy reiterates that the LORD directs his promises of restoration to all **Israel**, not just to those of the southern kingdom of **Judah** (v. 4). The LORD's promises regarding his people concern not only restoration but reunification. The division of David's kingdom was a direct result of the introduction of idolatry by King Solomon (1 Kings 11). A long history of rival claims to the LORD's promises had deepened the hostility between north and south, as evidenced by allusions to unfavorable comparisons between the two (see 7:15); but the root of the problem was idolatry. The elimination of idols (as called for by Jeremiah) should naturally open the way for the reunification of the kingdom.

The prophecy then proceeds in two phases. A depiction of Israel's destruction as comparable to labor pains (vv. 5-7) leads into a longer promise of the LORD's salvation of his people (vv. 8-11). The comparison of the people's anguish with labor pains is made a few other times by Jeremiah and other Israelite prophets (13:21; 22:23; 49:24; Isa 26:16-17; 66:7-11; Hos 13:13). It connotes the greatest pain imaginable.[4] There is some ambiguity in the text about when

---

[4]There might be an implied compounding of the pain, because male war-

this anguish occurs. The NIV translates all the verbs of verse 7 in the future tense, suggesting the suffering is yet to commence. In fact, the first two clauses are verbless clauses in Hebrew (verbs of being can merely be implied). The future tense is inferred from the final verb in the verse (**he will be saved**), which is expressed by the Hebrew imperfect form (denoting incompleted action). However, this sequence of clauses might just as well indicate that the people have already entered into the time of suffering and only the salvation is yet to come.

In any case, the final clause of verse 7 turns the attention of the reader from the people's suffering to the LORD's salvation. He promises to **break the yoke . . . and tear off their bonds** (v. 8; cp. Hos 11:4). These "yoke" and "bonds" refer to the domination of the Babylonians. The people now "serve" those foreign rulers, but soon they will be freed — **to serve the LORD their God** (v. 9). There is a strong connection between these lines and Jeremiah 2:20, where Jeremiah describes how the people had broken free from the LORD's "yoke and . . . bonds" to "serve" other gods rather than him (cp. 5:5). Now they are breaking free from the "yoke and bonds" of the Babylonians to "serve" the LORD once again.[5] These lines also fit nicely in the flow of the book, coming so soon after the account of Jeremiah's symbolic act of wearing a yoke as a way of calling nations to submit to Babylon (27:2). This announcement reverses that recently-mentioned event. This does not necessarily mean that this prophecy was originally given in response to that symbolic act. It could be that Jeremiah and Baruch remind the people of the symbolism here to show them how the hope the LORD holds out for his people is a reversal of their present distress.

This hopeful image includes **David their king** (cp. Hos 3:5). The promise of an eternal dynasty for David and his house is not retracted because of the actions of his descendants. Their actions have brought on this exile, but it constitutes only a temporary interruption in the fulfillment of that promise.[6] The LORD will once again

---

riors are enduring pain that is reserved for women alone. Brueggemann, *Jeremiah*, pp. 272-273.

[5]The line, "no longer will foreigners enslave them," is rendered more literally, "no longer will they serve foreigners" (cp. 5:19).

[6]The same is true of the promise to Abraham, that his descendants would inherit a particular land. Yet, at another level, the reiteration of the promises in this context point to a fulfillment of them in a way that transcends

raise up a king from the line of David to deliver them from foreign oppressors, just as he "raised up" deliverers in the days of the judges (Judg 2:16,18; 3:9,15).

As the train of thought progresses into verses 10-11, Jeremiah mixes the image of the servant with the language of divine appointment, particularly the language of Jeremiah's call. The LORD addresses the nation as **Jacob my servant** and **Israel** (cp. 46:27-28).[7] This might originally have been in reference to the northern tribes only, but it could also refer to all twelve tribes. This form of address is most common in the second half of Isaiah (Isa 41:8-9; 44:1-2,21; 45:4; 48:20; 49:3), but it does not constitute a "late" development in the thinking of the Israelites.[8] It is part of a larger complex of phrases used as far back as Deuteronomy and Joshua. There, the LORD refers to Moses as "my servant" (Josh 1:1-2). Moses had earlier told Joshua not to be "afraid" or "discouraged," because the LORD would be "with" him in all his battles (Deut 31:8). The LORD himself reiterates this to Joshua after Moses' death (Josh 1:5-9).[9] By the end of his life, Joshua too is called "the servant of the LORD" (Josh 24:29; Judg 2:8). The LORD's promise here to **save** his servant from **exile** would remind Jeremiah's listeners of Joshua as well, since the name Joshua means "salvation of the LORD." Moreover, they would have made an immediate connection between the LORD "raising up" someone (the Davidic king) and "saving" them, because the LORD "raised up" judges after Joshua, who "delivered" (= "saved") them from foreign oppressors (Judg 2:16,18; 3:9,15), giving them **peace**, or "rest" (שָׁקַט, šāqaṭ).[10]

Essentially then the LORD is promising his people the culmination of a new sequence of deliverance from Egypt (now Babylon)

---

the external and physical. It is not the possession of a physical land or the rule of a physical king that gives the promises their ultimate meaning. Instead, it is the realization of the sovereignty of the LORD, that he is the one who gives the land and appoints its ruler. Clements, *Jeremiah*, pp. 179-180.

[7]For further discussion of this parallel, see Parke-Taylor, *Formation*, pp. 119-126.

[8]Compare the comments of Thompson, *Jeremiah*, p. 557; Clements, *Jeremiah*, p. 182.

[9]Similar language is used by David to encourage Solomon, as they prepare for the transition of power in their time (1 Chr 28:20). The LORD often refers to David as "my servant" (Jer 33:21-22,26; 2 Sam 7:5,8; 1 Kgs 8:66; 11:13,32-38; 14:8; cp. 1 Kgs 3:6-9; 8:24-30).

[10]The difference with Isaiah and Jeremiah is the way they "democratize" this image by applying it to the whole nation.

and conquest of the land. In the earlier event, the LORD had demonstrated his "name," his twofold character of mercy and punishment (Exod 34:6-7). The two cannot be separated. There are definite echoes of that early revelation of the LORD's "name" in the final clause of verse 11 (**I will not let you go entirely unpunished**; see Exod 34:7). By referring to their punishment in these terms, he is intimating that he will also demonstrate his mercy (Exod 34:6) in this instance. Moreover, the story of the Exodus has its sequel in the story of Joshua's conquest in the land, a conquest that ends in peace and prosperity for the Israelites. In the same way, once they return to that land after the exile, they will enjoy the **peace and security** (וְשַׁאֲנַן שָׁקַט, šāqaṭ wᵉša'ănan; see Josh 11:23; 14:15; Judg 3:11,30; 5:31; 8:28) they enjoyed in the days of Joshua and the judges.

The echoes of Jeremiah's call add further assurance to this promise. The LORD had told Jeremiah, "Do not be afraid of them, for I am with you and will rescue [= "save"] you" (1:8). The people can see how the LORD has honored this promise throughout Jeremiah's long career, and so they can be reassured that he will also "save" them, as he is promising now (30:11).

30:12-17 The assumption about the two aspects of the LORD's "name" continues into this next unit. The object of the LORD's attention is Jerusalem personified (**Zion**, v. 17); the **you(r)** used throughout is feminine in form (cities are often spoken of as women). The unifying theme here is the **healing** of wounds (cp. 8:22; 10:19). Jerusalem has a **wound** (שֶׁבֶר, šeber; also v. 15) that cannot be cured, an **injury** (מַכָּה, makkāh; also v. 17) that will not heal (v. 12). The reason why it is incurable is the LORD himself inflicted it (v. 15). He has hurt them as punishment for their **sins** against him, and the punishment is equal in measure to the crime (vv. 14-15). Their sins are **great and many** (cp. 5:6), and so are their injuries. Since the LORD caused the pain, he alone can take it away; and now he promises to do so (vv. 16-17).

The shift from injury to healing is accompanied by a shift from **allies** (v. 14) to **enemies** (v. 16). The LORD refers to the latter in a fourfold expression of the reversal of fortunes which Jerusalem will enjoy. He has wounded Jerusalem by sending those who have **devoured**, those who have **exiled**, those who have **plundered**, and those who have **despoiled**. The healing will come when those agents of injury receive the same treatment themselves. The motivation for this shift is divine pity. Jerusalem is the LORD's chosen city, but now she is ridiculed. The other nations belittle the Israelites, as if their present condition is a reflection of their true worth. She has been declared an **outcast** ("one driven out"; cp. 40:12; 43:5) by those whom the LORD sent to punish her; they ridicule her because **no one cares** ("seeks") for her (v. 17; also in v. 14). The LORD knows that the Israelites' present condition exists only because he has decreed punishment and humiliation for them. Their true calling is to be a people that "belongs," not one that is "driven out." Their true calling is to be a people "sought" by others, yet here they are "despised and rejected." The LORD feels pity for those whom the world despises. Every human being is of great worth, and the LORD is tenderhearted toward those whose high value is not appreciated. It is the LORD's pity for his chosen people — not their renewed righteousness — that moves him here.[11]

30:18–31:1 The balance of the LORD's message shifts to the side of mercy in this unit. Several lines promising restoration climax with the LORD's declaration of the ancient covenant vows (vv. 18-22). He digresses briefly to describe the prerequisite destruction of Israel's foes (vv. 23-24), but then concludes by reaffirming his covenant vows with Israel in 31:1.[12]

These optimistic words begin with the broad promise, **I will restore the fortunes of Jacob's tents**. The phrase, "restore the fortunes" (שְׁבוּת שׁוּב, *šûb šᵉbûth*), is most common in this block of Jeremiah (30:3,18; 31:23; 32:44; 33:7,11,26; cp. 29:14; 48:47; 49:6,39; cp. Deut 30:3; Ps 126:4; Lam 2:14; Ezek 16:53; 39:25; Amos 9:14; Zeph 2:7).[13] It refers generally to the restoration of a nation's past glory. Things that are destroyed by invading armies are rebuilt, fields are replanted, everyday pleasures are enjoyed once again. Some of those things are specified here in the rebuilding of the city

---

[11]Brueggemann, *Jeremiah*, pp. 277-278.

[12]This verse also points the reader ahead to the following saying (31:2-6). The conclusion here is the same conclusion one finds in Hos 2:14-23, and Jer 31:2-6 echo the themes of Hos 2:14-23.

[13]The precise meaning of the phrase is disputed. The second term in the phrase most naturally comes from the root שָׁבָה (*šābāh*), meaning "take captive." If this is correct, the phrase reads, "return the captivity" (see 30:3; 31:23; 33:7, in the NIV) The sense is that the restoration will look like a reversal (mirror image) of the exile. Many scholars assert, however, that the second term is derived from שׁוּב (*šûb*), yielding a translation like "turn the turning." The sense here is that the LORD has "turned away" his people, and now he will "turn" them back to their land. Thompson, *Jeremiah*, pp. 555-556; Holladay, *Jeremiah 2*, p. 142.

and its palace, and in the singing of songs (in contrast to 7:34; 16:9; 25:10).[14] There is also a good deal of attention placed on a new leader (v. 21). The LORD does not specify here that this leader will be a descendant of David, but neither does he deny that. Instead, his remarks hint at the way in which the leader will fulfill the expectations for a king, as spelled out in Deuteronomy. The so-called "law of the king" (Deut 17:14-20) lists several requirements of Israel's kings, the first two being that he be chosen by the LORD and that he come from among the Israelites. It is these two requirements that the LORD mentions here. It is likely that the others mentioned in Deuteronomy are to be understood in Jeremiah as well. In the immediate context of exile, these comments serve a dual purpose. On the one hand, they remind the kings that they have not lived up to the expectations placed on them from the beginning. On the other hand, they hold out an element of hope, because Israel's rulers will once again be Israelites, not foreigners.

The primary emphasis in verse 21 is on the fact the LORD will choose Israel's ruler. He will be able to approach the LORD only because the LORD brings him near.[15] No man, not even the religious leader of God's people, can **devote himself** ("pledge his heart") to spiritual pursuits perfectly enough to be worthy to approach God on his own. It requires a dying to self, an acceptance of the need for the LORD's help in every aspect of one's life, for even the best of us to

---

[14]The precise meaning of the reference to "children" (v. 20) is uncertain. The English translation suggests a continuation from "them" and "their" in verse 19 (songs rising from the inhabitants of "Jacob's tents" and the city and palace) to "their" in verse 20. There is a transition in the Hebrew at the beginning of verse 20, however, to "his/its children" (not "their children"), etc. One possible antecedent for "his" is "the palace." The term for "palace" is better translated "citadel," probably referring to the special fortifications that protected the royal residence. It could be that Jeremiah is thinking of the palace district in Jerusalem as the "father" district, and other neighborhoods as the "children." The more common form of the metaphor, however, is to speak of main cities and outlying villages as "mothers" and "daughters" (e.g., Josh 15:47; Judg 1:27; Jer 49:2). For this reason, it could be that the antecedent of "his" is Jacob (v. 18). This, in effect, is the sense adopted by the NIV. See Holladay, *Jeremiah 2*, p. 178; Thompson, *Jeremiah*, pp. 561-562.

[15]There is a wordplay in the Hebrew of verse 21 that is missed in the English translation. The law requires that the king come "from among them" (מִקִּרְבּוֹ, *miqqirbô*). Then the LORD says of the king that he will "bring him near" (הִקְרַבְתִּיו, *hiqrabtîw*). Both derive from the root *qereb* ("near"). See "coming near," see Holladay, *Jeremiah 2*, p. 179.

be able to approach God.[16] This perspective is necessary for a proper interpretation of all these verses. The restoration of the LORD's people will be accomplished by the LORD himself. As he says, **I will restore the fortunes . . . I will add to their numbers . . . I will bring them honor.** These are not things they will accomplish on their own; it will be the LORD's doing.

This focus on the role of the LORD continues in verses 23-24. The cessation of the Israelites' oppression will come with the defeat of their conquerors. That can only be accomplished because the LORD himself will fight against those powerful foes. These events, which now seem impossible, will demonstrate how the will of the LORD cannot be thwarted. These verses have a parallel in 23:19-20. The two passages work nicely together, but in different ways, according to their respective contexts. In the context of chapter 23, the concern is with false prophets, who vainly encourage their listeners with their own wishful thinking. The focus there is on the human source of the people's unfounded optimism. Here, the concern is with people who see no reason for hope, who doubt the power and love of the LORD. The focus here is on the divine source for countering the people's shortsighted pessimism.[17]

The reiteration of the covenant vows in 31:1 (**I will be** [their] **God . . . and they will be my people**; cp. Hos 2:23) should now serve to reassure the people that their relationship with the LORD still stands, while reminding them of the two sides of that relationship. One side is the LORD's pledge to protect them and bless them. The other side is their own pledge to serve him wholeheartedly (see Deut 26:16-19). The people had lived their lives for generations with an eye to the first side, while minimizing the importance of the second. Jeremiah's central message to them is — as it always has been — that a community of believers cannot expect to enjoy the LORD's blessings without their own wholehearted devotion to him and his ways.[18]

---

[16]This thought is made clear in several NT passages. In particular, one might consider Heb 10:19-25, where "drawing near to God" is predicated on the purifying work of Jesus on our behalf.

[17]See also Parke-Taylor, *Formation*, pp. 85-89.

[18]It might seem that this point contradicts the one preceding, regarding the LORD's role in drawing people to him. This is not the case. Both require an active recognition of the LORD's sovereignty. In the first, the true believer recognizes the need for the LORD's help and mercy in being able to approach him. In the second, the true believer recognizes the need to submit one's ways to the LORD's ways, as laid out in his laws.

JEREMIAH 31

A. RESTORATION OF ISRAEL (30:1–31:40) (continued)

31:2-6 Once again, Jeremiah utilizes imagery from Hosea in weaving together themes from Israel's premonarchic period with the themes of his own prophetic call. Verse 2 mentions the transition from **desert** to **rest**,[1] which parallels the progression from Israel's days in the wilderness to the conquest and settlement of the land (cp. Hos 2:14-23). The talk of **love** and "drawing" Israel to the LORD in verse 3 echoes the language Hosea used in Hosea 11:4 to describe the wilderness period. The hopeful reference to the **planting** of **vineyards** (v. 5) also reminds one of Hosea's words of hope (Hos 2:15,23), yet these go beyond Hosea's words in true Jeremianic fashion by coupling the language of "planting" with the language of "building" (v. 4; cp. Jer 1:10; 24:6). The mention of **tambourines** and "dancing" (v. 4) suggests a reversal of the mournful images in some of Jeremiah's prophecies of doom (7:34; 16:9; 25:10). The triple use of **again** in verses 4-5 emphasizes how this is not something new, but a return to past glories and prosperity in Israel. This further implies that there had been a time of faithfulness to the LORD in the past. An intriguing aspect of this saying are the references to **Samaria** (v. 5) and **Ephraim** (v. 6).[2] These are the tribes of the north, but they are returning to **Zion**, the city of David in the south, to worship the LORD. The hope for all Israel entails again the leadership provided by the Davidic monarch (see 1 Kgs 12:26-27).[3]

---

[1]The term for "rest" (רֶגַע, *rega'*) is not the one commonly used in Joshua and Judges, but it is synonymous (cp. Jer 6:16).

[2]"Ephraim" occurs in Hosea more often than in any other OT book; it occurs in Jeremiah 31 four times (31:6,9,18,20), and only three times in the rest of the book (4:15; 7:15; 50:19).

[3]Thompson, *Jeremiah*, pp. 567-568.

31:7-14 A few allusions to the prophecies of Hosea can be seen in these verses as well. The strongest is in the father-son metaphor of verse 9 (cp. Hos 11:1-11). The pairing of **ransom** and **redeem** in verse 11 echoes Hosea 13:14 (cp. Exod 15:13; Deut 7:8; 9:26), a passage regarding the LORD's power over death itself, a passage quoted by Paul (1 Cor 15:55). It is also likely that the language of agricultural prosperity (**the grain, the new wine and the oil**; v. 12) has its antecedents in Hosea's prophecies (Hos 2:8,22; but see Joel 2:19). Still, Jeremiah supplements these agricultural metaphors with shepherding imagery (**the flocks and herds**; v. 12; cp. 3:24; 5:17). This is anticipated in the way the LORD talks of leading his people **beside streams of water on a level path** (v. 9; cp. Deut 8:7; Ps 107:7), which sounds similar to Psalm 23:2-3 (cp. Isa 40:11). He uses this shepherd metaphor again in verse 10, speaking of how he will **gather** those whom he has **scattered** (cp. 50:6-7,19).

Jeremiah expands on these images in other ways that are typical of him. His principal theme is the rejoicing that will replace the mourning and sorrow currently exhibited by the people of Jerusalem. One way Jeremiah brings out this theme is to talk about the return of **joy** to the people (vv. 7,12,13). Jeremiah had prophesied on earlier occasions about how "joy" and "gladness" would cease with the coming of the Babylonians (7:34; 16:9; 25:10; cp. 33:11). Now he is predicting a reversal of their misfortunes. These joyful people will come **from the land of the north** (v. 8),[4] a land currently known as the home of Judah's savage attackers (see 6:22-24). The weakest of the people (**the blind and the lame**) will be among those restored and rejoicing. There is a sense of completeness to this communicated by the inclusiveness of the designations in verses 13-14. These include female (**maidens**) and male, **young men and old**, **priests** and [common] **people**.[5] The whole nation will rejoice.

Unlike Hananiah (28:1-11), Jeremiah's message of hope can be greeted with confidence, because only Jeremiah has accurately predicted the misery which they now endure (see 37:18-19). These words of hope seem to carry much more weight and significance coming from Jeremiah, because he has said much which has made the people

---

[4]This particular construction is most common in Jeremiah (3:18; 6:22; 10:22; 16:15; 23:8; 50:9; cp. Zech 2:6; 6:6,8).

[5]This pairing of "priests" and "people" marks another reversal of a message proclaimed by Hosea (Hos 4:9) and reiterated by Jeremiah (Jer 1:18; 19:1; 23:34).

weep over the years. To hear such words of comfort from Jeremiah must have sounded extremely sweet to the people of Judah.

31:15 This short saying seems out of place in the present collection, because it is extremely brief and somber in tone. It is here primarily to set up the emotional context of verses 16-22 (see especially v. 16), which serve as a hopeful response to this description of Israel's sorrow.

Ramah had been an important religious and political city for centuries. It was the home of Samuel, and so it was involved in the history of the founding of the dynasties of Saul and David (see 1 Sam 7:15-17; 8:4; 15:34; 19:18; 25:1). Even though the city was located in Benjamin and thus part of the southern tribes, its history gave it connections to the northern tribes as well.[6] The reference to **Rachel** furthers this sense, as she was the mother of Joseph (from whom came two northern tribes) and Benjamin (a southern tribe). But this does not exhaust the significance of "Rachel" in this passage. Rachel is one of the great ancestresses of the people, so she represents their basic identity as a people and their most ancient hopes. If she is weeping, the nation itself has reason to weep over its present state. She also represents all the mothers currently in the nation. "Rachel" weeps because all the mothers of Israel and Judah weep. **Her children are no more**, meaning first of all that the tribes have been destroyed, but also reflecting the fact that so many Israelite mothers have seen their children die.

Matthew's citation of this "saying" in Matthew 2:17-18 should not be interpreted as a claim that Jeremiah was predicting the anguish endured by the people of Judea in the days of Herod. Jeremiah is speaking immediately of the anguish of his contemporaries over the final collapse of Judah. This could be an example of a prophet using one prophecy to speak of two separate occasions ("double fulfillment"). It could also be that Matthew is simply noting a parallel between the situation in the days of Herod and the situation during the time of Babylonian domination.[7]

31:16-22 This "saying" stands as a response to the preceding one. The LORD answers the dual reference to "weeping" in verse 15 with

---

[6]Some associate Ramah with Rachel's tomb. For discussion, see Holladay, *Jeremiah 2*, pp. 186-187. It is also the site where Jeremiah and other survivors were held temporarily by the Babylonians (Jer 40:1).

[7]For a discussion of the fulfillment of prophecy, see Terry Briley, *Isaiah, Volume 1* (Joplin, MO: College Press, 2000), pp. 111-122.

a dual statement of reassurance (see specifically **declares the LORD** and **They/Your children will return . . .** , vv. 16b-17). These together form a unified rationale for "Rachel" (**your** in v. 16 is feminine singular) to stop her "weeping." Her tears are regarded as **work** for which she will be compensated (**rewarded**), and this pay means **hope for your future**. The promise that serves as the basis for this hope is that the exiles will **return** from their captivity.

The words of the people[8] quoted in the following verses expand on this theme of **return** (שׁוּב, *šûb*). This term can mean "turn away" or "return, turn back." Further, a particular form of the verb (the causative form [Hiphil]) has the transitive meaning of "return, bring back." All three meanings are placed in the mouths of the people here (vv. 18-19). The flexibility of this term, used in combination with a few other key terms, should remind the reader of a couple of earlier prophecies. The theme of "return/restore" constitutes the central theme of one of Jeremiah's strongest condemnations, found in Jeremiah 8:4-7. There he talks about how the people "turned away" from the LORD, but then "refused to return" to him when he called to them (8:4-5). They refused to "repent" (נִחַם, *niḥam*), exposing how they "know" (יָדְעוּ, *yādᵊ'û*) less than a stork (8:6-7). Jeremiah reveals here that their attitude is changing as a result of the exile. Thanks to the LORD's help, the people have finally learned the lessons ("discipline")[9] they resisted earlier in his career. Now they pray for the next step: a "return" to their previous status as chosen child. They will **return** (אָשׁוּבָה, *'āšûbāh*), but only if the LORD brings them back (הֲשִׁיבֵנִי, *hăšîbēnî*, **restores**" them; 31:18). They admit that they **strayed** (שׁוּבִי, *šûbî*, "turned away"; 31:19); but since they **came to understand** (הִוָּדְעִי, *hiwwādᵊ'î*, "know"), they have **repented** (*niḥam*).

There are similar connections between 31:18-19 and portions of 3:11-4:4. In that earlier passage, the LORD mentioned "the weeping and pleading of the people of Israel" (3:21), and it is that same "weeping" which he now wishes to stop (31:16).[10] He used his role as

---

[8]The text specifically mentions only "Ephraim" (v. 18), the leading tribe of the North, but by extension it envisions both Israel and Judah. McKane, *Jeremiah*, pp. 802-803.

[9]The language of education fills the second line of verse 18. The "calf" that receives "discipline" (יֵסֵר, *yissēr*) had been "unruly" (לֹא לֻמַּד, *lō' lummad*, "not taught"; cp. Hos 10:11).

[10]The term for "moaning" in verse 18 implies "staggering about with grief."

"husband" (3:14; cp. 31:32) and "father" (3:19; cp. 31:20) to appeal to Israel to "return" to him (3;11,14,22; 4:1); now they are pledging to do so (31:18). He promised that the whole nation would "come from a northern land to. the land I gave your forefathers" (3:18), and he has just repeated that promise (31:8,16). The primary difference, though, comes in the sincerity of their repentance. He had called on them to "acknowledge" (דְּעִי, *dᵊʿî*, "know"; 3:13) their sins; now they truly do (31:19). They had even uttered words of regret, speaking of their "youthful" sins (3:24-25) and the "shame" (בֹשְׁתֵּנוּ, *boštēnû*) and "disgrace" (כְּלִמָּתֵנוּ, *kᵊlimmāthēnû*) which those sins had caused. They use the same terms to describe their feelings of regret here (31:19).

It would be natural to be skeptical of their sincerity here in view of the way they had made similar statements of regret in the past, only to see the hollowness of those statements in their subsequent actions. We must recognize, however, that the LORD received their pledge then in full awareness of the possible inability of the people to fulfill their pledge. He clearly reminded them then that their words of repentance must be accompanied with acts of repentance (4:1-4). The same is true here. He again accepts their words because he is a loving father (31:20). He also reminds them (implicitly) that they need to follow their words with deeds. This reminder is thinly veiled because he literally calls on them to **return to your towns** (31:21). This strictly physical "return" assumes a deeper spiritual "return" to a faithful relationship with the LORD. They must follow the **road signs** and **guideposts**, markers which point not only to the cities and towns of Israel, but also to the just and righteous behavior, the wholehearted worship, and the sincere honoring of their relationship with the LORD that a loving husband and father deserves.[11] The difference here, if there is one, is the recognition that true repentance requires the participation of the LORD in the process. Before they had said, "Yes, we will come to you" (3:22). Now they say, "Restore me, and I will return" (31:18). They had tried before to use human willpower alone to achieve repentance. Now they are humbling themselves to the transformative power of the LORD to produce true repentance (cp. 15:19).

---

[11]There are also some connections between 3:14-18 and 31:31-34. Only in 3:14 and 31:32 does the LORD make the statement, "I am your husband." The inclusiveness of the restoration is intimated in the references to "the house of Judah" and "the house of Israel" (3:18; 31:31).

Such a call (with its implicit promise) must have seemed hollow to the Israelites, under the present circumstances. They cannot expect to "return" to their hometowns, as long as the Babylonians forcibly occupy those towns. If they cannot "return" to those towns, the LORD cannot reasonably expect them to "return" to him. It is in this light that one must read the final, enigmatic statement of verse 22.[12] The LORD promises to do something completely new, something as unexpected as a woman "surrounding" (protecting) a man (the converse of a man suffering labor pains; 30:6). That new thing is the restoration of an exiled people to its original homeland. The people of Israel cannot lose heart because such a restoration had never happened before. This is the LORD making this promise. He is the Creator, the one who makes new things (cp. Exod 34:10; Isa 41:19-20; 43:18-19; 65:17-18).[13] If he says it can happen, it can happen. Similarly, true repentance can happen, if — and only if — the LORD is involved in the process. But it can happen with anyone, even with the hearts of the most obstinate of persons (Ps 51:10).

31:23-26 This brief oracle refers to the restoration of Judah only, describing three idealized (almost dreamlike?)[14] characteristics of the restored nation. One is the veneration of Zion/Jerusalem (**O sacred mountain**; cp. Ps 15:1; 43:3; 99:9). This is similar to the statements made regarding Jerusalem in 3:14,17, and in the writings of other prophets (Isa 2:2-4; 11:9; 27:13; 56:6-7; Joel 3:17; Micah 4:1-3; Zech 8:3). The precise nuance of the second characteristic is uncertain. The reference to farmers and nomads living **together** might imply the removal of animosity between settled and nomadic clans. Such groups are perennial opponents. They would serve here as a human example of irreconcilable foes, parallel to illustrations involving natural enemies elsewhere (Isa 11:6-8; 65:25). The reference to these groups could also intend to show the breadth of what the LORD is doing, as these groups represent the broad spectrum of agricultural livelihoods in the land.[15] Finally, the LORD promises to revive — phys-

---

[12]For discussions of possible interpretations, see Holladay, *Jeremiah 2*, pp. 192-195; ibid., "Jer xxxi 22b Reconsidered: 'The Woman Encompasses the Man,'" *VT* 16 (1966): 236-239; McKane, *Jeremiah*, pp. 806-807; Thompson, *Jeremiah*, pp. 575-576.

[13]The verb "create" is used only with the LORD as its subject in the Old Testament.

[14]Brueggemann, *Jeremiah*, p. 289.

[15]Holladay, *Jeremiah 2*, p. 196; McKane, *Jeremiah*, p. 809.

ically and, by extension, spiritually — those who are weak (1 Sam 2:4-8; Ps 113:7-9; Isa 40:27-31; cp. Matt 11:28). Putting these together, one sees the LORD enthroned securely as king, ruling over a kingdom known for its peace and prosperity (cp. Ezek 47:1-12). It is no wonder this vision leaves Jeremiah feeling quite content (v. 26).

31:27-30 The first half of this brief oracle is relatively straightforward. The LORD uses the language of Jeremiah's call (1:10) to describe the marked shift in his message from exile and destruction to return and reconstruction (cp. 24:6; 31:4-5; 42:10). Again, Jeremiah has developed a reputation as a faithful prophet because of his ability to predict the Babylonian Exile. More accurately, the LORD has been vigilant (**watching**) about punishing those guilty of sin; now he will be just as vigilant to ensure the nation's restoration (cp. 1:12). His "track record" should give the people confidence in the reliability of the current message of hope.

The second half (vv. 29-30) raises some significant theological questions. Jeremiah quotes a popular saying of the day, which Ezekiel also quotes (Ezek 18:2). Ezekiel's elaboration on the LORD's response to it is much more extensive than Jeremiah's (Ezek 18:3-32). His "bottom line" is that the LORD "takes no pleasure in the death of anyone" (Ezek 18:32). For this reason, he pledges to judge every person individually. No one will die as the result of another's sin.

This message needs to be considered in its immediate historical and theological context. Historically, the popular saying emerged as a response to the people's interpretation of what they were going through. The people obviously believe that they do not deserve the punishment they are enduring, that they are suffering (**the children's teeth are set on edge**) for sins committed by their ancestors (**the fathers have eaten sour grapes**). They have apparently rationalized their situation theologically by appeal to the ancient doctrine of God punishing the guilty "to the third and fourth generation" (Exod 34:7). They cannot understand how their behavior has been any worse than the behavior of preceding generations, at least to the degree that it would explain why they are exiled while others died in peace. They might also point to the comments of Jeremiah (Jer 15:1-4) and the author of Kings (2 Kgs 23:26; 24:3-4) as "proof" that the exile was most directly attributable to Manasseh and his generation. They, on the other hand, have not done anything to deserve this. They must be suffering, so they think, as "the third and fourth generation" of the guilty parties.

Such an interpretation suggests that the LORD is not living up to his name (Exod 34:6-7), that his vengeance and punishment surpass his mercy and forgiveness. The first half of this oracle (vv. 27-28) indicates that such an interpretation is merely shortsighted. The LORD has "uprooted . . . ," but he will also "plant. . . ." The people must wait (until the return from exile) to see the complete picture. These two verses reaffirm that the people will again see that the LORD's love and forgiveness predominate in the long-run.[16]

The second half of the oracle takes this a step further by suggesting that the punishment aspect of the LORD's "name" is being revised. The traditional rendering of that "name" suggests that a person's sins are automatically visited on that person's children and grandchildren (e.g., the suffering in David's house as a consequence of his sins against Bathsheba and Uriah). The present pledge (31:29-30) seems to constitute a change in "official policy." Such a change is allowed easily enough among humans but is completely inappropriate for God. It would imply that God changes, that he reconsiders how he deals with humans and decides another way would be better. This would consequently imply that he considers his previous "policy" to be less than perfect, and furthermore, that he had somehow been less than perfect in his dealings with past generations.

This is a very serious and complex question, which cannot be entirely answered in the present context. The reader is encouraged to consider Ezekiel 18 and reflect on scholarly discussions of that more detailed treatment.[17] A few observations seem necessary before leaving this passage, though. The first is the reminder that the LORD was not binding himself to an ironclad rule in talking about punishing "to the third and fourth generation." He did not *have* to punish to the third and fourth generations. He could, if he so desired, but he could also be more lenient (see Deut 24:16). For example, the LORD punished the generation that listened to the ten unfaithful spies by making them wander in the wilderness (Num 14:17-23), but he did not make the next three or four generations wander as well. Similarly, while the LORD brought suffering on

---

[16]McKane, *Jeremiah*, pp. 815-817; Brueggemann, *Jeremiah*, p. 291; Thompson, *Jeremiah*, pp. 578-579; Clements, *Jeremiah*, p. 189.

[17]For example, Herbert G. May, "Individual Responsibility and Retribution," *HUCA* 32 (1961): 107-120; Paul Joyce, *Divine Initiative and Human Response in Ezekiel*, JSOTSupp 51 (Sheffield: JSOT Press, 1988).

David's children because of his sins, that suffering did not continue beyond that generation. This does not contradict what is said about the LORD's "name," it merely demonstrates that the basic principle of that "name" (Exod 34:5-7) is that the LORD's mercy is shown to be greater than his punishment in the long run. One other consideration is about who is doing the talking in Jeremiah 31:29-30. It is the people who have interpreted their situation (v. 29) as an (unjust) application of the principle of punishing to the third and fourth generations. This merely reflects their perception of reality. They, in effect, appear to have deluded themselves into thinking that they are actually innocent. They then must conclude that what the LORD is doing to them in the exile is unfair. The intent in verse 30 is to show how the people's conclusions about what the LORD is doing will change. They now look upon the LORD as unfairly vengeful; later, they will see him as extremely merciful and their punishment as completely just.

31:31-34 This brief passage has had a profound influence in shaping Christian interpretation of the Old Testament, if not the whole Bible. It is on the basis of this passage, along with its interpretation in Hebrews 8–10, that Christians developed the terminology of "Old Testament" and "New Testament" ("testament" and "covenant" are parallel translations of the same term). It is according to common interpretations of this passage that Christians perceive the difference between the teachings of the Old Testament and the teachings of the New Testament. Unfortunately, quick readings of this passage have led many Christians to regard most of the Old Testament as irrelevant. A more careful examination yields the opposite result.[18]

The LORD here speaks of a "new covenant" (= "testament"), which Christians understand to be the covenant established by Jesus at the Last Supper (Matt 26:28; Mark 14:24; Luke 22:20). Certainly the characteristics of a covenant relationship described here are the characteristics of the covenant established by Christ with the Church; but one should not jump too quickly to the conclusion that the LORD here is announcing the founding of Christianity only, six centuries before that event. The matter is more complex than that.

The LORD announces that he is making **a new covenant with the house of Israel and with the house of Judah**. These two houses con-

---

[18]Brueggemann, *Jeremiah*, pp. 291-295. For discussions of technical issues, see McKane, *Jeremiah*, pp. 817-827; Holladay, *Jeremiah 2*, pp. 164-165.

note the totality of the twelve tribes, separated following the death of Solomon. The Old Covenant he identifies as the Mosaic/Sinaitic Covenant. This is the covenant mediated by Moses between the LORD and his people at Mount Sinai, immediately following the Exodus from Egypt, and extending through the laws spoken on the east bank of the Jordan River, recorded in Deuteronomy. It is the covenant that has governed the people since the days they entered the land under Joshua. It is this **covenant** which the people have **broken**, "provoking the LORD to anger." It is this covenant which Hosea refers to when he talks of the LORD as a husband and Israel as an adulterous bride, "sleeping with" other gods (Hos 2:2-13). The LORD called for a "divorce" at that time, which is realized in the Assyrian exile of the northern tribes. He then went on to talk about his plans to win the hearts of the Israelites again, making a covenant again with them and restoring them to their land (Hos 2:14-23). Jeremiah adopts the metaphor of a broken marriage to warn his listeners in the days of Josiah of the possibility of an exile of their own (Jer 3:6-18). He adapts the metaphor only slightly by speaking of Israel and Judah as sisters, both guilty of adultery, both sent out of the house by their husband, and both offered the possibility of reconciliation (cp. Ezek 16:1-63; 23:1-49). The references to "the house of Israel and the house of Judah" and to the LORD as their **husband** show an intentional link between this passage and that earlier one.

There are also links to a few earlier passages in Jeremiah. Perhaps the most pronounced parallels are those with Jeremiah 11:1-13. There the LORD talks about the covenant he made with "your forefathers when I brought them out of Egypt" (11:3-4,7). He accuses them repeatedly of not "obeying" ("hearing") "the terms of this covenant" (11:3,4,6,8,10), because of "the stubbornness of their evil hearts" (11:8). He says that "both the house of Israel and the house of Judah have broken the covenant" (11:10). It is this "broken covenant" which will be replaced by the "new covenant" in 31:31-34. Another link exists between these verses and Jeremiah 5:1-13. There Jeremiah talks about his inability to find honest men in Jerusalem, among either the poor or the rich (5:4-5 [= "from the least of them to the greatest"]), so that the LORD can forgive them (5:1,7; cp. 31:34). The LORD has "supplied all their needs" (5:7), as a husband would, yet "the house of Israel and the house of Judah have been utterly unfaithful" (5:11; cp. 31:31). So, the LORD plans to "punish them" (5:8). His promise of forgiveness in 31:34 represents the opposite of that earlier judgment.

In a similar way, Jeremiah 31:34 stands as a reversal of the LORD's previous judgment on the nation spoken in Jeremiah 14:10. Jeremiah had announced the LORD's rejection of his people there, declaring "he will now remember their wickedness and punish them for their sins." Jeremiah is now announcing the reversal of that earlier judgment. The hopeful attitude inherent to the New Covenant is foreshadowed in Jeremiah 24:6-7 (cp. 31:4-5), where there is a mixing of talk about the "heart" of God's people (cp. 29:13), about the expectation that they will "know" the LORD, and the use of "marriage" language to describe their relationship.

It is from this background that Jeremiah's audience would hear this prophecy. As he had done through Hosea, the LORD is talking about establishing again a covenant with his soon-to-be-exiled people. Yet he says that this **new covenant . . . will not be like the covenant I made with their forefathers**. This raises a natural question: How is this "New Covenant" different from the "Old Covenant" of Moses? It is in answering this question that Christians often veer off course in their interpretation of this passage. Verses 33-34 describe the essential characteristics of this New Covenant. Many readers assume that each of these characteristics is "new," but that is not the case. Once we realize this, the text forces us to reflect further (and with greater understanding) on what the LORD is saying here.

The description of the New Covenant (vv. 33-34) consists of four parts, each delineated in a pair of synonymous lines. (This is typical of Hebrew poetry, and those English translations that render this in verse rather than prose allow the reader to see this more easily.) The four parts can be summarized in this way:

(1) the laws of the covenant are to be internalized;
(2) the relationship between the LORD and his people will be like a marriage;
(3) each person will enjoy a personal relationship with the LORD, a relationship that manifests itself in every aspect of one's life; and,
(4) the LORD will forgive their sins.[19]

---

[19]Here is an enumerated rendering of these lines:
(1) I will put my law in their minds ("in their midst")
   and write it on their hearts.
(2) I will be their God,
   and they will be my people.

The wrongful conclusion that many draw from reading this passage in isolation is that the Mosaic/Sinaitic covenant was based on external obedience, that it was viewed as a master-slave relationship, that the people were not expected to have a personal relationship with the LORD ("know the LORD"), and that there was no forgiveness or, at best, it was given in anticipation of later events (i.e., the crucifixion of Christ). An examination of each of these characteristics exposes their existence in the Mosaic covenant. Recognizing this forces readers to take another look at what makes this covenant "new," which in turn will modify how they perceive the relationship between the Old and New Testaments.

The expectation of an internalization of the laws was an essential part of the Mosaic covenant. The clearest examples are in Deuteronomy 6:6 and 11:18. Moses tells the people, "These commandments that I give you today are to be upon your hearts," and, "Fix these words of mine in your hearts and minds." Moreover, Moses declared that the people could not be excused for disobedience, because "the word . . . is in your mouth and in your heart so you may obey ["hear"] it" (Deut 30:14; cp. Rom 10:8-10). There is a slight difference, however, in the way Jeremiah talks about this characteristic in regard to the New Covenant. Moses told the people to put the laws on their hearts themselves; the LORD now says that he will write them on their hearts (cp. Jer 24:7; Deut 30:6; Ezek 11:19-20; 36:26-27).[20] Jeremiah often remarks on problems with the hearts of the people in ways that echo the words of Moses in Deuteronomy. Instead of his laws (Deut 6:6; 11:18; cp. Ps 37:30-31; Isa 51:7), they have inscribed their sins on their hearts (Jer 17:1). They stubbornly refuse to keep the LORD's laws on their heart (3:17; 5:23; 7:24; 9:14; 11:8; 13:10; 16:12; 18:12; 23:17; cp. Deut 29:18-19; 30:17). Yet the LORD continues to hope that they will do as Moses had instructed their ancestors, giving their

---

(3) No longer will a man teach his neighbor or a man his brother,
saying, "Know the LORD,"
because they will all know me, from the least of them to the greatest.
(4) For I will forgive their wickedness
and will remember their sins no more.

[20]McKane (*Jeremiah*, p. 825) asserts that the passages in Deuteronomy call for the mere memorization of the laws. This seems to bend the interpretation to one's own preconceived conclusions. The result — the laws are on the hearts of the people — is the same in either case.

"whole heart" to the LORD (3:10; 4:4; 24:7; 29:13; cp. Deut 4:29; 6:5; 10:12; 11:13; 13:3; 26:16; 30:2,10), "circumcising" their hearts to him (4:4; cp. Deut 10:16; 30:6).[21] He reiterates this expectation here, in reference to the New Covenant, but in terms that seem more definite than with previous generations.[22]

The use of marriage language (wedding vows) to describe the relationship between the LORD and Israel is most evident in Deuteronomy, Hosea, and Jeremiah (Deut 26:16-19; 29:12-15; Hos 1:9; 2:23; Jer 7:23; 11:4; 24:7; 30:22; 31:1; 32:38). The people enter into it at Sinai (Exod 19:3-6; 24:3-8), the next generation reaffirms it on the Plains of Moab (Deut 26:16-19), and Joshua's generation begins the process of perpetuating it, in a ceremony at Shechem (Josh 8:30-35; 24:1-27; cp. Deut 27:1-8). The failure of later generations to maintain this covenant relationship is what prompts Hosea to announce the judgment he does against the northern tribes. A similar failure leads Jeremiah to announce a similar judgment against the southern tribes (3:6-10). This expectation in the New Covenant is again a reiteration of ancient expectations which the people had not been meeting.

The full implications of the third characteristic might not be obvious to many readers. Jeremiah uses the language of "knowing" the LORD, language which seems rather nebulous. Modern readers might assume this refers to a purely spiritual (or mental) phenomenon. Fortunately, Jeremiah clarifies some of what he means by this expression with his words in Jeremiah 22:15-17. There, to "know" the LORD is to "[do] what is right and just," to "[defend] the cause of the poor and needy" (cp. 9:24). The opposite is to have one's "heart . . . set only on dishonest gain, on shedding innocent blood, and on oppression and extortion." Elsewhere, Jeremiah can say about those living under the Old Covenant, "'They go from one sin to another; they do not know me,' declares the LORD" (Jer 9:3; cp. Hos 4:1,6). Or, he can say, "From the least to the greatest, all are greedy for gain" (Jer 6:13;

---

[21]When Paul talks to Christians about "circumcision of the heart" (Rom 2:28-29), he is affirming an Old Testament principle; he is not giving a new principle that supersedes what existed prior to Christianity.

[22]It could even be that the "old covenant" refers to the corrupted ways in which the Israelites have lived out the Mosaic Covenant, and that the LORD is simply calling them back to the kind of covenant relationship he originally intended them to have with him (see Thompson, *Jeremiah*, p. 581; cp. Matt 5:17-20).

8:10). The clear implication is that, in the New Covenant, each person will naturally "do what is right and just" so perfectly that no one — like Jeremiah, for instance — will ever have to encourage a "neighbor" or "brother" to such behavior (cp. Isa 1:3). These lines match the promise of the LORD regarding the "good figs" in 24:7, where he says, "I will give them a heart to know me," and, "[they will] return to me with all [their] heart" (cp. Joel 2:12).

This characteristic reminds us that a proper relationship with the LORD translates into proper relationships with one's fellow human beings. The two cannot be separated. This connection is implied throughout the book of Deuteronomy, especially in "the greatest commandment" (Deut 6:5). This command, in the context of the whole book, implies both unadulterated devotion to the Lord and the doing of "justice and righteousness" toward others (see Deut 4:5-8; 6:1-3,24-25; 7:12-14; 16:18-20). The expectation of the New Covenant is that the ideals of the Old Covenant will be realized, but there is no indication that those ideals have changed. The LORD has always called on those who "know" him to do "justice and righteousness." The difference in the New Covenant is the expectation that these ideals will be realized consistently by every person.[23]

The final characteristic of the new covenant is perhaps the one most prone to misrepresentation by some interpreters. There are several aspects of this characteristic which warrant clarification. The first matter for clarification is the meaning of **remember** in the final clause. The LORD is not speaking of a loss of mental recollections regarding past misdeeds. The expression "forgive and forget" — in the literal sense common in modern Western society — is not an appropriate interpretation of the intent here.[24] Rather, the LORD is pledging not to punish people as their sins warrant. The meaning of

---

[23]There is probably a connection here with Jer 5:4-5. The inclusiveness of "from the least of them to the greatest" is reminiscent of the references there to "the poor" and "the leaders." Holladay, *Jeremiah 2*, p. 198.

[24]The Hebrew terms for "remember" and "forget" refer to mental recollection *and* to the actions which automatically follow. To "remember" a past event entails reacting to that event in the "expected" way. For example, to "remember" a past wrong is to retaliate against those who committed it (Ps 137:7; Hos 8:13; 9:9). To "remember" covenant promises is to fulfill them (Jer 14:21; Gen 8:1; 9:15-16; 30:22; Exod 2:24; 6:5; Lev 26:42; Deut 9:27; Ps 111:5; Ezek 16:60). To "remember" persons implies acting toward them in a way that honors them (Luke 23:42; Heb 13:3,7; cp. Exod 20:8).

this bicolon is most clearly recognized by comparison with Hosea's remarks to his northern audience 150 years earlier. In Hosea 8:13 he says, "The LORD is not pleased with them. Now he will *remember their wickedness* and *punish their sins*. They will return to Egypt" (cp. Hos 9:9; Ps 25:7). Jeremiah says that the LORD will "*forgive their wickedness* and will *remember their sins* no more." It is clear in Hosea that "remembering wickedness" and "punishing sins" are inseparable (cp. Jer 14:10); the latter is the physical manifestation of the former. The LORD might think of a past wickedness, but until he punishes the guilty party, he has not "remembered" that wickedness. Conversely, the LORD shows he has truly "forgotten sins" by declaring that he will never punish the guilty party.[25] In sum, "forgive" and "forget" here are synonymous terms for a single act; they do not denote sequential and complementary acts.

The second matter for clarification involves a question about what the LORD means by **wickedness** and **sins**. It is possible to interpret these as references to the sinful acts which have led to the imminent exile. In other words, it could be that the LORD is promising forgiveness of the sins that led to the exile and an eventual end to the suffering and shame that the Israelite nation will endure at the hands of the Babylonians. This follows as well from the passages in Hosea. His words refer to the sins which led the northern tribes to be exiled, so "forgetting" those past sins would lead to a return from exile. Such a restrictive interpretation of Jeremiah 31:34 is probably not warranted, however. Forgiveness is an essential characteristic of the LORD (see Exod 34:5-7), so it is logical to assume that the promise regarding forgiveness in the New Covenant alludes to the perpetual display of this characteristic in the future (see Isa 43:25; 64:9). He will forgive the sins which led to exile, but also any sins subsequently committed.

Another important consideration for interpretation here is the first word of the line: **For.** This seems to make forgiveness of sins the prerequisite for the preceding characteristics. The people can internalize the laws *only* because the LORD forgives them; they can have a marriage relationship with him *only* because he forgives them; they

---

[25]There are also two theological difficulties with popular ideas about "forgive and forget." One is that it implies that humans can know ("remember") something that God does not. Second, it undermines divine mercy. If there is no memory of a past wrong, then there is no memory of forgiveness.

can do justice and righteousness *only* because he forgives them. It is not necessary to assume that one particular act of forgiveness will achieve these results, though. They naturally follow every act of forgiveness that is duly recognized by the human recipient.

This leaves perhaps the most significant question: Was there forgiveness of sins in the OT? Based in part on later interpretations of this passage, many Christians arrive at a negative response to this question. The assumption is that the LORD promises forgiveness in the New Covenant, therefore, it must not have been present in the old. The fact that the first three characteristics of the New Covenant were also characteristics of the Mosaic Covenant suggests that the same might be true with forgiveness. A quick look at any concordance will bear this out. The LORD promises repeatedly in the laws of Moses to forgive people of their sins (Lev 4:20,26,31,35; 5:10, 13,16,18; 6:7; 19:22; Num 15:25-28; 30:5,8,12), and later Israelites assume that he does (1 Kgs 8:30,34,36,39,50; Neh 9:17; Ps 78:38; 86:5; 130:4). It is logical to conclude, therefore, that forgiveness of sins was an essential characteristic of the Old Covenant, and that the LORD is promising here to maintain a posture of forgiveness in the New Covenant.

How, then, is the New Covenant different from the Old? There are two parts to an answer. The first is given in verse 32. The people "broke" (הֵפֵרוּ, *hēphērû*)[26] the Old Covenant (cp. 11:10), but they will not break the New Covenant. It is as simple — and as difficult — as that. The expectations of the Old Covenant will finally be realized by those living under the New.[27] The LORD has been living up to the things expected of him; now the people will also live up to what has been expected of them. This will not be the result of having "better" people, though. The LORD himself will write his laws on the hearts of the people, establishing a strong "marriage" relationship with his people, producing people who "do justice and righteousness" in their everyday lives, people who are freed from the dominance of unjust and unrighteous inclinations because the LORD has forgiven them.

The second part is a recognition of the deepening of forgiveness provided in the New Covenant. A key influence on Christian interpretation of Jeremiah's New Covenant is the interpretation discussed

---

[26]See McKane, *Jeremiah*, p. 818.

[27]"What is promised is not so much a radically different covenant but a renewed form of the earlier, broken covenant." Clements, *Jeremiah*, p. 191.

in Hebrews 8–10. The preceding comments should not be read as a questioning or refutation of that interpretation. They are meant to sharpen what the Hebrews writer is saying. The Hebrews writer does not say that every aspect of the Old Covenant is made obsolete or changed by the New (Heb 8:13). The writer is commenting on Jesus' role as high priest, and particularly on how the sacrificial system ("regulations for worship" in 9:1) has changed. The Hebrews writer is commenting specifically on the characteristic of forgiveness raised in Jeremiah 31:34. The sacrifices of the Old Covenant are made obsolete because they provided only external purification (Heb 9:13) for past sins (Heb 10:1-2,11), while Jesus' sacrifice establishing the New Covenant (cp. Heb 9:20 and Matt 26:28; Luke 22:20) "made perfect forever those who are being made holy" (Heb 9:14). The sacrifice of Jesus cleanses the consciences of believers (Heb 9:14), so that they no longer feel guilty for their sins (Heb 10:2). The sacrifices of the Old Covenant had to be repeated, because they brought forgiveness for past sins only; but they could not "take away sins" (Heb 9:26; 10:4, 11) in the way Jesus' sacrifice does. He offered his sacrifice "once for all time" (Heb 10:12). When individuals enter into this covenant, Jesus' sacrifice atones for their sins and removes their guilt, thereby eliminating the need for any other sacrifices.

This does have a transformative effect on the three preceding parts of the covenant, however, since they all are made possible by the fourth (see above). Forgiveness at this level gives one "confidence to enter the Most Holy Place" (Heb 10:19), where God dwells. Forgiveness at this level removes the feelings of guilt aroused by repeated sacrifices, allowing a more profound internalization of the laws, a deeper understanding of the "marriage" relationship with the LORD, and a stronger inclination to treat others with "justice and righteousness." Rather than looking for weaknesses in others as a means of elevating themselves before the LORD, Christians "spur one another on toward love and good deeds" (Heb 10:24).

An important consideration for Christians to ponder, then, after reading Jeremiah 31:31-34 in this light, is the extent to which they live up to the expectations of this New Covenant. If they do, they have only the LORD to thank for that. If they do not, they should look to the example of the Israelites of the Old Testament. Here are people who knew what the LORD expected of them, yet they did not live up to those expectations. Christians should analyze why the Israelites failed, then ask themselves if they are deficient in similar ways. In fact, Christians need to "pay more careful attention to what we have heard" (cp. Heb 2:1-3). The forgiveness ("salvation") provided by the New Covenant should make it more natural to live out the expectations of the covenant. If that is not the result, should they not expect a "just punishment" (Heb 2:2) that is harsher?

31:35-36 + 37 These two brief "sayings" make the same assertion in only slightly different ways. Both assert the LORD's unwavering allegiance to his covenant promises to Israel. His covenant with Israel is as certain as the movements of the sun, the moon, and other heavenly bodies, as dependable as the ocean tides. The foundation for this certainty is the LORD's function as Creator (v. 35; cp. Isa 45:7; Psalm 148). He established a "covenant" with the heavenly objects mentioned, which explains their regularity and reliability. The same reliability undergirds his covenant with Israel. The covenant will stand because the LORD has decreed it, just as the sun maintains its course because the LORD decreed it.[28]

31:38-40 The final oracle of this series speaks of Jerusalem's restoration in a couple of very practical ways. The first (vv. 38-39) is to supply a few details about the rebuilding of Jerusalem's walls. This gives some concreteness to Jeremiah's common but general promise about the LORD "building" the nation again. The use of **rebuilt** here and **uprooted or demolished** at the end of verse 40 betrays a conscious effort to remind the reader one more time of Jeremiah's call, particularly its positive components (1:10; cp. 24:6; 31:4-5,28; 42:10). The **never again** ascribed to the destructive terms puts an exclamation point on the chapter's message that the future, positive acts of the LORD on Israel's behalf will overshadow his current acts of judgment.[29] He then gives a somewhat surprising prediction about the Kidron Valley. This valley serves as the southeastern boundary of Jerusalem. The promise here forms a contrast to the earlier judgment oracle regarding the adjoining Valley of Hinnom (19:10-13).[30]

---

[28]Brueggemann speaks of tension between the "discontinuity" implied in verses 31-34 and the "continuity" implied in verses 35-37 (*Jeremiah*, pp. 295-296). Such a reading of verses 31-34 is a bit forced. The New Covenant is essentially a renewal of the Old. The LORD places no new expectations on the people; he is dealing with them as he always has. If there is discontinuity, it is in the people's vacillating faithfulness. Verses 35-37 imply the continuity of the LORD's faithfulness, and nothing in verses 31-34 contradicts that.

[29]Ibid., pp. 299-300.

[30]Thompson, *Jeremiah*, p. 584; cp. McKane, *Jeremiah*, pp. 833-835.

That passage connects the fate and function of Jerusalem with the fate and function of the Topheth, Jerusalem's dumping-ground. This one connects the fate and function of Jerusalem with the fate and function of the Kidron Valley. The future sanctification of the Kidron Valley implies the resanctification of Jerusalem as well (cp. Ezekiel 40–48; Zechariah 2, 8, 14).

JEREMIAH 32

B. JEREMIAH BUYS A FIELD (32:1-44)

The prose narratives of chapters 32–33 divide naturally into two parts, as reflected by the division into chapters. The justification for this in the text is provided in 33:1, where it says, "The word of the LORD came to him a second time." Both narratives are set in the days of Jeremiah's confinement in Jerusalem (32:1-2; 33:1; see chapters 37–38). This is during the final Babylonian siege of the city (588–586 B.C.). When there is no longer any hope that Jerusalem will be spared, Jeremiah speaks words of hope (for life after the Exile) to its inhabitants.

The first section (32:1-44) plays off the dark message of humiliation to speak about future prosperity. Just as surely as the LORD has brought this terrible destruction on his people and their land, so he will restore their fortunes in the days ahead. This he illustrates through Jeremiah's redemption of land. The narrator (Baruch) constructs the chapter around this transaction. Having explained the reason for Jeremiah's confinement in Jerusalem (vv. 1-5), he has Jeremiah describe how he had conducted the redemption transaction with his cousin and then handed the official documents over to Baruch, and how he had then prayed to the LORD for an explanation of this seemingly futile act (vv. 6-25). A lengthy prophecy of the LORD to Jeremiah serves as a response to Jeremiah's words. He affirms the inevitability of the completion of the destruction, but then he reassures him of the equally inevitable restoration of his people (vv. 26-44). Ironically, it is the fulfillment of Jeremiah's words of destruction which now serves to provide credence to the promise of restoration.

32:1-5 Some consider Jeremiah's redemption of property to be a sequel to the events recorded in 37:11-21. Jeremiah is trying to leave Jerusalem during the siege to "get his share of the property," when he is stopped and arrested as a deserter. It is possible that Hanamel's visit to Jerusalem (vv. 6-12) is to allow Jeremiah to sign the necessary documents, so that he can conduct his property business while he is being detained.[1] The text gives the "official" explanation for Jeremiah's arrest, probably reflecting the king's position in reaction to pressures from his advisors.[2] Additional details in chapter 37 reveal that Zedekiah's words do not reveal the full spectrum of his thoughts. The king quotes some of Jeremiah's words as a way of bringing charges of treason against him (cp. 20:4-5; 21:7; 34:2-3,21-22; 37:17; 38:3,18,23). A message of doom for Jerusalem and the king would discourage those defending the city, leading to discontent and desertions among the populace (see 38:4). There is no mention here of an official defense by the prophet.

32:6-25 Jeremiah's words are not spoken as a response to the king's charges, but for the benefit of his own friends and supporters. He tells how a visit regarding family business by his cousin has confirmed the LORD's words to him (vv. 6-8). His report of the redemption transaction has similarities to other symbolic acts (13:1-11; 19:1-15).[3] He does not reveal the divine message itself until the transaction with his cousin has been finalized (vv. 13-15).

The transaction is an act of redemption. The laws concerning such a transaction are found within the Jubilee laws of Leviticus 25 (esp. 25:25,47-53). These call for a near relative to "redeem" (buy back) property forfeited to a lender during times of poverty (cp. Ruth 3:10-13; 4:2-4). The goal is for an extended family to preserve the unity of property passed down from an ancestor and divided among his various descendants.[4] Jeremiah is careful to establish that the transaction is legal and accurate because this will substantiate the veracity of the subsequent prophecy. The proper amount of money changes hands as the weighing out verifies. There are witnesses to confirm the transaction and its validity, as well as the properly signed and notarized documents. There are two copies made, one sealed and one unsealed. The assumption is that the unsealed document can be consulted if there are any challenges to the

---

[1]Clements, *Jeremiah*, p. 194; McKane, *Jeremiah*, p. 838; Holladay, *Jeremiah 2*, pp. 287-288; Parke-Taylor, *Formation*, pp. 205-208.

[2]Thompson, *Jeremiah*, p. 587; McKane, *Jeremiah*, p. 837.

[3]Holladay, *Jeremiah 2*, pp. 211-212.

[4]Thompson, *Jeremiah*, p. 588.

redemption, while the sealed document serves as a "back-up," should anything happen to the unsealed copy.[5]

Jeremiah follows these actions with an instruction to store the documents (v. 14) and an explanation of the wider implications of this instruction. He calls for them to be stored **in a clay jar**. The Dead Sea scrolls survived in clay jars for two thousand years, demonstrating how well this system might work.[6] Jeremiah wants the documents to **last a long time** ("stand many days"). This warrants explanation because there is little reason to assume anyone will be there to challenge or defend a claim to the property. One could assume that the deeds would be worthless in a very short time. The justification for preserving the deeds entails the LORD's broader promise regarding the whole land. If Jeremiah's family will someday be able to claim ownership of their property again, then so will everyone else.

Jeremiah still speaks in the first person ("I") in verse 16, continuing his message in the form of a personal prayer. He hints at a question which must have been on the hearts of **Baruch** and his other friends (on Baruch, see Introduction and chapter 36). The question is whether the LORD can "deliver" on his promise to restore the Israelites to their land. He prefaces his reservations with a rehearsal of the LORD's previous mighty acts. He acknowledges the LORD as Creator, for whom **nothing is too hard** (v. 17; cp. v. 27; Gen 18:14). He alludes to the LORD's **name**, as revealed at Mount Sinai. He acknowledges the LORD as a God who is loving, yet who punishes sin (v. 18; cp. Exod 34:5-7; Deut 7:9-11), who demonstrated his "name" by bringing the people out of **Egypt** (cp. Deut 26:8-9; Ps 78:43; 105:27), giving them victory over their enemies in the Conquest, providing for them with prosperity, but then punishing them with exile for sinning continually (vv. 19-23). It is in spite of this recognition of the LORD's power — or perhaps because of it — that Jeremiah verbalizes his doubts regarding the present situation.[7] He says that "nothing is too

---

[5]There is also evidence that the two copies might have been written on a single piece of parchment. One part was rolled up and sealed to protect it, while the other could be unrolled for reference. Holladay, *Jeremiah 2*, p. 215.

[6]Thompson, *Jeremiah*, p. 589; Holladay, *Jeremiah 2*, p. 216.

[7]Brueggemann, *Jeremiah*, p. 304. Holladay assumes that Jeremiah's tone is one of "dismay," as if the prophet is disappointed that the LORD would change his message from destruction to redemption (*Jeremiah 2*, p. 211). The assumption here is that he is incredulous, not necessarily regarding the LORD's power, but regarding his mercy.

hard" for the LORD, but does he really believe it? His statements regarding the siege betray his doubts now. Yes, the LORD can do anything, but does that really mean *anything*? The most amazing display of the LORD's power had been given in the Exodus; the current situation seems to demand an even greater display than that.[8] The LORD's answer offers reassurance (cp. 23:7-8).

32:26-44 The LORD's message unfolds in three parts. He first reiterates his intention to destroy Judah and send the people into exile based on their continual pattern of sin (vv. 28-35). This is prompted perhaps by a temporary lifting of the siege (37:4-10). Then he gives the surprising promise to restore the people to their land (vv. 36-41). The reference to the land (v. 41) leads into specific confirming promises about the people of Judah again owning their family inheritances (vv. 42-44).

The theme is set in verse 27, in direct response to verse 17. As **the God of all mankind**, the LORD truly is the God who can do **anything**. His immediate plans call for the destruction of Jerusalem at the hands of the **Babylonians**. Such a display of destructive power is awesome, though not unprecedented in the military history of the ancient Near East. A prediction of it would not have been viewed as exceptionally remarkable by Israel's neighbors (see Jer 28:8). It was probably "hard" for the Israelites to believe that the LORD would use such power against Jerusalem, but only because they viewed the LORD's promises regarding Jerusalem and the House of David as unconditional. Even this was not **too hard** for him. What would be even more remarkable to all who heard it is the prediction of the deliverance of a small nation like Israel from the control of a much larger neighbor. This had happened in the Exodus, and the people of Israel had recognized in it the truly awesome power of the LORD. It is amazing to think that the LORD would do something just as awesome — if not more so — a second time; yet that is what is promised. An awesome display of destructive power (the exile) is now to be matched by an equally awesome display of redemptive power.[9]

The ominous warning of destruction begins routinely enough, as the LORD repeats some fairly standard statements of the impending

---

[8]Determining which act actually requires more power is not the issue. Jeremiah reflects a typical reaction. In spite of our knowledge of past demonstrations of God's power, an existing dilemma still seems impossible for even him to remedy.

[9]Brueggemann, *Jeremiah*, pp. 308-310; Holladay, *Jeremiah 2*, p. 212.

capture and **burning** of the **city** (vv. 28-29; cp. 34:2-3,22; 37:8-10). He then links the burning of their **houses** to the **burning** of **incense** to foreign **gods** on the **roofs** of those houses. This seems to open the floodgates of indictment, as the LORD rehearses once again a long list of the sins of Jerusalem, most reminiscent of the Temple Sermon. There is a bit of hyperbole in this. The people **have done nothing but evil** (v. 30); they have angered the LORD **from the day** [Jerusalem] **was built** (v. 31);[10] everyone is guilty of sin from the **kings** down to all **the people** (v. 32; cp. 1:18; 6:13; 8:1). Their sin has persisted over the years in spite of the LORD's repeated warnings (through his prophets; v. 33; cp. 7:25-26; 25:4; 29:17-19; 35:15; 44:4-5). They even defiled the Jerusalem temple itself with **their idols**, and they engaged in child sacrifice, something so heinous the LORD had never dreamed it would be done (vv. 34-35; cp. 7:30-33; 19:4-6).[11]

The change in verse 36 is surprising in light of the preceding indictment. The expected sentence for such crimes is **the sword, famine and plague** (cp. 19:15-19) as Jeremiah has been announcing for at least a decade.[12] The people are now wallowing in the middle of these miseries, expecting a future of nothing but woe and death when the LORD tells them that he is promising a reversal of their current situation. He is going to **gather them** and **bring them back** from the place where he has "banished them." This will lead to a renewal of the covenant, as mentioned in 31:31-34. Here again he mentions the covenant vows (cp. 30:22; 31:1). Here again there is an emphasis on the LORD working directly on the people, cultivating fear and obedience in their hearts. He will set them an example, promising to honor his part of the covenant **"with all my heart and soul"** (v. 41), the same way they are to love him with all their heart

---

[10]Historically speaking, Jerusalem was built by the Jebusites centuries before the arrival of the Israelites. David and his men took the city without destroying it. If one takes this remark very literally, one would have to say that the LORD is punishing the Israelites, in part, for the sins of the Jebusites. Obviously, this is not the intent. He is simply emphasizing the prevalence of sin from the early days of the monarchy. Similarly, there are no references to righteous people, even though we know there were always some among the Israelites.

[11]Parke-Taylor, *Formation*, pp. 192-195.

[12]The "you" at the beginning of verse 36 is plural. He is addressing the people of Jerusalem, who are repeating Jeremiah's words as part of a lament. They are watching with heavy hearts as his words are fulfilled. McKane, *Jeremiah*, p. 849.

and with all their soul (Deut 6:5). He also makes explicit the promise that this will be **an everlasting covenant** (cp. Gen 9:16; 17:7,13,19; 2 Sam 23:5; 1 Chr 16:15-17 [= Ps 105:8-10]; Isa 55:3; 61:8; Jer 50:5; Ezek 16:60; 37:26) in contrast to the earlier one that they "broke" (31:32; cp. Isa 24:5).

A pledge to **plant them in this land** in verse 41 gives way to thoughts about ownership of land, the theme with which this section began. The certainty of destruction — which they cannot deny — is now balanced by the certainty of a return to a normal, settled life.[13] Jeremiah's act of redemption serves as a model of what will happen throughout the land. Just as he has paid silver and formalized the transaction with signatures, seals, and witnesses (vv. 9-10), so others will do the same with their property. Jeremiah's deal involves property in the land of Benjamin; the LORD speaks of how this practice will encompass Benjamin and all the other parts of the nation. This is a welcome message for a people presently experiencing complete desolation (v. 43). It is only possible because the LORD **will restore their fortunes** (v. 44; see 29:14).

---

[13]Brueggemann, *Jeremiah*, p. 302; McKane, *Jeremiah*, p. 841.

JEREMIAH 33

C. PROMISE OF RESTORATION (33:1-26)

The second prose section of hope (chapter 33) consists of a series of oracles, similar in style and themes to chapter 32. Based on introductory clauses, one can discern six distinct oracles — 33:1-9,10-11,12-13,14-18,19-22,23-26.[1] The first three promise that Israel will be reinhabited, and the second three affirm the LORD's continuing commitment to his covenant with the royal and priestly houses. The first oracle is placed chronologically during the siege. It is likely, though not certain, that the remaining oracles come from the same time.

33:1-9 The reference to Jeremiah's confinement **in the courtyard of the guard** links this chronologically to the preceding section (32:2), and to the events recorded in chapters 37–38 (37:21; 38:13,28). Jeremiah sets the tone of reassurance by introducing the LORD as "Creator" (v. 2; cp. 32:17). The Hebrew text is actually a bit more general than the English suggests. Jeremiah describes the LORD as "the one making it" (עֹשָׂה, 'ōśāh), without specifying what "it" is.[2] Whatever "it" is — the earth, the heavens, a mighty nation like Babylon — the LORD is its Creator. Whatever he decrees, therefore, is certain to come to pass.[3] At present, he is promising to **do** (עֹשֶׂה, 'ōśeh) "good things" for the city and **provide** ('ōśeh) for it (v. 9). He sets a tone of hope, promising to **answer** when they **call.** Previously he had declared he would not "listen" when they "called" to him (11:14; cp. 7:16,23-27); now he says he will not only "listen," but "answer." And he will answer in unimaginably wonderful ways (v. 3).

---

[1]Some separate out verses 17-18 as a separate oracle, but the use of "For" at the beginning seems to unite this piece to the preceding verses. See Holladay, *Jeremiah 2*, p. 230; Brueggemann, *Jeremiah*, pp. 312, 319.

[2]The LXX supplies "earth" to fill out the sense of the statement. See McKane, *Jeremiah*, p. 855.

[3]Brueggemann, *Jeremiah*, pp. 312-313.

He begins, as in chapter 32, with a word of destruction (vv. 4-5). The current devastation of the land will continue to its full extent. The **city** that is being **torn down** will be **filled with the dead**. Verse 6 ushers in a reversal of all this. The reversal most obscured by translation is in the verb, **let them enjoy** (גִּלֵּתִי, *gillêthî*). This is from the same root as the word for "exile" (גָּלָה, *gālāh*). The basic meaning is "uncover." The form for "exile" conveys the sense of fully exposing something (to danger). The form for "enjoy" might be translated "reveal, show." Where the people now experience exile, he will "show" them **peace and security**. Where there is now death, they will find **healing** (cp. 30:17). He has sent them away, but he will soon **bring** [them] **back**.[4] He now is "tearing down" their houses, but he will **rebuild** them (v. 7). They have defiled Jerusalem, filling it with **wickedness**; he will **cleanse** the city and **forgive** its inhabitants of their unrighteousness (v. 8).[5] People now speak of it as "a reproach and a byword, an object of ridicule and cursing" (24:9); it will become a place of **renown, joy, praise and honor** for the LORD (v. 9; cp. Deut 26:18-19). This will be the Creator's "doing" (see v. 3).

33:10-11 This brief oracle reiterates the restoration of life to the cities of Judah (**I will restore the fortunes**, v. 11; cp. 29:14; 30:3,18; 31:23; 32:44; 33:7,26; **as they were before**, v. 11; cp. v. 7). The description of rejoicing is a standard way of referring to "happy times" (Ps 51:8; Isa 22:13; 35:10; 51:3,11; Zech 8:19); in Jeremiah's case, this constitutes a direct reversal of the punishment currently being meted out (7:34; 16:8-9; 25:10; cp. 31:13). The words of thanksgiving Jeremiah quotes are almost identical to the opening lines of Psalms 106, 107, 118, and 136 (see also Ps 100:5; 118:29). These psalms primarily juxtapose the LORD's mighty acts of deliverance against Israel's acts of rebellion. Psalm 106 even concludes with the petition, "Save us, O LORD our God, and gather us from the nations." Jeremiah is reminding the people here of a well-known theme of their worship, in which they celebrate the LORD's omnipotence and undying mercy toward them, in spite of their sinfulness.

33:12-13 This oracle complements the preceding one quite nicely. It repeats the language of desolation (cp. vv. 10 and 12), but now the reader's attention shifts from people to livestock. The previous

---

[4]The expression "bring . . . back from captivity" is the same as "restore the fortunes" (v. 11).

[5]Holladay sees this passage as a reversal of 19:3-13. *Jeremiah 2*, p. 223.

unit describes the return of humans to the cities, while this one describes the return of sheep to the hillsides of the various agricultural regions of Judah (see 17:26). This fills out the social picture of Judah (urban and rural), showing that all will be restored. It is possible that there is a double entendre in these verses. The reference to **flocks** dotting the hillsides can be taken literally, but it could also be an allusion to the people of Judah themselves (cp. 10:21; 23:1-4; 50:6; cp. Luke 15:3-7; John 10:1-18).

33:14-18 Jeremiah opens this oracle with a reference back to the prophecy recorded in 23:5-6 (see there for further comments).[6] The lines he quotes are part of an indictment against the "shepherds" of the people of Judah (23:1-4), with a strong hint that he is singling out King Zedekiah for judgment. There, he had gone on to compare the return from Babylon with the Exodus from Egypt (23:7-8). Here, he talks about the perpetuation of the royal and priestly houses. The promise to maintain the House of **David** is stated in terms common in Samuel and Kings (2 Sam 7:12-16; 1 Kgs 2:4; 8:25; 9:5; 2 Chr 6:16; 7:18; cp. Jer 35:19). The covenant with the **Levites** is less well known, but just as sure (Num 8:12-14; 25:10-13; Deut 10:8; 18:6-7; 1 Chr 15:2; 2 Chr 29:4-11; cp. Ezek 44:10-16).[7] There would have been some uncertainty in the minds of the people about the eternality of these covenants, as both are stated at times in conditional terms. The LORD here repeats his continuing commitment to both, in spite of the sins that have led to the Exile. Despite the people's unfaithfulness, the LORD is faithful to his covenant promises. There would be ongoing speculation about and interpretation of these promises in the centuries ahead, but both covenants achieve their ultimate fulfillment in the person and work of Jesus Christ.[8]

---

[6]One difference is the shift in the application of the name, "The LORD our Righteousness," from the king to Jerusalem. Since the king sets the tone for his city, this is a very minor difference. See Thompson, *Jeremiah*, p. 601; Parke-Taylor, *Formation*, pp. 55-60.

[7]There is much suspicion regarding the authenticity of these verses, in part because of this emphasis on the high profile given to the Levites. There is also the fact that none of verses 14-26 is preserved in the LXX. For discussion, see Holladay, *Jeremiah 2*, pp. 228-231.

[8]There is a lack of clarity among the Dead Sea Scrolls regarding the fulfillment of these covenant promises. Some speak of two messiahs, one a royal messiah and one a priestly messiah (perhaps originating with the "anointing" of priests in Lev 4:3,5,16). John J. Collins, *The Scepter and the Star: The Messiahs of the Dead Sea Scrolls and Other Ancient Literature* (New York: Doubleday, 1995), pp. 74-101.

33:19-22 This oracle reaffirms the permanence of these two covenants by comparing them to two others: the "**covenant**" with **night** and **day**, and the covenant with Abraham. The first is an implied covenant. By divine command, night and day were created (Gen 1:3-5). When the "covenant" with those ends, history and time as humans know them will end. Similarly, the covenants with the royal and priestly houses of Israel were established by divine command; they too will last "until the end of time" (see 31:35-37). The LORD furthers this by making promises to these houses which are identical in form to the LORD's promises to Abraham (Gen 15:5; 22:17; 26:4; 32:12; Exod 32:13). That covenant is eternal, so these are too.

33:23-26 This final oracle in the series reinforces some of the key elements of the one just before. The **people** who are despising Israel and ridiculing her for losing her chosen status are the neighboring nations (16:10; 22:8-9; cp. Deut 29:24; 1 Kgs 9:8-9).[9] They say the LORD has **rejected** Judah and Israel.[10] The LORD's response suggests that he takes this statement personally, that somehow his abilities as a God are being brought into question. To counter this charge, he supplements his preceding remarks by comparing the Davidic covenant with his "covenant" with **heaven and earth** (cp. Deut 31:28), flatly denying that he is "rejecting" his "chosen" people and king. To get the full impact of this, one must recognize that it would not be contrary to the LORD's character for him to "reject" someone he has "chosen." Jeremiah himself uses this language to explain the

---

[9]Some have argued that these "people" cannot be Gentiles, because they are too well informed about Israel's theology. (See McKane, *Jeremiah*, pp. 863-864, and Thompson, *Jeremiah*, p. 603, for discussion.) On the other hand, this is the kind of "information" one might expect the Israelites to use in their war propaganda, when defending themselves against outside invaders (see Isa 36:13-20).

[10]It is intriguing to find the reference here to the choosing of two nations. Some have suggested that the people of "Israel" actually consisted of two separate nations, Israel and Judah (see 3:6-10; Isa 8:14; Ezek 23:1-49; 37:15-19). Thus, some say, David and Solomon actually ruled from two thrones (see 2 Sam 11:11; 19:43). It seems more likely that the political situation of the Divided Monarchy is retrojected at times back onto the situation in the days of David and Solomon, so that the natural distinction between tribes looks more marked than it actually was. The LORD later (v. 26) responds to any questions about the unity of the people by referring to their common ancestry from Abraham.

LORD's actions against Judah (Jer 6:30; 7:29; 14:19; cp. 1 Sam 15:21,26; 2 Kgs 17:20; Ps 78:67-68; 89:38-39; Lam 5:22). The LORD can "reject" those who "reject" his laws. The fact that he does not "reject" Israel here is an act of mercy, which he explains in the closing clause. He will **restore their fortunes** because he has **compassion** (רֶחֶם, *reḥem*, "motherly love") for them (see 30:18).

Viewed together, these oracles show the LORD's merciful commitment to his covenants with Israel. It would be natural for the people to express doubts about these covenants, which might lead to questions about the faithfulness of the LORD. These oracles proclaim the LORD's mercy-based allegiance to the covenants. In the process, they demonstrate once again the complementary aspects of the LORD's character. He is a God of love and mercy, of faithfulness and forgiveness, yet he punishes sin. They are currently experiencing his wrath and punishment, but the dominant side is the side of his love and mercy. He has demonstrated this over and over again in his dealings with his people, and he will demonstrate it yet again in the Exile and Return.

JEREMIAH 34

VII. PERSECUTION AND DISPLACEMENT (34:1–45:5)

A. WARNING TO ZEDEKIAH (34:1-7)

34:1-7 The narrator envelops this two-part oracle regarding King **Zedekiah** (vv. 2-3,4-5) within historical notes (vv. 1,6-7) about the final Babylonian siege of **Jerusalem** (588–586 B.C.). Archaeological discoveries have confirmed the information regarding **Lachish and Azekah** (v. 7) provided here. Several letters written by the defenders of Lachish at this time confirm and supplement our knowledge of military activities, as disclosed in this and other biblical passages. One of those letters contains a hauntingly matter-of-fact reference to the subjugation of Azekah,[1] which would be followed by the collapse of Lachish and then Jerusalem itself.

This passage serves as a bridge from the ultimately hopeful words of the preceding chapters back into the gloom that hung over Jerusalem during and after the Babylonian siege of the city. It promises a silver lining to the dark cloud Zedekiah is under as a result of his persistent refusal to "hear the word of the LORD" from Jeremiah. Jeremiah probably gives this oracle while he is "in the courtyard of the guard," after the events and prophecy recorded in 38:14-27.[2] The first half essentially is a repetition of his prediction of the exile of Zedekiah in 32:3-5. The second half (vv. 4-5) puts a salve on the wounding prediction of Zedekiah's humiliation. Although he will be led away in chains to Babylon, he will still receive honors at his funeral. At least Zedekiah will have someone to **lament** his passing!

---

[1]James B. Pritchard, ed., "Lachish Letter IV," *Ancient Near Eastern Texts Relating to the Old Testament* (Princeton: Princeton University, 1969), p. 322.

[2]This is based on the certainty with which Jeremiah here says that Jerusalem will be burned (34:2). The possibility of sparing the city of that is still held out in 38:17-18. Cp. Holladay, *Jeremiah 2*, p. 234.

This seems like little to offer, but it is more than was offered to his brother, Jehoiakim (22:18-19; 36:30; cp. 22:10-12). One must wonder, however, whether this promise is itself conditioned on a favorable response from the king, which would be more in line with Jeremiah's tone toward Zedekiah elsewhere in the book (cp. 21:8-9; 32:5; 38:20-23). Also, Zedekiah is actually blinded and further humiliated when Jerusalem falls (39:5-7). For these reasons, many read verse 4a as the protasis of a conditional sentence — "[If you] **hear the promise of the LORD . . . this is what the LORD says. . . .**"[3]

B. FREEDOM FOR SLAVES (34:8-22)

The book's inspired compiler now presents a clear example of how the people do not "hear the word of the Lord," even as their nation faces its most dire military crisis in more than a century. It is the final Babylonian siege of Jerusalem (588–586 B.C.). There is a reference to a temporary withdrawal of the Babylonian troops (v. 21), probably in response to word of an approaching Egyptian force (see 37:5). This took place most likely in the middle of this eighteen-month siege. Prior to this temporary withdrawal, the people of Jerusalem had decided to enforce the ancient law regarding the manumission of Hebrew slaves (34:8-11; see Exod 21:2-11; Lev 25:39-43; Deut 15:12-18). They had been ignoring this law for many years, probably for economic reasons. The release could have had the dual intent of currying the Lord's favor and increasing the size of Jerusalem's standing army.[4] The withdrawal of the Babylonian troops follows soon after this, which the people of Jerusalem take as a sign of the LORD's deliverance (see on 37:4-10). They respond to this "deliverance" by reverting to their evil ways and enslaving those who had recently been freed (34:8-11). The balance of this passage contains the LORD's words of condemnation for this oppressive behavior. It falls into three parts: a reiteration of the people's offense (34:12-16), judgment on the people (34:17-20), and judgment on the king and his officials (34:21-22).

34:8-11 The **free**ing of Hebrew **slaves** is initiated by **King**

---

[3]See Holladay, *Jeremiah 2*, pp. 233-234; Brueggemann, *Jeremiah*, p. 324; Thompson, *Jeremiah*, p. 607.

[4]Holladay, *Jeremiah 2*, p. 239; Thompson, *Jeremiah*, p. 610.

Zedekiah. No reason is given in the text for this "policy" change.[5] Whatever the reason, the people enter into a covenant with the king for this change. Just as easily, they renege on this **covenant**. The most likely catalyst for this reversal is the withdrawal of Babylonian troops, mentioned in verse 21; but this connection is not explicitly drawn by the author. The term translated **changed their minds** (v. 11) is the verb שׁוּב (*šûb*), which is often used for "repent, return" (see 3:10,12,14,22; 4:1). The LORD had been looking for the people to repent, but not in this direction.

34:12-16 Several important themes from the preceding paragraph and elsewhere in Jeremiah are woven into the LORD's indictment against the people of Jerusalem. The king had **recently** entered into a **covenant** with the people regarding the freeing of Hebrew slaves. The LORD reminds them that he had made the very same **covenant** with them many centuries before (v. 13). This was something they should have been doing all along. Instead, as in many other areas of their lives, their ancestors **did not listen . . . or pay attention** to the LORD in this regard (cp. 7:24,26; 11:8; 25:4; 35:15). Finally, with the LORD's appointed executioners surrounding them, the people **repented and did what is right**. There is no record of such an evaluation of the people of Jerusalem after the reign of Josiah until here. But the smile on the LORD's face fades quickly. The people "repented" (*šûb*, **turned around**; see v. 11) again, reversing their recent good behavior. This second change "profanes the name of the LORD," because it makes light of the promise they had made **in the house that bears** [his] **Name**. They have no true respect for him and his authority.

34:17-20 Once again the LORD charges his people with not "hearing" him: **you have not obeyed** (שָׁמַע, *šāmaʿ*) **me**. He elaborates on this with two wordplays. The first and most obvious is the play on the "freedom" with which they so recently tormented their fellow Hebrews. They were not willing to give **freedom** to their **countrymen**, so he will serve as an example of a liberator for them — by "freeing" them to die as they choose. Their choices are expressed in the familiar triad of disaster — **sword, plague and famine** (see 14:12; 21:9; 24:10; 27:8,13; 29:17-18; 32:24,36; 38:2; 42:17,22; 44:13). A

---

[5]It is logical to conclude there were some palace officials who still held to the ideals of Josiah's Reform thirty years prior. Perhaps they convinced the king to make this change in hopes of appeasing the LORD.

second wordplay exists in Hebrew between **violated** and **walked between** in verse 18. The same Hebrew term is used for both (עָבַר, *ʿābar*) but with different nuances.[6] In this he reminds them that the reason for this judgment is their failure to **fulfill** covenant promises, covenants made with each other and with him. They apparently had entered into this covenant with the king through a ceremony involving the splitting of a **calf**, just as the LORD had done in reaffirming his covenant with Abram (Gen 15:10-11,17). One assumption of such a sacrifice is that those entering into it deserve the fate of the sacrificed animal, if they fail to abide by the terms of the covenant.[7] The LORD is simply holding them to their pledge in saying he will **treat** them as they treated the calf (v. 18). The closing curse, calling for the exposing of their bodies to **the birds of the air and the beasts of the earth**, is a fairly common one in Jeremiah and other writings (7:33; 15:3; 16:4; 19:7; cp. Deut 28:26; 1 Sam 17:44,46; 2 Sam 21:10; Ps 79:2; Ezek 29:5).

34:21-22 The judgment on **Zedekiah . . . and his officials** is directed at their overconfidence. Zedekiah looks on recent events as proof that he is another Hezekiah, whom the LORD favors. The "deliverance" of Jerusalem confirms again the royal family's claim to being "chosen," thus enjoying a special status — true — which makes them and their chosen city immune from divine wrath — not true. The LORD assures him the city will be burned, which he denies. At the same time, he reiterates a theme made popular by Isaiah in the days of Ahaz and Hezekiah, namely, that the LORD is the true king (e.g., Isa 6:1-5). He had demonstrated his kingship in Isaiah's day by controlling the actions of the Assyrian kings. He is claiming the same authority now by saying, **"I will bring** [the Babylonians] **back to this city."**

This episode seems to typify the attitude of disobedience held by the people of Jerusalem in Jeremiah's day. They ignore the commands of the LORD until their situation becomes extremely precari-

---

[6]Brueggemann (*Jeremiah*, p. 329) notes a third wordplay involving "cut" in verse 18. The Hebrew expression for "make a covenant" is, literally, "cut a covenant." This is balanced by the reference to the animal of the sacrifice that is "cut" into two pieces. Another possible wordplay exists between "each of you has *taken back* the . . . slaves" (v. 16) and "I will *bring* [the Babylonians] *back*" (v. 22). Holladay, *Jeremiah 2*, p. 242.

[7]The Aramaic inscription of Sefire alludes to such an understanding. J.C.L. Gibson, *Textbook of Syrian Semitic Inscriptions* (Oxford: Clarendon, 1971).

ous. Then they "repent" and follow his commands hoping he will come to their rescue. Once the situation improves, they assume the danger is past, that they no longer need the LORD's help, and so they "un-repent" to their former ways. There is no longer any "need" for obedience, because they no longer "need" God.[8] Sadly, such an attitude is not uncommon among believers, though they usually do not display it in so graphic a way as this.

---

[8]If things had not improved, they would have concluded that obedience to the Law was of no benefit to them. Either way, they can continue to be wicked and "justify" their behavior on utilitarian grounds.

JEREMIAH 35

C. THE RECABITES (35:1-19)

This story and the one that follows (Jeremiah 36) take place during the reign of Jehoiakim (609–598 B.C.), some ten to fifteen years prior to the events recorded in the surrounding chapters. They occur no earlier than 605 B.C. when the Babylonian armies and their allies first invaded this region (see 2 Kings 24:1-2). The number of particular details mentioned in this episode lead even the most skeptical of readers to concede the likelihood that it is historical.[1]

The story of the Recabites has been placed here in the book probably because it contributes to the theme of "hearing" the LORD. The positive example of individuals who "hear" ("listen to") the commands of their earthly leaders presents a stark contrast to the example of the people in the preceding chapter, who do not "listen to"/"obey" the LORD's commands to free their Hebrew slaves (34:14, 17), as well as a contrast to the king and his assistants in the next chapter, who refuse to "listen to" ("hear") the commands and warnings of the LORD through Jeremiah (36:31; cp. 7:13,26; 11:10; 13:10-11; 17:23; 25:4; 26:4-5; etc.).[2] The resultant divine blessing on the Recabites represents an unpleasant and constant reminder to the Davidic kings of what they could have enjoyed, if they had just "listened" to the LORD.

The chapter begins with the LORD instructing Jeremiah to confront the Recabites with a moral challenge, and Jeremiah carries out these instructions (vv. 1-5). In response, the leaders of the family voice their resolve to maintain their integrity (vv. 6-11). Their expressed integrity prompts a divine pronouncement of punishment

---

[1]Clements, *Jeremiah*, p. 208. Holladay places this episode in the final months of Jehoiakim's reign, but this is far from certain. Holladay, *Jeremiah* 2, p. 246; cp. Thompson, *Jeremiah*, p. 615.

[2]Brueggemann, *Jeremiah*, pp. 332-337.

on the people of Jerusalem for their own lack of integrity (vv. 12-17), and a pronouncement of blessing on the Recabites (vv. 18-19). These two pronouncements are parallel in form. The former consists of an indictment (vv. 12-16) and a formal pronouncement of judgment, each introduced by "Therefore, this is what the LORD Almighty, the God of Israel, says" (vv. 13,17); the latter consists of a commendation (v. 18) and a promise of blessing, each introduced by "Therefore, this is what the LORD Almighty, the God of Israel, says" (vv. 18,19).

35:1-5 We know very little about the individuals mentioned in the opening section. The tribal origin of the **Recabites** is not absolutely certain, although descent from the the Kenites — and the line of Caleb? — is most probable (see 1 Chr. 2:55; cp. 2:19,50-51; Judg 1:14-16).[3] There are no biblical references besides these to **Jaazaniah** or his immediate ancestors, nor is there any other reference to **Hanan** or his father, **Igdaliah**.[4] It is possible that the **Maaseiah** mentioned here is the same individual mentioned among those commissioned by King Josiah to repair the temple (2 Chr 34:8), but this is no more than a guess. Finally, we cannot be certain how far down Jonadab comes in the lineage of the Recabites. He might have been the actual son of Recab (that is, in the very next generation), although the designation "son" can refer to any descendant. The identification of this Jonadab with "Jehonadab son of Recab" (a northerner), mentioned as an ally of Jehu in 2 Kings 10:15,23, does not have much to commend it.

35:6-11 The abstinence from wine practiced by this family does not reflect a general moral prohibition or divine disapproval of wine. Rather, it is part of a restricted policy of **nomad**ism chosen by one man and imposed by him on his descendants (and only on them). He has forbidden them to participate in a sedentary agricultural lifestyle. The reasons for this prohibition are not given (see below). This sedentary lifestyle is represented by the owning of houses and the production of crops which require year-round and/or extended care (v. 7). The production of wine is particularly indicative of this lifestyle, because several years of continuous residence in one place are required before one can expect to enjoy the

---

[3]Holladay, *Jeremiah 2*, p. 246; Clements, *Jeremiah*, pp. 208-209.
[4]Igdaliah is identified as a "man of God," which implies that he was a prophet (cp. 1 Kings 13).

fruits of the grapevine. But it would be no more immoral in God's eyes for them to drink wine than it would be for them to live in houses or grow crops. In fact, all of the things forbidden by **Jonadab** are understood by the biblical writers to be signs of God's blessings on his people (Deut 6:10-12; cp. 1 Tim. 4:1-3). This point is made clear by the fact that Jeremiah brings the Recabites into the temple to offer them **wine** to drink. This likely is wine that had been brought to the temple as part of the tithe-offerings of the people, offerings which represent the abundance the LORD has provided and their gratitude for it. It would have served as part of the supplies which the priests themselves would enjoy or would distribute among the needy members of the society. If anything, the fact that Jeremiah offers the wine to them in the temple probably would have suggested to them the LORD's support for what Jeremiah was doing.[5]

Jonadab's command is intriguing because of the way it is worded. In it, he promises his descendants that, if they will follow his instructions, they will **live a long time in the land** (v. 7). This sounds similar to some of the exhortations given by Moses to the people of Israel in Deuteronomy, "that it may go well with you and your children after you and that you may live long in the land" (Deut. 4:40; 5:33; 11:9,21; cp. 4:26; 30:18). This raises several possible explanations for the supposed connection between what Jonadab commands and the promised outcome. One is that Jonadab is speaking to his family with the same authority — and for the same reasons — that Moses spoke to the Israelites. This seems doubtful, since Jonadab's directives seem directly contradictory to the words of Moses in some respects. A second possible explanation for this promise is that the nomadic life might have been thought of as more difficult, that those who lived it would recognize more acutely their dependence on God (cp. Deut. 8:1-5). Perhaps they felt that such acute awareness of their dependence on God would make divine blessing more likely. Another possibility is that there were some less direct benefits to living the nomadic life. Perhaps there were certain negative aspects of the sedentary life that were generally recognized, and so one way to avoid those negative aspects was to avoid the sedentary life altogether. A modern parallel to this way of thinking might be in the choice of some to "home school" their children, rather than expose them to certain unwanted influences of life com-

---

[5]Clements, *Jeremiah*, p. 209.

monly found in public schools. Or it might be seen in the decision not to own a television in order to avoid unwanted influences from modern media. Whatever the reasoning, the promise of long life in the land is reminiscent of Deuteronomy.

But one should not read into this promise that Jeremiah is suggesting that they do something against the moral standards of God. He is merely calling them to relinquish a somewhat ascetic way of life which they all acknowledge to be human in origin. The fact that they refuse to do so shows their basic integrity. The strength of their integrity is suggested rhetorically in their words to Jeremiah. Twice they claim to have been even more thorough in their adherence to the patriarchal command than the patriarch himself had envisioned. Jonadab called for them and their sons (**descendants**) to follow his regulations (v. 6). They expand on this when they say, **Neither we nor our wives nor our sons and daughters** have disobeyed Jonadab (v. 8). Similarly, Jonadab told them not to **build houses, sow seed or plant vineyards** (v. 7). They affirm that they have never **built houses . . . or had vineyards, fields or crops** ("seed") (v. 9). Both statements imply that they have perhaps gone beyond what was required in their zeal to adhere to their ancestor's directives.

Questions about their zeal would have been raised by their recent move to **Jerusalem**. They most likely have moved into houses, so one might naturally assume that they have renounced their ancestor's guidelines. Their response to Jeremiah shows that this is not the case. They are simply doing what is necessary under the present circumstances (i.e., the **Babylonian** invasion). Their continuing adherence to other parts of the patriarchal command reveal their intention to return to full nomadism whenever possible.

The most important part of the Recabites' response is their double assertion to have **obeyed** ("heard") their ancestor. The main part of their response essentially begins (v. 8) and ends (v. 10) with this assertion. Their current departure from his commands merely reflects a temporary necessity (v. 11) which should not be construed as disrespect for their ancestor and his words. Even though their ancestor was a mere mortal and even though it is clear that violating his command would not constitute an act of sin against the will of the LORD, they persist in their obedience to him. As such, the Recabites represent a model of obedience for all to emulate.

35:12-17 The LORD's indictment (vv. 12-16) highlights the sharp contrast between the obedience of the Recabites and the disobedi-

ence of the people of Judah. The verb **obey** ("hear") is used by the
LORD five times in these verses. He first appeals to them to **learn a
lesson and obey my words** (v. 13). He then turns to the example of
the Recabites and how they abstain from wine simply **because they
obey** their ancestor (v. 14). In contrast, the LORD has spoken to them
again and again, yet his words **have not** been **obeyed** (v. 14). He
goes on to say that they **have not paid attention or listened to**
("heard") **me**, in spite of numerous warnings (v. 15). He then summarizes his remarks, juxtaposing the obedience of the Recabites to
the disobedience of his own people (v. 16).

Other aspects of this indictment bring out the magnitude of
their disobedience. The Recabites have obeyed an earthly father,
while the people of Judah have disobeyed **the LORD Almighty, the
God of Israel** (v. 13). The Recabites obeyed their father the first
(and only?) time he gave them a command; the LORD has spoken
again and again to his people, and he has sent prophets to them
again and again, yet they continue not to obey. Further, God had
made the same promise to his people (**Then you will live in the
land. . . .**) that Jonadab made to his family; but even though the
LORD is much more able than Jonadab to deliver on such a promise,
the recipients of the LORD's promise have not taken it to heart the
way the Recabites had received their ancestor's promise.

The judgment pronounced on the Judahites (v. 17) is general but
direct. He will punish them **with every disaster I pronounced
against them**. This could be a reference to disasters announced by
Jeremiah on other occasions, or to the disasters mentioned in the
laws of Moses (e.g., Deut 28:15-68). He concludes with yet another
dual accusation of disobedience (cp. 7:13,27).

35:18-19 The LORD's commendation and blessing of the
Recabites parallels in form the indictment and condemnation of the
people of Judah (**This is what the LORD Almighty, the God of Israel
says. . . . Therefore, this is what the LORD Almighty, the God of
Israel says. . . .**). The main theme of the commendation is the
reverse of the preceding indictment. The people have not obeyed
the words of the LORD, but the Recabites **have obeyed the command**
of their ancestor. The promised blessing is communicated in terms
reminiscent of the dynastic promise to the Davidic House (see on
36:30; cp. 1 Kgs 2:4; 9:4-5). The fact that the promise to the Recabites is given in response to their "hearing" the command of their
ancestor should serve as a reminder to the Davidic king that the

promise which serves as the basis for his own position as king is itself conditioned on whether he "hears" the LORD's commands. His failure to "hear" Jeremiah forms the conclusion of the next chapter.

JEREMIAH 36

D. JEHOIAKIM BURNS JEREMIAH'S SCROLL (36:1-32)

This episode from Jeremiah's career provides some invaluable insights into the phenomenon of biblical inspiration, insights which were discussed in the Introduction. The following comments focus on some more immediate aspects of this text. The story recorded here spans a period of one to two years.[1] It begins with the LORD's command to Jeremiah to dictate to Baruch all his prophecies, spoken over the preceding twenty-three years (26:1-3). Jeremiah does this (vv. 4-7), and sometime in the following weeks or months, Baruch reads these prophecies to a sympathetic audience in a room in the temple, then to some of King Jehoiakim's officials, whose hearts are pricked by the message they hear (vv. 8-19). Those officials bring the scroll to the attention of the king, who shows his own impenitence by cutting and burning the scroll (vv. 20-26). This prompts the LORD to call for a second copy of the scroll to be made and to announce a personal judgment oracle against the king (vv. 27-32).

The writing of this scroll and its subsequent rejection by King Jehoiakim marks a significant shift in Jeremiah's career. Prior to this event, Jeremiah's words could be classified as "threats," as proclamations of what would happen *unless* the king and people had a change of heart. Those threats were not actualized, however, until the Babylonians gained the upper hand in the region. That happened in the year in which this story begins, when the Babylonians come into the territory of Judah and take some of the young men with them back to Babylon. The people can now see that Jeremiah has been speaking the truth in his words about an "enemy from the north." They should recognize the need to take Jeremiah seriously. Jehoiakim's base treatment of the scroll demonstrates how little

---

[1] Holladay, *Jeremiah 2*, p. 254.

regard he still has for Jeremiah and his message. His rejection of that message marks the beginning of the end of any hopes the nation might have of avoiding the disaster the LORD has been predicting through his prophet. Their window of opportunity is still not completely shut, but it is closing fast.

36:1-3 The LORD's initial instructions about dictating his prophecies come to Jeremiah **in the fourth year of Jehoiakim** (605 B.C.). This is the year that Nebuchadnezzar defeated the final remnants of the Assyrian army at Carchemish and established Babylonian dominance over the lands along the Mediterranean seaboard. This must have had a profoundly sobering effect on the people in Jerusalem, and it might have been the reason for the "day of fasting" mentioned later in the story (v. 6).[2] The LORD's instructions reveal that Jeremiah's prophetic work has been strictly oral until this time. He also reveals that there is still the possibility that total destruction can be avoided. The expressed goal in putting these prophecies into writing is to get the people to repent (**Perhaps . . . each of them will turn from his wicked way**), and then the LORD **will forgive** them (v. 3). The language here is very close to that of Jeremiah's Temple Sermon (7:1-15; 26:1-6).

36:4-7 Jeremiah dictates to **Baruch**, as **the LORD** has instructed him (v. 4), and then he gives similar instructions of his own to Baruch (vv. 5-7). He is not allowed to speak in the **temple**, so Baruch will speak in his place. The reason for the restriction is not given. It could be a general restriction against his family, going back to the banishment of Abiathar (1 Kgs 2:26-27); but the more likely reason is the "treasonous" nature of his prophecies concerning the fate of the temple.[3] The **day of fasting** when **the scroll** is to be read is not identified either. It probably is declared in response to some national threat, and the presence of the Babylonians in the land that year is the most likely reason for it. Jeremiah, like the LORD, expresses the hope that the people will repent (**Perhaps . . . each will turn from his wicked ways**) when they hear his message (v. 7).

36:8-19 The reading in the temple takes place **in the ninth month of the fifth year**, which would have been December, 604 B.C. Baruch is not in the main courtyard of the temple, but in a room

---

[2]See Thompson, *Jeremiah*, p. 620.
[3]So Holladay, *Jeremiah 2*, p. 255; Thompson, *Jeremiah*, p. 623. Jer 45:1-3 indicates that there was overt opposition to Baruch as well at this time.

reserved for **Gemariah son of Shaphan**. It was probably this Shaphan who had first made King Josiah aware of the discovery of the "Book of the Law" almost twenty years earlier (2 Kgs 22:8-10). And it was probably Gemariah's brother, Ahikam, who stood with Jeremiah at his trial (26:24). It is actually Gemariah's son, **Micaiah**, who is first touched by the message of the scroll. He calls it to the attention of his father and certain **other officials**, who respond as they should: they are afraid (cp. Hezekiah's response to Micah in Jer 26:19). These officials decide to bring the scroll to the attention of King Jehoiakim, but they realize before they even begin that **the king** will probably not respond as they have. While they have received the scroll with fear and reverence, they assume the king will be angry and strike out against the scroll's authors; so they advise Baruch and Jeremiah to **hide** (v. 19).

These reactions expose the existence of a religious-political rift within the Jerusalem officials. These men apparently still hold to the ideas which were central to the religious reforms of Josiah. They are sympathetic to Jeremiah's message, and they assume that Jehoiakim is not. One is left to wonder what was said and done "behind the scenes" when the reform policies of Josiah were undone by Jehoiakim. What opposing opinions were expressed, and how did the king deal with them? These individuals are still part of the palace establishment, yet they are not part of the king's inner circle. Those individuals, mentioned in the next scene, have a different reaction to the message of the scroll.[4]

36:20-26 The **scroll** is brought to **the king** by **Jehudi**. This apparently is the same individual who had brought Baruch to the royal officials in the preceding scene (v. 14). Jehudi reads the scroll in the presence of **the king and** certain other **officials** (**his attendants**, v. 24), while some of those who have already heard it look on. The reaction of these new hearers is completely different from the reaction of those who heard it in the temple. **The king . . . showed no fear** (v. 24; the verb here and in v. 16 is the same), even though there are advisors like **Gemariah** who urge him to rethink his reaction. The king's response is to treat Jeremiah's scroll as trash. He is cold, the scroll can provide fuel for his fire, so he burns it. In his mind, it has no other purpose, no other value. His reaction is in marked con-

---

[4]See J.A. Dearman, "My Servants the Scribes: Composition and Context in Jeremiah 36," *JBL* 109 (1990): 403-421.

trast to Josiah's reaction a generation earlier to a similar scroll (2 Kgs 22:11).[5]

There is a subtle play on the word "hear/listen" (שָׁמַע, *šāma'*) in these verses. Jehoiakim **heard** the words of the scroll (v. 24), but he responds with indifference. He has not really "heard" them as he should. He demonstrates his refusal to hear these words when **he would not listen** to Gemariah and the other officials who had come with the scroll. The text gives no explanation at this point for the king's rejection of Jeremiah's words. Later, we are told that the king questioned Jeremiah's prediction that the Babylonians "would destroy this land and cut off men and animals from it" (v. 29). It is likely that he and others around him have known of Jeremiah and his teachings for several years, and they already have an "official position" concerning him. One plausible interpretation is that some of the king's advisors are asserting the inviolability of Jerusalem, based on divine promises and events in the reign of Hezekiah. They would see the recent presence of the Babylonians as the typical or even full extent of the Babylonian threat to Judah. It is tantalizing to place some significance on the fact the king uses **a scribe's knife** (v. 23) to cut the scroll. Jeremiah mentions elsewhere the harmful influence of scribes on the way people react to the Law (and probably on how they react to his interpretation of its demands; see 8:8). Perhaps the identification of the knife as a scribe's knife implies it is ultimately other scribes (rivals to Baruch) who influence the king to ignore Jeremiah's words of advice.

The king's final reaction is similar to the reaction of the prophets and priests to Jeremiah's Temple Sermon (26:7-11). Jeremiah is viewed as a threat to the well-being of the city, even though he is the one presenting the only way the city's well-being can actually be preserved. He must be locked up, kept away from any audience (like Gemariah and the others) that might be swayed by his words. Among those whom he sends to track down Jeremiah and Baruch is **Elnathan**, one of those who had brought Uriah the prophet back from Egypt (26:20-23). Fortunately, **Jeremiah** and **Baruch** escape capture this time. They had **hidden** at the advice of the sympathetic officials. Baruch (the narrator) attributes their success here to the working of **the LORD** (v. 26).

36:27-32 The king's rejection and destruction of the scroll elicits

---

[5]Brueggemann, *Jeremiah*, p. 351; Thompson, *Jeremiah*, pp. 627-628.

a twofold response from the LORD. The first are instructions to Jeremiah for the making of a second copy of the scroll. Jeremiah does this, adding **many similar words** to the prophecies already recorded (v. 32). The other response is a pronouncement of judgment directed at Jehoiakim alone. The pronouncement begins and ends with the reason for the LORD's punishment on the king. He has apparently dismissed the possibility of Jerusalem's destruction (v. 29; see above), and he has not **listened** to the words of the LORD (v. 31). The details of the judgment announced lend further weight to the assumption that Jehoiakim believes in the inviolability of Jerusalem and the Davidic dynasty. The first half of the judgment is almost a reversal of the Davidic promise. That promise states that David "will never fail to have a man sit on the throne of Israel" (1 Kgs 2:4; cp. 2 Sam 7:12-16; 1 Kgs 8:25; 9:5). Now the LORD says Jehoiakim **will have no one to sit on the throne of David**. This does not take away the promise to David altogether, but it does take away Jehoiakim's participation in that promise.[6] The prediction of an ignoble burial has a parallel in 22:18-19. The second half of the judgment is against **Jerusalem** in particular, and **Judah** more generally. The pairing of the Davidic dynasty and Jerusalem as things divinely chosen goes back at least to the days of Solomon (1 Kgs 8:16; 2 Chr 6:5-6). The deliverance of Jerusalem in response to a prayer by the Davidic king confirmed their divine election in the minds of the people of Judah. Unfortunately, they had lost sight of the inherent conditionality of their ongoing participation in that election (but see Jer 33:19-26).

Finally, this judgment oracle presents an interesting contrast to the blessing pronounced on the Recabites, in the preceding chapter. David had been promised that he "would not fail to have a man" on the throne; now that promise is denied to Jehoiakim, because he has not "listened" to the LORD. In contrast to this, the LORD promises that the Recabites "will not fail to have a man" to serve him, because they have "listened" to their ancestor. The key — as Jeremiah often mentions — is "listening" to the LORD. Most of the people of

---

[6]This is fascinating, because Jehoiakim's son does reign after him, though only for a few months. But the messianic promise of an eternal kingdom is traced through this line down to Jesus. However, in Matthew's genealogy of Jesus, Jehoiakim is skipped and Jeconiah — Jehoiakim's son — is identified as the son of Josiah (Matt 1:11). Is it because of this prophecy?

Jeremiah's day "have ears, but they do not hear" (5:21; cp. Isa 6:9-10; Acts 28:25-28). There is a twofold message in this. For the immediate members of the House of David, there is reason to feel shame for what they have let slip away. Jeremiah and other prophets duly warned them, but they chose to ignore the warnings. Now they suffer the inevitable consequences and disgrace of their decision. Then there is a message for every subsequent generation of believers. That message is about the need to "hear the word of the LORD." The LORD makes promises of blessing and honor to all, but only those who "hear" him will inherit those promises.

JEREMIAH 37

E. JEREMIAH IN PRISON (37:1-21)

Jeremiah 37:1-2 ushers in the longest continuous prose section of the Book of Jeremiah. It begins with events and oracles from the time of Nebuchadnezzar's siege of Jerusalem (588–586 B.C.), briefly describes the destruction of the city, and then continues into the stories of Jeremiah's final years in Judea and Egypt. The overall thematic unity of these chapters suggests that they were originally written with the fugitive Jewish population of Egypt in mind. King Zedekiah serves as the "bad example" which the leaders of those fugitives are encouraged not to follow. Unfortunately, they do follow his example, and the narrative closes with Jeremiah predicting that Zedekiah's fate will eventually befall the Egyptian pharaoh.

The narrative can be divided into three major parts. The first part (37:1–40:6) concerns Jeremiah's interactions with King Zedekiah and other leaders in Jerusalem as that city is being conquered by the Babylonians. This part is literarily divided into an introduction (37:1-2) and six scenes (37:3-16; 37:17-21; 38:1-13; 38:14-28; 39:1-14; 39:15–40:6) by the repetition of the concluding statement, "Jeremiah remained" (37:16,21; 38:13,28; 39:14) or "stayed" (40:6) in a particular place.[1] The second part (40:7–43:7) briefly describes how Jeremiah was forced to move with some Judean refugees from Judea to Egypt. In this part, Johanan son of Kareah emerges as a potentially positive leader. Unfortunately, he turns out to be just like Zedekiah. The third part (43:8–44:30) repeatedly warns the refugees in Egypt that they are no safer there than Zedekiah had been in Jerusalem.

37:1-2 The introduction here is similar in form to what one finds throughout the Books of Kings when a new king is introduced (see

---

[1] These items are noted by Holladay and used by him to establish the overall structure of Jeremiah 37–44 (*Jeremiah 2*, pp. 282-284).

esp. 2 Kgs 24:17).[2] It represents an obvious temporal shift from the preceding chapter. That story took place in the fourth year of Jehoiakim (605 B.C.), while those beginning here occur during the reign of Zedekiah (597–586 B.C.). In fact, verse 4 indicates that we are in the final months of Zedekiah's reign, during the siege of Jerusalem. There might also be some significance to mentioning that **Nebuchadnezzar** had made **Zedekiah** king. As we discussed in Jeremiah 24, there are strong indications that Zedekiah and his advisors had concluded that they were a sort of remnant, that the LORD had spared them from punishment just as he had spared Hezekiah from the Assyrians a century earlier. Jeremiah had strongly contradicted such an interpretation of Zedekiah's situation. The note in 37:1 might strengthen this contradiction by implying that Zedekiah's hold on the throne is precarious, because a mere man (Nebuchadnezzar) — and not the LORD — had placed him there.

Verse 2 sets the tone for the entire block of stories that continues to 44:30. It imposes on them a general sense of foreboding with which the reader is to interpret the events described. No one **paid any attention** to Jeremiah's prophecies. More literally, they did not "hear" (שָׁמַע, *šāmaʿ*) **the words of the LORD. . . .** This refusal to "hear" the LORD is a recurring theme throughout the book, but here it takes on a rather specific application. It is the king and those close to him who refuse to "hear" the LORD's message through Jeremiah. Naturally, a calamitous fate awaits them.

37:3-16 This is the first of three times that **Zedekiah** "sends" for **Jeremiah** (see also 37:17; 38:14). Each time the statement serves to introduce a discernible scene of the story. This particular scene continues down to verse 16, where we are told that Jeremiah **remained a long time** in a dungeon. So this scene explains how he came to be in that dungeon.

We know tantalizingly little about the two men whom Zedekiah sends to Jeremiah. **Jehucal,** also called Jucal, is one of the "officials" who will later accuse Jeremiah of treason against the city (38:1-3). The same **Zephaniah** (not the biblical prophet) accompanied Pashhur, another "official" mentioned in 38:1, on a similar assignment at about the same time (see 21:1). Zephaniah apparently is a high-ranking priest (see 2 Kgs 25:18; Jer 29:24-32; 52:24), which might imply

---

[2]Ibid., p. 283; Bright, *Jeremiah*, p. 222; Nicholson, *Jeremiah, Chapters 26–52*, p. 114; Thompson, *Jeremiah*, p. 631.

that he looked upon Jeremiah as a troublesome prophet and a member of a rival priestly house. On the other hand, the reference in Jeremiah 29:24-32 reveals that he was ordered to silence Jeremiah, but that he chose to warn Jeremiah instead. Apparently, he had some sympathy for Jeremiah and his message. These two represent to some extent the competing inclinations that seem to be at war inside Zedekiah during the siege. On the one hand, Zedekiah "hears" his advisors who counsel squelching Jeremiah's message; on the other hand, he repeatedly "sends" for Jeremiah, as in this case. He asks Jeremiah to **pray to the LORD our God for us.** This exposes the truly tragic nature of Zedekiah's character. He represents those who yearn to "hear" the word of the LORD and yet are not willing to "hear" that word when it comes. He has "ears to hear," but he does not "hear."[3]

Verses 4-5 represent a brief interruption in the central flow of the narrative. Jeremiah's response to Zedekiah's request (v. 3) begins in verse 6, but these verses postpone that to specify the exact time this takes place. Jeremiah has **not yet been** imprisoned, and the **Babylonian** siege has been temporarily lifted at word of an Egyptian force in the region. For the earliest readers, this would place a minor event (the imprisonment of Jeremiah) in a context that was more widely known (the temporary reprieve during the siege).

This could have been a time of great anticipation for the citizens of Jerusalem. An amazingly similar situation had developed in the days of Hezekiah (701 B.C.; see 2 Kgs 18:17–19:37; Isaiah 36–37). The Assyrians had laid siege to Jerusalem, expecting to destroy it as they had all the other cities they had besieged. King Hezekiah had "sent" to Isaiah, asking him to "pray for the remnant" left in Jerusalem (Isa 37:2-4). An Egyptian army was marching out at the time to confront the Mesopotamian attackers, who went out to meet the Egyptians and never returned. The LORD decimated the Assyrian army before they could engage the Egyptians in battle, and they returned home to Nineveh, disillusioned.

It would not be surprising to find King Zedekiah's advisors pointing out these parallels. Isaiah, a true prophet in the days of Hezekiah, had advised a response of trust in Yahweh in the face of a siege. King Hezekiah had shown his trust, and he became known

---

[3]As Brueggemann says, he wants the LORD's "aid" but not his "command." Brueggemann, *Jeremiah*, p. 355.

as the king who "trusted in the LORD, the God of Israel" (2 Kgs 18:5) more than any other king had trusted in him. The same series of events seems to be unfolding right before the eyes of Zedekiah and his advisors. They could easily suppose that they are going to see Yahweh's wondrous salvation of his people once again. They might broadcast a similar appeal to trust in the LORD, and they would expect any true prophet to do the same.[4] But this is not to be Jeremiah's inspired message.

Jeremiah's message comes in two parts. The first half (vv. 7-8) states what the LORD has decreed will happen: The Egyptians will **go back** (שׁוּב, *šûb*) to **their land**, and the **Babylonians** will **return** (*šûb*) to **attack** and **burn** Jerusalem.[5] This message contrasts sharply with the one Isaiah delivered to Hezekiah more than a century earlier. Isaiah prophesied that the king of Assyria would "return" (*šûb*) to his homeland in shame (Isa 37:7); Jeremiah says that the king of Babylon will "return" (*šûb*) in triumph over Jerusalem. The second half of Jeremiah's response makes this even more certain. There could be a false sense of hope emerging that the Babylonians will "leave" for good, as the Assyrians had. Some 185,000 of the Assyrians had perished by the LORD's hand in one night, and the remaining Assyrian troops — who were still healthy — had gone home to Nineveh. Jeremiah tries to dispel such hopes by declaring that even if the Babylonians had **only wounded** soldiers left, **they would come out and burn this city down.**

The narrator now turns the reader's attention to how Jeremiah's message affects Jeremiah personally (vv. 11-12). It is possible that this is related to the incident recorded in Jeremiah 32, when Jeremiah redeems a field from his cousin. There, Jeremiah is already

---

[4]There might be some considerations of a more personal nature involved in these competing expectations. Isaiah's call vision takes place in the temple (Isa 6:1). Since only priests were allowed in the temple, it is likely that Isaiah was a priest before becoming a prophet (unless he merely has a vision of being in the temple). If Isaiah was a priest serving in the temple, he almost certainly was of the Zadokite family. This would make Isaiah an ancestor of the priests whom Jeremiah now found as his opponents. They would naturally see Jeremiah as one who questioned the teachings of their beloved prophetic ancestor.

[5]It is tempting to see a contrast between the way in which Judah's enemies "return" according to God's commands and the way that God's people "refused to return" to God (see 8:5). But this verb is so common, that this could also be a simple coincidence.

incarcerated in **the courtyard of the guard** (see 37:21). It is possible that Jeremiah is going out for that purpose here, but that **Irijah** prevents him from doing so. It could also be that there are simply several family property matters with which Jeremiah is having to deal at this time. The text is not specific enough about Jeremiah's purpose here to draw any firm conclusion.

Even though the Babylonian army has withdrawn, guards stop Jeremiah and charge him with desertion (vv. 13-15). Apparently, his message of doom is well known. It could be that this guard is a brother to Jehucal, who is also identified as **son of Shelemiah**. However, the specification of Shelemiah here as **son of Hananiah** might suggest that this is a different Shelemiah. In any case, Jeremiah's message precedes him, and Irijah is suspicious (or angered) enough to detain him. There is no waiting to see if Jeremiah's prophecy will be fulfilled or not. He must endure the same treatment as Micaiah had suffered at the hands of Ahab, who put Micaiah in prison for being the only prophet to prophesy (correctly) Ahab's impending death (1 Kgs 22:26-28).

Irijah accuses Jeremiah of **deserting** ("falling") **to the Babylonians,** a charge which Jeremiah adamantly denies. But Irijah, true to the character of those in power in Jerusalem, does not **listen** (*šāmaʿ*) **to him.** Instead, he takes Jeremiah to certain **officials** (see on 38:4, below). This reaction by Irijah is not that hard to understand. Jeremiah has been warning people for some time that Jerusalem would soon fall to the Babylonians, and he had been urging people to surrender to avoid "the sword, famine and plague." Shortly after this, King Zedekiah is going to express his fear of those who had already surrendered to the Babylonians (38:19). And the Babylonians show great leniency to Jeremiah when he is captured (39:11-12), suggesting that even they have heard about Jeremiah advising people to surrender. So, it would not be surprising to find that Jeremiah had a reputation as a Babylonian sympathizer.

They (v. 15) refers to the officials, who take over from Irijah at this time, spearheading the opposition to Jeremiah for the remainder of the siege. The term for **officials** (שָׂרִים, *śārîm*) is a rather flexible term in the Old Testament as a whole, but it seems to connote military officials in particular in Jeremiah. They are mentioned in the book alongside several other groups which do not perform specifically military functions, which would make it more likely that these persons do (see 1:18; 2:26; 4:9; 8:1; 24:1; 26:10-12; 29:2; 32:32;

34:19). The term is used frequently in chapters 37–44 for Babylonian and Judahite military leaders (e.g., 38:17,22; 39:3,13; 40:7,8,13; 41:11,13,16; 42:8; 43:4,5).

It makes sense that military leaders would be leading the opposition to Jeremiah at this time. Their pride in particular would have been hurt by Jeremiah's pronouncement that even an injured Babylonian army would overthrow Jerusalem (37:10). This would make them highly incensed by Jeremiah, and they would be the most likely group to have the authority to prevent him from exiting the city, accuse him of "falling" to the enemy, and then **beat** and **imprison** him. He is placed in the house of a certain **Jonathan**, who is described only as a **secretary** (סֹפֵר, sōphēr), or "scribe." This fact also brings out the cooperation going on between the royal scribes (see 8:8) and the military establishment of Jerusalem. It seems most likely that the scribes were among those who had convinced people in the palace that the LORD would never allow Jerusalem to be conquered, and this belief strongly influenced the military strategy of the nation.

The official reaction to Jeremiah's attempt to warn his audience is to punish Jeremiah (v. 16). The officials have "heard" the warning, but their response shows that they actually refuse to "hear" it. They refuse to believe that the LORD could act in the way that Jeremiah relates. A precise translation of Jeremiah's place of confinement (**vaulted cell in a dungeon**) is impossible. Two terms are used, one of which occurs only here in the Old Testament ("vaulted cell"). The term translated "dungeon" literally means "house of the cistern" (see 2:13). The conditions inside this dungeon are not described, but Jeremiah's great desire to be out of it suggests some significant unpleasantness. The statement **where he remained for a long time** marks the end of this first scene.

37:17-21 Verse 17 relates the second time that **Zedekiah** sends for Jeremiah. With this scene, the reader's attention begins to shift from Jeremiah to the king. The king has to act with stealth. He knows that his officials have incarcerated Jeremiah for his prophecies, yet he still believes in Jeremiah's prophetic gift. Also, he wishes now to speak with Jeremiah directly rather than through his officials, as he had with the previous prophecy. It is likely that the king's actions are being controlled here more by his fear of those officials than by his opinion of Jeremiah.

Jeremiah's response is simple and direct, concerning the king alone. One wonders what prompted the question. Perhaps the Babylonian army has returned from its confrontation with the Egyptians. The question that the king asks does not necessarily imply that he wants to know what the LORD has in store for him personally, although the private audience might suggest that. In any case, Zedekiah is the object of Jeremiah's answer. (On the significance of **handed over** in these chapters, see on 38:3.)

In spite of the bad news Jeremiah has just delivered to the king, he asks for the king's help (vv. 18-20). He appears to be shifting the focus of the conversation from the king to himself; yet, the question actually places the spotlight on the character of the king. Will the king do what he knows is just, or will he act unjustly because he fears the wrath of his misguided advisors? The triad of king-officials-people is the same as those accused in the general introduction (v. 2) of not paying attention to Jeremiah's words. They are truly the ones with power, because they have the authority to imprison a prophet. Yet even the king knows that there is no justification for this imprisonment.

The truly unjust nature of Jeremiah's imprisonment is brought out in his second question. He is the only prophet whose predictions have come true, but he is the only one who is imprisoned. The "lie" of the false prophets is now made clear. They have said that the Babylonians would not even come to Jerusalem, much less conquer it. Their falseness is already evident. They cannot even pass the first test of the true prophet — predicting something that actually happens. Yet they are honored and Jeremiah is silenced.

The king has a bad track record when it comes to "hearing" Jeremiah, but Jeremiah tries again anyway. Again, the reasons for the request are not explained. The conditions in **the house of Jonathan** probably were known to be the most severe of any place that might be used as a prison, because Jeremiah fears for his life and the king responds favorably to his petition without any hint of hesitation.

Zedekiah's actual concern and respect for Jeremiah is demonstrated in his actions in verse 21. He leaves Jeremiah in confinement, but he considerably lessens the discomfort of this ordeal. The reference to **the street of the bakers** seems to suggest that the king is concerned to see that Jeremiah get food until the city's supplies are entirely depleted. The narrator has already made it clear that Jeremiah is in this courtyard; the seemingly redundant final statement (**Jeremiah remained in the courtyard of the guard**) serves the literary function of marking the end of the scene (see 38:13,28; cp. 37:17; 39:14; 40:6).

JEREMIAH 38

F. JEREMIAH THROWN INTO A CISTERN (38:1-13)

There are two more scenes in this chapter, demarcated again by the repetition of the statement that "Jeremiah remained in the courtyard of the guard" (38:13,28). The former scene (the third in the series begun in Jeremiah 37) falls into two parts, hinging on Jeremiah's descent into and ascent from a second cistern. In this, a conversation between antagonistic military officials and the king (38:4-5) leads to Jeremiah being lowered into the cistern "by ropes" (בַּחֲבָלִים, bahăbālîm, 38:6). This is balanced by the second half, a conversation between Ebed-melech (a eunuch) and the king (38:9-10), which leads to Jeremiah being lifted out of the cistern by ropes (bahăbālîm, 38:13). The latter scene consists of a long conversation between Jeremiah and the king, a conversation separated into two parts by a prophetic oracle. The first half of the conversation focuses on Jeremiah and his concerns about how he might be treated (38:14-16). Those concerns are slight in comparison to Zedekiah's fears about how the Judean people might treat him if he surrenders to the Babylonians (38:19-26). In between these two parts is a prophetic oracle which offers one last ray of hope for the king (38:17-18). The king shows his ultimate lack of faith by instructing Jeremiah to lie to the officials about the nature of their meeting (38:27).

38:1-13 What an ironic statement to begin Jeremiah 38! These opponents of Jeremiah **heard** what Jeremiah said; however, their reaction to what they **heard** shows that they did not truly "hear" it. They "hear" it but do not accept it as true for reasons that will be explored shortly. The first two **officials** (v. 4) listed here are not mentioned anywhere else in the Bible. The third is the same man sent with Zephaniah in 37:3. The fourth apparently is a priest of some importance. His descendants among the priests are mentioned as being among the first of those who return to Jerusalem following the exile (1 Chr 9:12; Neh 11:12). More significant for the interpretation of this episode is the fact that this Pashhur (not the one who had him placed in stocks; Jer 20:1-6) was sent by Zedekiah to Jeremiah to "inquire of the LORD" (21:1-2). Part of the response given by Jeremiah at that time is quoted here by these officials, as they try to convince King Zedekiah that Jeremiah needs to be silenced. This gives a strong indication that that story (chapter 21) also took place during the final siege.

Verse 2 gives a direct quote of one verse (21:9) from the oracle pronounced on Jerusalem when **Pashhur son of Malkijah** and others are sent to Jeremiah by the king (21:1ff.). The king's request included the suggestion that the LORD might be poised to deliver Jerusalem once again, as he had in the days of Hezekiah. Jeremiah's message is intended to dispel such false hopes. But Jeremiah is not telling this to the messengers alone; he is **telling all the people** (v. 1). All this time he is confined to the courtyard of the guard; so, it is likely that "all the people" refers primarily to military personnel. This would have seemed a serious threat to military "officials," because a prophet is encouraging them to surrender to the enemy. They have come to the king to have Jeremiah restricted to some place where he will not be able to influence the morale of the troops.

There is the intriguing possibility of a significant wordplay in this first quote. It contrasts the fate of **whoever stays** to the fate of **whoever goes over** ("the one going out") **to the Babylonians**. The person who "stays" (יֹשֵׁב, *yōšēb*) in Jerusalem **will die**; the one who "goes out" (יֹצֵא, *yōṣē'*) will live. These terms are paired in Jeremiah only in this prophecy (38:2; cp. 21:9). The closest parallel is later in this chapter, where the king is given the option of "going out" or "not going out" (38:17-18). Isolating who actually stays and who goes out in these stories reveals a great irony to the story. Jeremiah was "free to come and go" ("was coming and going out") among the people when the story begins (37:4), but he is arrested because he tries to "go out" through the Benjamin Gate. He then is forced to "stay" ("remain") in the city until after the Babylonians have captured it. The significance of this irony is highlighted by the fact that the narrator closes each scene by noting where Jeremiah **remained** (37:16,21; 38:13,28; 39:14; 40:6). The only other person who "remains" during the story is King Zedekiah. He is **sitting** (יֹשֵׁב, *yōšēb*) in the Benjamin Gate when Ebed-melech comes to him on Jeremiah's behalf (see below). The one who advises everyone to "go out" of the city (Jeremiah) is the one who ultimately "remains" there longer than anyone else; and the one who "remains" in the Benjamin Gate (Zedekiah) is the one who eventually suffers when he goes out because he did not "go out" when he was advised to do so.

At first glance, the second quote (v. 3) looks like the conclusion (21:10b) of the oracle quoted in the preceding verse. On the other hand, the final clause in verse 3 (**who will capture it**) points to antecedents in either 32:3 or 32:28. Jeremiah is speaking in chapter 32 while he is "in the courtyard of the guard" (32:2), which would fit perfectly in the context of 38:1-3. It looks like these officials are quoting the most inflammatory statements from Jeremiah's words to the soldiers around him. Again, it is likely that Jeremiah's message raises concerns about talk of desertion among those troops, and this is what motivates these officials to bring Jeremiah before Zedekiah a second time.

The core of what is quoted in this verse is that Jerusalem "shall be given into the hand of" the Babylonians. Perhaps it is a coincidence, but the most concentrated use of the term for **hand** (יָד, *yad*) – especially in the phrase, "into the hand of" – in Jeremiah is found in these two chapters and in Jeremiah 32. The LORD declares repeatedly "by the hand of" Jeremiah (37:2) that King Zedekiah and the city will be given "into the hand of" the Babylonian king and his army (37:17; 38:3,18). Zedekiah places Jeremiah "into the hands of" his officials (38:5; cp. 38:16), but then "into the hand of" Ebed-melech (38:10-11). Zedekiah is afraid of falling "into the hand of" his own people more than being captured by the Babylonians (38:19,23). It is as if everyone's life is "in the hand of" someone else.

Jeremiah's words are **discouraging** ("weakening the hands of") **the soldiers who are left in this city** (v. 4).[1] They are unable to take anyone "into their hand." Here again there are echoes of the days of Hezekiah. These soldiers represent a "remnant" to the officials; they are the ones who **are left** (both words derive from the same Hebrew root שָׁאַר (*šā'ar*). Those who were saved in Hezekiah's day were the "remnant" who trusted in the LORD. These officials see the **soldiers who are left** as another remnant, one which needs prophetic encouragement of the sort given by Isaiah.

This brings out a fundamental problem with common interpretations of the prophecies of Jeremiah. Jeremiah is often cited in the ways that he speaks out against "false" prophets. But modern readers

---

[1] On this clause, see Thompson, *Jeremiah*, p. 637; Holladay, *Jeremiah 2*, p. 289.

need to be cognizant of the nature of the "false" message they were propagating. A part of it was a call to trust in the LORD to protect them against enemy attack. What made that message "false" is that it did not come from the LORD. It was his message to Jerusalem in the days of Isaiah and Hezekiah; but he had a different message for the people in the days of Jeremiah. Actually, the message is the same in essence, but different in its details. The essence of the message was: Trust in the LORD. In Isaiah's day, that meant they were to trust in him to spare Jerusalem from her attackers; in Jeremiah's day, that meant they were to trust in him to use their attackers to take care of them. The people mistakenly assumed that the specific way in which trust was manifested should be the same in every similar situation. Such is not the case. Trust in the LORD is simply that — trust in the LORD. One cannot know ahead of time what the LORD is going to require in a given situation; only he knows that. That is why one must simply trust in him.

Zedekiah shows his ultimate weakness (and fear) in his response to his officials (v. 5). He shows in other moments that he does not share the officials' opinion of Jeremiah, yet he gives in to them here. It is probable that the military threat against Jerusalem has served to increase the powers of the military officials momentarily; yet this still does not excuse the king's actions here. He is responding out of a stance of fear, rather than from a stance of faith. He relies more on the officials than on the LORD for his well-being.

It is likely that the **Malkijah** mentioned in verse 6 is the same man whose son is mentioned in verse 1, although we cannot be absolutely certain. Furthermore, we do not know why one **cistern** rather than another is used for this purpose.[2] Excavations have shown that such cisterns were fairly common in Israelite homes, being carved out of the soft limestone which one finds throughout much of the region. They were used to catch and store rainwater for the long dry months of summer. It is not surprising to find one with a silt-covered bottom.

---

[2]Some commentators argue that Jeremiah 38 is an alternate version of the story told in Jer 37:11-21. This would mean that Jeremiah was arrested only once, that he was placed in only one cistern, that he was rescued (by the king? by Ebed-melech?) once, and that he had only one private audience with the king. So Bright, *Jeremiah*, pp. 232-233; Nicholson, *Jeremiah 26–52*, p. 118; Thompson, *Jeremiah*, pp. 636-637; Clements, *Jeremiah*, p. 220. Holladay gives strong arguments against that view (*Jeremiah 2*, pp. 282-283).

Ebed-melech enters the scene without introduction. His name means "servant of the king." We are not informed until later that the reason for his concern for Jeremiah is that he was one who "trusted in (the LORD)" (39:14), meaning he accepted Jeremiah's message that the LORD was working through the Babylonians to fulfill his purpose. The NIV gives a footnote indicating that the term translated **official** here (סָרִיס, *sārîs*) is different from the term for the **officials** (שָׂרִים, *śārîm*) who had put Jeremiah in the cistern.

The **Benjamin Gate** would be a gate leading north out of the city, since Benjamin lay to the north. Some have suggested that Zedekiah probably was there in a judicial capacity, providing Ebed-melech with the opportunity to approach the king on Jeremiah's behalf.[3] Ebed-melech accuses the other officials of wrongdoing, but he does not call for any action against them. He probably knows that, realistically, one cannot expect action to be taken against those officials. Instead, he merely petitions the king to correct the wrong that has been done before it is too late. The NIV translation suggests that there still is **bread** to be found in Jerusalem, but the Hebrew could also be saying that they have already run out. The king's response might support the latter.

Zedekiah's answer is swift and favorable. The number of men commissioned to accompany **Ebed-melech** in getting **Jeremiah out** suggests that he was concerned about protecting Jeremiah (from the officials) after he was out.[4] Taken together, these considerations further support the impression that Zedekiah had had Jeremiah imprisoned out of fear, rather than from a personal denial of Jeremiah's prophetic office.

The narrator reports the successful rescue of Jeremiah from the cistern (vv. 11-13); no mention is made of any opposition posed by the other officials. Perhaps they are too preoccupied with mounting Babylonian pressure to bother with this troublesome prophet.

G. ZEDEKIAH QUESTIONS JEREMIAH AGAIN (38:14-28)

38:14-28 This is the third and last time that **Zedekiah** sends for **Jeremiah** (v. 14; see 37:3,17). Like the second, this is a summons to

---

[3]Bright, *Jeremiah*, p. 231; Thompson, *Jeremiah*, p. 639.
[4]There is some textual evidence for reading "three" instead of "thirty," and the former reading is adopted by many. See the translations; cp. Bright, *Jeremiah*, p. 231; Thompson, *Jeremiah*, p. 640.

a very private audience with the king. One wonders, though, why the king sends for Jeremiah. As Jeremiah says in verse 15, **Even if I did give you counsel, you would not listen to me.** This points us to the fact that the writer wants the reader to see that we have reached something of a climax in this part of the story. Here is a specific example of the main point of these stories: that the king (like his followers) did not "listen to the words of the LORD" (37:2). He does not listen, we will soon see, because he is afraid of his own people.

Jeremiah has his own fears, which he expresses before directly addressing Zedekiah's request. He fears that he will be killed for telling the truth. Zedekiah solemnly reassures him with a strong oath (**As surely as the LORD lives, who has given us breath**). He further shows that he does not agree with his officials' opinion of Jeremiah by distancing himself from them, from **those who are seeking your life** (v. 16).

Zedekiah is offered one last opportunity to "go out" (**surrender**; v. 17; cp. v. 2). The opportunity involves a narrow range of options and outcomes. Zedekiah must place himself either in the hands of the **officers** (*śārîm*) of **Babylon** or into the hands of his own officials (*śārîm*). The former option carries with it a promise that the royal **family will live** and the **city will not be burned**. This does not mean that it is possible that the Babylonians will leave in defeat. They will still take control of Jerusalem, and they will still capture the royal family; but the ill treatment of both will be lessened. In another sense, Zedekiah is being asked to act in the best interests of those under his care (his family and the city) rather than according to his own, short-term self-interests.

Zedekiah also stands figuratively for the entire nation in this instance. He is being told to place his personal welfare into the hands of his enemies. The LORD has declared that only there will he be safe. Jeremiah has been proclaiming the same message to the rest of the people. The LORD has decreed that safety lies in the hands of the Babylonians. Those who surrender to them, who put their lives in the hands of their enemies, will find the LORD's care there.[5] Those who refuse to do so are looking forward to certain death.

---

[5]Brueggemann expresses very well the sense of disharmony that must have been felt in Jeremiah's message of hope in surrender (*Jeremiah*, pp. 360-363). But this would not be the first time that Jeremiah stood in opposition to people who believed that God would never let his chosen city fall to invaders (see Jer 7:1-15).

Zedekiah finally admits to the root problem in his heart: he is **afraid** (v. 19). Such fears show a lack of faith in the LORD. A prophet whom he believes to be a spokesman for the LORD is telling him that the LORD will protect him from those whom he fears, but he does not trust the message. In this, he is even ignoring the example that Jeremiah has just set for him. Jeremiah feared the royal officials, but those fears are assuaged by the promises of protection by the king. But Jeremiah trusts more in the king than the king trusts in the LORD; he is ruled by his fears. His fears are certainly understandable, but only to a degree. The people might blame him for their suffering and take out their frustrations on him. But they probably would not be angry at him for surrendering. After all, they themselves have surrendered, seeing it as the prudent (if not divinely commanded) thing to do. They have done what Jeremiah had been accused of doing, they had **gone over to the Babylonians** (see 37:13-14). In addition to all that, the king has a "personal invitation," the personal promise of the LORD. But it is to no avail, because he refuses to listen.

The prophet's initial message to Zedekiah (vv. 20-22) is a partial reversal of his previous conversation with the king, when he said that the king would be handed over to the Babylonians (37:17). Now he says he **will not** be **handed over** to his own people. Jeremiah then addresses Zedekiah's fears in a positive way. He draws on the language of Deuteronomy (**it will go well with you**) to present this as an opportunity for Zedekiah, an opportunity to learn to have faith and consequently receive the LORD's blessing. This implies that the blessings previously promised for those who lived in the Promised Land are being perpetuated in a different land, the land of the Babylonians. But the same condition exists if this promise is to become a reality: he must **obey the LORD** ("hear the voice of the LORD"). The reader has already been warned that this is not going to happen, and Jeremiah has recently indicated his belief that it would not happen. So, it is not surprising that there is a much longer section to follow which spells out the consequences that will follow if Zedekiah does not "hear."[6]

Once again Jeremiah mentions the need for the king to "go out" (**surrender**). Of course, he is not going to do so, so Jeremiah now

---

[6]Even though Zedekiah "sends" to Jeremiah for advice, he does not "hear" that advice when it is given (as Jeremiah says in 38:15). See Thompson, *Jeremiah*, p. 631; Clements, *Jeremiah*, p. 218; Holladay, *Jeremiah 2*, p. 287; Brueggemann, *Jeremiah*, p. 355.

explains in greater and more humiliating detail what will happen. First of all he brings up the **women** who are under Zedekiah's care. These women should have been the persons he treasured and protected most diligently; yet, because he fears his own officials more than the Babylonian officials, the women are going to be taken out of his hands and placed into the hands of his enemies.

The words of the women here recall some of the things that have already happened to Jeremiah. The suffering endured by Jeremiah at the hands of the Judean officials will now be suffered by the king at the hands of the Babylonian officials.[7] The women say that Zedekiah will **sink** (טָבַע, ṭābaʻ) in the **mud** (בֹץ, bōṣ), just as Jeremiah "sank" (ṭābaʻ) in the "silt" (טִיט, ṭîṭ) at the bottom of the cistern (v. 6). Furthermore, Zedekiah had handed over Jeremiah to his officials because he was "unable" (אֵין יוּכַל, ʼên yûkal) to resist them (v. 5). Soon, the women of the vision say, the king's own friends will **overcome** (יָכְלוּ, yākᵊlû) him. The phrase **trusted friends** (אַנְשֵׁי שְׁלֹמֶךָ, ʼanšê šᵊlōmekā, "your men of peace") is rare (see Jer 20:10; Obad 7). In this context, it might be an allusion to the official named Shelemiah. Similarly, the name "Jucal" (38:1; Jehucal in 37:3) means "he overcomes." Maybe this taunt is to suggest that "He Overcomes" will someday "overcome" the king.

The prophet's final warning (v. 23) brings together several elements of previous statements. It reaffirms the suffering awaiting the royal family, suffering which could have been avoided had Zedekiah "gone out" to the Babylonians (v. 17). Because of his refusal to "go out," his family will be "made to go out" (**brought out**). He could have "escaped" by surrendering (v. 2), but now he **will not escape** (see v. 18). Likewise, the city will not be spared, but will instead be **captured** and **burned down** (37:8; cp. 37:10; 38:3).

Zedekiah's response (vv. 24-26) takes us back to the beginning of this scene. He had promised Jeremiah that he would not be killed for what he might say; now he makes that promise contingent on Jeremiah not "saying" anything to the officials. Moreover, the words he places in his officials' mouths (**do not hide it from us or we will kill you**) are essentially the words he had used to get Jeremiah to speak to him. How typical this is: for a man to expect someone else to be honest with him and to hold confidentialities with him, but

---

[7]See Nicholson, *Jeremiah 26–52*, p. 123; Thompson, *Jeremiah*, p. 643; Holladay, *Jeremiah 2*, p. 290.

then to demand the opposite of that person when he interacts with others. His final statement is meant to make it look like he agrees with their opinion and treatment of Jeremiah, that the king had been considering returning Jeremiah to the place from which he had actually had him extricated. Again, he shows that he is most afraid of his own officials.

Zedekiah is the most complex character in these two chapters. He is to be pitied, to some extent, because there are logical reasons for Zedekiah to doubt the veracity of Jeremiah's message (e.g., Jerusalem's fate under Hezekiah). On the other hand, as Jeremiah points out, only he had correctly predicted the coming of the Babylonians. Zedekiah vacillates between his personal inclination to trust in Jeremiah as a true prophet (probably because of his "track record") and the strong pressures of his officials to reject the Lord's words. In the end, he gives in to those pressures and does not "hear" Jeremiah. For that crucial reason, he is a character whom the reader is not to emulate. He knows what to do, but he is afraid to do it. He is a man of cowardice who tries to wear a mask of faith at times, somewhat like King Saul (1 Samuel 13). His own indecisiveness contrasts to the (misguided) decisiveness of his officials. And his weak will, which derives from that indecisiveness, contrasts to the courageous humanitarianism of Ebed-melech. It is a lack of courage which leads him to "hear but not hear" the message of Jeremiah. The ultimate fate of Jerusalem, described in the chapters immediately following, is thus placed squarely on his weak shoulders.[8]

Verse 27 raises a couple of unanswerable questions. Some could charge Jeremiah with being weak and faithless himself, because he protects himself from additional suffering by corroborating the king's lie. This would seem to condone lying in certain circumstances (cp. 1 Kgs 22:19-23). We cannot know for sure, however, because we do not know the LORD's opinion of Jeremiah's cooperation with the king in this instance.

The literary conclusion (v. 28) of the scene has been expanded in this case to form a bridge to the next scene, which describes the taking of Jerusalem (39:1-14). There is a minor textual problem in this. The short sentence at the end (which has been attached in the NIV to 39:1) is not found in many early Greek manuscripts. It

---

[8]Nicholson, *Jeremiah 26–52*, p. 124; Thompson, *Jeremiah*, pp. 631, 642-643; Clements, *Jeremiah*, pp. 218-221; Brueggemann, *Jeremiah*, pp. 354-368.

consists of four words in Hebrew, three of which are simply repeating the end of the preceding sentence (the words **captured** and **taken** are translations of the same Hebrew word). Structurally, the short sentence is a typical subordinate clause, used to introduce the main clause of a sentence (39:1); however, that sentence already has an introductory clause. Also, the chronological note in 39:1 first takes the reader back to the beginning of the siege, before the events described in 37:3-5. From a literary standpoint, 39:1 seems to introduce the telling of a completely separate story. This leaves the impression that 38:28b is secondary. It is possible, then, that 38:28b was originally a marginal note, intended to clarify the connection between 38:28a (which looks ahead to the fall of Jerusalem) and 39:1-10 (which records the fall of Jerusalem). Then again, it could be that 38:28b is original, composed to tie together two stories, and that it was omitted accidentally by a copyist because of an eye-skip between similar clauses, or intentionally because it seemed redundant.

JEREMIAH 39

H. THE FALL OF JERUSALEM (39:1-18)

The expanded form of the concluding formula in Jeremiah 38:28 points ahead to Jeremiah 39. Other literary clues suggest that 39:1-40:6 are to be read as a continuation of or sequel to chapters 37-38. Two of these clues are the additional notes about where Jeremiah "remained" (39:14; 40:6). Another is the record of Jeremiah's prophecy concerning Ebed-melech, which could have fit just as well in Jeremiah 38.[1] This suggests a slightly different demarcation of the text than is given in the NIV. In this, the "Fall of Jerusalem" ends in 39:14, describing the fate of the inhabitants of the city, particularly Zedekiah and Jeremiah. But 39:15-18 and 40:1-6 are out of place chronologically because they relate details of what happened prior to Jeremiah being placed in the care of Gedaliah (39:14). Literally, these verses constitute an aside relating the treatment of Ebed-melech and Jeremiah, two individuals who received special treatment because of their trust in the LORD.

39:1-14 The narrator describes the entire siege and capture of Jerusalem, from beginning to end, in a very few lines (vv. 1-3; cp. 2 Kgs 25:1-21). He only goes into detail when giving the names of the Babylonian **officials** who orchestrated the actual occupation and destruction of the defeated city. In so doing, he implies the humiliation of Judah's own officials, the officials who had refused to hear the words of Jeremiah in the preceding episodes. The writer's primary focus is on the humiliation of **Zedekiah** (vv. 4-7), which will be bal-

---

[1]Holladay wants to move 39:15-18 back into Jeremiah 38 because of chronological considerations (*Jeremiah 2*, pp. 282-284). Others speculate that the placement of this oracle intends to verify that Ebed-melech survived the destruction of Jerusalem, as predicted in the prophecy (Brueggemann, *Jeremiah*, pp. 373-374; Nicholson, *Jeremiah 26-52*, p. 129; Thompson, *Jeremiah*, p. 649).

anced by the special treatment given to Jeremiah (vv. 11-14). Finally, Zedekiah has followed Jeremiah's advice and has **left** ("gone out of") **the city,** but he is too late. He travels just a few miles from Jerusalem before the **Babylonians capture** him, as Jeremiah had prophesied. They hand him over to the **king of Babylon,** who orders Zedekiah's family to be killed in front of him before having **Zedekiah's eyes** gouged out. The last thing the king sees is the horrifying fulfillment of Jeremiah's words of warning (cp. 32:4; 38:17,23).

The description of the fulfillment of Jeremiah's warnings continues in verses 8-10. As he had predicted, the city is burned by its conquerors (21:10; 37:10; 38:18,23). The remnant ("those who remained"), made up of those who had **gone over** ("fallen") to the Babylonians previously and those just captured, are now exiled to Babylon. Only the landless are left with anything when the Babylonians have finished. The only hopeful aspect of this picture is that Jeremiah has told the people that the future of the LORD's people is in the hands of these Babylonian conquerors.

We do not know how the Babylonian king came to know about **Jeremiah.** The most likely proposal is that some of the Judean captives had mentioned him to their captors. These officials do for him what the Jerusalem officials should have done: they release him from **the courtyard of the guard** (vv. 11-14). Their treatment of Jeremiah in some sense prefigures the essential fate of all the people of Judah who now find themselves in the hands of the Babylonians. If they will put their faith in the LORD as Jeremiah has, ultimately they will be released as well.

Gedaliah, the new Babylonian-appointed governor, is mentioned here without introduction. The reader is simply supposed to know of him and his family (see 36:11-12). Exactly where Jeremiah goes here is difficult to determine. The double use of "his" in the translation suggests that he goes back to his family's home territory; but the Hebrew text does not contain this pronoun in either instance. He goes from the courtyard to **the house** (of Gedaliah? of his people?), and he **remained among** [the] **people.** The same result is given in 40:6, indicating that the main story line picks up again there. Jeremiah 40:1-6 thus constitutes an expansion of what is recorded here. The use of a statement about where Jeremiah **remained** (39:14) again marks the conclusion of a literary scene.

39:15-18 The reference to **the courtyard of the guard** takes the reader back to the stories just before the capture of Jerusalem.

Literarily, this section represents a brief respite from all the noise and anguish of the bigger story that is being told. In the midst of the chaos and despair of Jerusalem's demise, a couple of small lights glow. The main parts of this section are two prophetic oracles (**the word of the LORD**) regarding people who are spared from the LORD's judgment. Both involve foreigners. The first has the foreigner as its object (**Ebed-melech**; 39:15-18); the second is communicated by a foreigner (Nebuzaradan) to Jeremiah (40:1-5).

The Lord uses this time of Jerusalem's military collapse to reassert his sovereignty over war. He is **the LORD Almighty** ("LORD of Hosts"). He can still protect Ebed-melech from the military might which the Babylonians are exerting. His authority is primarily demonstrated, however, in the destruction of Jerusalem, not in its salvation. This runs counter to the prevailing wisdom of the men of the day, who assumed that the LORD would always bring them **prosperity** ("good") and not **disaster** ("evil"). But as with Amos's message to the people of the North, this "day of the LORD" is a day of "darkness, not light" (Amos 5:18). It is a time of shame and destruction, not of hope and peace.

Against this dark background, the LORD promises to **rescue** Ebed-melech, thereby giving to him the same promise he had thus far given to but one other person: Jeremiah (1:8,19; 15:20-21; cp. 42:11). He also reverses the language of defeat which characterizes his message to Zedekiah and the people during the final days of Jerusalem, saying that Ebed-melech **will not be handed over** (see on 38:3) to the Babylonians. He promises this to Ebed-melech, in spite of the fact Ebed-melech is afraid. Here again, one might see a parallel with Zedekiah. Zedekiah did not "go over" to the Babylonians because he was afraid of his countrymen (39:19). One might suspect that fear on the part of Ebed-melech betrays a lack of faith; but the following verse dispels that idea. Apparently it is possible to be afraid and yet trust in the LORD. The difference is that Ebed-melech did what Jeremiah advised in spite of his fear.

Jeremiah's words in verse 18 again show how Ebed-melech faces a fate that is opposite to what Zedekiah and the rest of the population of Jerusalem were facing. He **will not fall by the sword.** This is in contrast to what Jeremiah typically prophesied regarding the fate of the people, when he said they would die "by the sword, famine and plague" (21:9; 24:10; 27:8; 32:24; 38:2; etc.). Further, Jeremiah tells Ebed-melech, "(you) **will escape with your life**." This promise is also given to one other of Jeremiah's supporters, Baruch (45:5). The justification for this different treatment is given in the final clause: **you trust in me, declares the LORD**. Again, this does not mean that Ebed-melech is without fear; rather, he acts in spite of his fear when he does what Jeremiah advises. This verb ("trusts") also takes the reader back to the story of Hezekiah and the Assyrian invasion of 701 B.C. The writer of Kings emphasized there that Hezekiah and his people were spared by the LORD because they "trusted" in him (see 2 Kgs 18:5,19-22, 30). Now Jeremiah gives the same explanation for the "deliverance" of Ebed-melech.

JEREMIAH 40

I. JEREMIAH FREED (40:1-6)

40:1-6 The introductory phrase (**the word . . . from the LORD**) indicates that the following words of the Babylonian commander are a divine oracle from the LORD to Jeremiah. This is unusual, but it suggests that such oracles did not always come to Jeremiah simply through direct revelation or by the LORD speaking directly to Jeremiah alone. Sometimes, the LORD's word could be revealed to Jeremiah through the words of someone else.

It is unclear where this conversation takes place in the chronological sequence of the story. Jeremiah 39:14 mentions Nebuzaradan (and others) taking Jeremiah out of the courtyard and then placing him under Gedaliah's protection. In this episode he is found among other Judahite prisoners, but he ends up with Gedaliah at the end. It could be that this conversation takes place sometime after the events in 39:14, and that in the interim Jeremiah had gone to Ramah and been incarcerated along with other survivors by some Babylonian soldiers. It seems more likely, however, that 39:14 relates the beginning and end of the Babylonians' treatment of Jeremiah, and these verses relate some of what happened in the interim that led up to his finally coming into Gedaliah's care.

The enemy commander makes an amazing statement here. First, it is amazing that he does not credit the gods whom he worships with the Babylonian victory. Second, what he says implies some level of belief that Israel's LORD truly is God, because only the true God could bring about what he has predicted. Third, he gives an inspired explanation for why this fate has befallen Jerusalem.

These words validate Jeremiah's message on several levels. On a literary level, they confirm the fulfillment of the words of the prophecy to Ebed-melech just reported (39:16). On a more immediate level, they serve to reassure Jeremiah (if he needs to be reas-

sured) that the LORD is working through the Babylonians. It is as if
the LORD has occupied the body of the Babylonian, winking and
whispering to Jeremiah to let him know that the LORD is there with
him. The same is true on another level, as these words would suggest to the book's readers that they, like Jeremiah, should be looking to the Babylonians to be the instruments for carrying out the
LORD's plans for his people. Furthermore, this Babylonian echoes
the words of Jeremiah himself. He says that the LORD has brought
this upon Jerusalem, and that he has done so because the people **did
not obey him** ("listen to his voice;" cp. 37:2; 38:20). This also should
confirm to the readers that Jeremiah is a true prophet and that his
words regarding the current exile in Babylon should be heeded.

The treatment by this Babylonian official is in marked contrast
to his treatment at the hands of the officials of his own people. They
had confined him, while this man allows him complete freedom to
choose where he will go. They had placed Jeremiah in a cistern and
apparently were not concerned that he could easily have died there;
he pledges to take care of Jeremiah personally, if that is necessary.

The presence of a footnote with an alternate reading in the NIV
points to some uncertainty regarding the beginning of verse 5. The
Hebrew text is elliptical, actually lacking the phrase, **Nebuzaradan
added,** even though it is clear that he is speaking the words which
follow.[1] This leaves the sense of the transition here uncertain, and
no convincing proposal to explain it is forthcoming. Perhaps something was accidentally skipped by a copyist.

Nebuzaradan's directive to **go back** can be understood in a couple of ways. It could imply that Jeremiah had already been staying
with Gedaliah for a while (39:14) and that Nebuzaradan is advising
him to return there. It might also simply reflect the direction which
he himself is now taking, that he has "set his face" to go to Babylon.
From that perspective, to stay in Judah would mean "going back,"
even if he has not left yet. Gedaliah is not identified at greater
length. He is **Gedaliah son of Ahikam, the son of Shaphan.** This
points to a long-term relationship between Jeremiah and a leading
family in Jerusalem. This Shaphan probably is the one who brought
the scroll containing "the book of the covenant" to King Josiah
(2 Kgs 22:3-13; cp. Jer 3:10). Gedaliah's uncle, Gemariah, had

---

[1]The text literally reads, "And still he would not go back. 'And go back to
Gedaliah . . .'"

advised King Jehoiakim not to burn Jeremiah's first scroll (Jer 36:25), a scroll brought to the king's attention by Gedaliah's cousin, Micaiah (36:11). Jeremiah had entrusted another of Gedaliah's uncles, Elasah, with the letter that he sent to the early exiles (29:3).[2]

We have already pointed out that verse 6 represents the last reference to where Jeremiah "stayed" during the Fall of Jerusalem, thereby marking the end of a literary section in the book. The repetition of this concluding formula also reminds the reader that Jeremiah still "remains," even after Jerusalem has fallen and the people have been led away. The establishment of **Mizpah** as the center for the new Babylonian province of Judah stands as something of an inclusio for the history of Israel's monarchy (see also 2 Kgs 25:23). This Mizpah (not to be confused with another one in Gilead) was a gathering-place for the tribes in the days of the judges (Judges 20–21) and Saul (1 Samuel 7), and it was the site of Saul's public anointing ceremony (1 Sam 10:17-25). As such, it stands as one of the last central places utilized by the tribes before there were kings, and it now reverts to that same capacity once Israel's time of kings has come to an end.

J. GEDALIAH ASSASSINATED (40:7–41:15)

The events in Jeremiah 42–44 show how the bad example set by Zedekiah is followed by Johanan son of Kareah, the man who eventually emerges as the leader of those who flee to Egypt. The present section (40:7–41:15) forms a bridge to those later stories, describing how Johanan came to be the sole leader of the renegade Judeans left behind by the Babylonians. Jeremiah is not mentioned in this section, nor is the LORD. This contributes to the impression, later verified, that these people are living their lives apart from the LORD's guidance. A shortened version of Jeremiah 40:7-9 appears in 2 Kings 25:23-24, and 2 Kings 25:25-26 summarizes Jeremiah 41–43.

40:7-10 We are not told how these small bands of Judean soldiers manage to escape the Babylonian troops. Apparently, once Jerusalem has been captured and the "official" Judahite resistance has been squelched, these troops are allowed to move about the country relatively easily, because they are able to come to the head-

---

[2]Thompson, *Jeremiah*, p. 653.

quarters of the highest appointed official. Perhaps the Babylonians no longer viewed them as a threat. The army officers listed here (and in 2 Kgs 25:23) are not mentioned in any other context. It is possible, but not likely, that **Ishmael** is the brother of the man who read Jeremiah's scroll to King Jehoiakim (Jer 36:14,21-23).

It is unlikely that **Gedaliah** could have made the promise in verses 9-10 unilaterally. The Babylonians probably had informed him that they would be lenient toward any refugees who surfaced, as long as they were not disruptive.[3] The message of Gedaliah again is the same as that previously given by Jeremiah: **serve the king of Babylon** (e.g., Jer 27:8). The promise that **it will go well with you** resonates with the exhortations of Deuteronomy; but this must have sounded rather hollow and mocking to these men. The Deuteronomic promise assumed a free nation and was based on fidelity to the laws of the LORD; Gedaliah's promise is directed to a subject nation, in subjection because of their infidelity. Still, it indirectly perpetuates the message of Jeremiah by implying that the hopes formerly associated with the Promised Land are now to be realized through their Babylonian conquerors.

The surprise in verse 10 is in the final phrase. It indicates that these soldiers **have taken over** ("seized") certain towns in Judea. One would expect a response by the Babylonians, but there has been none. The impression is that these events are too insignificant in the eyes of the Babylonians to warrant a response. It also suggests that these men are not really concerned about restoring a united nation of Judah. They are not trying to rally all refugees under a common banner with which they might attempt to withstand the Babylonians. They are making enemies with their own people, using their military might to help themselves at the expense of their countrymen.

Gedaliah encourages them to follow the course of economic rebuilding, indirectly suggesting they give up any military schemes. He tells them to **harvest** and store away crops that are staples in the region. These were things that had traditionally been the backbone of the local economy. They are to be doing this agricultural work and not relying on others to provide goods for them. They are to be preparing for peace, not war. The political problems (namely, the Babylonians) would be handled by Gedaliah, who apparently has enough respect from both sides to be trusted by both.

---

[3]Brueggemann, *Jeremiah*, pp. 377-380.

40:11-12 These **Jews** (better, "Judeans") must have fled to these neighboring countries prior to the final siege and destruction of Jerusalem. The number of people involved in this return is unknown, but it probably was no more than a few thousand. The reference to a **remnant** being left behind is rather ironic. These are not the "remnant" in the same sense in which Isaiah uses the term, when he talks about the LORD leaving behind a group to perpetuate his people and his covenants with them. This **remnant** has been left by the king of Babylon, not by the LORD. Further, Jeremiah has made it clear that the future for Judah lies in the land of Babylon, not in the people left behind. Those in Babylonian exile are the true "remnant" of the LORD's people (Jeremiah 24; Ezekiel 11).

There is also uncertainty as to how much time has passed since the end of the siege. It seems illogical to assume that this is the same year that Jerusalem fell. The crops they gather require some tending throughout the year, so it is unlikely they could produce a "bumper crop" just a few weeks after Jerusalem was destroyed. Also, these people have had time to hear about the fate of Jerusalem, then hear about the appointment of Gedaliah, and then move back to their homeland and harvest a crop. Therefore, it seems plausible that these events transpire over the period of a year after Jerusalem has been sacked.[4]

40:13-16 The "abundance of wine and summer fruit" should have been taken as an indication that Gedaliah's advice was sound. Unfortunately, it was ignored by at least some of the Judeans left in the land. The veracity of this part of the story is supported by the fact that **Johanan** does a heroic thing in trying to warn **Gedaliah**, yet he later proves not to be a hero. His actions here could be construed (by a skeptic) as an attempt by the author to build up the reputation of Johanan. But Johanan's actions shortly after this are not heroic at all, showing that the author's ultimate assessment of him is negative.

Johanan mentions a rumored plot fomented by **Baalis** the Ammonite. The reality of the plot becomes apparent shortly. The likely reason for this insurrection is that Baalis would somehow benefit from a disruption of the fragile stability in Judea. In later generations, neighboring groups such as the Ammonites looked on

---

[4]There is reference to a subsequent deportation of Jews in 582 B.C. (Jer 52:30). Some associate that deportation with the assassination of Gedaliah (41:1-3; Thompson, *Jeremiah*, p. 657).

such stability as a threat to their own economic ambitions in the region (see Nehemiah). It is likely that the same sort of motivation lies behind this plot by Baalis.[5]

A second warning (vv. 15-16) reinforces the portrayal of Johanan as one who is not involved in the plot against Gedaliah. Johanan's comments suggest two possible insights into this situation. He assumes that striking a blow against the appointed governor will likely bring the wrath of the powerful Babylonian military down around the heads of the entire Judean population. It would be a blow in the name of the people (even if the people do not support it), and so the people as a whole would suffer retaliation. He wishes to diffuse this, but his motivation is not clear. It might be that he is in full support of Gedaliah's stated policy, wanting to accept Babylonian domination and make the best of the situation. He could also be more sympathetic to the nationalist zeal of Ishmael, but fearful that Ishmael is striking a blow too soon. A less obvious aspect of this situation is that Gedaliah's dismissal of his warnings might reflect fear rather than confidence. His initial disbelief (40:14) might suggest that he is confident of his own security, that he believes no one would dare to strike out against him because of the Babylonians.[6] But Johanan's offer to kill Ishmael in a way that would not attract notice suggests that Gedaliah might be less fearful of Babylonian reprisals than he is of persons who were sympathetic to Ishmael. These individuals could have been so loyal to Ishmael and his (nationalist?) sentiments that they would have reacted to an accusation against Ishmael as a ploy to neutralize his growing strength. So, perhaps Gedaliah is more fearful of his own people than he is of the Babylonians.

---

[5]For recent archaeological finds relating to Baalis, see Robert Deutsch, "Seal of Baalis Surfaces: Ammonite King Plotted Murder of Judahite Governor," *BAR* 25 (Mar-Apr 1999): 44-49, 66.

[6]Thompson, *Jeremiah*, p. 657.

JEREMIAH 41

I. GEDALIAH ASSASSINATED (40:7–41:15) (continued)

41:1-3 The warning of Johanan now proves to be well-founded, as **Ishmael** and his followers massacre **Gedaliah** and his associates. This event is placed **in the seventh month**, but the year is not specified. The preceding chronological marker dates the breaching of the walls of Jerusalem in the fourth month of Nebuchadnezzar's nineteenth year (July 586 B.C.; Jer 39:2), with the razing of the city in the following month (2 Kgs 25:8-9). If this is the seventh month of the same year, it would mean that Gedaliah served as governor for no more than two months. This is certainly possible, although a term of at least fourteen months seems more likely (see on 40:12).

We find out here for the first time that Ishmael is **of royal** descent and the son of a palace official in the recently ousted regime. This means his attack is likely to be construed by the new administration as a political move, an attempt by the Davidic family to reestablish its fallen kingdom.[1] The narrator further indicts Nethaniah by specifying the victims as **the one whom the king of Babylon had appointed . . . as well as the Babylonian soldiers who were there.** It is clear that this is to be viewed as an act of direct rebellion against the sovereignty of Nebuchadnezzar. It is also something of a statement against the faith of many refugees. Even **all the Jews who were with Gedaliah** are killed. Ishmael is pitting those Jews as allies with the Babylonians against his own troops, the "true" patriots of Judah.[2]

41:4-10 The subsequent section strengthens and clarifies this interpretation. Worshipers from a few northern cities (northern tribesmen,[3] or settlers who had been moved there by Josiah; see

---

[1]Brueggemann, *Jeremiah*, pp. 382-383.
[2]Ibid., p. 380.
[3]Thompson, *Jeremiah*, p. 659.

2 Chr 34:6-9) are heading toward the ruined city to lament and offer sacrifices at **the house of the LORD** (v. 5). Ishmael's small force tricks and then ambushes them. There is a sarcastic tone to Ishmael's statement, **"Come to Gedaliah son of Ahikam,"** which indicates his disdain for Gedaliah, these worshipers, and the reason for their visit. His disdain is further demonstrated when he dumps his victims' bodies into the cistern there. The fact that the cistern had been dug in a defensive move by Asa against Baasha (v. 9; see 1 Kgs 15:16-22) points to the likelihood that this was a large cistern, important for the entire town of Mizpah. The dumping of corpses there would have polluted and defiled it, preventing it from being used for some time to come. Such an attitude suggests that Ishmael rejects the political position of Gedaliah, a position also held by Jeremiah and based on the assumption that Babylonian domination was the LORD's will at the moment. It is likely, then, that Ishmael was one of those in Jerusalem who had never accepted Jeremiah's message, that he rejected the notion that the LORD would hand his people over to their enemies and allow Jerusalem to be destroyed. This notion had also spurred on Josiah's Reform, because no reforms would have been deemed necessary if Jerusalem were inviolable. It is likely, then, that Ishmael had resented those reform measures (see Jer 3:6-10) and had not opposed the return to idolatry under Jehoiakim. In his mind, worship of the LORD allowed for the worship of other gods as well, and the defeat of Jerusalem only confirmed the power of those other gods.

Two groups are spared by Ishmael and his men. There are ten of the eighty pilgrims who bribe him with provisions they have stored away, and they are spared. Then there are other people left in Mizpah who are taken captive. The writer highlights the presence of **the king's daughters** in this group. It is likely that Ishmael sees a political advantage in claiming control of these women, similar to Absalom's control of David's concubines (see on 2 Sam 16:21-22). Indirectly, it would have been viewed as part of Ishmael's claim to sovereignty over the local population; more directly, it was an act of defiance against the orders of **Nebuzaradan commander of the imperial guard**. Ishmael sets out to take all these captives **to the Ammonites**, confirming Johanan's warning to Gedaliah about collusion with Baalis and lending further credence to the suggestion that Ishmael put some faith in foreign gods.

41:11-15 Johanan and his followers respond swiftly to the news of Ishmael's attack. They catch up with the fleeing assassins and their captives at **Gibeon**, just a few miles south of Mizpah (see 2 Sam 2:12-16). The captives break free of Ishmael's men, who turn and run without a fight, taking advantage of their now lightened loads to escape the rest of the way to Ammon.

K. FLIGHT TO EGYPT (41:16–43:13)

Believing that the Babylonians will want to seek vengeance on those left behind for the death of their appointee, Johanan and his followers flee to Egypt. Before they leave, however, they decide to seek the advice of Jeremiah, waiting ten perilous days for his reply (42:7). The faith which this petition apparently supposes soon shows itself to be transparent, like the faith of Saul and the faith of Zedekiah. It is in this episode that one sees the strongest parallels between Johanan and the late king, Zedekiah. It is possible, in fact, that this section was written particularly with Johanan and his followers in mind as readers. By showing them how Zedekiah's failure to "hear the word of the LORD" led to his downfall (37:1–39:7), the writer might be warning Johanan and those with him about what fate awaits them if they do not "hear the word of the LORD" from Jeremiah now. They initially pledge that they will listen to whatever message Jeremiah delivers, but their refusal to accept his words in Jeremiah 43 shows how weak their faith truly is.

41:16-18 Johanan and his followers perhaps have better political judgment than **Ishmael**, but they initially demonstrate no more (or less) faith than Ishmael in their actions. They understand that the **Babylonians** will want to seek revenge for the death of their appointee upon whomever they can capture. They also understand that they have thwarted the plot of the Ammonite king and can expect no help from that quarter. The most practical option is to turn to a nation with the greatest ability to provide them with shelter: Egypt. They have gone several miles to the south (**Geruth Kimham near Bethlehem**), nearing the east-west road that they will take to Egypt, when they stop to consult with Jeremiah.

JEREMIAH 42

J. FLIGHT TO EGYPT (41:16–43:13) (continued)

42:1-6 It is intriguing to realize that Jeremiah almost certainly has been among those captured at Mizpah,[1] yet he is not mentioned until this moment. He had given no word of warning (that we know of) to Gedaliah; he is not killed by Ishmael and his men; and yet the sparing of his life is not noted either. He is just one of "all the people Ishmael had taken captive at Mizpah" (41:14). Why the people turn to him now is not revealed.

The main part of the people's request sounds very similar to Zedekiah's initial inquiry of Jeremiah in 37:3. They ask him to **pray to the LORD your God for this entire remnant** (v. 2), just as Zedekiah had earlier asked him to "pray to the LORD our God for us."[2] There are two noteworthy differences. The first is that Johanan's people refer to him as Jeremiah's God rather than their own God. This does not necessarily mean that they do not worship the LORD; in fact, it is probably the case that they do. Instead, their statement reveals that they believe that Jeremiah enjoys the LORD's favor, while their own status before him is less certain. The second item of note is their self-designation as a "remnant," a designation which they justify at some length. This is probably an appeal (not so subtle) for divine mercy. Their history and the words of previous prophets has taught them that the LORD is especially merciful toward remnant groups, toward a small number of people whose size will not obscure his working in the world through them and for them. Their request is fairly open-ended; they do not limit the LORD

---

[1]Thompson wonders whether Jeremiah was originally among them, or was simply met by them as Johanan led them from the region (*Jeremiah*, pp. 661, 663).

[2]Holladay speaks of this as an inclusio for these chapters (*Jeremiah* 2, pp. 282-283).

with few options, but simply ask **where we should go and what we should do**.

The response of Jeremiah (v. 4) and the counterresponse of Johanan's people (vv. 5-6) accentuate the shame and disappointment associated with the fear and disobedience of the people's subsequent rejection of Jeremiah's words (43:1-3).[3] Jeremiah says, **"I have heard you."** This points to the main issue at hand, whether they will hear him. He has shown them the respect of listening to what they have to say; there is an undertone of an admonition to them to listen just as respectfully to what he will say. He then says he is going to **pray to the LORD your** [plural] **God**, changing slightly — but significantly — the wording of their request. The LORD is not just Jeremiah's God ("your [singular] God", vv. 2-3), he is their God as well. He then pledges to **keep nothing back** from what the LORD says. The implication is that they must be just as willing to "hear" whatever the LORD has to say.

The people immediately pick up on Jeremiah's meaning, and so they call on **the LORD** himself to serve as a **witness against** them if they fail to "hear" (**act in accordance with**) everything he has to say. They reiterate their resolve in verse 6. **Whether it is favorable or unfavorable** ("good or bad"), **we will obey** ("hear") **the LORD our God**. The same designation (**the LORD our God**) is stated twice in this verse. He is no longer just Jeremiah's God; the people claim him as their own. Moreover, they acknowledge that their well-being depends on their obedience to ("hearing") him. Sadly, their words will soon be shown to be hollow (see especially 43:4). Jeremiah lives up to his pledge in the stark message he delivers in 42:7-22, while the people's reaction in 43:1-3 shows how their own words are without substance. They have already decided what is best, and no contrary words will be heeded.[4]

42:7-22 Following a narrative introduction (vv. 7-8), Jeremiah's message to Johanan and his followers falls into three parts, each more strident than the one before. He begins with the LORD's directive to the people to **stay in** their **land**, coupled with a promise to protect them from the Babylonians (42:9-12). The LORD then shifts

---

[3]The author "uses the example of ostensive obedience in order to demonstrate rank disobedience" (Brueggemann, *Jeremiah*, p. 389).

[4]Thompson proposes that they assert their willingness to obey only because they are convinced that God wants them to go to Egypt (*Jeremiah*, p. 667).

to a warning about what will happen to them if they ignore his directive and **go** on to **Egypt** (42:13-18; cp. 24:8). Jeremiah concludes with
his own warning to the people for refusing to obey the LORD's directive (42:19-22). The hopeful anticipation of the first part gives way
to the possibility of disappointment in the second and finally to a
preemptive accusation of disobedience in the third.[5] This third part
is reminiscent of Jeremiah's remarks to Zedekiah before Zedekiah
has had a chance to hear Jeremiah's message (cp. 38:15).

The prophetic word comes to Jeremiah after **ten days**. This
seems like a long time to wait. It might point to a high level of faith
on Johanan's part, for surely this was long enough for the
Babylonians to hear about the recent assassination of Gedaliah. But
Jeremiah's words at the end of the chapter point to the likelihood
that the wait was actually detrimental to their faith.

The words of encouragement to the fugitives are drawn from the
earliest days of Jeremiah's prophetic career. The LORD says, **I will
build you up and not tear you down; I will plant you and not
uproot you** (Jer 1:10; cp. 18:7-10; 24:6). It is very likely that these
people have heard these words from Jeremiah on previous occasions, so they should know how trustworthy they are. The subsequent admonition, **Do not be afraid . . . for I am with you and will
save you and deliver you**, also echoes the LORD's words to Jeremiah
at his call (1:8,19). The fact that Jeremiah has survived the fall of
Jerusalem, in fulfillment of that early promise, should further
encourage his present listeners. The LORD concludes this section
with a promise of **compassion**, compassion which he will infuse in
Nebuchadnezzar. It is as if the LORD's "maternal instincts" are coming out here, because the term for "compassion" (רַחֲמִים, *raḥămîm*)
comes from the same root as the word for "womb" (רֶחֶם, *reḥem*).
This marks a definite shift in the LORD's feelings toward his people,
so it is not altogether surprising to find the recipients unsure of its
veracity. He had declared earlier his decision to withdraw his "love
and pity" ("compassion") from the people (13:14; 16:5), and he said
he would hand them over to the Babylonian king, who would show

---

[5]Brueggemann sketches out the rhetorical structure of 42:7-17. The initial
positive words consist of an "if-then" proposition (vv. 10-12), while the warning of the second (vv. 13-17) is constructed upon two such "if-then" statements. This puts greater weight on the second prospect, thus leading into
Jeremiah's own negative (pre-) assessment. Brueggemann, *Jeremiah*, p. 389.

them "no mercy or pity or compassion" (21:7); but now, all that has changed. He attributes this shift in his attitude to being **grieved** (□□, *niḥam*; see on 18:7-10)[6] by their recent suffering (v. 10). His heart has been touched. Unfortunately, their hearts will not be touched by his words of compassion.

The possibility that they will not be moved by these words prompts the stern warning in verses 13-18. Egypt appeals to them because it looks to be a place of peace and prosperity (**we will not see war . . . or be hungry for bread**). But moving to Egypt constitutes disobedience; they are not "hearing" the LORD. If they "will not hear the voice of the LORD" (**disobey the LORD**; v. 13), they will have to **hear the word of the LORD** which follows (v. 15). That "word" is the same that the rest of the nation has already "heard" — they **will die by the sword, famine and plague** (cp. 15:2; 21:7,9; 24:10; 38:2). They are the **remnant of Judah**, having avoided this "word" so far. But in Egypt they will escape no longer. This thought is carried further in verse 18, as the LORD directly refers to the fate of Jerusalem as a warning for Johanan's people. They too will become a **cursing and horror** and a **reproach** (cp. 24:9-10; 25:9,18; 29:18), an example to be avoided by all around.

Jeremiah's rebuke (42:19-22) almost seems out of place.[7] The people have had no chance to react to the LORD's words, no opportunity to demonstrate whether they have heard what he is saying to them. His harsh remarks would seem to make more sense after 43:3, after the people have voiced their rejection of the prophecy. It could be that Jeremiah is simply stating a "hunch" he has (again see 38:15) based on his experiences with other recipients of such messages. It could also be that he knows the mood of the people, what they have been saying for the past ten days, and so he already knows how they will respond. Or perhaps they are displaying nonverbal signals while he speaks, signals that show their frustration and disbelief. Whatever the reason, Jeremiah's words prepare the reader for the people's rejection of the prophecy. He says they even **made a fatal mistake**[8] in seeking the LORD's advice. The mistake is not that they asked,

---

[6]For differing interpretations of this verb, see Thompson, *Jeremiah*, p. 666, and Brueggemann, *Jeremiah*, p. 390.

[7]Bright, *Jeremiah*, pp. 252,256; Thompson, *Jeremiah*, p. 667.

[8]The NIV footnote reads "you erred in your hearts." The reading is, more literally, "you erred in your souls."

because they should seek the LORD's advice; it is a mistake because their imminent rejection of it means that they now have an additional reason for the LORD to be angry with them. Their rejection is so obvious that he talks about it in the past tense (**but you still have not obeyed the LORD**), even before it has been verbalized. Then he reiterates the sentence against them, using the terms already used by the LORD.

JEREMIAH 43

J. FLIGHT TO EGYPT (41:16–43:13) (continued)

43:1-7 The people's rejection is forcefully stated by **Azariah son of Hoshaiah and Johanan. . . .** There is some textual evidence (LXX) that Azariah is the same man identified as Jezaniah in 42:1. They could also be brothers. Neither is mentioned elsewhere in Jeremiah. It is probably significant that Azariah is mentioned here before Johanan. It suggests that Azariah might have been influencing Johanan to flee to Egypt, while Johanan on his own might have been more receptive to Jeremiah's promises of security in Judea (cp. his earlier warning of Gedaliah). Whatever the case, their words come off as desperate to the careful reader of Jeremiah. They accuse Jeremiah of **lying** ("speaking a lie"), a charge which Jeremiah has repeatedly and appropriately leveled against his opponents (cp. 7:4; 8:8; 14:14; 23:25-26).[1] Like Zedekiah (37:19), these people are more willing to "hear" the words of lying prophets; now, they have taken the next step and called Jeremiah a liar. Moreover, they accuse Jeremiah of being part of a conspiracy spearheaded by **Baruch**. One can only speculate about the reasons behind such an accusation. It is plausible to conclude that Baruch was more significant in the Judean political scene than Jeremiah, and he had probably had a role in spreading Jeremiah's pro-Babylonian rhetoric. Perhaps the general population now interprets Baruch's position as political maneuvering calculated to enhance his standing in the eyes of the new lords of the land.

The writer follows with a quick report of the people's move to Egypt (vv. 4-7). Practically everyone is mentioned: **Johanan, the army officers, the remnant of Judah, the king's daughters,** even **Jeremiah** and **Baruch**. They end up in the eastern delta town of

---

[1]Brueggemann, *Jeremiah*, p. 396.

Tahpanhes. The report is not entirely objective, though, as it also gives an (inspired) explanation for the move. The report begins with a comment about how **Johanan . . . and the people disobeyed** ("did not hear") **the LORD's command** (43:4), and it ends with a comment about how they went there **in disobedience to** ("did not hear the voice of") **the LORD** (43:7).

Clearly, Johanan has the same "hearing" problem which plagued Zedekiah. Both men ask Jeremiah to pray to the LORD for them; both men are given the opportunity to be spared from the fate suffered by the rest of the nation; and both men refuse to "hear" what they are told. Johanan and his followers represent something of a second chance. They should have learned from the downfall of Zedekiah and his people that "hearing" the LORD's message is crucial to their survival and success. Unfortunately, they refuse to "hear" the LORD, and so the fate that befell Zedekiah now ominously awaits them.

But we must be careful not to dismiss these unbelieving leaders too quickly. Both could have adduced sound reasons — drawn from Israel's past — not to "hear" what Jeremiah was saying. In Zedekiah's case, he could point to the faith of Hezekiah, king during a previous siege of Jerusalem (Sennacherib's invasion, one hundred fifteen years earlier), as encouragement to stand steadfastly against the Babylonians. The word of the LORD in Isaiah's day had been to trust in Yahweh to deliver Jerusalem; now, the word of the LORD through Jeremiah tells people to surrender, with no expectation of divine deliverance. In Johanan's case, Jeremiah had been telling people for years to "go out" of Jerusalem. Now, after the governor has been assassinated and Johanan's people are prime suspects, Jeremiah advises them to "remain" in Jerusalem.

Someone might contend, based on these differences, that the LORD's word is inconsistent from one generation to another, that it is difficult for one to "hear" what the LORD is saying because the message changes over time. But this seeming inconsistency is only superficial. There is an underlying consistency in the need to trust in the LORD. Trusting in the LORD ("hearing" him) in the days of Isaiah and Hezekiah meant trusting in him to deliver Jerusalem. Trusting in the LORD ("hearing" him) in the days of Jeremiah and Zedekiah meant believing that he would take care of his people in Babylon. Zedekiah can only see the LORD working when his people are politically successful, and so he is captured and humiliated. A few years later, Johanan's people adopt the same narrow assumption and suffer a similarly humiliating fate.

43:8-13 The second half of Jeremiah 43 stands in close relationship to what follows, but its only connection to what immediately precedes is the reference to Tahpanhes.[2] It is the first in a series of prophecies delivered by Jeremiah to the Jews in Egypt. In an indirect way, Jeremiah is repeating the prediction (42:15-17) that the destruction which has already come to Jerusalem will now come to the disobedient Jews seeking refuge in Egypt.

This is an oracle concerning a Babylonian invasion and subjugation of **Egypt**, stated in terms that have been heard before in regard to Jerusalem; but this subjugation of Egypt never takes place.[3] The language of the oracle betrays the fact that it is primarily a warning to the Jews there, for it is most similar to Jeremiah's earlier warnings to the people of Jerusalem. These items together indicate that the words are not really a prediction, but are merely meant to say to the people that they in Egypt are no more righteous than their neighbors in Jerusalem had been. Jeremiah buries **some large stones** under the pavement in an Egyptian temple (**the temple of the sun**) and declares that **Nebuchadnezzar**, who is identified as the LORD's **servant**, will set up his throne on the "foundation" which Jeremiah has laid. The Babylonians never do this, but they had done something very similar when Jerusalem fell (39:3). The warning in verse 11 is almost identical to the one in Jeremiah 15:2 (**those destined for death . . .**), while verse 12 echoes the warning of 32:29 (**will set fire to the temples** ["houses"] **of the gods of Egypt**). Egypt is like a second Jerusalem.

---

[2]On the other Jewish communities mentioned in Jer 44:1, see Thompson, *Jeremiah*, pp. 674-675.

[3]Thompson, *Jeremiah*, pp. 671-672.

JEREMIAH 44

L. DISASTER BECAUSE OF IDOLATRY (44:1-30)

This final chapter of the narrative that began in Jeremiah 37 consists of divine admonitions enveloping a sort of theological debate between the Jews in Egypt and Jeremiah over the reasons for their sad condition. The LORD speaks an admonition through the mouth of Jeremiah in 44:1-14; the Jewish men and women reject this with bitterness in verses 15-19; Jeremiah rebukes them for their attitude in 44:20-23; and then the LORD closes with a second admonition and a sign in verses 24-30. The tone is more strident, as the LORD becomes increasingly exasperated with the people's growing obstinance. Familiar words, words whose fulfillment has been witnessed before, are ignored once again. And in the end, an all too familiar fate awaits Jeremiah's hard-hearted audience.

44:1-14 The admonition of the LORD in these verses is filled with expressions common to Jeremiah and the Books of Kings. First, he describes what has happened to Jerusalem (vv. 2-6): He says he brought **great disaster** on the people of Judah (v. 2; cp. 2 Kgs 21:12; Jer 11:11) because **they provoked** [the LORD] **to anger** (v. 3; cp. 2 Kgs 17:11,17; 21:6,15; 22:17; 23:26; Jer 7:18,19; 11:17; 25:6-7; 32:29-32) **by burning incense** (cp. 2 Kgs 17:11; 22:17; 23:5,8; Jer 1:16; 7:9; 11:12,13,17; 19:4,13; 32:29)[1] **and by worshiping other gods** (cp. 1 Kgs 9:6; Jer 16:13); he sent his **servants the prophets** to warn them (v. 4; cp. 2 Kgs 9:7; 17:13,23; 24:2; Jer 7:25; 25:4; 26:5); **but they did not listen or pay attention** (v. 5; cp. Jer 7:24,26; 11:8; 17:23; 25:4; 34:14; 35:15); so, his **fierce anger was poured out** (v. 6; cp. 2 Kgs 22:13,17; Hos 5:10; Jer 7:20; 10:25; 42:18; Ezek 20:8,13,21, 33,34) on **Judah** and **Jerusalem** (cp. 7:17; 11:6). He now transitions

---

[1]This term is used ten times in this chapter alone. Apparently, it was seen as the epitome of the idolatrous worship practiced by the Jews in Egypt.

to an indictment of the present audience, using some similar expressions in accusing them, but also piling on additional common phrases (vv. 7-10): he says they are bringing **great disaster** on themselves (v. 7), such that they will leave themselves **without a remnant**; they too have **provoked** his **anger** (v. 8) by **burning incense to other gods**; and so they will become **an object of cursing and reproach** (cp. Jer 24:9; 25:18; 26:6; 42:18; 49:13), just like their **fathers** and **the kings and queens of Judah** (v. 9). The LORD then passes sentence on the Jews in Egypt, summarizing what has already been said and adding a little more to it (vv. 11-14): he will **bring disaster** on them, just as he had on Jerusalem (v. 11); he will do away with **the remnant** who have gone to **Egypt** (vv. 12,14), rather than rebuild the nation with it; none of them will **return to** their homes. Instead, these people will suffer the same humiliating fate as those before them: they will die by **the sword, famine and plague** (v. 13; cp. Jer 14:12; 21:7,9; 24:10; 27:8,13), and **they will become an object of cursing and horror, of condemnation and reproach** (v. 12; cp. Jer 24:9; 25:18; 29:18,22; 42:18).

The overall effect of using these common expressions is to place these fugitives in the mainstream of Israel's apostate sinners. They have escaped the Babylonians for the moment, but they are no better than their relatives and neighbors who have already been exiled. In fact, the LORD's words are so filled with these expressions of condemnation that Jeremiah's current audience appears to be the worst of the lot. Only the most evil King Manasseh receives harsher criticism. The most probable reason for the harshness of these words is that these people have been given the most opportunities to repent, yet they still refuse. They should know by now that faith in other gods leads to destruction; they should recognize that the fall of Jerusalem was a result of the LORD's wrath for their idolatry; they should know the importance of "hearing the word of the LORD." But they still refuse.

44:15-19 The response of **the men** (vv. 15-18) is one of open defiance. They make no denials and offer no apologies for their sinful actions. They admit that their predecessors in Jerusalem worshiped **the Queen of Heaven,**[2] and they openly say, **"We will not listen . . ."**

---

[2]This designation is associated with the worship of Astarte/Ishtar, a goddess of fertility and health in Canaanite and Mesopotamian religions. Clements, *Jeremiah*, p. 240.

(v. 16). Zedekiah's humiliation for not listening (37:2) has had no effect on them. In their warped perception of past events, prosperity accompanied idolatry, and decline came with the worship of the LORD. The reader sees that they stand to suffer the same fate as Zedekiah, and their parallel response to Jeremiah's warnings foreshadows the fact that they will suffer that fate.

The interpretation of verse 19 is difficult. The Hebrew text does not include the opening phrase, **The women added**; it comes from other early manuscripts. In addition, the first half of the statement is made in the masculine plural, as if the men are still talking. If that is the case, then the women's words begin with **did not our husbands know . . . ?** This would suggest that both halves of the crowd (see v. 15) are defiantly declaring that they will continue in their idolatrous practices.

There might be something more implied in the women's words about **making cakes like her image. . . .** These and other references to women in these verses might indicate that the women led the way in worshiping the Queen of Heaven.[3] That women in particular would be tempted to worship a female deity is not surprising. There even seems to be some hint that they perpetuated this cult during the days of reform. The reference to their husbands "knowing" what they were doing suggests that, even at a time when it was considered unacceptable by the religious leaders in the nation, they continued to prepare what amounted to sacrifices to a foreign god, with the full knowledge of their husbands. If this is a correct interpretation, it betrays the true hypocrisy of the people's defiance. They have been arguing that they fared worse when they gave up their idolatrous practices, yet they now admit that they never really stopped those practices. This, of course, would explain why the LORD regarded the reform as halfhearted (Jer 3:10).[4]

44:20-23 Jeremiah answers the people's arguments with a straightforward and typical (for him) reappraisal of the situation. The LORD has brought Jerusalem down because of the idolatry of its inhabitants (v. 21). If there was prosperity while idolatrous practices were being performed, that simply shows the LORD's patient mercy. But **when the LORD could no longer endure** their sinful practices, he brought upon them the destruction he had been warning about

---

[3]Thompson, *Jeremiah*, p. 680.
[4]Ibid., p. 674.

for so long (v. 22). So Jerusalem did not fall because its inhabitants turned away from their idols (as these people claimed) but because they have not **obeyed** ("heard") the LORD or **followed his laws or his decrees** (cp. v. 10). Like Zedekiah, they exemplify what happens to those who "hear" the LORD's commands but refuse to "hear" ("obey") them.

44:24-30 The LORD now throws up his hands in disgust and pronounces a final judgment on the people. Their words of apostasy have been realized in their actions (vv. 24-25), so he hands them over to their sinfulness rather than wasting his time with any more calls for repentance (cp. Rom 1:21-23). He knows for certain that they will not "hear" him. He tells them to fulfill their oaths, and then he follows this with an ironic oath of his own. He swears by his own **great name** that none of them there will ever swear by his name again (v. 26). To swear by the LORD's name was a right reserved for (and an opportunity accorded to) his people and nobody else (Deut 6:13; 10:20). Now, that right and opportunity has been taken away.

With verses 27-28, a small thread of the LORD's prophecies tying together the Book of Jeremiah is brought full circle. The LORD assures the people that his prophecies will be fulfilled by speaking of **watching over** his listeners. This theme was introduced at Jeremiah's call (1:12), when he told Jeremiah that he would be *"watching* to see that my *word* is fulfilled."* This theme of **watching** was then used in Jeremiah 31:28 as reassurance to those going into exile that he would one day bring them back to their land. Now it is used in the opposite sense, as he is *watching* **over them for harm**, and their decimation will show them **whose *word* will stand.**[5]

The LORD then closes this final message of judgment with a **sign**, something not used anywhere else in Jeremiah (cp. 2 Kgs 19:29; 20:8-9). The sign takes the reader back to the beginning of this narrative section. The Egyptian **Pharaoh** will suffer the same basic fate as King **Zedekiah**, by falling into the hands of **his enemies.**[6] Zedekiah's shadow has already fallen across the career of Johanan; now it extends to the reign of **Hophra** as well. The Jewish refugees

---

[5]Brueggemann (*Jeremiah*, pp. 408-409) remarks that God has not abandoned his people. He is still "with them," still "watching over" them when he is punishing them.

[6]Hophra was later killed when one of his generals usurped his throne. Thompson, *Jeremiah*, p. 682.

have fled to Egypt for protection from the wrath of the LORD, but even those who are expected to provide protection there are endangered by their apostasy.

This section presents to the reader an example of the basic struggle of faith: Whom a person will serve (cp. Josh 24:14-15).[7] Faith is crucial because much of our life is lived in anticipation of what the LORD will do for us, based on promises he has made to us. "We walk by faith, not by sight." But there are other "powers" in our life that make promises to us. For example, economic conditions and political conditions and health conditions affect the quality of our lives. People consider competing economic forecasts and philosophies, opposing political ideologies and platforms, and a complex spectrum of physical and mental health traditions in deciding how to live their lives. All those things lay claim to some power, to the ability to improve our lives. Among the various choices available, some conform to the will and commandments of the LORD. Every person has to decide whose position to follow, based on their belief about "whose word will stand." That belief is based in turn on whose word has stood in the past. A major component of the Bible is the presentation of the LORD's past deeds, deeds which are recorded to give readers the motivation to believe that the God who has worked for the good of humanity in the past is working still. Jeremiah's audience chooses to reject that evidence. The challenge posed by the book to contemporary readers is not to make the same wrong decision.

---

[7]Brueggemann, *Jeremiah*, pp. 410-413.

JEREMIAH 45

M. A MESSAGE TO BARUCH (45:1-5)

Jeremiah's short message to Baruch has been removed from any chronologically-based location and placed here to form a contrast to what precedes it in the text. Just as the fate of Ebed-melech and Jeremiah (39:11–40:6) stands in contrast to the fate of Zedekiah (39:1-10), now the fate of Baruch (45:1-15) stands in contrast to the fate of Johanan and his followers (43:1–44:30).

45:1-5 This little section is set in the fourth year of Jehoiakim (605 B.C.), which means that it could have been placed within Jeremiah 36; but the compiler of the book chose to place it here instead. The small glimmer of hope in it stands in stark contrast to the extremely dark and hopeless tone of the preceding sections. Baruch's own words (v. 3) resound with the kind of hopelessness which the people in Egypt must have felt. He speaks of adding **sorrow to pain**, of **groaning** and finding **no rest** (cp. Job 3:24-26). The first part of the LORD's response (v. 4) would not serve to relieve the anguish of the Jews in Egypt. Even though the words were spoken to an audience thirty years prior, they would carry a special sting to those now in exile. He uses the language of Jeremiah's call to describe the devastation of the land: **I will overthrow what I have built and uproot what I have planted** (cp. 1:10; 24:6). There is even a foreshadowing of the recent prophecy of doom in the LORD's pledge to **bring disaster on all people** (v. 5a). The only hope is held out for Baruch himself. The LORD promises, **I will let you escape with your life** (v. 5b).

There are at least four significant aspects to this small message of hope. One is the parallel to the prophecy to Ebed-melech. Virtually identical phrases are used to comfort Ebed-melech at the time Jerusalem falls (39:18) and Baruch here. The literary structure for all of Jeremiah 37–45 which this suggests has already been mentioned. This also points toward a second literary connection in that this promise functions literarily as a response to the accusations of the people in 43:1-3. Their slander against Baruch betrays their misguided belief that the LORD was on their side and against Baruch. This prophecy to Baruch exposes the error of that belief. A third aspect of this passage is the way that it shows how the LORD is faithful to his promises. This promise was actually made to Baruch many years before he was taken to Egypt; its placement here shows the LORD's intention to honor it still. Moreover, the same promise had been made to the people who surrendered to the Babylonians, the people now in Babylonian Exile (21:9; 38:2). In that regard, this passage serves to encourage those other exiles.[1]

Finally, it is tempting to see this brief passage as a sort of conclusion for the whole book. The final chapter (Jeremiah 52) is almost identical to the ending of 2 Kings, which makes it look more like an appendix to the book. Similarly, Jeremiah 46–51 contain the only prophecies in Jeremiah directed toward other nations. The LXX even places those prophecies at another location in the book. They too function something like an appendix. If we read Jeremiah 45 as the final word of the book — at the least, as the final words to the people of Israel — then we see that word to be a word of destruction for most, but a word of hope for a chosen remnant.[2]

---

[1]Clements (*Jeremiah*, p. 243) speaks of Baruch as "an archetype of 'the wandering Jew.'"

[2]Cp. Brueggemann, *Jeremiah*, p. 30.

JEREMIAH 46

VIII. ORACLES TO THE NATIONS (46:1–51:64)

A. A MESSAGE ABOUT EGYPT (46:1-28)

46:1 Jeremiah 46:1 stands as a literary introduction to all of chapters 46–51, a series of prophecies concerning other nations.[1] These oracles exhibit Jeremiah's ordained role as "a prophet to the nations" (1:5,10). They show that the LORD is sovereign over all the nations of the region, not just Judah and Israel.[2] He communicates his word to all those nations through the same prophet, Jeremiah. His message is primarily one of judgment, but there are occasional promises of blessing in the future (46:26; 48:47; 49:6,39). That he chooses to speak to them at all shows not only his sovereignty, but his concern for each of them. "The LORD disciplines those whom he

---

[1] It is clear that the lengthy oracle(s) concerning Babylon originally stood independent from the others (see 51:59-64). The presence of several section-headings (46:1; 47:1; 49:34; 50:1) and the different ordering of the oracles in the LXX make it likely that written copies of these oracles circulated independent of each other for a while before being placed here in the book.

The order of these oracles apparently is of little significance, as they appear in a different order (and location; see 25:13) in the LXX (see Thompson, *Jeremiah*, pp. 29-30, 117-118, 687; McKane, *Jeremiah*, pp. 1108-1111; Holladay, *Jeremiah 2*, pp. 313-314). There might be some significance to the placement of Egypt and Babylon at either end, since these represent the two empires who made prisoners of the nation of Israel during their history. It could also be that Egypt is placed first because the preceding chapters have to do with Judeans in Egypt, while Babylon is placed last because the account of Babylon's capture of Jerusalem immediately follows.

For similar groupings of oracles against foreign nations, see Isaiah 13–23, Ezekiel 25–32, Amos 1:3–2:3. On these, see D.L. Christensen, *Transformations of the War Oracle in Old Testament Prophecy* (Missoula, MT: Scholars, 1975 [on Jeremiah 46–51, pp. 183-280]).

[2] Brueggemann, *Jeremiah*, p. 426.

loves" (Prov 3:12; Heb 12:6). Still, one cannot miss the fact that Israel is his favorite. Many of the condemnations pronounced against these other nations are for various atrocities, some committed against Israel. Some are announced without specific accusations of wrongdoings being given. The LORD occasionally finds ways to speak words of comfort to Israel in these oracles (46:27-28; 48:27; 49:1; 50:4-7,17,33 34; 51:5,34-35).

There apparently are three separate oracles to Egypt (46:2-12,13-24,25-28). All three come in the wake of military confrontations between Egypt and Babylon, but not necessarily the same confrontation each time. The first two predict Egypt's humiliation by Babylon; the third focuses on how these events will affect Israel. The LORD mentions these events to take the credit for causing them, attempting in the process to convince the Egyptians (and the readers) of his sovereignty over them.

46:2-12 The heading (46:2) speaks of Egypt's defeat at the hands of the Babylonians in 605 B.C. Egypt had marched to **Carchemish** to aid the Assyrians in their last-ditch effort to repel the Babylonians (see 2 Kgs 23:29-30), but their efforts proved unsuccessful.[3] Egypt's brief hegemony over Judah (2 Kgs 23:34-35) is now over. Nebuchadnezzar's forces put him in firm control of the entire region.

Jeremiah opens by reciting commands typical of battle. The lines are terse, the mood tense, evoking the sense of apprehension that is the prelude to combat (vv. 3-4; cp. Nah 2:1; 3:1-3). The prophet is the watchman (v. 5), standing on the walls of the city to see the outcome of the battle and report it to those waiting anxiously inside. He describes an army retreating in disarray. **There is terror on every side**. The Israelites must have rejoiced at this news, because the same Egyptians had recently humiliated them and killed their king (2 Kgs 23:29-30). Any joy will be short lived, however, because Jeremiah will soon use the same words to describe their own defeat at the hands of the Babylonian army (6:25; 20:4; see 49:29). This is an army that overtakes the swift and overpowers the strong. None can withstand its onslaught.

There is a sequential digression in verses 7-9, which serves to emphasize the significance of this defeat from an Israelite perspective. Jeremiah compares the Egyptian forces with the **Nile** itself, suggesting enormous and unrelenting power. Men from throughout

---

[3]Holladay, *Jeremiah 2*, p. 319.

Egypt (**Cush, Put, Lydia**) had marched proudly out to face the Babylonians, expecting a resounding victory. What had gone wrong? The answer comes in verse 10: **The LORD** has decreed their defeat. This is "the day of the LORD," the time when he takes **vengeance** on his enemies. This proud army has marched out wonderfully adorned, supposing itself to be an honored guest at a feast; but the LORD intends for it to be the **sacrifice** (cp. Zeph 1:7-9).

The closing lines (vv. 11-12) suggest a measure of bitterness toward Egypt on the part of the Israelites. The call to **get balm** from **Gilead** is a taunt. Gilead was known for its medicinal products (8:22; see Gen 37:25).[4] It would be natural for wounded troops to seek soothing ointments there. Jeremiah advises them they will find no relief in Gilead this time. This might reflect a move by the retreating Egyptians to salve their wounded egos by pillaging weak Israelite settlements on their way back to Egypt. This will not hide the **shame** of their defeat, though.

46:13-24 The scene shifts from the Battle at Carchemish to a subsequent confrontation between Babylon and Egypt, either the following year or some twenty or more years later (see 37:4-8).[5] The mighty **sword** of the Babylonians, which also terrorizes Judah, is "devouring" Egyptian soldiers (see v. 10; 2:30). They try to **stand**, but they **will stumble** and **fall** (v. 16; see vv. 6,12) because **the LORD will push them down**.[6] Everyone sees the Egyptians routed, and they assume the Babylonians are the cause. Jeremiah asserts, before it has actually happened, that the real "victor" is Israel's God. This is all part of his plan. Once the Egyptians realize the futility of resistance, they will run to the safety of home (**our native lands**, "the land of our birth"), where they will blame their **Pharaoh** for their defeat

---

[4]Thompson, *Jeremiah*, p. 690.

[5]Holladay, *Jeremiah 2*, p. 328; McKane, *Jeremiah*, pp. 1125-1126; Thompson, *Jeremiah*, p. 691; Clements, *Jeremiah*, p. 248. A central problem with the historical location of this prophecy is that the Babylonians never actually invaded and devastated Egypt.

[6]The object of "push" (v. 15) is singular in the Hebrew. Some account for this by dividing the words of the first line differently. The word for "laid low" is נִסְחַף (*nishaph*), a passive form. If this is divided into two words (*ns + ḥp*), it reads, "Apis [an Egyptian deity] has fled." The word for "your warriors" can also mean "your Bull," which is a common designation for a deity in the ancient Near East. The resulting reading is, "Why has Apis fled? Your Bull did not stand. . . ." Thompson, *Jeremiah*, p. 690; McKane, *Jeremiah*, pp. 1127-1128; Holladay, *Jeremiah 2*, pp. 328-330.

(v. 17). The words they speak contain one or two derogatory puns to this effect. The less likely one is a play on the name Hophra, an Egyptian Pharaoh (589–574 B.C.). This name is similar to the root for **missed** (הֶעֱבִיר, *he'ĕbîr*, "passed by") **his opportunity**. The idea is that Hophra "does not honor his appointments" on the battlefield.[7] Another possibility is that this insinuates how the Pharaoh was expected to be a "warrior" (אַבִּיר, *'abbîr*, v. 15), but instead he has "passed by" (*he'ĕbîr*) without fighting.

The LORD then issues a royal decree (he, not Nebuchadnezzar, is the true king here) about the outcome of the upcoming campaign. He makes his point by stringing together several metaphors, some of which are very "Egyptian" in their imagery. Nebuchadnezzar is like a prominent mountain towering over the surrounding plains (**Tabor** or **Carmel**, v. 18). The Egyptians will be like stampeding **calves**, "spooked" by the sting of a **gadfly** (vv. 20-21). **Egypt will be like** a cobra, hissing as it flees from an attacker (v. 22). Egypt will be felled like a dense **forest** (vv. 22-23; cp. Isa 10:33-34), overrun by **locusts** (v. 23; cp. Ps 105:34; Nahum 3:15). This heaping up of destructive images helps to convey the certainty of the Egyptian defeat and the relentless nature of the Babylonian attack.

There are also a few elements which would be most meaningful to an Israelite reader. One is the LORD's self-identification (v. 18) as **the King** (see 8:19; 10:7,10; 48:15; 51:57; cp. Isa 6:5; 33:17,22; 41:21; 43:15; 44:6) and **the LORD Almighty** ("LORD of Hosts," "LORD of the Armies"). Both would evoke the sense that this is a royal decree by a powerful monarch, who cannot be challenged (see 2:19; 10:16; 11:20; 20:12; 31:35; 32:18; cp. Ps 24:7-10; Isa 6:3,5; Amos 4:13). Israelites would also have identified well (though not happily) with the language of verse 19. The references to **exile** and to cities that are **laid waste** and **without inhabitant** are a common refrain in Jeremiah's prophecies against them (2:15; 4:7; 44:22; see also 9:11; 17:6; 18:16; 19:8; 25:9,11,18,38; 26:9; 29:1,16,18; 33:10; 34:22; 42:18). These, together with the repeated references to danger **from the north** (vv. 6,10,20,24), serve to cultivate a sense of parallel fates between Judah and Egypt. Similarly, the title, **Daughter of Egypt** (v. 24, see v. 11), is like the commonly used titles for Israel, "Daughter of Zion"/"Daughter of My People" (4:11,31; 6:2,23,26; 8:11,19,21,22; 9:1,7; 14:17). The two are "sisters" in their struggles against Babylon.

---

[7]Thompson, *Jeremiah*, p. 692; but see McKane, *Jeremiah*, pp. 1129-1130.

The use of all these phrases must have been intended to evoke a strong empathy in the Israelites for the Egyptians in their humiliation. Such language also could have increased their own anxiety when the LORD's attention was turned to them. If the LORD could direct the Babylonians to humiliate the powerful Egyptians, then he could easily destroy the Israelites in the same way. When Jeremiah uses the same language later to predict their own fall, they should be very concerned. They should not rejoice at the Egyptian collapse, for they should see their own fate in the current fate of Egypt.

46:25-28 There is no indication of the occasion for this final oracle concerning Egypt. It takes a small note about the future resurgence of Egypt to promise a similar resurgence for Israel. He gives a fairly general prediction of the defeat of Egypt and its allies (vv. 25-26), but he closes with a promise that **Egypt will be inhabited** again (cp. v. 19). This seems to open the door just enough to allow in the theme of hope for the future, a theme which the LORD then expands in reference to Israel (vv. 27-28). These verses are virtually the same as 30:10-11 (see there for comments). It is impossible to determine whether Jeremiah repeats himself here to a slightly different audience, or whether the book's editor (Baruch) repeats the promise of 30:10-11 here to draw a comparison between the ultimate fate of Egypt and the ultimate fate of the LORD's people.[8] In either case, it is at the LORD's prompting that this comparison is made. The desired outcome is twofold. On the one hand, the defeat of Egypt should serve as proof to Judah that the LORD is using Babylon, as Jeremiah is saying. On the other hand, once the people recognize the veracity of Jeremiah's words, they should have even more reason to believe his words of hope. As Egypt resurges, they should recognize it as proof that the LORD is going to bring them back to glory as well. And the future glory promised for Israel exceeds that of any other. Israel is still the LORD's favorite.

---

[8]McKane, *Jeremiah*, p. 1137; Parke-Taylor, *Formation*, pp. 119-126.

JEREMIAH 47

B. A MESSAGE ABOUT THE PHILISTINES (47:1-7)

47:1-7 The occasion for this brief oracle concerning the Philistines[1] is **before Pharaoh attacked Gaza** (47:1). It is most likely that this refers to an attack by the Babylonians, although the attackers could also be the Egyptians, as they retreat from the Babylonians following their defeat at Carchemish (see comments on 46:11).[2] The oracle moves from the battle seen (vv. 2-3) to that which is unseen (vv. 4-7), the "behind the scenes" workings of the LORD (**For** at the beginning of v. 4 marks this transition). Coursing through it all is the overwhelming despair felt by the Philistine people. They **cry out** and **wail** (v. 2; see 25:34). The hands of Philistine fathers, overwrought by the display of Egyptian might, **hang limp** as their children die (v. 3). The people of **Gaza** and **Ashkelon** (two of the five leading Philistine cities; see 25:20; 1 Sam 6:17) perform extreme acts to express their grief, shaving their heads and cutting themselves in utter despondency (v. 5; see 16:6; 41:5; 1 Kgs 18:28). They address **the sword of the LORD** — which, in this case, would be the invading army — longing wistfully for it to tire of its work (v. 6).[3] Ironically, in this world of destruction revolving around a faithless Israel, this for-

---

[1]"Caphtor" is thought to have been Crete (cp. Deut 2:23). According to Egyptian records, the Philistines migrated south with other "Sea Peoples" from the northern islands of the eastern Mediterranean shortly after 1200 B.C. Holladay, *Jeremiah 2*, pp. 337-338.

[2]It makes sense to see the Babylonians here, because they are often the enemy that comes from the north, and there is clear evidence of a Babylonian destruction of Ashkelon in 604 B.C. (Thompson, *Jeremiah*, pp. 696-697; McKane, *Jeremiah*, pp. 1141-1144; Brueggemann, *Jeremiah*, 439). On the other hand, one is left to wonder why there is no reference to the Babylonians in the introduction. See Clements, *Jeremiah*, pp. 250-251; Holladay, *Jeremiah 2*, pp. 336-337.

[3]McKane, *Jeremiah*, p. 1153.

eign "sword" is faithfully fulfilling the LORD's orders (v. 7). Because of this foreign military power and its obedience to the LORD's command, there is no note of comfort, no solace to be found in Jeremiah's words.

There are a few significant similarities between this prophecy and the first oracle concerning Egypt (46:3-12). One is the metaphor of a river to describe an invading army (v. 2; cp. 46:7-8). The sheer volume of the attacking force seems like an overpowering river to the smaller nations of the region. One finds a second parallel in the military allusions (v. 3), which evoke the feel of battle (cp. 46:3-5). Readers can almost see and hear the battle, even though they are not there. Third, and most significant, there is a transition in the middle of the oracle where Jeremiah "pulls back the curtain" to reveal the LORD's role in the battle. It is the LORD's **day** (v. 4; see 46:10). It is the LORD, not the attacking army, who is going to destroy **the Philistines** (v. 4). It is the LORD's sword which strikes down its victims (v. 6), which slashes without **rest** because **the LORD has commanded it** (v. 7). This is his doing, a deed performed by the invaders at his command. The LORD is using one nation, which he perhaps has just punished, to mete out judgment on another nation. There is no mention of Israel in this; he is dealing with these nations for their own sake. There is not even an indictment for wrongdoing mentioned here. Apparently, that is not important for the believing reader to know. It is enough to know that the LORD does work through nations to discipline nations, even when those nations do not realize it. Believers are to recognize it, and stand in awe of the power and wisdom of the LORD.

JEREMIAH 48

C. A MESSAGE ABOUT MOAB (48:1-47)

Moab was a "cousin" people to the Israelites, being descended from Lot (Gen 19:30-38). The royal house traced some of its ancestry to this nation (Ruth 1:1-22; 4:18-22; 1 Sam 22:3-4). In spite of David's family ties, the two nations had been at odds since the time of Israel's reentry into the region under Moses and Joshua (Numbers 21–24; Deut 2:8-19; Judg 11:14-18). The subsequent centuries found them often at war (Judg 3:12-30; 2 Sam 8:2; 2 Kgs 3:4-27; 2 Chr 20:1-30), as the two nations squabbled over territory. Many of the cities of Moab mentioned here (vv. 1-2,18-21,32-34) had been claimed by the tribes of Reuben and Gad at one time (Num 32:1-5,34-38; Josh 13:8-28; 21:36-39; 1 Chr 6:78-81). The primary concern of the biblical writers does not involve this political rivalry, but the corrupting influence of Moab on Israel's religious faithfulness (Num 25:1; 31:13-18; Deut 23:3-6; 1 Kgs 11:1,7,33; 2 Kgs 23:13; Micah 6:5). Another more immediate catalyst for antagonism is Moab's ridiculing posture toward Jerusalem as the Babylonians destroy the city (v. 27). Moab falls to Babylon a few years later, probably following the assassination of Gedaliah.[1]

A somewhat superfluous editorial note marks the end of this lengthy "judgment on Moab" (v. 47b). There is little evidence of literary breaks within the section to warrant its division into smaller units. Only the introductory words of verse 40 suggest a new beginning there. The preceding verses probably comprise a single oracle, which moves back and forth between words of lament for the towns of Moab (48:1-10,18-25,29-39) and the use of wine-related analogies to talk about Moab's humiliation (48:11-17,26-28). It appears that several literary features in this oracle (esp. vv. 29-39) have been bor-

---

[1]Thompson, *Jeremiah*, p. 701.

rowed or adapted from Isaiah 15–16 (cp. Zeph 2:8-11). The shorter oracle (48:40-47) declares the inevitability of destruction, but concludes with a promise of restoration.

The primary oracle (vv. 1-39) emphasizes the theme of Moab's destruction. This was the theme of the introduction of Isaiah's oracle against Moab, written more than a century earlier. Isaiah begins, "Ar in Moab is ruined [שֻׁדַּד, *šuddad*] . . . Kir in Moab is ruined" (Isa 15:1). Now Jeremiah intones, **Woe to Nebo, for it will be ruined** (*šuddad*; 48:1; cp. 4:13). Nebo is not alone in its fate. **The destroyer** (שֹׁדֵד, *šōdēd*) **will come against every town** of Moab (v. 8). Despite the efforts of her valiant warriors, **Moab will be destroyed** (*šuddad*; v. 15). The proud city of Dibon will fall, because **he who destroys** (*šōdēd*) **Moab** will conquer it too (v. 18). The big news item on the lips of every man and woman is **that Moab is destroyed** (*šuddad*; v. 20). Moab has prided itself for years in its vineyards, but now **the destroyer** (*šōdēd*) has descended on its crops and ruined the land (v. 32). Jeremiah's listeners are familiar with the devastation of Moab that constituted the fulfillment of Isaiah's prophecy. This oracle promises even greater devastation.

48:1-10 This great devastation is announced on behalf of the divine warrior, **the LORD Almighty, the God of Israel** (v. 1; cp. v. 15; 46:18; 51:57). There is no hope that he can be repulsed. The Babylonian army, which serves as his instrument here, is actually weak in comparison to his military might. The defeat of Moab is certain. Most of the lines in the first ten verses, then, describe some aspect of this military collapse. Strongholds are **captured** (v. 1); **the sword** pursues its victims (v. 2); one hears **cries of great havoc and destruction** (שֹׁד, *šōd*; v. 3); there are the sights and sounds of people in flight (vv. 4-6); **Chemosh**, their protector deity, **will go into exile** (v. 7); there is no **escape** for any settlement (v. 8). As a culminating sign of conquest, **salt** will be poured on the whole nation (v. 9). This was done to prevent a land from being useful for many years to come (see Deut 29:23; Judg 9:45; Ps 107:33-34; Jer 17:6).[2]

Jeremiah uses several wordplays in verses 1-5, which those unfamiliar with Hebrew would miss (see Micah 1:10-15). The verb for **plot** (חָשַׁב, *ḥāšab*) is the root of the name of the city **Heshbon** ("they plot evil against Plots-town;" v. 2). The town of **Madmen** (this is a

---

[2]Thompson, *Jeremiah*, p. 704; McKane, *Jeremiah*, pp. 1164-1165; Holladay, *Jeremiah 2*, p. 357.

transliteration of a Moabite name, not the English word for the insane) in the following line comes from the root for **be silenced** (דָּמַם, *dāmam*, "even Silent-town will be silenced"). Verse 4 forms a nice inclusio with the final clause of verse 5: "Moab is broken (נִשְׁבְּרָה, *nišbᵊrāh*), her little ones cause a cry to be heard (הִשְׁמִיעוּ זְעָקָה, *hišmî'û zᵊ'āqāh*); . . . they heard the distress of a cry of breaking" (צָרֵי צַעֲקַת־שֶׁבֶר שָׁמֵעוּ, *ṣārê ṣa'ăqath-šeber šāmᵊ'û*).

The subsequent verses reveal the impetus behind this destruction, bringing out the undeniable sovereignty of the LORD. The Moabite people have been relying on their idols (**Chemosh**) and their **deeds and riches** to protect them (see Ps 115:8; 135:18; Prov 11:28; Ezek 16:15). All these things will be taken away, signifying how utterly powerless they really are. This line of thinking raises a small problem, though. The powerlessness of Moab's god is demonstrated by the nation's defeat and exile. One could easily argue that the same should be true for Israel and Judah. If those nations are exiled, then the LORD must also be powerless. The answer provided by this text is that the invasion and exile have been called for by the LORD, the God of Israel. Perhaps the false prophets of Chemosh have been predicting his protection of the Moabites, like the false prophets of Jerusalem who opposed Jeremiah. The difference between the two sets of false prophets is that the message of the Jerusalem prophets is countered by the words of Jeremiah, who claims to speak on behalf of the LORD just as they do. It is the veracity of Jeremiah's words regarding Jerusalem which make the words of the LORD through him to Moab worthy of notice. It is at the LORD's command that the Moabites are taken away (v. 8). He is the ultimate power here, the ultimate cause for Moab's humiliation. He is the divine commander who has given the order to attack; anyone who dares ignore this order will suffer the harshest recriminations (v. 10) as the fate of Jerusalem should prove to all.

48:11-17 This portion moves from the analogy between Moab and a jar of wine (vv. 11-13) to the divine announcement of the nation's demise (vv. 14-17). In the process, the contrasting words of the Moabites and her neighbors (vv. 14 and 17, respectively) illustrate the difference between a nation's hopes and history's reality.[3]

Moab lives with an inflated sense of herself. She has never suffered as the Israelites have; she has never been forced to leave her

---

[3]Holladay, *Jeremiah 2*, p. 350.

land. Jeremiah compares this situation to an undisturbed jar of **wine**, which has lost none of its potency by being **poured from one jar into another**.[4] Now she will not only be poured, she will be poured onto the ground, emptied, and shattered. Jeremiah justifies this again on the basis of their trust in something that will ultimately fail them (see. v. 7). The people of Israel can identify with this, because their current suffering comes as a result of their trusting in things which are "false" (5:17; 13:25; 28:15; 29:31), which cannot deliver. The northerners **trusted in Bethel** (v. 13; see Amos 3:14; 4:4-5), and the southerners trusted in the inviolability of their temple (7:4,14). In the same way, the Moabites have been trusting in their "false" god, Chemosh, and in their own military abilities (their "deeds," v. 7; see Isa 31:1; 36:4-7). Rather than making them proud, though, these will bring them only shame.

The proud claims of the Moabite soldiers (v. 14) betray their deluded egos. They ignore the reality of their predicament, their own weakness in contrast to the overwhelming military might of Babylon, the LORD's agent. The LORD asserts his ultimate sovereignty by announcing Moab's eminent humiliation in the name associated with his military might: **the** (true) **King . . . the LORD Almighty**. The divine commander has given the order; it cannot be countered. He then calls on Moab's neighbors to have an attitude of sympathy toward Moab. They are not to gloat (as Moab did in regard to Israel's destruction; v. 27), but they are to **mourn**. They are to lament the fact that the symbols of Moab's military strength, **the mighty scepter** and **the glorious staff**, are being broken.[5]

48:18-25 The LORD addresses the people of Moab here, using several statements and literary devices to communicate the completeness of Moab's destruction. He starts by addressing the people of **Dibon**, one of the best fortified cities of the land. They feel like they are "above" all that is about to happen. The LORD tells them they will have to **come down**, because the present "destroyer" will **come up** even over them (v. 18).[6] He then directs the listeners' attention to **Aroer**, another "secure" city, but one from which people will soon be **fleeing**. They bring with them the shocking news of that

---

[4]But see McKane, *Jeremiah*, pp. 1166-1168; Holladay, *Jeremiah 2*, p. 358.

[5]Brueggemann, *Jeremiah*, p. 446.

[6]The "glory" of Moab probably implies a "seat of honor." McKane, *Jeremiah*, pp. 1174-1175.

city's defeat. This bad news mushrooms out from the border (**the Arnon**) to a dozen of the principal cities of the country. The listing of city after city graphically illustrates the totality of the current destruction. The references to Moab's **horn** and **arm** summarize this, indicating the nation's "strength" is broken.

48:26-28 This brief portion probably brought a little comfort to the suffering people of Israel. Moab ridiculed her unfairly when she was overwhelmed by those whom the LORD sent. Now it is Moab's turn. This proud nation will humiliate itself like a man in a drunken stupor. Their swagger is turning into a stagger. They must abandon the cities in which they have taken pride, slinking away in shame to live like weak animals in **the rocks** and **caves**.

48:29-39 These comments regarding the replacing of Moab's glory (v. 18) with shame (vv. 26-27) lead naturally into the lines of verses 29-39. Much of this is taken over from Isaiah 16. Jeremiah 48:29-33,36 closely parallels Isaiah 16:6-11[7] (see chart). Some of the surrounding verses (vv. 34-35,37-38a) are based somewhat less loosely on Isaiah 15:2-6 (see Jer 48:5). A comparison of the two passages shows an important development. In Isaiah, Moab's humiliation prompts her to grieve for herself (Isa 16:6-7). In Jeremiah, it is the LORD himself who grieves. What a beautiful illustration of the LORD's compassion for all peoples! He is bringing great destruction on a "Gentile" nation because of its sinfulness, yet he still grieves with that people over their losses.

ISAIAH 16:6-11	JEREMIAH 48:29-33,36

We have heard of Moab's pride—
  her overweening pride and conceit,
her pride and her insolence—
	"We have heard of Moab's pride—
	  her overweening pride and conceit,
	her pride and arrogance
	  and the haughtiness of her heart.
	I know her insolence but it is futile,"
	  declares the LORD,

but her boasts are empty.
Therefore the Moabites wail,
  they wail together for Moab.
Lament and grieve
  for the men of Kir Hareseth.
The fields of Heshbon wither,
  the vines of Sibmah also.
The rulers of the nations have
  trampled down the choicest vines,
	"and her boasts accomplish nothing.
	Therefore I wail over Moab,
	  for all Moab I cry out,
	I moan for the men of Kir Hareseth.

---

[7]McKane, *Jeremiah*, pp. 1192-1193; Parke-Taylor, *Formation*, pp. 131-135.

which once reached Jazer
    and spread toward the desert.
Their shoots spread out
    and went as far as the sea.
So I weep, as Jazer weeps,
    for the vines of Sibmah.
O Heshbon, O Elealeh,
    I drench you with tears!
The shouts of joy over your ripened
    fruit
    and over your harvests have been
      stilled.
Joy and gladness are taken away from
    the orchards;
    no one sings or shouts in the vine-
      yards;
    no one treads out wine at the presses,
    for I have put an end to the shout-
      ing.

My heart laments for Moab like a harp,
    my inmost being for Kir Hareseth.

I weep for you, as Jazer weeps,
    O vines of Sibmah.
Your branches spread as far as the sea;
    they reached as far as the sea of
      Jazer.

The destroyer has fallen
    on your ripened fruit and grapes.

Joy and gladness are gone
    from the orchards and fields of
      Moab.
I have stopped the flow of wine from
    the presses;
    no one treads them with shouts of
      joy.
Although there are shouts,
    they are not shouts of joy. . . ."

"So my heart laments for Moab like a
    flute;
    it laments like a flute for the men of
      Kir Hareseth.

This part of the oracle makes most explicit the arrogance of Moab, which the LORD will deflate. There is an initial piling up (puffing up?) of terms to refer to the people's inflated national ego. They are filled with pride, conceit, arrogance, haughtiness, and insolence. They pointed to their continuous occupation of their land as proof of their god's powerful protection. This they celebrated, and in this they rejoiced. The LORD, the true God and King, will soon turn their joy into sadness, their celebration into lament and wailing.

The closing verses (vv. 38b-39) refer back to some of the main ideas of the oracle. Moab is **broken . . . like a jar** (48:38b; see 22:28), a jar whose contents have been poured onto the ground (see vv. 11-12). She is **shattered** (חַתָּה, *ḥattāh*; see vv. 1,20),[8] and so people **wail** at the sight of her (see vv. 20,31). She is filled with **shame** (see vv. 1,13,20), **an object of ridicule** (see vv. 26-27; 20:7) rather than praise.

48:40-47 This shorter oracle against Moab speaks directly of the nation's capture and exile. Babylon is portrayed as **an eagle** (v. 40).

---

[8]The term for "object of horror" (מְחִתָּה, *məḥittāh*) at the end of the verse comes from the same root as this verb.

This probably is a vulture, a bird that feeds on the bodies of those slain in battle. Jeremiah moves from this allusion to a battlefield strewn with the bodies of the dead to talk about forts **captured** and **taken**, to soldiers who have lost their courage (**hearts**). This confident, arrogant people went too far, defying the LORD himself (v.42). There is a crescendo from **terror** to **pit** to **snare** (vv. 43-44) to illustrate the inevitability of their coming humiliation (cp. Amos 5:19; Isa 24:17-18). These **noisy boasters** have always found protection **in the shadow of Heshbon** (cp. Judg 9:15; Ps 17:8; 36:7; 57:1; 63:7; 91:1; 121:5; Isa 30:2-3; 32:2; 49:2; 51:16; Hos 14:7), but now they stand there as helpless **fugitives**. They have relied on Chemosh to protect them, but he shows his powerlessness by allowing their children to be **taken into exile** (see Num 21:28-29).

Verse 47 ends this oracle — in fact, the entire **judgment on Moab** — on a hopeful note. This is the formula used several times by Jeremiah to give hope to the soon-to-be-exiled people of Judah (29:14; 30:3,18; 31:23; 32:44; 33:7,11,26). The Moabites have been rebuked for gloating over Judah's collapse. They will suffer the same humiliation as Judah. They will also enjoy the same renewal.

JEREMIAH 49

D. A MESSAGE ABOUT AMMON (49:1-6)

49:1-6 This brief oracle against the **Ammonites**[1] falls into three parts on stylistic grounds. Verses 1-2 are addressed to an unspecified audience, announcing the future fall of **Rabbah**, capital of Ammon (site of present-day Amman, Jordan). The LORD's attention turns directly to the people of Ammon in verses 3-5 as he calls on them to **mourn** their fall. A brief promise of restoration in verse 6 concludes the oracle. The first and third parts contain the typical prophetic formula, **declares the LORD** (יהוה נְאֻם, *nᵊ'um YHWH*; vv. 2,6), while the more extended (and militaristic) identifier is used in the second part (צְבָאוֹת יהוה אֲדֹנָי נְאֻם, *nᵊ'um 'ădōnāy YHWH ṣᵊbā'ôth*, **declares the Lord, the LORD Almighty**; v. 5; see 46:18,25; 48:15).

The oracle begins with a series of three rhetorical questions. This is a popular style in Jeremiah (2:14,31; 8:5,19,22; 14:19; 22:28). The third question points to a situation that should not exist, based on the information gathered by the first two. The first two establish that Israel has **sons, heirs** (יוֹרֵשׁ, *yôrēš*, "possessors") who "possess" the land. The surprising situation raised, then, is that **Molech** (= Milcom, national deity of the Ammonites; Lev 18:21; 20:2-5; 1 Kgs 11:7; 2 Kgs 23:10; Jer 32:35)[2] has **taken possession of** (יָרַשׁ, *yāraš*) portions of Israel's territory. The divine response to this comes at the end of verse 2, where the LORD says **Israel will drive out** (*yāraš*, "take possession of") **those who drove her out** (יֹרְשָׁיו, *yōrᵊšāyw*, "his possessors"; see Deut 2:16-19; Judg 11:24). Rabbah will become an uninhabited **mound** ("tel"). It is intriguing to have a reference to Israel

---

[1] The Ammonites were perennial enemies of the Israelites (Gen 19:36-38; Deut 2:16-19; Judg 11:4-33; 1 Sam 11:1-11; 2 Sam 10:1–11:1; 12:26-31; 1 Kgs 4:13-19; Amos 1:13-15).

[2] It is possible that "Molech" is not a proper name in every case. The name literally means "their king." McKane, *Jeremiah*, p. 1204.

(not Babylon) as Ammon's conqueror. This raises the possibility that Jeremiah has taken an old prophecy against Ammon (vv. 1-2) and is expanding on it here.[3]

The LORD's address to the people of Ammon is similar in some ways to preceding oracles, particularly the oracle concerning Moab. He calls on the people of Ammon to **wail** (v. 3; see 48:20,31,39) and **cry out** (48:3,5), because their city **is destroyed** (48:1,15,20).[4] They are in a panic, because their deity and his religious attendants are to be exiled (48:7). Like the proud Moabites (48:29-30), the Ammonites have been boasting about things that have no real glory, trusting in their **riches** (v. 4; see 48:7) to protect them. They arrogantly ask, **Who will attack** ("come against") **me?** The LORD himself responds, **I will bring terror** ("cause terror to come"; vv. 4-5).

The Israelites should also recognize a bit of themselves in these words addressed to the Ammonites. The call to lament in verse 3 resonates strongly with the LORD's words to Judah in 4:8-9 (with "Molech" here paralleling "king" in 4:9; see n. 2, above). The designation, **unfaithful** ("ever-turning") **daughter** (v. 4) is used elsewhere only in reference to Israel (3:14,22; 31:22; 50:6). The threat to bring **terror** (פַּחַד, *paḥad*) **from all those around** (סָבִיב, *sābîb*; v. 5) is similar to the LORD's threat of "Magor-Missabib," announced in 20:3-4,10 (see 6:25; 46:5; 49:29). The spiritual failings of Israel's enemies are present among the Israelites themselves (see 9:25-26), leading to similar punishments. The Israelites might be tempted to point a finger of accusation at those around them, but they need to hold a mirror up to themselves first, because there they will see many of the same features in their own spiritual faces. It is from this perspective that they can honestly recognize, and rejoice in, the LORD's promise to **restore the fortunes of the Ammonites** (v. 6). It requires the same mercy for the LORD to forgive his people as it does for him to forgive the Ammonites. It takes the same mercy for the LORD to save someone raised in a Christian home as it does to save someone raised in paganism (see Acts 15:11; Rom 3:21-24).

---

[3]For an opposing opinion, see Holladay, *Jeremiah 2*, p. 367.

[4]Heshbon seems to have been a border town, with ties both to Ammon and Moab (48:2,34,45); but see McKane, *Jeremiah*, pp. 1206-1207.

E. A MESSAGE ABOUT EDOM (49:7-22)

The Edomites were the descendants of Esau, who occupied territory to the south of Judah (Gen 36:1-43). They too, like the Moabites and Ammonites, had a long history of antagonism toward the people of Israel, going back to Israel's days in the wilderness (Num 20:14-21; 2 Sam 8:14; 1 Kgs 11:14-22; 2 Kgs 8:20-22; Ps 60:8-9; 108:9-10; 137:7; Lam 4:21-22). The lack of remorse over the downfall of this proud nation is striking.[5] They suffer extensively at the hands of the Babylonians, yet they survive, being the Idumeans of later centuries. Jeremiah's message concerning Edom consists of three oracles proclaiming the inevitability of Edom's demise. A brief poetic oracle announcing the LORD's plans to devastate Edom (vv. 7-11) is followed by a briefer prose oracle of similar tone (vv. 12-13). The final and longest oracle expands on these themes, incorporating illustrations and images used elsewhere in Jeremiah's prophecies.

49:7-11 The Edomites are occasionally associated with wisdom (Obad 8).[6] Eliphaz, one of Job's "comforters," is a Temanite, and **Teman** is a leading city or region of Edom (Gen 36:15,34,42; Amos 1:12). The Edomites would have taken as a personal insult the statement that **wisdom** had failed in Edom (v. 7). Here is something that even their great wisdom cannot prevent. It is not a matter of understanding, but of accepting the inevitable. The LORD is bringing punishment, so they need to **hide in deep caves** (vv. 8,30). This is not to imply that they can actually hide from the LORD (v. 10), but it infers that the sight of the destruction will be so horrendous, they will not want to look on it; so they should hide from the sight. Verses 9-10 draw from Obadiah 5-6 to convey the completeness of this destruction. **Pickers** always **leave** a little bit of the unwanted fruit behind (6:9; Deut 24:19-22), and **thieves** leave behind items that are not worth taking. The LORD's devastation on Edom will be more thorough than that. None can hide, none can escape. Yet, the LORD is not without mercy. Even here, his concern for **orphans** and **widows** will temper his anger (v. 11).

49:12-13 This brief prose oracle shows how strong are the ties between these oracles concerning other nations and Jeremiah 25.

---

[5]McKane, *Jeremiah*, p. 1230; Thompson, *Jeremiah*, p. 720.
[6]Holladay, *Jeremiah 2*, p. 374.

Jeremiah 49:12 summarizes the primary thought of 25:15-29, in which some of the cities of Edom are mentioned (25:23). They must all **drink the cup** of the LORD's wrath; none will be excused. Verse 13 then furthers this, adopting some of the strongest language concerning Judah's devastation to describe Edom's (see 24:9; 25:9; 29:18; 42:18; 44:8,12,22; cp. 25:18).

49:14-22 Jeremiah develops two motifs in this main oracle. The first (in vv. 14-18) draws heavily from Obadiah 1-4.[7] It revolves around the notion of bringing down the one who is high up. The LORD summons nations to attack Edom with the words, **"Rise up for battle!"** This battle is against a nation that is "high-hearted" (proud) and lives high up, like an **eagle**, in **the heights of the hill**, among the rocky crags (a topographical description of certain parts of Edom). Edom will be "brought down" in two senses. Its defenders will be brought down from their posts among the steep mountains; also, their national pride will be brought down by this humiliating defeat (see 18:16; 19:8). Passersby will compare the land to the region of **Sodom and Gomorrah** (23:14; 50:40; Gen 19:1-29; Deut 29:23; Isa 1:9; 13:19; Amos 4:11; Zeph 2:9). The second motif compares the Edomites to young sheep (v. 20) who are attacked by a ravenous **lion** (v. 19). No **shepherd** (king) will be able to protect them from this attack. The final two verses tie this motif back to previous ones. He again speaks of **their fall**, an event so momentous it feels like an earthquake. Then he uses the **eagle** (נֶשֶׁר, *nešer*; cp. v. 16) in a different way. Now the eagle is not Edom, nesting high up for protection; it is once again Babylon (see 48:40-41), **swoop**ing **down** on Edom to carry away any of the devastated flock that might still survive. Once again, the proud heart of Israel's enemies (v. 16) becomes overburdened with pain, **like the heart of a woman in labor** (v. 22; see 13:21; 22:23; Isa 13:6-8; 26:16-18; Hos 13:13). At the center of all this is the assertion/reminder that this is all assured because the LORD has commanded it (see 18:7-10; 50:44-46; Isa 14:27; 23:9). These events ultimately display his sovereignty. This is a decree of "the LORD Almighty" (v. 7).

---

[7]McKane, *Jeremiah*, p. 1222.

F. A MESSAGE ABOUT DAMASCUS (49:23-27)

49:23-27 This brief oracle concerning **Damascus** is relatively straightforward. Damascus, capital of Aram (Syria), lay between Israel and her Mesopotamian invaders. It prospered at times from trade because of its proximity with Assyria and Babylon, but it also faced repeated threats of invasion for the same reason. It too was a perennial enemy of the Israelites (Gen 15:1-2; 2 Sam 10:6-19; 1 Kgs 20:20-29; 2 Kgs 7:4-16; 8:28-29; 9:14-15; 12:17-18; 16:5-12; Isa 7:1-9). It had been conquered by the Assyrians in the mid-eighth century B.C. (Isa 7:16-17), but the collapse of Assyria a century later had apparently allowed the nation to reassert its independence.

One senses the approach of the Babylonians as the oracle progresses. The cities of **Hamath and Arpad** (Isa 10:9; 36:19; 37:13) lay between Damascus and the Babylonian invaders. Their discouragement spawns a similar reaction among the citizens of Damascus. Like the Edomites (v. 22), their **anguish** is analogous to **labor pains**. Onlookers are amazed that anyone still remains there (v. 25),[8] because no one would want to see their beautiful hometown humiliated as this one inevitably will be. As with the other nations, **the LORD Almighty**, the divine king of all nations, has decreed it. The LORD himself will take the credit for burning down the outer defense-walls — made of mud-brick over a frame of wooden beams — and then, finally, the inner fortifications surrounding the royal complex (**the fortresses of Ben-Hadad**; see Amos 1:4,7,10,12,14; 2:2,5),[9] the very heart of the Syrian nation.

G. A MESSAGE ABOUT KEDAR AND HAZOR (49:28-33)

49:28-33 The main question raised by this oracle is geographical. It concerns the identification of **Hazor**. The only known site bearing this name was a large Canaanite city-state captured by Joshua (Josh

---

[8]The negative Hebrew expression ("Why has the city of renown not been abandoned?") might be a positive expression of amazement ("How abandoned is the city of renown!"). Thompson, *Jeremiah*, pp. 723-724; McKane, *Jeremiah*, pp. 1233-1235; Holladay, *Jeremiah 2*, pp. 380-381.

[9]The chief deity of Syria was (Baal-)Hadad. Several kings of Syria wore the honorific title, Ben-Hadad ("son of Hadad").

11:10-11; cp. Judg 4:2; 2 Kgs 15:29). It is puzzling to find a reference
to **the kingdoms** (plural) of Hazor, to pair them with **Kedar**, a tribe
of northern Arabia, and to call their inhabitants **the people of the
East** (v. 28). It is most likely that a minor scribal error has occurred
in the process of transmission. The term חָצֵר (*ḥāṣēr*) refers to
unwalled settlements, and it is used in conjunction with Kedar in at
least one other passage (Isa 42:11, "the settlements [*ḥăṣērîm*] where
Kedar lives"). Most commentators conclude, therefore, that this oracle concerns various Arab tribal groups, situated south and southeast of Judah, attacked by Nebuchadnezzar around 599 B.C.[10] This
fits well with the nature of the destruction predicted in this oracle
(cp. Isa 21:13-17; Ezek 25:12-14). Descriptive comments throughout
this oracle indicate that those being attacked are a nomadic type of
people. They have **tents, flocks, camels**, and **herds** (vv. 29,32). There
are no **gates** or defense-works that one finds in cities (v. 31).

The oracle itself falls into four pieces. The LORD twice addresses
the Babylonian attackers, encouraging them in their efforts (vv. 28b-
29,31-32a). In between, he advises those being attacked to seek shelter in caves (v. 30). The oracle closes with a divine announcement of
coming desolation (vv. 32b-33; see v.18). There is no promise of
restoration. This final section reminds the reader that the devastation might be executed by the Babylonians, but it is ultimately the
LORD who is ordering and causing it.

There are a few elements in this oracle which have direct ties to
other oracles in Jeremiah. One is the use of the expression, **Terror
on every side** (v. 29). Jeremiah uses this indicator of the pervasiveness of suffering in reference to Pashhur the priest and others who
will fall to the Babylonians (6:25; 20:3-4,10; 46:5). There appears to
be a verbal link to 49:32 as well ("disaster on them from every side"),
but that exists only in the English translation. Completely different
Hebrew terms are used in these two clauses. The mention of
Nebuchadnezzar "plotting" and "devising a plan" (v. 30) might be a
bit misleading. Elsewhere in Jeremiah, these terms sometimes imply
something devious or underhanded (11:18-19; 18:18); but more
often the term for "plot" (חָשַׁב, *ḥāšab*) can simply mean "plan, strategy" (see 18:8,11; 26:3; 36:3; 48:2; 49:20; 50:45). Nebuchadnezzar is
not using "covert operations" to overthrow these regions; he is

---

[10]Holladay, *Jeremiah 2*, pp. 382-383, 385; Thompson, *Jeremiah*, pp. 726-727;
McKane, *Jeremiah*, p. 1238; Brueggemann, *Jeremiah*, p. 459.

devising military strategy. **Plunder** and **booty** (v. 32) form a common word-pair (Isa 8:1,3; 10:6; 33:23; Ezek 29:19; 38:12-13). As with the oracle concerning Ammon (49:1-6), the Israelites should readily identify with the desolation described in the closing of this oracle (**haunt of jackals** [see 9:11; 10:22; 51:37; Isa 34:13; 35:7], **a desolate place** [see 4:27; 6:8; 9:11; 10:22; 12:10-11; 25:12; 32:43; 33:10; 34:22; Isa 1:7; 6:11; 64:10], **no one will live there** [see 2;15; 4:7; 9:11; 17:6; 26:9; 33:10; 34:22; 49:18]).

H. A MESSAGE ABOUT ELAM (49:34-39)

49:34-39 Elam was at its height in the second millennium B.C., lying to the southeast of Babylon, between Babylon and Persia. It is mentioned among the nations that are to drink from the LORD's cup of wrath (25:25), but it had very little contact with the Israelites over the years. This makes the inclusion of this oracle somewhat curious (Gen 10:22; 14:1-12; Isa 11:11; 21:2; 22:6; Ezek 32:24; Dan 8:2). Equally curious is the use of a "major" literary introduction (v. 34; see 1:2; 14:1; 46:1; 47:1; 50:1).[11] It could be that this region, with its capital in Susa (see Neh 4:1), later would become associated with Persia, which would also dominate the Jewish people.[12] This introduction dates this oracle approximately to the year 597 B.C. There is limited evidence of a Babylonian campaign against Elam a few years later. That would likely be the fulfillment of the present prophecy. It could be that this prophecy served to eliminate any hopes the Israelites might have had of help from the Elamites in getting out from under Babylon's control.[13]

This prophecy too is a royal edict pronounced by the divine king, **the LORD Almighty**. Every statement is made in the first person. The LORD is declaring his direct involvement in the defeat of Elam. There are several allusions in these few verses to ideas that would

---

[11]The LXX arrangement places these oracles concerning foreign nations after 25:13, with this oracle coming first. Those who believe the Greek texts represent an earlier form of the book can explain this introduction on that basis, but that then leaves the need to explain the introductions in 46:1 and 47:1.

[12]McKane, *Jeremiah*, p. 1248.

[13]Thompson, *Jeremiah*, p. 728; Clements, *Jeremiah*, pp. 258-259; Holladay, *Jeremiah 2*, pp. 388-389.

have been particularly pertinent to Elam. The Elamites were famous for being an "ancient" kingdom, with strong kings and powerful armies. That is all eclipsed now by the LORD's actions. He will overpower them militarily (**I will break the bow of Elam** [v. 35]. . . . **I will pursue them with the sword** [v. 37]), and he **will set** up his own **throne** in place of theirs (v. 38; cp. 1:15; 39:3; 43:10). Verse 36 makes mention of **the four winds** and **the four quarters of heaven** (see Isa 11:12; Ezek 37:9; Dan 7:2; 8:8; Zech 2:6; 6:5; Matt 24:31; Rev 7:1; 20:8). These allude to the vast expanse of the Mesopotamian plain, on the one hand, and to the vastness of Elam's dispersion, on the other. The Elamites once thought of themselves as a nation that extended its power over many lands; now they will be extended — as exiles — over many lands. As with Moab and Ammon (48:47; 49:6), there is a final note of hope, as the LORD promises the eventual resurgence of this once powerful land (v. 39).

JEREMIAH 50

I. A MESSAGE ABOUT BABYLON (50:1-51:64)

50:1 The concluding narrative paragraph (51:59-64) sets this lengthy section in the context of the reign of Zedekiah (c. 594 B.C.), several years before the fall of Jerusalem. It identifies this as a single "message" (דָּבָר, *dābār*, "word") of Jeremiah, yet various introductory statements indicate that this "message" is made up of several originally separate oracles (50:2-32,33-46; 51:1-32,33-35,36-57,58).[1] The introduction in 50:1 similarly identifies what follows as **the word** (*dābār*) spoken **through Jeremiah**. This label is common in Jeremiah and other prophetic books, where it normally refers to a group of independent "sayings" collectively as "the word of the LORD" to a prophet (1:1-2; 7:1; 14:1; 46:1). What this particular group of "sayings" has in common is that **Babylon** is the ultimate object of the prophet's remarks.

It is likely, but not certain, that all these oracles were delivered originally within a short time frame, during the first half of Zedekiah's reign (see 51:59). There are occasional allusions to peoples exiled by the Babylonians, but this was a long process, begun early in the reign of King Nebuchadnezzar.[2] A more significant consideration is the place of Babylon in Jeremiah's teachings. It is particularly during

---

[1]Many scholars eschew any attempt to identify individual oracles here, but that is predicated in part on their attempts to separate "authentic" statements of Jeremiah from secondary additions. I am starting with the assumption that all is authentic, and I am trying to use the literary clues supplied by the text to discern smaller units within the "word" as a whole. For a supporting clue, compare the ending of Jeremiah 21 with 50:31-32.

[2]Clements, for example, reads verse 28 as an allusion to the final exile of Jerusalem in 586 B.C. (*Jeremiah*, pp. 260-261). It could also refer to the earlier stage of 597 B.C., when Jehoiachin was taken. Mention of Nebuchadnezzar (v. 17) points to a date prior to his death in 562 B.C. Thompson, *Jeremiah*, pp. 731-732.

the reign of Zedekiah that Jeremiah encourages his audience to submit to Babylonian control, that the future for God's people lies with those who go over to Babylon (see chaps. 21, 24, 27–29, 37–44). Predictions of the ultimate collapse of Babylon seem out of place in such a context. On the other hand, the rationale for Jeremiah's judgment on Babylon is that nation's arrogance. The Babylonians are being used by the LORD to punish Judah and other peoples, yet they believe they are acting of their own accord. These oracles merely put the relationship between the LORD and Babylon in its proper perspective.

50:2-32 The LORD is interacting with three groups of characters in this complex oracle. Together they form the same, large scene. One group consists of several nations "from the north," whom the LORD is calling to attack and defeat Babylon (vv. 2-3,8-10,14-16,21-22,25-27,29-30). A second group is the people of Israel, portrayed as wandering sheep who are being avenged by those invading nations (vv. 4-7,17-20,28). The third group is the people of Babylon, Israel's "foe from the north," who is about to be overrun by her own northern enemies (vv. 11-13,23-24,31-32).

Although criteria are somewhat arbitrary, there seem to be at least two likely ways to understand the overarching structure of the units within this "word."[3] One is to break it down into three cycles, each shifting the reader's attention from the nations to Israel, back to the nations, and finally to Babylon.[4] A more comprehensive way is to see in it two sets of concentric circles. The first (vv. 2-22) has Babylon at its center (vv. 11-13), with comments regarding the nations (vv. 8-10,14-16), then Israel (vv. 4-7,17-20), then the nations again (vv. 2-3,21-22), surrounding the center. The second (vv. 23-32) has Jerusalem at its center (v. 28), with comments regarding the nations (vv. 26-27,29-30) and Babylon (vv. 23-25,31-32) surrounding

---

[3]For other proposals, see Holladay, *Jeremiah 2*, pp. 411-415; Brueggemann, *Jeremiah*, pp. 464-471; McKane, *Jeremiah*, pp. 1250-1283; Thompson, *Jeremiah*, pp. 731-743.

[4]The three cycles fall out according to the following arrangement:

nations (vv. 2-3)/Israel (vv. 4-7)/nations (vv. 8-10)/Babylon (vv. 11-13)

nations (vv. 14-16)/Israel (vv. 17-20)/nations (vv. 21-22)/Babylon (vv. 23-24)

nations (vv. 25-27)/Israel (v. 28)/nations (vv. 29-30)/Babylon (vv. 31-32).

it.[5] The resulting picture is a contrast between the mood in Babylon (**ashamed**, humiliated) and the mood in Jerusalem (avenged). The most extensive verbal link between the two parts is the statement, **Do to her** [Babylon] **as she has done** (vv. 15,29). Babylon has meted out justice on other nations, but now it is the Babylonians' turn; **their day has come** (vv. 27,31).[6] Along the same lines, there is also the parallel repetition of **vengeance** in verses 15 and 28 (see 11:20). Ultimately, then, the future defeat of Babylon is portrayed as divine retribution on Judah's conqueror. More than a century before, the LORD had stopped the Assyrians short of their goal of conquering Jerusalem (Isaiah 10), thereby showing his ultimate love for his people. Now he is reasserting that covenant love by destroying those whom he has used to punish his people.[7]

The LORD's words regarding the **nations** (vv. 2-3,8-10,15-16,21-22,26-27,29-30) weave together several ideas. These nations come **from the north** (vv. 3,9), just as Babylon had been Jerusalem's "foe from the north" (1:13-15; 4:6; 6:1,22; 10:22; 13:20; 25:9).[8] They are not to spare Babylon at all, leaving no remnant, but filling their hands with her goods (vv. 2-3,9-10,21,26,29).[9] There is only the

---

[5]There are verbal cues tying together the various concentric circles. The command to "attack" (עָלָה עָלֶיהָ, *'ālāh 'ālêhā*, "go up against her") ties together verses 2-3 with verses 21-22, the outermost circle. Verses 4-7 and 17-20, regarding Israel, mirror one another in the double clause, "In those days, at that time" (vv. 4,20); meanwhile, the remaining verses (vv. 5-7 and vv. 17-19) speak of Israel as sheep. The inner circle regarding the nations (vv. 8-10,14-16) mirror one another with calls to "flee" from Babylon (vv. 8,16). The repetition of "how" in verse 23 marks the transition to a different structure. The only verbal evidence of concentricity is in the divine name, "the Sovereign LORD Almighty" (vv. 25,31).

[6]The words used to describe Babylon's destruction of Edom (49:17) and Judah (18:16; 19:8) are now employed against Babylon (50:13). The same logic is implied with verse 30. The description of Babylon's defeat is the same as that decreed on Damascus (49:26), and Babylon had been the one to defeat Damascus (see also 50:32 and 21:14). Parke-Taylor, *Formation*, pp. 152-153, 158-159, 172-173.

[7]Brueggemann, *Jeremiah*, pp. 461-463.

[8]There is uncertainty as to whether Babylon's enemies actually come "from the north." This could simply be a stock phrase for an inevitable conqueror. McKane, *Jeremiah*, p. 1253; Thompson, *Jeremiah*, p. 733.

[9]"Marathaim" and "Pekod" (v. 21; see Ezek 23:23) are two regions in southern Babylonia, named perhaps because they would be the "safest" in the case of a northern attack. McKane, *Jeremiah*, pp. 1273-1274; Thompson, *Jeremiah*, p. 741.

briefest reference to the Babylonian deity, **Marduk** (a.k.a. **Bel**, v. 2; see Isa 46:1). The Babylonians hailed Marduk as the most powerful being of all, the great warrior god who gave victory to Babylon.[10] Here he is shown to be nothing, as he is **put to shame** and terrified by the Lord through these northern nations. It is he, **the [Sovereign] Lord Almighty** (vv. 18,25,31; see 46:18; 49:5,26,35), the great divine warrior, who has called out his troops to show the true powerlessness of this tool he is wielding (v. 18).

The words addressed to Babylon (vv. 11-13,23-25,31-32) intend to "put Babylon in her place." The parallel drawn between these nations and Babylon as attackers "from the north" signal to Babylon that she is just like those other countries. The arrogance of Babylon regarding her status as the "foe from the north" is now brought back on her own head. Babylon had come to think of herself as the nation without compare (Isa 47:8-10); now, **she will be the least of the nations** (v. 12). She prided herself in her agricultural productivity and wealth; now she will become a **desert** land, without inhabitants (vv. 12-13; see vv. 16, 26; Hos 2:3), **desolate . . . among the nations** (v. 23). She had been home to impressive **granaries** (v. 26); now she will be "consumed" (v. 32). She had been **the hammer of the whole earth**, shattering other nations with her mighty blows; now she will be **broken and shattered** (v. 23). Babylon had been standing tall and proud and **arrogant**, but now she will **stumble and fall** (vv. 31-32). All this will happen because Babylon has offended the Lord. The Lord's anger will cause her to be deserted (v. 13). Although the Lord used Babylon to punish his people, Babylon has **opposed** and **defied** him (vv. 24,29). The Lord will assert his own authority and power by destroying this mighty opponent.

The ultimate effect of relegating Babylon to the same status as all other "nations" is that the Lord reaffirms the status of Israel as his chosen people. This is at the core of the passages here regarding them (vv. 4-5,17-20,28). He confirms his continuing desire for **an everlasting covenant** with them (v. 5; see 31:31-34). There will be a general reversal of their image among the other nations. Their **shepherds** (v. 6; see 22:22; 23:1-2) had **caused them to roam** (שׁוֹבְבוּם, *šôbᵊbûm*; v. 6; see 3:14,22; 31:22), but the Lord will **bring Israel back**

---

[10]The Babylonian creation myth of Enuma Elish depicts Marduk as the great warrior god, who defeated the ancient goddess of chaos, Tiamat, thereby bringing order and stability to the universe. King Cyrus attributed the success of his own conquest of Babylon to Marduk.

(וְשֹׁבַבְתִּי, wᵉšōbabtî) to graze in **his own pasture** (v. 19). They were punished because **they sinned against the LORD** (v. 7), but now no sin **will be found** in them (v. 20; see 30:15-17; 31:34). The LORD will bless **the remnant** of Israel (v. 20), while he will **leave no remnant** to Babylon (v. 26). Whereas the Babylonians had **devoured** (אָכַל, 'ākal) the Israelites earlier (v. 7), now the LORD's **fire . . . will consume** ('ākal) them (v. 32; see 30:16).

50:33-46 This oracle proceeds in two movements. The first (vv. 33-40) communicates the LORD's orders for the destruction of Babylon. The second (vv. 41-46) anticipates the nature of the execution of the LORD's orders. Again, one finds the primary theme to be "what goes around comes around." Babylon will suffer at the hands of invaders in the same way Israel and Judah have suffered at the hands of their Babylonian invaders. References to Babylon's invaders and the suffering they bring borrow heavily from previous oracles regarding Babylon's own invasion of other nations.

This oracle, too, is spoken by the divine warrior, **the LORD Almighty** (v. 33). He comes as **Redeemer** for his people (v. 34; see Exod 6:6; 15:13), doing for them what they are unable to do for themselves. There are a couple of wordplays in the Hebrew used to convey these thoughts. First, there is one with a strong legal overtone. A "redeemer" functions officially in a court of law, speaking and acting to support the legal rights of a relative who is economically destitute (see Lev 25:25-55; Ruth 4:1-12). The LORD steps forward — as a relative, not just as a generous neighbor — to **vigorously defend their cause** (רִיב יָרִיב אֶת־רִיבָם, rîb yārîb 'eth-rîbām). This phrase involves the triple use of the term rîb ("to file suit"), emphasizing the forcefulness of the LORD's actions (see Prov 23:11). A second wordplay describes the intended results. To the land of Israel he will **bring rest** (הִרְגִּיעַ, hirgîaʻ), but to the Babylonians he will bring **unrest** (הִרְגִּיז, hirgîz).

A strongly militaristic tone imbues the following lines (vv. 35-40), as the LORD exposes the powerlessness of the major Babylonian leaders and gods with his **sword**, and **overthrows** this seemingly powerful city. Their wise **prophets** will become **fools**; their brave **warriors** will flee in **terror**, behaving like **women**; the mighty **waters** of the Euphrates will **dry up**.[11] All of this exposes the powerlessness

---

[11]The word for "drought" (חֹרֶב, ḥōreb; v. 38) is very close to the word for "sword" (חֶרֶב, ḥereb; vv. 35-37).

of these people, and even more, the powerlessness of their false gods. Their abundant lives, which they attribute to their gods, will be stripped away, and Babylon will become another **Sodom and Gommorrah**, the epitome of death and destruction (see 49:18; Isa 13:19-22).[12]

The second half, describing the execution of these orders by the LORD, would remind the Israelite readers of previous prophecies, when Babylon was the one meting out the LORD's justice. Verses 41-43 are taken straight out of 6:22-24, except that the one formerly inflicting the punishment is now receiving the punishment. Similarly, verses 44-46 are taken almost wholesale from 49:19-21. There, Babylon is meting out the LORD's justice on Edom. Now it is Babylon's turn to receive her just punishment.[13]

---

[12]The reference to "desert creatures and hyenas" (םִיִּא־תֶא םִיִּצ, ṣiyyîm 'eth 'iyyîm; v. 39) might actually be an allusion to mythical demons and spirits in Babylonian thought, rather than physical creatures. This would make this a jeering taunt of Babylonian beliefs. Thompson, *Jeremiah*, p. 744; McKane, *Jeremiah*, p. 1292; Bright, *Jeremiah*, p. 355; Holladay, *Jeremiah 2*, pp. 420-421.

[13]Parke-Taylor, *Formation*, pp. 155-157, 175-177.

JEREMIAH 51

I. A MESSAGE ABOUT BABYLON (50:1–51:64) (continued)

51:1-32 This oracle can be broken into three sections. The first (vv. 1-13) emphasizes the coming destruction of Babylon, destruction justified as vengeance for Babylon's violence against Judah. Jeremiah introduces the theme of "destruction" (from the verb הִשְׁחִית, *hišhît*) in verse 1. The LORD is bringing a **destroyer** (מַשְׁחִית, *mašhît*), who will be a terror **on every side** (v. 2; see 46:5; 49:29) against the Babylonians,[1] just as Babylon has been a terror all around Judah (4:17; see 6:25). There follows a series of three units, each beginning with a pair of battle commands. The first pair (v. 3) are orders for the total destruction of the Babylonian forces. The justification for this is the LORD's desire to show that he has not abandoned his people (v. 5). He is seeking **vengeance** (נְקָמָה, *nᵊqāmāh*) for his suffering people (see v. 36). His continued devotion to his people is not a blind love, however, because he recognizes the extent of their sins. This vengeance on Babylon is an act of mercy toward his people. The people of Judah should be particularly aware of this, because he says both **Israel and Judah** are being avenged. The people of Judah tended to look on the people of Israel as the apostate ones, whom the LORD had abandoned more than a century earlier (cp. 7:15). The fact that the LORD is acting on their behalf would be recognized by the people of Judah as a sign of his mercy. The fact that he acts on behalf of both nations suggests to the people of Judah that their deliverance is just as much an act of mercy as is the deliverance of the northern kingdom of Israel. The second pair of commands (v. 6) is addressed to non-Babylonian peoples liv-

---

[1]"Leb Kamai" (v. 1) is an Athbash for Chaldeans (כשדים=לבקמי), i.e., Babylon. See McKane, *Jeremiah*, p. 1295.

ing in Babylon.[2] These are the nations who were forced to drink the **wine** of God's wrath from the **cup** of Babylon (v. 7; see 25:15-29). Now, the cup will **fall** and break, and it **cannot** be mended. Again, the reason for Babylon's fate is the LORD's desire to exact **vengeance** for his people (vv. 6,10). The third pair of commands is doubled (vv. 11-12). It again addresses the invading armies, instructing them to make certain their victory. And again, this is explained as the LORD's doing, an act of **vengeance** on behalf of his people (v. 11). There is no escape for this wealthy nation. For the first time, the invaders are identified (v. 11; see v. 28). They are the **Medes**, a people to the north and east of Babylon who incorporated with the Persians under Cyrus to establish the Persian Empire (539 B.C.).[3]

The center section of this oracle (vv. 14-24) consists of a dual oath in verses 14 and 24, enveloping a strong self-affirmation by the LORD of his divine sovereignty. The oath is given by God as the divine warrior, **the LORD Almighty** (v. 14). He pledges a victory over Babylon, as judgment on Babylon for her evil deeds against Jerusalem. The following verses (vv. 15-19) quote from 10:12-16 to expand in grand style on the certainty of an oath being sworn by the LORD.[4] The LORD declares his unique divinity. He is the true Creator, who displayed his great **wisdom** and **understanding** in establishing the world. He still commands the forces of nature, as evidenced by the **thunder** and **clouds** and **lightning** and **wind** (v. 16). The idols and their makers have no sense or real **knowledge** at all. There is no life, **no breath in them** (vv. 17-18). But Israel's God — **the Portion of Jacob, Maker of all things** — gives and sustains life. As Creator, he can assume the role of divine warrior — **the LORD Almighty is his name** (v. 19). In light of these truths, his oath cannot be challenged. It is as Creator that the LORD commands and controls the actions of Babylon, even though Babylon is not aware of it (cp. Isa 45:1-7). As he had done with Assyria more than a century before, the LORD has been using Babylon as his **weapon for battle** (see Isa 10:5-19). She has been his **war club**, his "shatterer" (מַפֵּץ, *mappēṣ*), with which he has "shattered" (נִפַּצְתִּי, *nippaṣtî*) **nations** and **kingdoms** (see 1:10) and all the peoples — men and women, young

---

[2]Or, as many commentators conclude, Israel and Judah are still being addressed. See McKane, *Jeremiah*, p. 1299.

[3]Thompson, *Jeremiah*, pp. 752-753.

[4]Parke-Taylor, *Formation*, pp. 177-179.

and old, aristocrat and peasant — living in the lands Babylon has conquered (vv. 20-23). This impressive series of nine "shatterings" (cp. the use of "sword" in 50:35-37) concludes with the LORD's pledge to **repay** (see 50:29; 51:56) Babylon for all the **wrong** עַר, *ra'*, ("hurt, evil") she did against Zion (v. 24).[5] The LORD will "shatter" Babylon, just as he has used Babylon to "shatter" others.

The third section of this oracle (vv. 25-32) resumes the theme of destruction (הִשְׁחִית, *hišḥîth*). Now the full scope of this theme is discerned. It is Babylon which has been known as the "destroyer," but now it will be destroyed (v. 25). This final section remains focused on the topic of Babylon's defeat. Nothing will be left that could be used for future rebuilding (v. 26). The soldiers will surrender, and there is nothing but bad news to be reported to the Babylonian king (vv. 30-32). This outcome is certain because it is not a plan arising solely from the minds of **the kings of the Medes** and their allies among the **nations** and **kingdoms**; these are **the LORD's purposes against Babylon** (v. 29).

51:33-35 Although the speaker here is God as divine warrior (**the LORD Almighty**), he speaks as the collective body of Jerusalem (v. 35). The images he uses are not common, but the point is clear. The first image (v. 33) simply indicates that Babylon's "time" is near, the **time** when she will be "harvested" for her sins. The second image (v. 34) portrays the ugliness of what Babylon has done to Israel, comparing Babylon to a snake that has eaten and regurgitated Israel. The concluding imprecation summarizes the central message of all these oracles: **Babylon** is to suffer just as she has caused **Jerusalem** to suffer.

51:36-57 The primary function of this substantial oracle is for the divine warrior (**the LORD Almighty**, v. 57) to assert once more the inevitability of Babylon's collapse. Secondarily, Jeremiah explains the LORD's desire to avenge the destruction of Jerusalem. These two motifs also dominate 51:1-13, suggesting a strong thematic unity to these oracles. Tying this particular oracle together is a dual use of the metaphor of drunkenness (see v. 7). Babylon will become **drunk, then sleep forever and not awake** (vv. 39,57). This again is to be

---

[5]The NIV translation might be a bit misleading here. The phrase "before your eyes" comes after the phrase "in Zion," in the Hebrew. This is not a promise that they will see the repayment, but a reference to the destruction they have already seen.

connected to the cup of wrath the LORD has been demanding every nation to drink (25:15-29). For those other nations, Babylon is the drink itself, the means by which the LORD inflicts his judgment on them. Now Babylon will become drunk with herself. Babylon will at first celebrate the humiliation of her enemies, but eventually that celebration will result in her own drunkenness and death.[6] Even Babylon's patron deity, **Bel** (a.k.a. Marduk, see 50:2; Isa 46:1), will vomit from the surfeit of wine (v. 44). Babylon will suffer the same fate as those over whom she is now celebrating; she will be consumed by what she has been feeding others — military conquest.

As in the earlier oracles of this section, some of the imagery and rhetoric used against Babylon here is the same as that used previously against other nations. For example, the densely-populated city will be deserted, left to the wild animals (v. 37; cp. 4:7; 9:11; 10:22; 25:9,18; 26:9; 29:18; 44:22; 49:33);[7] her attackers will come from **the north** (v. 48; see 50:3,9,41); the fighting will produce the sounds of **great destruction** (v. 54; see 48:3).

Then there are additional images. Babylon is to be slaughtered like common livestock (v. 40; cp. Ezek 39:18); she is to be **captured**, like a runaway slave, or like a soldier fleeing from battle (vv. 41,56). The most pervasive image is the image of the sea, an image which changes in meaning. The LORD will **dry up** Babylon's **sea** (v. 36; see v. 13), but then he will bring the sea to **cover her** (vv. 42,55). Such imagery evokes the LORD's victory over the Egyptians at the sea (Exodus 14–15).[8] The deliverance of Israel from Babylon will be like a second exodus, only more amazing (see 23:7-8). Another important image is found toward the end, as the oracle crescendos to its climax with several references to **destroyers** (vv. 53-56). At first

---

[6]There is a parallel usage of "Sheshach" (v. 41) to refer to a drunken Babylon in 25:26.

[7]Thompson, *Jeremiah*, p. 764.

[8]This is only one of three possible interpretations. A second equates the "sea" with the Euphrates River, overflowing its banks and inundating the great city which it has nurtured for so many years (cp. Isa 8:7-8). See McKane, Jeremiah, p. 1331. A third interpretation identifies the "sea" as the primeval waters of creation. According to Mesopotamian myth, the god Marduk (= Bel) subdued these waters in creating the earth. For the Babylonians, these lines might have suggested a reversal of creation, the disintegration of their world. Holladay, *Jeremiah 2*, p. 429; Brueggemann, *Jeremiah*, p. 481.

glance, this appears to link back directly to 51:1-13; but the Hebrew term for "destroyer" in these verses is different from the term used earlier. Here it is שֹׁדֵד (šōdēd; vv. 48,53-56). Jeremiah uses the term frequently to describe the fate other nations suffer at the hands of the Babylonians (47:4; 48:1,8,15,18,20,32; 49:3,10). It seems only fitting that Babylon now should suffer the same fate.

Jeremiah explains Babylon's destruction as recompense primarily for the suffering of Israel and Judah; the other nations are barely brought into it (v. 49). The LORD begins the oracle with a pledge to **avenge** his people ("I will avenge your vengeance," v. 36; see vv. 1-13). He warns them (**my people**, v. 45) to flee from Babylon to avoid its destruction. He exhorts them not to **lose heart** (v. 46), that he will eventually punish Babylon. He encourages them to think about Jerusalem, not with shame because of her current desecration, but with hope because of her future restoration. The climax to these thoughts comes with the section that begins, **But days are coming** (v. 52). The LORD will "take care of" Babylon's idols (see 50:2). The current state of affairs would suggest to the uninformed observer that Babylon's idols actually hold power and authority, that Babylon's success is to be attributed to them. This is the third time in this oracle (see vv. 44,47) that the LORD promises to **punish** (פָּקַד, pāqad, "take care of") these false gods in which the Babylonians trust. The threefold use of **punish** in this oracle, with its climax here, might intend to remind the reader of Jeremiah 5:9,29 and 9:9. There, the LORD repeats a pair of rhetorical questions regarding Judah: "Should I not punish them for this? Should I not avenge myself on such a nation as this?" Perhaps the same questions are now being applied to Babylon (see v. 36). The answer to such questions comes in the lines that follow, with their repeated warnings of "destroyers" coming against Babylon.[9] With the humiliation and destruction of Babylon, the LORD — **the King, whose name is the LORD Almighty** — will have **repaid in full** (שַׁלֵּם יְשַׁלֵּם, šallēm yᵉšallēm; v. 56, see v. 24) the suffering of his people.

---

[9]There is no stopping these "destroyers." To communicate this, Jeremiah alludes in verse 53 to the Tower of Babel. The intended height of that tower was a symbol of its invincibility. The LORD made a mockery of their feelings of invincibility then by confusing their speech. This reminder of that past act should encourage Jeremiah's audience that the LORD can bring down such a great city again. Holladay, *Jeremiah 2*, pp. 430-431; McKane, *Jeremiah*, p. 1343.

51:58 This final and brief word is somewhat obscure. The second half probably is borrowed from Habakkuk 2:13.[10] The fiery destruction of Babylon is plain enough, but there is ambiguity regarding the comments about **the peoples** and **the nations**. If these are Babylon's enemies, one would expect their work to be useful and effective, as the LORD uses them to punish Babylon. It is more likely that the plurality of "peoples" here points to the ethnic diversity among Babylon's citizens. Thus, it is the work of the ethnically-varied inhabitants of Babylon on behalf of Babylon which is futile.

51:59-64 This concluding note implies that all that precedes in Jeremiah 50–51 was sent at one time (c. 594 B.C.) by Jeremiah to the exiles in Babylon. The courier is identified as **Seraiah son of Neriah son of Mahseiah**. Apparently, he is the brother of Baruch, Jeremiah's friend and scribe (32:12). He is said to be accompanying King **Zedekiah** on an otherwise unmentioned trip to Babylon. It is logical to assume he embarked on this trip as a result of the gathering of kings in Jerusalem that is the occasion for Jeremiah's yoke-oracle (27:1-3).[11] Seraiah is to **read** the **scroll** (to the Babylonian leaders?), call on the LORD to fulfill his words of destruction,[12] then **throw** the scroll **into the Euphrates** River as a final symbolic act, demonstrating the ultimate fate of the great city. Obviously, a second copy of the scroll is retained.

The timing of this reading and symbolic act seems curious at first. Jeremiah is strongly advising King Zedekiah and his cohort nations to submit to Babylonian rule (27:4-11) because the LORD has decreed that Babylon shall punish these nations. It seems curious that he would simultaneously announce to Babylon that it would fall. This pairing makes sense, however, as part of Jeremiah's broader message to Zedekiah. The reason for Zedekiah's resistance to Jeremiah's call for submission is his ill-advised conviction that submission to Babylon indicates a lack of faith in the LORD. In reality, the opposite is true. Jeremiah's oracles against Babylon show that the destruction of Jerusalem is not the end of the story. Submission is only a means to an end, that end being the restoration and glori-

---

[10]Parke-Taylor, *Formation*, pp. 182-183.

[11]See McKane, *Jeremiah*, pp. 1351-1359, for discussion of the historical background to this unit.

[12]Seraiah's prayer that the LORD "destroy" Babylon (v. 62) employs a different term than the ones used in 51:1,11 or in 51:53-56. The term used here means "cut off" (כָּרַת, *kārath*).

fication of a purified and redeemed Israel. Therefore, the message of Babylon's destruction emerges primarily as an encouragement to King Zedekiah of Jerusalem, assuring him that Judah's submission to Babylon will be a temporary situation. The final scene of this play will be the restoration and glorification of Judah in her homeland.[13]

---

[13]Clements, *Jeremiah*, pp. 266-268.

EXCURSUS

THE ORACLES AGAINST THE NATIONS
AND MODERN INTERPRETATION

One would be remiss not to pause for a moment to reflect on modern (particularly American) appropriations of Old Testament prophecies in the light of Jeremiah 46–51. It has been a fairly common practice in certain American Christian circles to read Old Testament prophecies as speaking indirectly to this nation, associating America with ancient Israel. In other words, promises of prosperity given to Israel are seen as indirectly "fulfilled" when America is prospering, being attributed to America's "Christian" origins and America's adherence to Christian values. Similarly, prophecies of judgment against Israel for her idolatry and oppressive practices have been applied to parallel American phenomena (a misguided trust in material wealth [false gods], ignoring the plight of the poor, etc.) and used as warnings of divine judgment. Such interpretations, though generally appropriate (see Jer 18:7-10), probably overstate the connection between ancient Israel and modern America. They often assume that the material blessings America has enjoyed are the direct result of living as "one nation under God," that the LORD has blessed or punished America on the basis of her relative righteousness, because America is "God's nation," just as Israel was in the Bible.

These oracles raise another possibility. In them, the powerful and blessed nation is Babylon. It was raised up by the LORD for him to use in punishing Israel and other nations. There is the possibility that America has been raised up for similar reasons, that the "blessings" America enjoys are not directly attributable to her status as God's nation. Perhaps the LORD is merely using this political entity — in which many thousands of righteous Christians just happen to live — to work out his plans, as he has done with many other nations in the past. American Christians should not bind themselves, however, to the assumption that the well-being of America represents the well-being of God's people. The place of Christians in the world is more complicated than that.

JEREMIAH 52

IX. JERUSALEM IS CAPTURED (52:1-34)

A. The Fall of Jerusalem (52:1-30)

The book closes with a rather straightforward account of the exile, one that parallels the account in 2 Kings (see Excursus, below). It introduces King Zedekiah (52:1-3), then focuses on the fate of the king and his family (52:4-11), the fate of Jerusalem (52:12-16), the fate of the temple and its furnishings (52:17-23), and the fate of Jerusalem's leading officials (52:24-27). A final "accounting" of those taken prisoner closes this section (52:28-30).

52:1-3 The introduction of King **Zedekiah** is typical for kings of Judah in the Book of Kings. It gives his age at his accession, the length of his reign, his mother's name, and a general religious evaluation of his deeds. The reference to **all** that **happened** (v. 3) is anticipatory, setting the stage for the destruction that is to follow. It is evidence of **the LORD's anger**, not his negligence of his people.[1] It is because he is so "watchful" (see 1:12; 31:28; 44:27) that they suffer as they do. He is going to **thrust them from his presence**, just as he had the northern tribes (7:15; cp. 2 Kgs 17:20). There are no references to Jeremiah's prophecies, but the reader recognizes that the king's rebellion against the Babylonians is tantamount to rebellion against the LORD (5:23; 27:12-15).

52:4-11 The siege lasts eighteen months (Fall 588 B.C. to Spring 586 B.C.; cp. 39:1-2), ending when the people have run out of food (see 37:21). The note in 39:4 indicates that **the whole army** (52:7) might refer only to the king's guards. The rest of this piece repeats information about the humiliation of Zedekiah given in 39:5-7, adding only that the king remained in **prison** until **his death** (52:11).

---

[1]Holladay, *Jeremiah 2*, p. 440.

52:12-16 This paragraph provides an expanded rendition of information given in 39:8-10. Two supplementary facts are noteworthy. One is the length of time (one month) between the breaching of the walls of the city and the completion of the destruction, which included burning all buildings and tearing down defensive walls. The other is a reference to the destruction of **the temple**. One can easily assume in chapter 39 that the temple was burned, but here there is an explicit reference to it. This is followed with an account of the plundering of various parts of the temple.

52:17-23 The writer describes the looting of the temple in two phases (see 27:19-22). In the first phase, he inventories the **bronze** articles that are destroyed, moving from larger articles to smaller ones (52:17-18); then he lists the **gold** and **silver** articles (52:19). He returns to the large bronze articles in the second phase, giving details about their size and adornment (52:20-23; see 1 Kgs 7:15-37). Such a description adds to the sense of grief felt by those who witnessed this destruction.

52:24-27 The writer now returns to the other leaders who are executed. These include **priests**, **advisors**, and **officers** and their assistants. As a group, these appear to be those who opposed Jeremiah and his message (1:18; 2:26; 4:9; 5:31; 6:13; 13:13; 23:33-40; 26:7-16; 32:32), but the ones named here are known to have been sympathetic toward him. **Seraiah** was a grandson of Hilkiah, priest in the days of Josiah (2 Kgs 22:3-14; 23:4; 1 Chr 6:13-15). His grandson played a leading role in the rebuilding of the temple (Ezra 5:2; Haggai 1:1,12; 2:2,4; Zech 3:1-10). **Zephaniah** is probably the priest who shielded Jeremiah from other priests who opposed him (29:24-32; 37:3).[2] Perhaps these two eventually turned against Jeremiah as well, and this is why their execution is noted. Or perhaps they are noted to show that even some of Jeremiah's supporters lost their lives in this catastrophe (cp. 39:15-18; 45:1-5).

52:28-30 This final numbering of the exiles speaks of three phases. The first and largest concerns the time that Nebuchadnezzar exiled Jehoiachin and his court, setting up Zedekiah as his successor (597 B.C.; 2 Kgs 24:12; Jer 24:1; 29:2).[3] The second is at the conclusion of

---

[2]Thompson, *Jeremiah*, p. 782.

[3]There appears to be a one-year discrepancy in some of these chronological references. The explanation concerns how one counts the "first" year of a king's reign. Sometimes, the "first" year is counted from the day a king

the main siege of Jerusalem (586 B.C.; see 52:12; 2 Kgs 25:8). The final phase comes five years later, probably in response to the assassination of Gedaliah (see on 41:1). A question naturally arises about the numbers of people given. Surely there were more than 4,600 prisoners taken to Babylon. Second Kings 24:14 reports the deportation of ten thousand in the first phase alone. It is easy to speculate about ways to reconcile these figures. One might suppose, for example, that the smaller numbers reflect only the number of males or the number of families exiled. Even this yields a relatively small total. It could be that only certain segments of the population are being counted here (**Judeans** in vv. 28 and 30, **people from Jerusalem** in v. 29). Perhaps many more were killed than we realize, or perhaps the depopulation of the land has been exaggerated in our minds.[4]

B. JEHOIACHIN RELEASED (52:31-34)

52:31-34 Jehoiachin is introduced without reference to how he came to be in Babylon (see 2 Kgs 24:8-17). The new **king of Babylon** (**Evil-Merodach**, 561–560 B.C.) initiates a different policy toward the Judean king, elevating him above all other captive kings. No reason for this shift is given, but it evidently signals new reasons for the people to hope for better treatment for themselves. The previous Babylonian monarch served as the instrument of the LORD's wrath. This one seems to serve as the instrument of the LORD's mercy (see on 31:28; 32:26-44). King Zedekiah, who represented the sin and destruction of the preceding generation, lived as a prisoner "till the day of his death" (52:11). Now Jehoiachin is treated with special honor **till the day of his death** (v. 34). These parallel clauses, not found in 2 Kings 25, highlight the contrast between the LORD's treatment of these two men. Together, they clarify the LORD's positive intentions toward the whole nation in the years ahead.

---

takes the throne; sometimes that is year "0", and the "first" year begins on New Year's Day of the following year. See Thompson, *Jeremiah*, p. 774; McKane, *Jeremiah*, p. 1382. It is also worth noting that the chronological base shifts from Zedekiah's reign (52:4-5) to Nebuchadnezzar's reign (52:12). This corresponds to the shift in political power in Jerusalem. Brueggemann, *Jeremiah*, p. 490.

[4]McKane, *Jeremiah*, pp. 1382-1383; Holladay, *Jeremiah 2*, p. 443.

EXCURSUS

JEREMIAH 52 AND 2 KINGS 25

The final chapter of Jeremiah is almost identical to the ending of 2 Kings. The only significant difference between the two is after 52:27 (// Kgs 25:21). The Kings account there (2 Kgs 25:22-26) provides a summary of Jeremiah 40–41, describing how the Babylonians appoint Gedaliah governor of Judea, and then Ishmael assassinates him. There is no mention of Jeremiah's role in that summary. The account in Jeremiah (52:28-30) ignores these events, giving instead a brief numbering of those exiled. Besides this variation, almost all the differences between Jeremiah 52 and the ending of Kings involve slightly longer readings in Jeremiah.[5] These do not alter the account appreciably; they only clarify certain points. It is usually assumed that the existence of longer readings in Jeremiah betrays that it is a later, revised version of the Kings account.[6] It is possible, however, that the Kings account is a later, more "economical" version that has eliminated extraneous words and phrases.

---

[5]The following is a list of the "additions" in Jeremiah:
"they left the city at night" (52:7)
"Zedekiah" (52:8)
"in the land of Hamath" (52:9; cp. v. 27)
"There at Riblah the king of Babylon" (52:10)
"he also killed the officials of Judah" (52:10)
"where he put him in prison till the day of his death" (52:11)
"all" (52:14,17)
"some of the poorest people" (52:15)
"Nebuzaradan" (52:16)
"sprinkling bowls" (52:18)
"basins . . . pots, lampstands, dishes and bowls used for drink offerings" (52:19)
"and the twelve bronze bulls under it" and "King" (52:20)
Measurements of circumference and thickness (52:21-22)
All of 52:23
"till the day of his death" (52:34)

There are three discrepancies regarding numbers: "the tenth day" in Jer 52:12 is reported to be "the seventh day" in 2 Kgs 25:8; "seven royal advisors" in Jer 52:25 is reported to be "five royal advisors" in 2 Kgs 25:19; "the twenty-fifth day" in Jer 52:31 is reported to be "the twenty-seventh day" in 2 Kgs 25:27. Most other variants involve a difference in only one letter in a given Hebrew word.

[6]Thompson, *Jeremiah*, p. 773; Holladay, *Jeremiah 2*, p. 439.

The reason for this duplication is an enigma. It seems most likely that one writer is borrowing wholesale from another (most likely, the compiler of Jeremiah from Kings). This should be no cause for concern, as biblical writers occasionally mention the use of written "sources" at their disposal (Josh 10:13; 2 Sam 1:18; 1 Kgs 11:41; etc.). Parallels between Kings and Chronicles (like the Synoptic Gospels) provide numerous examples of this practice. There will always be questions regarding "variants" in such parallels, questions about the accuracy (and, for some, the inspiration) of these documents. It is impossible to resolve such questions. We do not know the state of the documents biblical writers were using as sources for their information, nor can we ascertain the (inspired) writer's (lack of) concern for "correcting" any incidental differences that might have arisen in the process of transmitting from one text to another, or from one copy of a text to another.[7] For example, in this particular case, it is most likely that the writer of Jeremiah 52 has been inspired to use additional phrases to clarify the information he is reporting. It is also possible that the writer of 2 Kings 25 was inspired to give a slightly more abbreviated account for some other reason. There are several instances where one can see that such differences are purposeful, giving a slightly different nuance to a story, (probably) for the benefit of a different audience (see on 52:34). Other differences are inconsequential to one's interpretation.

The presence of Jeremiah 52 raises a different set of questions, questions regarding the inclusion of the chapter in the Book of Jeremiah. On the one hand, it suggests the possibility of a literary connection between Jeremiah and Kings. Such a connection is well-recognized at the level of phraseology, as the two share many words and phrases in common.[8] It is quite possible, in fact, that Baruch or someone else close to him and Jeremiah is responsible for writing Kings. Beyond that, though, one is left to wonder about why this chapter is included in Jeremiah. It seems to serve no purpose in the overall structure of the book, having no connections linguistically or thematically to any other part. Perhaps its purpose, then, is not so

---

[7]The LXX readings are consistently shorter than the Hebrew of both Jeremiah 52 and 2 Kings 25 in many instances. This would seem to suggest that the LXX is an abbreviated (and secondary) text.

[8]See especially, M. Weinfeld, *Deuteronomy and the Deuteronomic School* (Oxford: Oxford University, 1972), pp. 320-361.

much to add to the message of Jeremiah, but to influence one's interpretation of Kings.

One of the ongoing discussions regarding Kings is how the ending affects the tone of the whole work. Some argue that the ending is negative, because the history of the people ends with their exile. Others argue that the closing reference to Jehoiachin (2 Kgs 25:27-30 // Jer 52:31-34) intends to suggest a thin ray of hope for the future, that Jehoiachin's release portends a more general release of his people (see on 52:31-34). The placement of this chapter in Jeremiah would seem to support the latter interpretation. Jeremiah's prophecies show that exile in Babylon will not be the final chapter in the history of Israel. There is still a glorious future for the LORD's people. He will "restore their fortunes" and bring them back to their land. He will "plant" them in their land again and "rebuild" them. He will make a "new covenant" with them, and once again, he will be their God, and they will be his people. The parallel between the ending of Kings and the ending of Jeremiah suggests that both books are to be read with this understanding of Israel's history.

LAMENTATIONS

INTRODUCTION

The traditional Hebrew title of this book is *'Ekah*, derived from the first word in the book ("How . . . ," 1:1; also in 2:1; 4:1). There is also an ancient practice of giving it the title "Lamentations." This title and the traditional Jeremianic authorship of the book probably derive from 2 Chronicles 35:25. "Jeremiah composed laments for Josiah, and to this day all the men and women singers commemorate Josiah in the laments [קִינוֹת, *qînôth*]. These became a tradition in Israel and are written in the Laments [*qînôth*]." There is no compelling reason, however, to accept a direct association between the laments of this book and Jeremiah's laments. The laments in the Book of Lamentations say nothing of Josiah. Instead, they voice reactions to the Fall of Jerusalem, which took place more than twenty years after that king's death.[1] There are only a few literary links between Jeremiah and Lamentations that can be discerned (especially in Lamentations 4), but there are just as many links to other Old Testament books. The absence of any specific hope in these laments ignores the hopeful oracles of Jeremiah and Ezekiel (Jeremiah 30–33; Ezekiel 25–48), which should make one cautious about attributing these laments to either of those prophets. Most scholars have concluded, in fact, that Lamentations is a collection of laments, composed by different authors (comparable to the Book of Psalms) concerning the same event.

The historical setting for all five Lamentations is the years immediately following the destruction of Jerusalem (c. 585–560 B.C.). The same pervasiveness of despair that seems to preclude Jeremianic authorship also suggests a time well before there is any widespread hope of return from Babylonian Exile (c. 540 B.C.). These are individuals who fondly remember Jerusalem prior to her collapse, and who are pessimistic about any restoration of the city in the near future.

---

[1]There are laments for Josiah's sons in Jeremiah (Jer 22:10-30) and Ezekiel (Ezek 19:1-14), but none for Josiah alone.

The primary aspect (besides historical context) that ties these Lamentations together is the acrostic structure that underlies each one. The structure of four of the five chapters is based entirely on the twenty-two letters of the Hebrew alphabet.[2] The first two chapters build around this structure in the same way. Each consists of sixty-six lines, organized in groups of three lines each. Each three-line group is called a tricolon. In the present versification, each verse represents a tricolon (three lines) of Hebrew. The first line of the first tricolon (v. 1) begins with the first Hebrew letter, *'aleph* (א), the first line of the second tricolon (v. 2) begins with *beth* (ב), and so forth. Chapter 3 triples this pattern. Again there are sixty-six lines, but now each of the first three lines begins with *'aleph*, each of the next three lines begins with *beth*, etc. The versification reflects this by giving a separate number to each line (each verse in 3:1-3 begins with *'aleph*, each in 3:4-6 with *beth*, etc.).[3] The fourth chapter is slightly simpler. In this chapter, each verse begins with the letters of the alphabet in succession, as in chapters 1-2, but now each verse consists of only two lines (called a bicolon).[4] The fifth chapter is not an acrostic, but it does consist of twenty-two lines, one for each of the twenty-two letters in the Hebrew alphabet.

Besides the acrostic frame, there is little similarity in the overall structure of the different chapters. Each says something about the suffering associated with the destruction of Jerusalem and/or its inhabitants, and each looks to God for ultimate justice. But there is only general consistency in the ways the writers verbalize their thoughts. There is not a particular expression that is repeated throughout the laments, tying them all together. Instead, the same general sentiments are expressed in five different ways. Whether the order in which the Lamentations are arranged is significant is a matter of much speculation.

Considerable attention has been given to the literary form of the

---

[2]Other examples of this structure include Psalms 9-10, 25, 34, 37, 111, 112, 119, 145, and Proverbs 31:10-31.

[3]Psalm 119 is the most elaborate acrostic. Each of its twenty-two stanzas is made up of eight lines, and every line within a stanza begins with the same letter of the alphabet. The first eight lines begin with *'aleph* (119:1-8), the next eight begin with *beth* (119:9-16), and so on.

[4]The order of two letters (*'ayin* [ע] and *pe* [פ]) is reversed in chapters 2, 3, and 4 (also Psalms 9-10). This could indicate a regional variation in the alphabet.

poems in the book. In this enterprise, modern form critics distinguish between a "lament" and a "dirge."[5] The former bemoans the suffering of one still alive, while the latter expresses grief over one who has died. Both terms have been applied to various parts of the Book of Lamentations. One who looks at the use of the term קִינָה (qînāh, "lament," plural qînôth) in the Old Testament must recognize the arbitrary nature of such a distinction. Ezekiel gives a series of qînôth over the city of Tyre (Ezek 26:17-18; 27:1–28:19) before the Babylonians conquer that city, while David sings a qînāh over Saul and his sons, after their deaths at Mount Gilboa (2 Sam 1:17-27). Similarly, Jeremiah composes his qînôth for Josiah after that king's death.[6] The latter two examples should be "dirges," according to the categories of modern form critics; but the biblical writers put the same label on all these songs. There seems little point, then, in distinguishing between "laments" and "dirges."

Researchers have shown that biblical laments typically consist of five parts: (1) a direct invocation of God, (2) a "complaint," describing the speaker's current hardships, (3) a declaration of trust in God, (4) a petition for help in specific terms, and (5) a pledge to praise God for his positive response to the petition. This helps one see the "big picture" when reading a lament. In particular, this helps one recognize that the "complaint" aspect of a lament does not exist in isolation from trust in God. In fact, such "complaints" are made because one trusts in God. They assume that God is compassionate, that he will hear the complaint, and that he will act on behalf of the petitioners to relieve their suffering.[7]

It is unnecessary to assume that all these elements must exist in a single poem, in order for that poem to be a "lament." For example,

---

[5]C. Westermann, *Lamentations: Issues and Interpretations,* trans. Charles Muenchow (Edinburgh: T. & T. Clark, 1994), pp. 1-23, 58-61, 81-85; but see E. Gerstenberger, *Psalms, Part 2, and Lamentations,* FOTL 15 (Grand Rapids: Eerdmans, 2001), pp. 477-478.

[6]The term קִינָה is found in 2 Sam 1:17; Jer 7:29; 9:10,20; Ezek 2:10; 26:17; 27:2,32; 28:12; 32:2,16; Amos 5:1; 8:10.

[7]One should be skeptical about attempts to modify an existing text to get it to "fit" the typical structure of a lament. Westermann, for example, argues that Lamentations 3 is an amalgam of parts of laments that have been artificially brought together under an acrostic rubric, while Lamentations 4 is not a true "lament" because it lacks a section of petition (Westermann, *Lamentations,* pp. 172-173, 197).

David's *qînāh* over Saul's family contains no invocation of God (2 Sam 1:17). This does not mean, however, that he is not addressing God in his lament. Israelite listeners would be familiar with laments, and they would know to whom a lament is addressed. Similarly, some of the Lamentations consist primarily of complaints describing the suffering the people are enduring. Such complaints are made in assumption of the other components of a typical lament. They assume, for example, trust in a God who is compassionate and merciful. So, even though Lamentations 3 alone has a clear declaration of faith in the LORD's mercy, this does not mean that the other Lamentations do not assume such a faith.

Finally, it is often difficult for present-day readers to appreciate, or even accept, some of the extreme sentiments expressed in these laments. In particular, many modern Christians are uneasy with the imprecatory elements, where the speakers call on the LORD to bring on their neighbors and enemies the same level of suffering that the Israelites are currently experiencing. Christians have been told to love their enemies, to pray for those who persecute them. Such compassion seems inconceivable to these writers (cp. Psalm 137). We must keep in mind the immediate context in which these sentiments are verbalized, as well as the exact nature of the imprecations (that the LORD punish those who truly are deserving of divine punishment). Similarly, we must remember the immediate context when we confront the despondency that overshadows most of these laments. These are a people who have learned to evaluate their standing with God solely in terms of physical conditions. They might have promises of a return from exile, but they do not yet have any physical proof to back up those promises. They are like Abraham prior to the birth of Isaac. He had promises from God about descendants and land, but he did not see the physical proof to support those promises for many years. In that context, Abraham could occasionally express some uncertainty about those promises (see Gen 15:1-8). But such expressions of doubt did not prompt God to turn his back on Abraham. In the same way, the LORD is understanding of these writers when they express uncertainty about the fulfillment of his latest promises. The only difference for these writers is the history of God's past dealings with his people. They still have reason to hope in the LORD's mercies. This is implied by the fact they are voicing their griefs and grievances to him, and it is made explicit in the middle of chapter 3 (see Psalm 79).

Overshadowing that hope for the moment is the recognition of the righteousness of the LORD's present punishment on them. They are not uncertain that the LORD is merciful, but they are deeply concerned that their sinfulness has surpassed even his mercy. If their exile never ends, they cannot blame that on some failing of the LORD. This is their doing.

These laments should not be ignored, however, on the grounds that they reflect a sort of "uninformed" understanding of life. Quite the contrary, they demonstrate how important it is for believers to express their true feelings regarding community-wide (or individual) disasters. Laments like these reflect the true feelings of individuals when they are hurting deeply. God does not want such feelings ignored, pushed aside, diminished, or belittled in any way. He is a God who "weeps with those who weep." He is "the God of all comfort," accepting these expressions of grief, and then responding to them in a way that will bring comfort to those currently suffering. Even the questions raised at such a traumatic time are welcomed by him. "Lamentations is a book for those willing to risk honesty and who are able to admit that sometimes our experiences call into question our deepest held beliefs about God."[8] The resolution of those questions is not always rational, is not always in a verbal answer. It often comes in the form of future divine actions. In this case, the resolution will come when the Israelites return from Babylon and the LORD offers them another chance at being his chosen people. Until then, their uncertainty is quite understandable.

---

[8]John M. Bracke, *Jeremiah 30–52 and Lamentations,* Westminster Bible Companion (Louisville, KY: Westminster/John Knox Press, 2000), pp. 223-224.

OUTLINE

SELECTED BIBLIOGRAPHY

Bracke, John M. *Jeremiah 30–52 and Lamentations*. Westminster Bible Companion. Louisville, KY: Westminster/John Knox Press, 2000.

Davidson, Robert. *Jeremiah, Volume 2, and Lamentations*. Philadelphia: Westminster Press, 1985.

Gerstenberger, Erhard. *Psalms, Part 2, and Lamentations*. Forms of Old Testament Literature 15. Grand Rapids: Eerdmans, 2001.

Hillers, Delbert R. *Lamentations*. Second, Revised Edition. Anchor Bible 7A. New York: Doubleday, 1992.

Westermann, Claus. *Lamentations: Issues and Interpretations*. Trans. by Charles Muenchow. Edinburgh: T. & T. Clark, 1994.

LAMENTATIONS 1

I. JERUSALEM THE WIDOW (1:1-22)

This first acrostic personifies the city of Jerusalem as a woman who has recently been widowed. The initial speaker is an anonymous narrator, describing Jerusalem's grief and humiliation (vv. 1-9b,10-11b,17). He gives way by the second half of the poem to personified Jerusalem herself (vv. 9c,11c-16,18-22). The words of these two speakers can be further divided according to who is being addressed. Many of the narrator's lines are directed toward an undefined audience (probably, the nations; vv. 1-7,17), but some lines are directed toward the LORD (vv. 8-9b,10-11b).[1] Jerusalem addresses the same undefined audience in the majority of her statements (vv. 12-16,18-19), but the isolated lines at the end of verses 9 and 11 are directed toward the LORD, as are the final three verses (vv. 20-22). The mixing of speakers and addressees in this chapter suggests that it might be helpful to read it as a short play or some other dramatization.[2]

There is only a general progression of thought in this first chapter, from one block of material to the next (vv. 1-7,8-11,12-16,17,18-19,20-22). Each block, however, should be read as a single thought, without expecting any linear progression within it.[3] The first seven verses describe personified Jerusalem's suffering. There is a shift in verse 8 to a listing of charges against Jerusalem. This shift might denote a change in addressees, from a generic audience to the LORD. It is obvious that the LORD is the addressee in verse 10, but

---

[1]See below for an explanation of these delineations.

[2]But see D. Hillers, *Lamentations,* AB (New York: Doubleday, 1992), p. 80. He says such a proposal "seems speculative to the extreme."

[3]Some despair completely of finding a structure in this chapter. For various proposals, see Westermann, *Lamentations*, p. 114; Hillers, *Lamentations*, pp. 78-79.

most commentators do not entertain the possibility that he is also being addressed in verses 8-9b and 11a-b. It would make sense in the lines surrounding verse 10, however, to have the speaker advocating to the LORD on behalf of Jerusalem, hoping to evoke the LORD's sympathy on her behalf. It would also make the most sense to have Jerusalem's own impassioned pleas to the LORD (vv. 9c,11c) voiced in the context of an address by the narrator to the LORD. The second plea leads into the first extended speech by Jerusalem (vv. 12-16). This is directed toward the undefined audience (a jury of sorts), again describing the unparalleled suffering the city has endured. Verse 17 provides a brief interlude which stresses that Jerusalem's suffering has been "decreed" for her by the LORD in his general judgment against the nation of Judah (see below). Jerusalem now confesses her own sinfulness, calling on the audience to heed her own example as a warning of what soon could befall them (vv. 18-19). Finally, she turns to the LORD, describing her (well-deserved) affliction and calling on him to extend his hand of judgment to others who are just as deserving of it (vv. 20-22).

1:1-7 These opening verses introduce the reader to an incredible scene. A once great lady has become a **widow**, a **queen** has become a servant girl; **her friends . . . have become her enemies,**[4] her rivals have gained the upper hand,[5] **her children** have been carried off, and her many possessions have been lost. What makes it all the more horrifying is the absence of any comforting hand. There is no shoulder to cry on, no heart to grieve along with her in her time of loss. Instead, the neighbors only laugh in derision.[6]

There are hints here of allusions to some important women in Israel's history. Jerusalem had been a **queen** (שָׂרָתִי, *śārāṯî*), a term from which "Sarah" is derived. The intent might be to link personified Jerusalem to a woman who in some sense embodied the whole nation (cp. Jer 31:15). The laughter with which Sarah greeted her child (Gen 21:1-6) is now reversed in the grief of Jerusalem. There

---

[4]This is a common motif in laments. Hillers, *Lamentations*, pp. 81-82.

[5]Verse 5a reads more literally, "Her foes have become [the] head." This echoes Deut 28:43-44. Bracke, *Jeremiah 30–52 and Lamentations*, p. 195.

[6]Verse 7 is the only one that consists of four lines rather than three. Most interpreters propose removing the second line in the Hebrew, leaving "Jerusalem remembers the days of her affliction and wandering, when her people fell into enemy hands, and there was no one . . ." Westermann, *Lamentations*, p. 112; Hillers, *Lamentations*, pp. 68-69.

are also terms that might evoke memories of the life of Ruth. The term for Jerusalem's **friends** (רֵעֶהָ, *rēʿêhā*; v. 2) is derived from the root for the name "Ruth." At the same time, Jerusalem's anguish is **bitter** (מַר, *mar*), a term which Naomi applies to herself (Ruth 1:20). The ultimate hopefulness of that story is crushed here, however, because Jerusalem's "friends" (the "Ruths" in her life) have become her enemies (see below).

1:8-11 The reference to the neighbors' laughter seems to move the narrator to direct his comments to the LORD in the succeeding verses. He acknowledges that **Jerusalem has sinned greatly**; nevertheless, is the LORD not embarrassed by his people's suffering? His primary responsibility toward his city is that of protection. Yet he has allowed many nations to plunder her, even permitting them into his personal **sanctuary**. The fact that he is responsible for protecting his people is why, even though the LORD has brought their suffering on them, they still call twice to him to relieve them of their distress (vv. 9c,11c). Parts of these verses imply sexual connotations, which would serve to heighten the urgency of these pleas. Jerusalem has been exposed naked to those around her (v. 8; cp. Hos 2:10; Ezek 16:35-39); a loving husband would not allow this to continue. She is **unclean** (v. 8), probably in reference to a female discharge (Lev 20:21).[7] This brings embarrassment on her husband as well, because a good husband would provide her with clean clothes. The description of the desecration of the temple (v. 10) hints at sexual violations of a wife by strangers. A husband's greatest responsibilities toward his wife involved his protection and honoring of her sexuality. Such a graphic description of the dishonoring of a wife would be the most likely to rekindle a sense of obligation in the heart of the angriest of husbands. One would expect him to avenge this violation of his wife, but no such response seems forthcoming.

1:12-16 Jerusalem's remarks highlight the intensity of her **suffering** and that her suffering has been **brought on** her by **the LORD**. The intensity of her suffering is brought out in the numerous references to parts of the human body in these verses. The LORD sends destruction into her **bones**. He has tripped her **feet** (v. 13). He has placed the burden of her **sins** on her **neck** (v. 14), and her **eyes** are filled **with tears** (v. 16). The fact that he has inflicted her with these injuries intensifies their pain. Her suffering is incomparable because

---

[7]Hillers, *Lamentations*, pp. 85-86.

he — not her earthly enemies — has brought them on her (v. 12). They came **from on high** (v. 13), they were tied around her neck **by his hands** (v. 14), they were produced **in his winepress** (v. 15), and they were inflicted on **the Virgin Daughter of Judah**. The self-righteousness of such a name is glaring, but it explains why she weeps so bitterly (v. 16). She was not expecting such harsh treatment from her husband. She is looking for sympathy from anyone, for something that will give her a reason to go on living, something that will **restore her spirit**.[8]

1:17 This brief interlude plays a vital role in the progression of thought in the chapter. This is the only time in the chapter that the suffering people are referred to in the masculine gender (as **Jacob**). This serves as a sort of reminder to the feminine city of **Jerusalem** that she is part of a larger body, the nation of Judah. It is the nation which the LORD is punishing, and Jerusalem is a part of that nation. If the LORD is justified in destroying the nation, then he is justified in destroying the city as well. It is clear from Jeremiah (Jer 24:1-10) and Ezekiel (Ezek 11:14-16) that many of the people of Jerusalem had come to see their city as inviolable, as an area that enjoyed a special promise of protection. Even if the rest of the nation were destroyed, they expected Jerusalem to remain, as it had in the days of Hezekiah. But Jerusalem is not inviolable. It too **has become an unclean thing**; therefore, just like any other wicked city, it deserves to be destroyed.

1:18-19 The city finally acknowledges the justness of her suffering. She had **rebelled** against a **righteous** husband. He has been treating her only as she deserves. She points out her suffering now as an object lesson to other cities. A righteous God shows his righteousness by bringing suffering on the wicked.

1:20-22 It is only a small step, then, for Jerusalem to turn from repentance to a two-part appeal to God for vindication. The first part is that he be merciful, so she points out her sufferings to him (v. 20). There is always reason to appeal to the LORD's mercy (see 2 Sam 12:22), so the people do so here, in spite of the justness of their punishment. The second part of their appeal is that he will further prove his righteousness by punishing all the other nations which deserve it (vv. 21-22). She is suffering for her **sins**, and justly

---

[8]The expression, "restore my spirit" (v. 16), uses the same phraseology as the expression, "to keep themselves alive" (vv. 11,19).

so; but this implies that others should suffer as well.[9] This would bring her some measure of comfort, the comfort in knowing that she is not the only recipient of God's righteous wrath. Furthermore, we know from other texts that Jerusalem's neighbors taunted her when she fell, gloating over the misery she endures (2:15-16). Those insults would fuel the sentiments expressed here (cp. Ps 79:9-13; 137:7-9).

On a different level than this general progression, there are numerous verbal links present in this acrostic lament.[10] The most common of these come together at the end of the acrostic to bring out the sense of grief the people are feeling. The first to be introduced utilizes various forms of the Hebrew term רַב (rab, "great, large"). Jerusalem had been **full of people** (רַבָּתִי עָם, rabbāthî 'am); she was **great among the nations** (רַבָּתִי בַגּוֹיִם, rabbāthî baggôyim; v. 1). Now she has been forced into **harsh labor** (רֹב עֲבוֹדָה, rōb 'ăbôdāh, "great work"; v. 3) because of **her many sins** (רֹב פְּשָׁעֶיהָ, rōb pᵉšā'êhā, "great transgressions"; v. 5). The only thing about her that remains "great" is her **many groans** (רַבּוֹת אַנְחֹתַי, rabbôth 'anḥōthay; v. 22). There is similar significance to the repetition in this chapter of the term for "groan" (אָנַח, 'ānah). The priests of Jerusalem **groan** (נֶאֱנָחִים, ne'ĕnāḥîm; v. 4); Jerusalem **herself groans** because of her deep sense of shame (נֶאֱנָחָה, ne'enḥāh; v. 8); she looks for others to comfort her because of her **groaning** (נֶאֱנָחָה, ne'ĕnāḥāh; v. 21), but no one responds; and the chapter ends with a reference to her many **groans** ('anḥōthay; v. 22), as her physical and emotional strength seeps away.[11]

The absence of "comfort" is probably the most obvious verbal theme in the chapter. Lady Jerusalem says at the end of her first speech, **No one is near to comfort me** (רָחַק מִמֶּנִּי מְנַחֵם, rāḥaq mimmennî mᵉnahēm, "Far from me is a comforter"; v. 16). This is similar to a statement made twice previously by the narrator: **There is none**

---

[9]Bracke, *Jeremiah 30–52 and Lamentations*, p. 202; Westermann, *Lamentations*, pp. 206-208.

[10]I am not commenting on the single repetition of several expressions; for example, "the LORD has brought her grief" (vv. 5,12), "unclean thing" (vv. 8,17), "my suffering" (vv. 12,18), "faint" (vv. 13,22), etc.

[11]One could point to several other synonymous terms, which together form a constellation of expressions for anguish. Jerusalem "weeps bitterly" (v. 2), her roads "mourn" (v. 4), her maidens "grieve" (v. 4), her sons are "destitute" (v. 16), her heart is "disturbed" and "faint" (vv. 20,22), etc.

to comfort her (לָהּ מְנַחֵם אֵין, *'ên mənaḥēm lāh*; vv. 2,9; also, **there was no one to help her**, v. 7). The same statement is repeated a third time in the narrator's transitional interlude in verse 17, and one final time by Jerusalem in her closing appeal to the LORD (v. 21). Instead of a "comforter," in each case, Jerusalem is confronted by her **enemies** (vv. 2,9,16,21; "foes" in v. 17). The choice of this term for "comfort" (נִחַם, *niḥam*) is intriguing. Several biblical writers use it to describe the LORD's feelings when he changes his plans (Jer 18:7-10). It connotes a change both in one's thought and in one's attitude. The repeated use of the term here suggests that the feelings of grief are so profound, they will never go away.[12]

---

[12]R. Davidson, *Jeremiah, Volume 2, and Lamentations* (Philadelphia: Westminster, 1985), p. 180. These statements find their counterpoint in Isaiah 40:1-2, which opens a section of that book addressed to those about to return from Babylonian Exile. Isaiah (and history) points to how God will comfort his people in the days ahead. See also Isaiah 51:17-20.

LAMENTATIONS 2

II. COMPLAINT AND APPEAL (2:1-22)

This lament places a much greater emphasis on the LORD's role in the destruction of Jerusalem.[1] In fact, the Babylonians receive no credit at all for what has happened. This is strictly an act of divine wrath. This recounting of evidence of the LORD's anger evokes a parallel tone of anger, directed toward the LORD, in the people's words at the end of the poem. Such a tone is not "irreverent" or "unbiblical." It is an honest reflection of the feelings of a people who have lost all. To speak otherwise would be hypocritical. One must not miss, however, the faith that is intertwined with such expressions of anger. They are directed toward the LORD in anticipation of his sympathetic response.

> "Trust in him *at all times*, O people,
> pour out your hearts to him,
> for God is our refuge." (Ps 62:8).

The poem falls into four parts. The first (vv. 1-10) contains the poet's description of the destruction the LORD has angrily brought on his people. An unidentified speaker then grieves in the first person over the pitiable suffering endured by the inhabitants of Jerusalem, addressing the entire city as a woman as he speaks (vv. 11-16). The third part returns to the theme of the first, but the poet now infuses his description with a call to the sufferers to appeal to the LORD for mercy (vv. 17-19). The poem then concludes in ways that remind one of the first poem, as Jerusalem herself expresses

---

[1]Westermann identifies this as an "accusation against God" (*Lamentations*, pp. 91-95, 147), which is a common component of laments. This label might be a bit misleading, however, because the purpose is to evoke pity, not to convict of wrong; "complaint" is better. Gerstenberger, *Psalms, Part 2, and Lamentations*, p. 485.

grief over the loss of her inhabitants, implicitly seeking the LORD's mercy (vv. 20-22).[2]

2:1-10 The predominant message in the poet's remarks in this first part is the ferocity of the LORD's destruction. The poet identifies the LORD as the author of their destruction twenty-eight times in these thirty lines.[3] He **covered** the city **with the cloud of his anger,**[4] and he **hurled** the city down (v. 1). He acted **without pity** (v. 2) and **in** [his] **fierce anger** (vv. 3,6), **pouring out his wrath like fire** (v. 4), a **fire that consumes everything** (v. 3). He has **swallowed** the city (v. 5), **laid waste** to it, **destroyed** it (v. 6). He **rejected** his people (v. 7).[5] He **has withdrawn his right hand** of protection (v. 3),[6] using it instead to draw back the bowstring to shoot arrows at them (v. 4). Now he does not **withdraw his hand from destroying** them (v. 8). Augmenting this message of the ferocity of the destruction is the undercurrent of references to the fact that this is the LORD's people, that the people he has so ferociously destroyed had been very dear to him. The writer repeatedly refers to Jerusalem as **the Daughter of Zion** (vv. 1,4,8,10; cp. vv. 13,18).[7] This city was his **footstool** (v. 1), the place he had always guarded with his own right hand (v. 3). This had been **his dwelling**, **his place of meeting** (v. 6), **his altar**, **his sanctuary**, his **house** (v. 7). Sadly, this "dream home" had turned out to be a disaster, so the owner has been forced to demolish it completely and start over. All the memories, good and bad, of life in that first home now lie in a heap of rubble at his feet.[8]

---

[2]Gerstenberger suggests it is helpful to read this poem as a liturgical performance, as others have suggested for the first poem (see above). *Psalms, Part 2, and Lamentations*, p. 490.

[3]Bracke, *Jeremiah 30–52 and Lamentations*, p. 206.

[4]For other renderings of this line, see Hillers, *Lamentations*, p. 96.

[5]The charge that the LORD has "rejected" his people is found in several laments in the Psalms (Ps 43:2; 44:9,23; 60:1,10; 74:1; 77:7; 88:14; 108:11). The terms for "rejected" and "abandoned" are used in succession in Ps 89:38-39, in reference to the LORD's possible rejection of the Davidic monarch (1 Chr 28:9). The same thought is expressed with a different term in 1 Samuel 15:23 and 16:1.

[6]There are several references to "right hand" in military contexts as a symbol of strength (Exod 15:6,12; Ps 17:7; 18:35; 20:6; 21:9; 44:3; 60:5; 77:10; 78:54; 98:1; Isa 41:10).

[7]This is a rather common title for Jerusalem (2 Kgs 19:31; Isa 1:8; 10:32; 16:1; 37:22; 62:11; Jer 4:31; 6:2,23; Micah 1:13; 4:8,10,13; Zeph 3:14; Zech 2:10; 9:9).

[8]In many subtle ways, this poem hints at the undoing of the covenants the

The results have been devastating to people and property. The **splendor of Israel** is gone (v. 1), **every horn**[9] has been cut off (v. 3), **all who were pleasing to the eye** are no longer to be seen (v. 4). The festive holiday gatherings with which the people worshiped the LORD have come to an end (v. 6). All **dwellings, palaces,** and **strongholds** have been demolished. **Princes** (vv. 2,9), **king and priest** (vv. 6,9), and **prophets** (v. 9) lie silent. The few commoners who remain, from **the elders** to **the young women,** sit on the ground and mourn in silence (v. 10).

2:11-16 The identity of the speaker in this section is uncertain. It could be the poet, speaking as an aggrieved citizen of Jerusalem.[10] The prophets speak at times in this way on behalf of the Israelites, expressing their common grief at what has happened (Isa 30:26; Jer 6:14; 8:11,21). This writer could be doing the same here. This might also be the LORD speaking.[11] If so, there is an added element of anguish here. The reference to Israel as "my people" is most often associated with the language of marriage ("I will be your God, and you will be my people"; Deut 26:16-19; Jer 30:22; 31:1,33; 32:38; Hos 2:23; Zech 13:9). This suggests that this punishment of his people was an act of love, that he has brought tremendous grief on himself in destroying this city (see Jer 4:19-22; 15:7). Either of these interpretations flows naturally from the first section.

The speaker conveys the depth of his grief by describing the plight of Jerusalem's **children**. They are **faint**, dying **in the streets**. Some of the poignancy of the picture being drawn here is lost in the translation. The term for **infants** in verse 11 is more literally, "nursing child" (יוֹנֵק, *yōnēq*). Their lives **ebb away** ("are poured out in all directions") as they lie motionless **in their mothers' arms** (חֵיק, *ḥêq*, "bosom"). No image tugs harder at the heart than that of mothers unable to provide food for their starving children. We have seen pictures of such scenes from destitute parts of Africa and Asia. The

---

LORD had established with his people. Davidson, *Jeremiah, Volume 2, and Lamentations*, pp. 182-183.

[9]An animal uses its horns for both defense and attack. The "horn" is often used to refer to those among a people who protect the rest from attack. It implies strength and courage. Hillers, *Lamentations*, pp. 97-98.

[10]Westermann, *Lamentations*, pp. 153-154; Bracke, *Jeremiah 30–52 and Lamentations*, p. 209; Hillers, *Lamentations*, p. 106; Davidson, *Jeremiah, Volume 2, and Lamentations*, p. 185.

[11]Gerstenberger, *Psalms, Part 2, and Lamentations*, pp. 487-488.

mother, dying of starvation herself, stares blankly ahead, unable to nurse the appallingly thin and weeping child in her arms (see 4:3-4).[12] There is nothing like it, nothing to which it can be compared, so that the sufferer can find little comfort in the possibility that others might understand her grief. This grief cannot be fathomed; it is **as deep as the sea** (v. 13). In view of the deaths of the children of Jerusalem, it is no wonder the people conclude, "Our bones are dried up and our hope is gone" (Ezek 37:11).

The speaker blames this situation on the **false** prophets of Jerusalem (v. 14). This reminds one of the numerous occasions on which Jeremiah harshly criticizes his fellow **prophets** for not endeavoring to change the wicked practices of the people (Jer 5:30-31; 6:10-14; 8:10-12; 12:16; 4:11-16; 23:9-40; 28:1-17; cp. Ezek 13:1-23).[13] What Jeremiah warned about has now come to pass. Adding insult to injury is the way Jerusalem's neighbors are relishing the sight of Jerusalem's suffering (vv. 15-16).[14] This explains in part the sentiments of vengeance expressed in 1:20-22.

2:17-19 This short section recapitulates some of the main themes expressed earlier in this poem. Contrary to the promises of the false prophets, this destruction (not the deliverance they promised) is the fulfillment of the LORD's will.[15] Their enemies gloat over their misery. They cry without relief, as their children die in the street. Added to this recapitulation is a series of imperatives, calling on the sufferers to appeal to the LORD, the one who has brought this suffering on them, to relieve them of their suffering (see Jer 9:10; Ps 62:8). This sets the stage for the closing section of entreaty.

2:20-22 The words of Jerusalem try to "put a face" on the calamity that has befallen her. It affects everyone. Mothers are reduced to cannibalizing their own **children** (see Deut 28:53-57; 2 Kgs 6:24-31); **prophets** and **priests** die in the performance of their rituals. **Young and old**, male and female; all die. Yes, the city's suffering is incom-

---

[12]Davidson, *Jeremiah, Volume 2, and Lamentations*, p. 185.

[13]The Hebrew word for "worthless" (v. 14) is better translated "whitewashed" (see Ezek 13:8-10). Hillers, *Lamentations*, p. 100; Davidson, *Jeremiah, Volume 2, and Lamentations*, pp. 185-186; Westermann, *Lamentations*, p. 145.

[14]The last line of verse 15 is a quote from Psalm 48:2, a psalm glorifying Jerusalem. Its use by Jerusalem's enemies is a merciless slap in the face. It would be like using a line from the song, "New York, New York," to gloat over the destruction of the World Trade Center.

[15]Westermann, *Lamentations*, p. 155.

parable; but that is because the LORD has treated this people more harshly than he has ever treated a people before. He has shown no **pity**, only **anger**. There are **terrors on every side** (v. 22). The plural noun in the phrase intends to connote something more severe than the "total" misery Jeremiah pronounced on his audiences (Jer 6:25; 20:3-6; 46:5; 49:29). In the long and cruel history of conquests, this one is the most appalling.[16]

---

[16]For references to laments over the destruction of other cities, see Hillers, *Lamentations*, pp. 102, 105-106; Gerstenberger, *Psalms, Part 2, and Lamentations*, pp. 486-490.

LAMENTATIONS 3

III. COMMUNAL SUFFERING GIVEN A FACE (3:1-66)

This is the most complex lament of the book. It too is acrostic in form, and it contains the same number of lines as the other three acrostics. The most obvious difference is that the acrostic pattern has been tripled. The lines appear as tricola (groups of three lines). Each of the three lines of a tricolon begins with the same letter of the alphabet. Each of the first three verses begins with 'aleph, each of the next three verses begins with *beth*, etc. The analysis which follows assumes the poetic unity of each tricolon. The bigger difference in this lament is that it is presented as personal lament, whereas the others are communal laments (vv. 42-47 are part of a communal lament quoted by the individual).[1] The speaker is not Judah personified, but perhaps one who embodies in his own sufferings the sufferings that the entire nation is experiencing. This is similar in some respects to the figure of the suffering servant in Isaiah 40–55, except that this speaker does not suffer on behalf of others. This speaker's suffering is representative, not vicarious. He might be a royal or prophetic figure (see on v. 1), but there is no redemptive aspect to the suffering he endures. Some have interpreted the speaker as a collective, as the whole nation speaking as an individual entity. (There have been parallel discussions regarding the "laments of the individual" in the Psalms.) In this sense, the speaker is really no different from the "I" of Jerusalem in Lamentations 1:12-16.[2]

The overall progression of thought in the acrostic is similar to that found in the first two. There is not so much a flow from verse to verse as there is a flow from section to section. There appear to

---

[1]Gerstenberger, *Psalms, Part 2, and Lamentations*, pp. 494-495.

[2]For further discussions of authorship, see Hillers, *Lamentations*, pp. 120-123.

be three basic movements in the poem, from hopeless despair over
suffering (vv. 1-18) to reassurance of the LORD's mercy (vv. 22-36) to
a petition for relief through divine punishment on others (vv. 40-
66).[3] In between these are two transitional pieces (vv. 19-21,37-39),
forming bridges of logic between the sections. The first section is a
"complaint," describing how the LORD has afflicted this one man.
The first bridge (vv. 19-21) initially appears to be a simple continuation of this as he talks about "remembering" his sufferings. But
there is a shift by the end of this tricolon. It is as if the speaker cannot think about "remembering" without being reminded of other
passages which encourage believers to "remember" the merciful
deeds of the LORD.[4] This seems to open a curtain in his thoughts,
allowing in a ray of hope, as the tone becomes decidedly optimistic
in the verses that follow (vv. 22-36). Such optimism is heavily muted
in the other laments of this book. The speaker declares that, in spite
of his suffering at the hand of the LORD, he still believes in the ultimate mercy and goodness of the LORD. These qualities reside at the
heart of the LORD's character. As the speaker reflects further on the
LORD's character, as revealed in many passages of the Old Testament (Exod 34:6-7; Num 14:18-19; Jonah 4:1-2; etc.), he realizes the
righteousness of his suffering.[5] The LORD is merciful, but he also
punishes sin. A statement of the righteousness of the LORD's anger
against sin (vv. 37-39) forms a bridge to a call for the LORD to punish others, who have been adding insult to Israel's injury. Thus, verses 37-39 set the stage for the final lengthy section of petition (vv. 40-
66). This petition falls into two parts. The first part presents the
speaker verbalizing a model communal lament for the whole nation
(vv. 40-48). The second part resumes the perspective of the individual speaker alone (vv. 49-66). Both parts of this section contain a
mixture of complaint about present sufferings at the hands of
Israel's enemies and petition for vindication through divine judgment on those enemies. Surely those enemies are no less deserving

---

[3]There is no consensus about the structure of this chapter. One can consult the various commentaries for other proposals. On the more extreme
side, Westermann (*Lamentations*, pp. 168-169) argues that the different sections come from disparate writers whose works have been brought together here. This seems far-fetched, in light of the unifying nature of the
acrostic.
[4]Gerstenberger, *Psalms, Part 2, and Lamentations*, p. 493.
[5]Hillers, *Lamentations*, pp. 128-129.

of punishment from a righteous God.[6] There is a strong undertone of confidence in the LORD in these lines, a confidence brought on by the remarks in verses 22-36.

3:1-18 This opening section paints a graphic picture of personal humbling at the hands of the LORD. The actual inflicting of the wounds was done by humans, but they were simply acting on the LORD's behalf. The notion that the LORD disciplines through personal hardship is found in the remarks of Job (Job 9:33-34; 21:9). A specifically military aspect of this notion goes back at least to the days of Israel's judges, when "the anger of the LORD burned against Israel" repeatedly, provoking him to discipline them with their enemies. The present suffering is yet another example of such discipline.[7] There is a strong connection to be made between this verse and Isaiah's remarks concerning the Assyrian invaders of his day. The LORD describes that nation as "the rod of my anger" and "the club of my wrath" (Isa 10:5; cp. 10:24). There is in these lines the possibility of a direct allusion to the LORD's punishment of the Davidic monarch. He warns David through Nathan that he will punish a disobedient member of the Davidic line "with the rod of men" (2 Sam 7:14; Ps 89:32). Two centuries later, Micah declares that a foreign power "will strike Israel's ruler . . . with a rod" (Micah 5:1). The speaker in Lamentations 3:1 might be intending to relate that prophecy to himself. If so, this would imply that he is a member of the royal family (Jeconiah?) or a spokesman for that family. This would not be surprising because kings often stand as representatives for their nations. What happens to him is one example of the kinds of things happening to all his people. There is also the strong possibility that this is a prophetic figure. This chapter is attributed more often than the others to Jeremiah. Not only is there the longstanding tradition of Jeremianic authorship for the entire book, but there are strong similarities between some of the lines of this lament and some of the words of Jeremiah (see below). This is not strong enough to argue for definitive proof that Jeremiah is the author, however, because there are similarities to other prophetic writings as well.

---

[6]Hillers sees all of verses 42-66 as a "collective prayer." A shifting back and forth between the individual and the group is not uncommon in laments. Ibid., pp. 131-133.

[7]There are several references to a "rod" being used to discipline misbehaving children (Prov 10:13; 22:15; 29:15).

One can see the same connectedness between the individual and the group in the verses which follow. The references to being placed **in darkness** (vv. 2,6) are the reverse of the remarks of Isaiah in Isaiah 9:2. Isaiah foresaw the people's transition from death to life, and this writer has seen his own transition from life to death. (Similarly, this might be seen as the "negative" of Psalm 23.)[8] Just as Samuel warned the whole nation when the first king was appointed (1 Sam 12:15), the LORD has **turned his hand against** this individual who has ignored his commandments (v. 3).[9]

Some negative phrases in these verses are better understood in comparison with their positive counterparts. For example, the LORD has made the speaker's **skin and . . . flesh . . . old** (v. 4), rather than renewing his life (Job 10:10-12; cp. Ps 38:2-3). He has **walled** him **in** and **barred** his **way** (vv. 7-9), rather than putting him in a "broad" or "spacious" land (Exod 3:8; 2 Sam 22:20; Neh 9:35). The LORD has made his way **crooked** (v. 9), rather than "smooth" or "straight" (Ps 5:8; 107:7; Prov 3:6; 8:15; Jer 31:9). Rather than filling his people with "abundance" and "bounty" (Jer 31:14), he has filled this man with **bitter herbs** and **gall** (v. 15).

Other lines allude to statements of despair voiced by previous biblical writers. The mention of an ambush by a **bear** or **lion** (v. 10) most easily reminds one of Amos's warning of the certainty of Israel's destruction in Amos 5:18-19 (cp. Hos 13:8). This man is a **laughingstock** among his **people** (v. 14), just as Jeremiah was derided by his own relatives (Jer 20:7). Just like Job (Job 3:26), this man is **deprived of peace** (v. 17).

The final verse of this section (v. 18) raises a couple of themes which set the stage for the hopeful sentiments of the following section. The speaker feels that his **splendor is gone**. This is an intriguing declaration. The term for "splendor" (נֵצַח, nēṣaḥ) is used elsewhere in this sense only of God (1 Sam 15:29; 1 Chr 29:11). Its more common meaning is "perpetuity" or "everlastingness" (Jer 3:5; 15:18; 50:39). This implies that what was expected to be eternal has now been brought to an end. He clarifies his understanding of this in the second half of the verse by speaking of what **I had hoped from the LORD**. The "everlastingness" to which he laid claim was

---

[8]Hillers, *Lamentations*, pp. 124-125; Davidson, *Jeremiah, Volume 2, and Lamentations*, pp. 190-191.

[9]Hillers, *Lamentations*, pp. 124-125.

something promised from the LORD. Is the LORD not eternal? Are his promises not eternal? This is what is at stake.

3:19-21 The turn in the speaker's thinking comes with the repetition of **remember** (זָכַר, *zākar*) in verses 19-20. His "short-term memory" fixes his thoughts on his present sufferings. He seems incapable of thinking of anything else. But this apparently is a man steeped in the language of Deuteronomy. He cannot use the word "remember" twice without being reminded of the many places there that Moses encourages the people to use their "long-term memory" to "remember" their past experiences with the LORD. They are repeatedly told, "Remember that you were slaves in Egypt and that the LORD your God brought you out" (Deut 5:15; 15:15; 24:18,22; cp. 7:18; 8:18).[10] The current suffering endured by this man and his fellow Israelites is similar to the enslavement in Egypt, so they should be encouraged by the Exodus to hope in the possibility of a similar salvation now (cp. Psalm 77).

3:22-36 Hope is the theme of this next section. Suffering such as this man is experiencing is not eternal. What is eternal is the LORD's **love**, his **compassions**, his **faithfulness** (vv. 22-23). This suffering is like the darkness of the night; but just as the sun rises **every morning**, the LORD will faithfully show love and mercy to his people.[11] This is a temporary **yoke** that the speaker must bear (v. 27); but it has been imposed on him by **the LORD** (v. 28), the God who is "compassionate and gracious, abounding in love and faithfulness" (Exod 34:6).[12] Yes, he punishes the guilty, but for a very short time, in comparison with his displays of love. Therefore, the sufferer must endure, realizing that the LORD will not show the one (anger) without the other (love; vv. 28-33).

Verses 34-36 have a dual meaning, moving the speaker toward the second bridge in verses 37-39. The speaker asks rhetorically if a

---

[10]This memory was supposed to induce obedience to his will (Deut 16:12), but the people have stubbornly resisted that (see Jer 11:6-8). The confession of sin in the second bridge (vv. 37-42) brings out this thought, setting the stage for the subsequent petition for divine mercy and vindication.

[11]This is the heart of the speaker's hope. He remembers the LORD's past actions, "therefore I will wait" (v. 21). The LORD's mercy comes like the rising of the sun, "therefore I will wait for him" (v. 24). The wording of these two clauses is identical, except the latter adds the prepositional phrase, "for him."

[12]Bracke, *Jeremiah 30–52 and Lamentations*, pp. 217-218.

merciful LORD would not take notice of oppression. The obvious answer is yes. In asking this, the speaker would initially identify with the oppressed. He is one of the **prisoners in the land** of Babylon. His rights have been denied, he has been **deprived of justice**. Yet, because he is being honest with himself, he realizes that these references to oppression also apply to those whom the Israelites had been oppressing over the preceding centuries. The prophets persistently talked of the injustices committed by certain Israelites against their brothers and neighbors. The LORD had "seen" those injustices (Isa 5:7; Jer 7:11; 13:27; Hos 6:10), and so he had brought punishment on Israel.[13]

3:37-39 The speaker generalizes this in the second bridge. The LORD sends **both calamities and good things**, in consideration of his self-proclaimed character (Exod 34:6-7; Isa 45:7) and in reaction to the good and bad deeds of people. The LORD is being true to his divine character when he punishes sin. This speaker is honest enough with himself to realize that his present suffering is deserved punishment, not a mistake. Therefore, he should not complain of unjust treatment.[14] This also has a dual meaning, though. The LORD is just to punish his people when they sin, but he should be even-handed in his punishment. This means he should be just as "just" with the other nations, because they are just as sinful as Israel. It is this line of thinking which drives the remainder of the lament.

3:40-66 The speaker now calls on his fellow Israelites to take inventory of their past deeds, abandon any sinful ways, and **return to the LORD** (vv. 40-42). They are finally admitting their guilt, as

---

[13]Westermann contends that the parenetic style and doctrine of silent suffering espoused in the central portion of this acrostic do not fit the time of the early exile. He dates it instead to the days of Ezra and Nehemiah (*Lamentations*, pp. 177-181; cp. Gerstenberger, *Psalms, Part 2, and Lamentations*, p. 496). This is subjective, however, and is based in large part on an assumed postexilic date for the Book of Deuteronomy. One can just as easily argue for an earlier date. Like Jeremiah, this writer calls to repentance an audience that blames its suffering on the sins of others (Jer 31:27-30; cp. Ezek 18:1-2). See Bracke, *Jeremiah 30–52 and Lamentations*, p. 221.

[14]Westermann argues that the middle of this chapter does not fit the rest because it undermines the speaker's right to complain at all (*Lamentations*, p. 180). But one always has the right to "complain" to the LORD, i.e., to lament when one is suffering. What is denied here is the legitimacy of any accusation of unfairness on the part of the LORD. See Davidson, *Jeremiah, Volume 2, and Lamentations*, p. 197.

Jeremiah had encouraged his audience to do (Jer 3:6–4:4; cp. 5:20-
25; 14:19-22). They confess their sin and rebellion, which should
make them more accepting of their current punishment. The final
clause of verse 42 inserts another aspect of this, however, which is a
bit troubling to many modern Christians. The speaker sounds accusatory as he states, **and you have not forgiven**. It is true that the people have failed (the covenant) by sinning against the LORD, but their
words imply he in turn has "failed" by not forgiving them. Their
motivation for such an accusation is explained in the following verses (vv. 43-48).[15] It seems as if the LORD has specially singled them out.
He hurts them **without pity** (v. 43); he does not accept their prayers
(v. 44). This is not characteristic of the LORD (however, see Jer 11:11;
14:11-12; 15:1). If the LORD has forgiven them, their enemies should
be punished just as the Israelites are being punished. The absence
of such punishment leads Israel's neighbors to ridicule them and
their faith (v. 46), questioning the power and justice, if not the very
existence, of Israel's God. The LORD would be affirming his divine
nature and the merciful side of his character — to Israel and Israel's
neighbors — by punishing Israel's neighbors on behalf of Israel.
Ultimately, then, the final clause of verse 42 is not so much an accusation against the LORD as it is an appeal for vengeance against those
who have cheered the suffering of Israel (cp. Ps 79:12; 137:7-9).

The individual speaker resumes in verse 48. The close association of the suffering of this individual to the suffering of the people
as a whole furthers the impression that this is a royal or prophetic
individual, one who embodies the feelings of the whole nation in his
individual person. He begins his remarks with a description of his
grief (vv. 48-51). His **tears flow** like **streams** from his **eyes** (v. 48).
These are perennial streams, not just seasonal wadis which flow only
when it rains.[16] The cause of his grief is the pitiless abuse he has
received from his **enemies** (vv. 52-54). He was thrown into **a pit**

---

[15]Westermann, *Lamentations*, pp. 166-167; Davidson, *Jeremiah, Volume 2,
and Lamentations*, p. 199.

[16]There is a fundamental association in the Hebrew language between
streams and crying. The Hebrew word עַיִן (*'ayin*) is used to refer to "eye"
and "spring." A "spring" is an "eye" in the ground. The stream that flows
from a "spring" is the tear emerging from the "eye" and rolling down the
"cheek" of the land. What is more, *'ayin* is the name of a Hebrew letter ע
(originally depicted as an oval with a dot in its center), and each of verses
49-51 begins with an *'ayin*.

(figuratively? literally?) like Jeremiah (Jer 38:6-13; cp. Ps 35:7-8; 57:6), stoned, and almost drowned (see Ps 69:2; Jonah 2:3-5; Isa 8:6-8). This evoked from him an appeal to the LORD for rescue, an appeal which the LORD has acknowledged only verbally so far. The incompleteness of this response occupies most of the rest of the poem (vv. 55-64). Much like Abram between age 75 and 100, this person is having to live totally in faith, without having seen the fulfillment of what has been promised. He persists at this stage on the basis of what the LORD has told him, rather than what the LORD has actually done for him. He points out how the situation has not yet changed; the LORD has not answered the **insults**, **plots**, **whisper**ings, and **mock**ings of his enemies. They have no reason to rethink their remarks. So the speaker closes by petitioning once again for the LORD to avenge their words (vv. 64-66). Like Jeremiah, he calls on the LORD to "pay back" his enemies **for what** they **have done** to him (Jer 51:6,24). The final line then forms a loose inclusio back to verse 43. Clothed **in anger**, the LORD had **pursued** his people (see Jer 29:18); now, he is asked to **pursue** the speaker's (and Israel's) enemies **in anger and destroy them**.

LAMENTATIONS 4

IV. CONTRASTS (4:1-22)

The imagery in this fourth acrostic is quite elegant, making the grief of the nation all the more poignant. As in the previous chapters, there is a very general flow of thought from part to part, but not a tight movement forward within each part. Instead, the individual verses in each section work together as pieces of a larger picture, which should be viewed in its totality. The general flow of the poem is in four parts. The first part (vv. 1-10) describes the many stark contrasts between life in Jerusalem in its former times of glory and life in Jerusalem during the Babylonian siege and destruction.[1] The second part (vv. 11-16) provides an explanation for these dramatic changes: the LORD has punished his sinful people.[2] The third (vv. 17-20) expresses the collective sense of futility felt by the people, as they witness the collapse of their beloved city and capture of their king. Then, like the previous chapters, this one closes (vv. 21-22) with words of condemnation for one of Judah's jeering neighbors, Edom (see Obad 1-21).

4:1-10 The poet describes in haunting beauty the devastating reversals of fortune suffered by **my people** (vv. 3,6,10; see 2:11; 3:14,48; Jer 8:19-22). This section is full of contrasts. The people had been valued like **gold** or **sacred gems**, but now they are mere **clay** (vv. 1-2). They had eaten the finest foods and worn the finest clothes, but now they are dressed in rags and begging for food on the streets (v. 5). They were clean and well-tanned, but now they are blackened with **soot** and dirt, their skin **shriveled** by overexposure to the sun

---

[1]Westermann, *Lamentations*, p. 200; Bracke, *Jeremiah 30–52 and Lamentations*, p. 226.

[2]The final verses of the second and fourth parts are marked by a common phrase in Hebrew, "he will not continue to (לֹא יוֹסִיף לְ, *lō' yôsîph lĕ*) watch over them/exile them."

(vv. 7-8).[3] The overwhelming concern is with food. They are so hungry, they have less compassion for their young than **jackals** do (vv. 3-4; see 2:12; Job 39:13-16).[4] Jeremiah's repeated threats of "sword, famine, and plague" (Jer 15:2; 24:10; etc.) have been realized, and the people now realize **the sword** would have been their preferred means of death (v. 9), as they slowly starve to death (see Jer 52:6). The famine was so desperate, truly **compassionate women** – mothers who truly loved their children – were reduced to cannibalism (v. 10; see 2:20; Deut 28:53-57; Jer 19:9). The depth of inhumanity to which they have been driven is jarring. The grief sweeps over those who watch, seeming to drown them in its wake. This is worse than the suffering experienced by the people of **Sodom** (v. 6). There, death came swiftly; here, it is agonizingly and horrifyingly drawn out.

4:11-16 This part of the poem begins and ends with straightforward statements about **the LORD** bringing this devastation on Jerusalem. He was **vent**ing **his wrath, pour**ing **out** his **anger**, "scattering them."[5] The rhetoric of the inviolability of **Jerusalem** (see on Jer 7:1-15; 21:1-2) was well-publicized, which explains the surprise of other nations at the collapse of the city. This writer also charges Jerusalem's **priests** and **prophets** with provoking the LORD's anger (v. 13; see 2:14,20; Jer 2:26; 32:32). They have perpetuated the evil tradition of "shedding innocent blood" (2 Kgs 21:16; 24:4; Ps 106:38; Isa 1:15; Jer 7:6; 19:4; 22:3,17; 26:15). The priests should have been purifying with sacrificial blood, but instead they have **defiled** with **the blood of the righteous**. They have made people **unclean**, when they should have been cleansing them.[6] They are so impure, that even people of other nations will not allow them to enter their "camps" (see Lev 13:45-46; Isa 6:5). These **priests**, along with the **elders** of the various households and clans, should be the most honored individuals in the community (v. 16; see 1:19). Instead, they are dishonored and out of **favor**. This is made clearer in the Hebrew of 4:16, where one discovers a contrast being made between "the face of the LORD" and "the faces of the priests." The

---

[3]Hillers, *Lamentations*, pp. 147-148.

[4]Ibid., pp. 146-147.

[5]Gerstenberger, *Psalms, Part 2, and Lamentations*, p. 498.

[6]Davidson, *Jeremiah, Volume 2, and Lamentations*, pp. 205-206; Bracke, *Jeremiah 30–52 and Lamentations*, p. 232; Hillers, *Lamentations*, pp. 149-150.

"face of the LORD" is set against the priests, so that he has "scattered" them (see Lev 20:3,6; 26:17; Ps 34:16; 80:16; Ezek 14:8), while
"the faces of the priests" are not "lifted up" by others (see Deut
28:50; Job 22:8; 2 Kgs 5:1; Isa 3:3).[7]

4:17-20 One notices an immediate shift in speakers in verse 17.[8]
References to the people of Jerusalem move from the third person
(they/them/their) to the first person (we/us/our). Their comments
express their despair, but also the underlying problem of a misdi-
rected faith, which led to their destruction. The people despaired,
saying, **from our** watch**towers we watched** (צִפִּינוּ בְּצִפִּיָּתֵנוּ, *bᵉṣippiyyā-
thēnû ṣippînû*) **for help**, but none was coming (see 1:7). They were
stalked wherever they turned, they were **chased** by swift **pursuers**;
there was no place to hide, even in the **mountains** or **desert**. There
was no escaping the fierce anger of the LORD. This anger is made
more understandable when one steps back and notices the objects
of the people's faith in their moment of despair. They are looking
to some other **nation** to save them (v. 17). They rely on natural
obstacles (the mountains, the desert) to hide them from their attackers (e.g., Zedekiah, in Jer 39:4-5; 2 Kgs 25:4-6). They look to **the
LORD's anointed** – but not to the LORD himself – for protection.[9]
Jeremiah expresses a similar judgment when he accuses the people
of trusting in the temple (Jer 7:14).

4:21-22 The speaker now responds to the mocking applause **of
Edom** over the Babylonian victory. She had better celebrate while
she can, because she will soon have to "taste" the bitterness of defeat
herself (v. 21). Echoing the words of Jeremiah (Jer 25:15-17,20-21,27-

---

[7]Hillers, *Lamentations*, p. 143.

[8]Westermann says this entire section is about the capture of the king
(*Lamentations*, pp. 198-199, 203-205). Hillers marks verse 18 as the first reference to the pursuit of the king (*Lamentations*, p. 145).

[9]The evidence for this is that other passages speak of seeking shelter in
the shadow of the LORD (Ps 17:8; 36:7; 57:1; 63:7; 91:1; Isa 49:2; 51:16; Hos
14:7; cp. Isa 30:2-3). Each of the options mentioned here makes some sense
from a human standpoint, but the presupposition lying behind each is the
belief that the LORD cannot save them. Or is it that he "will not" save them?
This is possible, based on the preceding verses; but their turning to the
LORD's anointed suggests some lingering belief in the LORD's willingness to
help them.
On the metaphorical references to the king, see Hillers, *Lamentations*,
pp. 151-152. Gerstenberger interprets this as a frustrated messianic expectation (*Psalms, Part 2, and Lamentations*, p. 499).

29; 49:7-13),[10] he predicts humiliating drunkenness and nakedness for Edom (Hab 2:15-16). Edom, too, must "drink the cup of the LORD's wrath." The closing verse draws a strong poetic contrast between Edom and Israel, which is seen very clearly in Hebrew. "[The punishment for] your iniquity is completed, O Daughter of Zion" (תַּם עֲוֹנֵךְ בַּת־צִיּוֹן, *tam 'ăwōnēkā bath-ṣiyyōn*) is contrasted to "He punishes your iniquity, O Daughter of Edom" (פָּקַד עֲוֹנֵךְ בַּת־אֱדוֹם, *pāqad 'ăwōnēkā bath-'ĕdôm*). Jerusalem's humiliation is past, while Edom's is yet to begin. The same point is implied in the second half of each line. The LORD will not continue to **exile** (לְהַגְלוֹת, *l°haglôth*) Jerusalem, but Edom's sins will be **exposed** (גִּלָּה, *gillāh*). These are two forms of the same verb (גָּלָה, *gālāh*), as "exile" is a way of "exposing" a people to various hardships. Edom is taunting Jerusalem for what has happened, not realizing that the same fate will soon befall her. Perhaps Edom would have been more sympathetic, if she had realized this.

---

[10]There are some significant verbal links between these final lines and Jer 49:7-13 — "punish" (Jer 49:8; Lam 4:22), "uncover" (Jer 49:10; Lam 4:22), and "cup" (Jer 49:12; Lam 4:21). There are also shared references to "eagle" (Jer 49:22; Lam 4:19) and "Sodom" (Jer 49:18; Lam 4:6).

LAMENTATIONS 5

V. THE COMMUNAL COMPLAINT (5:1-22)

This final chapter breaks from the mold of its predecessors by not following an acrostic pattern; yet, it still consists of twenty-two verses. Much of the poem is like a typical communal lament, except for the uncertainty of its ending.[1] The invocation of God (v. 1) leads into a lengthy recounting of the troubles experienced by the lamenters (vv. 2-18). Verse 19 moves to a statement of trust in God, but this is countered by a dual question of the LORD's seeming non-response to the present distress (v. 20). Similarly, when the speakers finally voice their petition (v. 21), they couple it with an expression of doubt about the efficacy of such a petition (v. 22). Perhaps they are wasting their breath. Perhaps those who are mourning will not live to see another morning, radiant with the LORD's compassions (3:23). This precludes any thoughts of the typical pledge of thanksgiving for God's anticipated deliverance.

5:1-18 The opening verses contain many allusions to Israel's early history. The initial appeal to the LORD is that he **remember** their situation. This reminds one of the introductory note in Exodus 2:23-25. The people were crying out to the LORD for help, and he "heard their groaning and he *remembered* his covenant with Abraham" (see 6:5). There are numerous other references to the LORD "remembering" his people in their times of distress (Gen 9:15-16; Lev 26:42; 1 Sam 1:11,19; 2 Kgs 20:3; Ps 98:3; 105:8; 106:45; 111:5; 136:23; Jer 14:21). It is part of his covenant faithfulness to do so. For the LORD to"remember" their suffering now would be for him to act again as he had in the Exodus and other salvific events.

---

[1] Gerstenberger categorizes this as a "communal complaint," because certain elements of the lament are missing (*Psalms, Part 2, and Lamentations,* pp. 502, 504; cp. Ps 44, 79).

They are calling to "the LORD who brought the Israelites up out of Egypt" (Jer 23:7) to do something consonant with his name again. He used the leadership of Moses and Joshua to drive other nations out of the land, giving it to the Israelites "as their inheritance" (Deut 4:21; 19:10; 20:16; 21:23; 24:4; 25:19; 26:1; 1 Kgs 8:36; Jer 3:18), because of the wickedness of those nations (Deut 4:37-38; 9:4-5); but the **inheritance** has now reverted to its previous inhabitants (v. 2). He showed himself in the past to be a God who "defends the cause of the fatherless and the widow" (Deut 10:18), but now he has brought this fate on his own children (v. 3). The warning of Deuteronomy 28:43-44 has become a reality. They are reduced to paying for their **water** and **wood** (v. 4), as they had been in the Wilderness (Num 20:19; Deut 2:6,28), rather than using the foreigners in their midst to haul wood and water for them (Josh 9:23,27). They were supposed to find **rest** in their promised land (Deut 3:20; Josh 1:13). They are having to borrow from their powerful neighbors for food (v. 6), rather than being the one to lend to other nations (Deut 15:6; 28:12).[2]

The sentiment of verse 7 suggests that they are still "in denial" to some degree about their present state. This is not their fault; their ancestors sinned, but they are suffering for it. This parallels the "sour grapes" proverb quoted and discussed by Jeremiah (Jer 31:27-30) and Ezekiel (Ezek 18:1-2). It reflects a common human reaction. Somebody else's crimes always seem worse than our own. Some other car was going faster than ours, but the traffic cop has pulled us over. Only toward the end of the chapter (vv. 16b,22) is there some glimmer of acceptance of their own responsibility (see below).[3]

The next several verses express the appalling state of affairs. Foreign servants — not even foreign kings — **rule over** them (v. 8; see Isa 3:4,12). They are desperate for food, as they face military threats not just in their cities, but in the farthest reaches of the desert (vv. 9-10). Then they describe how each segment of the nation's social fabric suffers shame and despair. All **women**, both married and **virgins**, have been sexually violated (v. 11). Neither royal leaders (**princes**)

---

[2]For a similar analysis, see Bracke, *Jeremiah 30–52 and Lamentations*, pp. 236-237. Hillers observes that the sequence of "inheritance" to "homes" to "water" in verses 2 and 4 parallels the same sequence in Deuteronomy 6:10-11 (*Lamentations*, p. 163).

[3]Westermann, *Lamentations*, p. 215.

nor traditional family leaders (**elders**) **are shown** the honor they deserve (v. 12). The **boys** should be enjoying their youth, but they are being made to do the work of adults (v. 13). One does not hear the typical sounds of young and old (**young men** and **elders**) in city life (see 1 Sam 18:6; 2 Chr 36:17; Ps 30:11; 149:3; 150:4; Jer 31:4,11-14; 49:26; 50:30; 51:22). There is no **joy**, no **dancing**, no wearing of **crowns** in honor and celebration (Job 19:9; Jer 13:18).

This leads to a wide swing in the pendulum of their emotions. Such a swing suggests great agitation in the hearts of the people. First, there is a momentary turn toward repentance (v. 16b). There is a general admission of guilt, but the absence of any specification makes one wonder how clearly they see their sins. Rather than focus on that, they return to the suffocating suffering they endure. Their "faint hearts" and "dim eyes" suggest the imminence of death. Jerusalem is left to the wild animals, the scavengers (Isa 13:19-22; Micah 3:12; Zeph 2:13-15).[4] Surely their own death must follow shortly after the death of their beloved city.

5:19-22 The pendulum swing of the closing lines of the preceding section continues into this closing section. A traditional lament usually moves from complaint to a statement of faith. Such a statement is given in verse 19. The **LORD** is still king, his **throne** still **endures**, even though his temple is destroyed (Ps 11:4; 45:6; 47:8; 89:4,14; 93:2; 97:2; 103:19; 132:12; see 1 Kgs 22:19; Isa 6:1; 66:1; Jer 17:12; Ezek 43:7). But the speakers cannot hold on to this thought. They swing back to despair. So what if the LORD is king? He appears to have forgotten and forsaken his people (v. 20) even while they call on him to "remember" them (v. 1).[5] This is not something that a good king would do, and it contradicts what the LORD had repeatedly promised he would do (Josh 1:5,9; 1 Kgs 6:13; 8:57; Ps 37:28; 94:14; Isa 41:17). They call on him to **restore** (הֲשִׁיבֵ, *hāšîb*) them, as he has been promising through Jeremiah (Jer 12:15; 15:19; 16:15; 23:3; 24:6; 27:22; 28:6; 41:16). He has said that he will "restore" them, but they must "return" to him (שׁוּב, *šûb*; Jer 3:12,14,22; 4:1).[6] Now they say that they will **return**, if he will **restore** them. Is each waiting for the other to make the first move? Or have the people learned that their own attempts to "return" (Jer 3:22-25; 14:19-22)

---

[4]Hillers, *Lamentations*, pp. 159-160, 165.
[5]Bracke, *Jeremiah 30–52 and Lamentations*, p. 236.
[6]Davidson, *Jeremiah, Volume 2, and Lamentations*, pp. 212-213.

have failed because they have (again) tried to do it without the
LORD's strength (Jer 31:18)?

The lament then closes on a note of uncertainty. The concern is
that the LORD has **rejected** them completely. There are examples in
their history of the LORD "rejecting" or threatening to "reject" those
whom he had previously chosen. He rejected Saul for rejecting his
commands (1 Sam 15:23,26; 16:1). David warned Solomon that the
same could happen to him (1 Chr 28:9). The LORD rejected the
northern priests in Hosea's day for ignoring God's laws (Hos 4:6; cp.
1 Sam 2:30), and he rejected the northern tribes for their continued
idolatry (2 Kgs 17:20). Now, according to Jeremiah, he has rejected
the people of Jerusalem (Jer 6:30). The question which they then
pose is whether he has rejected them completely (Jer 14:19). In spite
of the people's words of repentance (14:20-22), the LORD says he is
still sending them away (15:1-4). And so, the people are left with the
thought — with the haunting question — that the LORD might have
rejected them forever. Is the LORD's response to Jeremiah in
Jeremiah 15:1-4 his "final answer," or is there still another chance
for Judah?[7] Jeremiah later comes back to them with words of hope,
yet they must learn the meaning of faith all over again before, fifty
years later, they see the realization of those hopes.

The uncertain note on which this lament — and the entire book
— ends is fitting; and in its own way, it foreshadows a reason for optimism. Yes, the covenant promises made to Abraham are eternal.
Yes, the LORD has made promises through prophets like Jeremiah of
a future restoration. Much of the chapter, then, represents a challenge to the LORD's faithfulness. These terrible things would not
have happened, they assert, if the LORD had been faithful to protect
his people. These sufferings are the very things he had promised to
prevent. The fact that they have happened is reason to question his
faithfulness. Or so it seems to the people. They have done nothing
worse than their ancestors ever did. In fact, from their perspective,
"Our fathers sinned . . . and we bear their punishment" (v. 7).

The final verse shows the beginning of a turning in their thinking. Maybe their suffering is justified. Maybe they have been too
hasty in their self-evaluations. If the LORD has **utterly rejected us**, is

---

[7]"[It] is traditional [in Jewish liturgical practice] not to end public reading
of this scroll with this somber verse, but to repeat after it the prayer of v 21."
Hillers, *Lamentations*, p. 161.

that unwarranted? Or is it fully within the realm of possibility, based on their lives and the lives of their ancestors? They have aroused his great wrath, and the LORD does not anger easily. It must be for good reason. Being willing to accept that they might really deserve their punishment is the first step in the right direction. It will be almost fifty years before there is any physical indication that his anger has cooled and he is blessing them again. If they are truly honest with themselves during this long and painful exile, the people will have to wonder whether they had even exhausted the mercy of the God of all mercies. When they do experience his blessings again, after such a spiritual drought, they should finally understand the truly merciful and gracious nature of those blessings.[8]

---

[8]The prophecies of restoration in Jeremiah (Jer 23:1-8; 30:1–33:26) need to be read as responses to the sentiments expressed in Lamentations. The people are questioning the faithfulness of the God of their ancestors. Jeremiah (and Ezekiel) tries to encourage them to be hopeful – and obediently faithful as well – about what the LORD has in store for them. Much of what he says can be read as an answer to their doubts.